The European Court and Civil Society

D1139939

The European Union today stands on the brink of radical institutional and constitutional change. The most recent enlargement and proposed legal reforms reflect a commitment to democracy: stabilizing political life for citizens governed by new regimes, and constructing a European Union more accountable to civil society. Despite the perceived novelty of these reforms, this book explains (through quantitative data and qualitative case analyses) how the European Court of Justice has developed and sustained a vibrant tradition of democratic constitutionalism since the 1960s. The book documents the dramatic consequences of this institutional change for civil society and public policy reform throughout Europe. Cichowski offers detailed empirical and historical studies of gender equality and environmental protection law across fifteen countries and over thirty years, revealing important linkages between civil society, courts and the construction of governance. The findings bring into question dominant understandings of legal integration.

RACHEL A. CICHOWSKI is Assistant Professor of Comparative Politics and Law in the Department of Political Science and the Law, Societies and Justice (LSJ) Program at the University of Washington. She is co-editor of the book *State of the European Union: Law, Politics and Society* (2003) and her research is published in various journals, including *Comparative Political Studies, Law & Society Review* and *Journal of European Public Policy*.

Themes in European Governance

Series Editor
Andreas Føllesdal

Editorial Board

Stefano Bartolini	Ulrich Preuss	Helen Wallace
Beate Kohler-Koch	Thomas Risse	Albert Weale
Percy Lehning	Fritz W. Scharpf	J. H. H. Weiler
Andrew Moravcsik	Philip Schlesinger	

The evolving European systems of governance, in particular the European Union, challenge and transform the state, the most important locus of governance and political identity and loyalty over the past 200 years. The series *Themes in European Governance* aims to publish the best theoretical and analytical scholarship on the impact of European governance on the core institutions, policies and identities of nation states. It focuses upon the implications for issues such as citizenship, welfare, political decision-making, and economic, monetary, and fiscal policies. An initiative of Cambridge University Press and the Programme on Advanced Research on the Europeanisation of the Nation-State (ARENA), Norway, the series includes contributions in the social sciences, humanities and law. The series aims to provide theoretically informed studies analysing key issues at the European level and within European states. Volumes in the series will be of interest to scholars and students of Europe both within Europe and worldwide. They will be of particular relevance to those interested in the development of sovereignty and governance of European states and in the issues raised by multi-level governance and multi-national integration throughout the world.

The European Court and Civil Society

Litigation, Mobilization and Governance

Rachel A. Cichowski

CAMBRIDGE UNIVERSITY PRESS
Cambridge, New York, Melbourne, Madrid, Cape Town, Singapore, São Paulo

Cambridge University Press
The Edinburgh Building, Cambridge CB2 8RU, UK

Published in the United States of America by Cambridge University Press,
New York

www.cambridge.org
Information on this title: www.cambridge.org/9780521671811

First published 2007

Printed in the United Kingdom at the University Press, Cambridge

A catalogue record for this book is available from the British Library

ISBN-13 978-0-521-85585-3 hardback
ISBN-13 978-0-521-67181-1 paperback

This book is dedicated to Ed

Contents

Figures

Tables

Acknowledgments

This book is the product of considerable support: financial, intellectual and personal. I am grateful to the following foundations for their generous support of my research: German Marshall Fund, Woodrow Wilson Foundation, MacArthur Foundation, Council of European Studies (CES), University of California Center for German and European Studies, University of California Institute on Global Conflict and Cooperation (IGCC), Women in International Trade, and DeutscherAkademischerAustauschDienst (DAAD). Further, the project involved considerable time conducting research in Europe and I would especially like to acknowledge the support and hospitality of various individuals and institutions. In particular, I am grateful to Yves Mény and Alec Stone Sweet who made it possible for me to work as a visiting fellow at the Robert Schuman Center for Advanced Studies, European University Institute, Florence, Italy (1998–1999). I would also like to extend my gratitude to Adrienne Héritier who was extremely gracious in her support and welcome while I was a visiting fellow at the Max Planck Institute in Bonn, Germany (2000). These were both superb intellectual environments and I have no doubt this research project was significantly shaped and improved by the time spent at both of these institutions. Finally, the study has greatly benefited from ongoing conversations with my colleagues at the University of Washington in the Comparative Law and Society Studies Center, Law, Society and Justice Program, European Union Center and Political Science Department. Special thanks also go to John Haslam, Senior Editor at Cambridge University Press, and his excellent support team, Assistant Editor Carrie Cheek and Production Editor Jo Breeze, and equally invaluable were the suggestions and comments from the anonymous reviewers.

Intellectually, I have been inspired, challenged and encouraged by too many to list. However, I want to extend my appreciation to my mentors while I was at the University of California, Irvine. My own professional and intellectual development owes much to Russell Dalton, who not only provided invaluable feedback on my research, but who never ceased to

xiv

inform me of and encourage participation in conference and research travel opportunities. Wayne Sandholtz provided an invaluable source of clarity and reliability in my moments of intellectual confusion. I also want to acknowledge Alec Stone Sweet; his generous spirit was integral to the completion of this project – from use of his data and office space to the hospitality that was so graciously extended to me in Irvine, Oxford and Florence. But most of all, Alec shared with me his intrigue and curiosity for law, courts and politics, a gift that deeply influenced this book.

This study could not have been completed without the personal support of my close friends and family. My brother, sister and close friends deserve acknowledgment not only for listening to my musings but also for providing breaks into the world beyond this book. I also would like to acknowledge my parents, Mary C. Clare and Bob Cichowski. Whatever my latest endeavor, wherever it might be in the world, they continue to provide me with an invaluable gift of love, respect and pride. Whether she knows it or not, my daughter Lucia, who was born during the duration of this book, gave me an invaluable gift of perspective, delightful distraction and motivation that made the completion of this project possible. Finally, I am dedicating this book to Edward Rejzek, my husband and best friend. Few individuals possess the strength to truly let go of the thing you love the most. Ed does. His endless encouragement and support for my adventurous spirit – which often puts us on opposite ends of the globe – is testimony to this. Completion of this book relied on this love and friendship.

1 Introduction: institutions, organizations and actors

In the late 1950s, moved by the hope for peace and economic prosperity in Europe, six governments constructed the foundations of an unprecedented form of supranational governance: the European Community. Heads of governments negotiated the rules and organizations that would govern what was largely an international economic agreement. Interest groups and civil society were not directly involved in these negotiations and public interest issues were not on the agenda.

Today, in the year 2006, this same supranational space – the European Union (EU) – possesses an ever-expanding net of public policies, including women's rights and environmental protection.[1] These policy areas have consistently been guarded by national governments, who have been hesitant to let the EU legislate in the area of national social policy and environmental preservation. Today, public interests groups and civil society – from feminist activists to environmental groups – and increasingly powerful EU organizations, such as the European Court of Justice (ECJ) – are equally present in this supranational policy arena. Individuals possess enforceable rights under EU law and public interest groups are now permanent participants in EU policy processes. This book explains how this remarkable transformation took place – how an international treaty governing economic cooperation became a quasi-constitutional polity granting individual rights and public inclusion. I argue that the ECJ and civil society were integral to this transformation.

This book examines the emergence and evolution of supranational governance in Europe. How does supranational governance – characterized by a set of binding rules and procedures governing actors and organizations in a supranational policy arena – emerge and institutionalize? By institutionalization, I mean the process by which these rules

---

[1] For consistency and clarity, this study will refer to the institutions and organizations of the European Union by this newer name, despite the historic nature of this research. Further, consistent with this etiquette, I will utilize the post-Treaty of Amsterdam numbering and parenthetically cite previous numbering as relevant.

and procedures become increasingly formalized and are supported by actors and organizations with increasing competence to change these rules.[2] The objectives are twofold: first, to explain the sources and consequences of the institutionalization of two EU policy domains – social provisions and environmental protection. Second, the book evaluates this evolution in terms of its effects on the intergovernmental nature of the EU. Do national governments retain control over the direction of European policy development or are EU policy spaces filled with supranational organizations and civil society who can independently affect policy evolution? I examine the processes of litigation and mobilization to answer this question.

The study comes at a critical time in the EU. The voice of civil society and the people of Europe are more important than ever before to the future of European integration. The development and final ratification of the Constitutional Treaty stalled in 2005 due to the voice of the people – a resounding NO vote in public referenda in France and the Netherlands.[3] At the core of this outcome was a protest – a demand that the integration project was moving forward at a pace and level that left the people of Europe too far removed from the process. Thus, many might record this as another historic moment where the integration project came to a halt or at least lost momentum and began to slow. I would disagree. Certainly, the new institutions, organizational improvements and perhaps a sense of European pride and identity that might have come with a Constitution are now on hold. Yet, constitutionalism in the EU remains vibrant; and individuals, civil society and the ECJ are at the core of this positive trajectory.

Understanding supranational governance

Like many systems of governance, the emergence and evolution of supranational governance in Europe can be characterized by a complex relationship between social actors, organizations and institutions (March and Olsen 1989; North 1990; Stone Sweet, Sandholtz and Fligstein 2001). The processes by which institutionalization in the EU

---

[2] See Stone Sweet and Sandholtz (1998: 9).
[3] The Constitution for Europe (or Constitutional Treaty) was ratified by fourteen member states in 2005: Austria, Belgium, Cyprus, Germany, Greece, Hungary, Italy, Latvia, Lithuania, Luxembourg, Malta, Slovakia, Slovenia and Spain. Following the rejection of the Treaty in public referenda in France (29 May 2005) and the Netherlands (1 June 2005), member states have decided to enter a "period of reflection, discussion and explanation" with the hopes of successful ratification in the future (European Council, 16–17 June 2005).

takes place are many, and explanations of who controlled these processes vary. Scholars have focused on institutional change through treaty amendments (Moravcsik 1998; Tsebelis and Garrett 2001), the role of EU organizations in rule creation (Pollack 2003; Tsebelis 1994; Stone Sweet 2004; Cichowski 2004) and the significance of transnational actors in policy innovation (Sandholtz 1998), to name just a few. Their findings consistently demonstrate that the EU today embodies a complex set of EU institutions, EU organizations and, increasingly, private actors.

The debate

There is much less agreement over *how* this complex system emerged and to what degree EU policy processes remain controlled by member state governments. Regional integration scholarship has largely developed out of an attempt to theorize the interactive effects that policy actors (national government executives and transnational actors) and EU organizations (the ECJ, Commission, Parliament or Council) have on the process of European policy making (the production of new European rules through secondary legislation, treaty revisions and the ECJ's jurisprudence). Neofunctionalists argued that new areas of supranational policy would emerge from the transnational activism of interests, the policy innovations of supranational organizations and the pressure these groups put on national governments (Haas 1958; 1964). Supranational organizations and transnational society are instrumental components of this explanation of how EU rules become institutionalized and subsequently "spill over" to other policy domains, ultimately shifting policy competence to the supranational level.

Conversely, intergovernmental approaches privilege the role of national government executives in the integration process (Moravcsik 1998; Garrett 1992). Domestic policy actors, in particular, commercial and economic interests, are important to the extent that they influence national government preferences and thus affect policy preferences asserted at the bargaining table. But ultimately, supranational governance is a product of the relative bargaining power of member state governments as constrained by decision-making rules. Consistent with regime theory, intergovernmentalism argues that EU organizations stabilize supranational policy coordination between national governments by reducing the costs of information and policy innovation (Keohane 1984). In this explanation, supranational organizations and organized interests do not exert any autonomous or direct influence on EU rule making.

An alternative approach

While both of these explanations recognize that governance in the EU contains both supranational and intergovernmental elements, there is a clear need for explanatory theory that can account for this variation. Motivated by this problem, this study further develops a theoretical approach that examines supranational governance as a process of institutional change. Explicit in this approach, and consistent with new institutionalism scholarship more generally, the constituent elements of institutional evolution are a dynamic interaction between institutions, organizations and actors – the macro, meso and micro levels in any political space. For the purposes of this analysis, I adopt the generally agreed distinctions between these three entities (see North 1990; Hall and Taylor 1996):

- **Institutions** constitute the macro level. They are complexes of rule systems that pattern and prescribe human interaction. In the EU, these are treaty provisions, secondary legislation, ECJ precedent and the procedures that govern rulemaking.
- **Organizations** make up the meso level and they are more or less formally constituted spaces occupied by groups of individuals pursuing collective purposes. The ECJ is an example of an EU organization.
- **Individual action** occurs at the micro level. In the EU, these are individuals and groups involved in transnational action.

This approach is consistent with neofunctionalism in that it privileges the role of EU organizations and transnational society in integration processes. Integration evolves in any given policy sector as a result of the growing intensity and presence of three factors: EU rules, EU organizations and transnational society. In particular, Stone Sweet and Sandholtz argue that movement along these three dimensions constitutes a shift from intergovernmental politics to supranational politics (1998: 11). Furthermore, growth on any one of these dimensions may stimulate movement within the other elements. For example, an expansion of EU organizational power can provide new opportunities that actors will be motivated to exploit, thus expanding transnational society. In response to these new supranational rules, societal actors will adjust their behaviors and in doing so these rules are reinforced. Neofunctionalism helped us understand why there was a functional demand for supranational governance, yet it tells us little about how and when this may develop. While my approach is consistent with neofunctionalism, it differs by not *a priori* suggesting that European integration will move forward smoothly; instead it provides the heuristic device to examine individual policy areas, over time, and evaluate whether they are more or less intergovernmental and how this may change over time.

I utilize this framework to examine the sources and consequences of the institutionalization of EU social provisions and environmental protection policies. Furthermore, the research evaluates this institutional evolution in terms of its effects on the intergovernmental nature of EU governance. In particular, I ask whether the institutional and organizational changes associated with these public policy developments affected public access and participation in the EU, and subsequently I ask how this may alter the balance of power in EU politics between member state governments, EU organizations and citizens. How do we measure this process of institutionalization? Using the above theoretical argument as a guide, institutionalization can be measured in three ways:

- **Institutions**. Institutionalization in a given policy sector can be measured in terms of whether the EU institutions (rules and procedures) governing that legal domain become more binding, precise and enforceable and whether they expand in scope. We know institutionalization is occurring when EU rules increasingly govern and sustain the activities (at both the national and transnational level) between social, political and economic actors in a given policy sector.

- **Organizations**. EU organizations will exert greater influence on supranational policy outcomes and processes the greater degree of institutionalization that occurs in a given area. In a fully institutionalized space, EU organizations act autonomously, that is, they are able to exert independent influence on policy outcomes.

- **Actors**. We know institutionalization is occurring when there is an increasing intensity and presence of transnational actors in supranational policy processes. In intergovernmental politics, domestic actors exert pressure on national governments to bring supranational policy change. National governments remain the mediators between domestic actors and supranational policy decisions. In sites of supranational governance, we would expect these actors to pressure for change at both the national level and the supranational level. In particular, we would expect greater institutionalization in a policy area the extent to which this action becomes more formally organized and collective and increasingly permanent.

Litigation, mobilization and governance

This study moves beyond the existing European integration scholarship by analyzing how institutionalization can occur through the processes of supranational litigation and transnational mobilization. I argue that much like domestic politics, litigation and social activism in the EU provide avenues for institutional change. By this I mean that these processes can lead to a change in the rules and procedures that govern any particular policy arena (i.e. change in opportunity structures). Litigation enables individuals and groups, who are often disadvantaged in their own legal systems, to gain new rights at the national and EU level. Judicial decisions can be particularly powerful in the extent to which they expand the scope or alter the meaning of treaty provisions – rules that are otherwise relatively immune to alteration. This is not unique to the EU, as courts and processes of legalization are increasingly shaping supranational and international governance (Alter 2006; Slaughter 2003, 2004; Cichowski 2006a; Scheppele 2004). Further, EU citizens who may be excluded from EU politics can gain new power and voice through the mobilization of transnational public interest groups. This action can shape policy development as well as expand the boundaries of EU politics by giving civil society a voice and place in EU politics. A similar dynamic is evolving at the global level as civil society and transnational activists are increasingly present and participating in international politics (Keck and Sikkink 1998; Tarrow 2005).

Institutional change in the EU takes place through a host of processes, such as intergovernmental treaty negotiations (Moravcsik 1998), parliamentarian policy agenda setting (Tsebelis and Kreppel 1998) and policy development by the Commission (Pollack 2003). Unlike these other integration processes, litigation and mobilization introduce a dynamic in which institutional change can occur from below. The interaction between law, politics and society has been an important avenue of institutional change in Europe (Cichowski and Börzel 2003). Further, the analytic focus of this study provides a test for scholarship that argues European integration is best understood by the "formal" interaction of EU organizations, an approach that may operate above the radar of citizen politics (Tsebelis and Garrett 2001: 388). Instead, beyond high politics, this study complements research illustrating why courts may provide a more responsive institutional form of democracy for the public than do traditional representative organizations (e.g. Graber 1993; Lovell 2003; Zemans 1983). To be clear, litigation and mobilization do not replace the importance of legislative and executive decision-making processes, but instead complement and enhance these equally important modes of democratic governance.

In any system of governance, litigation and mobilization present avenues for institutional change, and thus are particularly fruitful for exposing the many processes through which supranational governance can evolve. Litigation enables actors to question existing rules and procedures. And the court's judicial rulemaking can lead to the creation of new rules and procedures that sometimes serve as new opportunities for action (Shapiro

1981; Stone Sweet 2000). By judicial rulemaking, I mean, *a court's authoritative interpretation of existing rules and procedures, which results in the clarification of the law or practice in question.* Mobilization processes involve the strategic action of individuals and groups to promote or resist change in a given policy arena (Tarrow 1998; Marks and McAdam 1996). This study examines public movement activism. By movement activism, I mean *sustained challenges, by individuals or groups with common purposes, to alter existing arrangements of power and distribution.* I adopt this general definition to examine the importance of both individual and group activism.[4] Rule change occurs through mobilization when activists utilize available opportunity structures to pressure governing organizations to create or amend rules that will satisfy their goals. In particular, movement activism has historically operated to expand the boundaries of politics, a strategy that can lead to change in the rules and procedures that impact who has access to these policy spaces (Dalton, Kuechler and Burkin 1990).

Theoretically, we would expect to find complex linkages between litigating, mobilization and rulemaking in the EU (Börzel and Cichowski 2003; Stone Sweet and Caporaso 1998; Cichowski 2004). As EU rules and the ECJ present social activists with the opportunity to bring new legal claims, we would expect activists to mobilize and exploit these new opportunities. This litigation in turn can empower the ECJ by providing the opportunity to clarify and construct new EU rules. In response to these new supranational rules, actors adjust their behaviors in a way that makes these institutions increasingly difficult to change. Furthermore, once these actors gain some access to this new arena, they will push for greater inclusion. As the policy process becomes more dependent on this increasingly present transnational civil society, for legitimacy and efficiency reasons, we can expect the rules to change in a way that formally includes these actors in the supranational policy space. Through these processes supranational governance can emerge and evolve. By further developing a theoretical approach that understands supranational governance as multiple processes of institutional change involving varying actors and organizations, this study brings into question theories that limit the emergence and evolution of European integration to a set of intergovernmental bargains and policy decisions dominated by national governments (Moravcsik 1998; Garrett et al. 1998).

---

[4] Alongside collective action taken by movement organizations, scholars highlight the importance of activities carried out by individual activists who are often bound together in informal networks, but whose challenging action can be equally as effective as collective action by movement organizations (e.g. Katzenstein 1998a).

In the remaining part of this chapter, I elaborate the approach that underlies this study.

The litigation dynamic

In this section, I focus on the various stages of the litigation dynamic. First, I suggest the necessary conditions for litigation. This is followed by a discussion of the feedback effects of litigation on governance (the rules and procedures). Finally, I explore how this litigation dynamic can affect mobilization.

The necessary conditions for litigation: making a legal claim

The litigation dynamic begins as a result of strategic action by individuals who are either disadvantaged or advantaged by an available set of rules. This stage is characterized by both action and at least some necessary rule or procedure that is invoked in the legal claim. In particular, social movements have experienced relative success at utilizing litigation as an avenue to pressure for social change and have done so by utilizing an explicit or implied set of rights (McCann 1994; Handler 1978; Vose 1959; Walker 1990; Kluger 1975). In the United States, there is a long tradition of marginalized groups utilizing the courts as an opportunity to challenge existing governance structures and exclusionary policies. Most notable are the activities of the early civil rights movement on issues such as school segregation (for example, the *Brown v. Board of Education* decision, see Morris 1984) and also a host of other social movements, including the American labor movement (Forbath 1991; Tomlins 1985), the women's movement (Costain 1992; O'Connor 1980), the welfare movement (Piven and Cloward 1977), and the animal rights movement (Silverstein 1996).

There is a considerably shorter history of this type of litigation in Europe. From what we know generally about public interest litigation in Europe, environmental and women's group activation of courts is minimal, yet present (Krämer 1996; Harlow and Rawlings 1992; Cichowski 1998; 2004; Kelemen 2006; Cichowski and Stone Sweet 2003). Unlike a long tradition of social movement use of the courts in the United States, many European legal systems have only recently provided *locus standi* for groups (for France and the United Kingdom see Harlow and Rawlings 1992). However, in the area of environmental protection we do find groups throughout Europe increasingly engaging in legal action despite sometimes restrictive access to justice rules (e.g. Führ and Roller 1991; CEC 2002a) and with increasing success utilizing EU law to bring legal proceedings against their own governments (Cichowski

1998; Krämer 1996). Similarly, women's rights litigation utilizing EU gender equality law may benefit from the organized interests and activists that generate this seemingly individual litigation (Hoskyns 1996; Harlow and Rawlings 1992; Cichowski 2001). Although not class action suits in terms of a vast general interest, EU gender equality litigation increasingly involves multiple litigants, who may or may not work for the same employer, but who share a common complaint. These interests are joined not by chance, but through strategic organization.[5]

Stated generally, the litigation dynamic begins with the following two factors:

- the strategic action on behalf of an individual or group interest, in our case movement activists, to invoke this rule and make a claim before a court.
- at least some necessary rule or procedure, embodying an explicit or implied right.

Without these two factors, we might expect this process to fail, or rather that there would be less public interest litigation in a given legal system relative to others. In this study, I explore and elaborate the underlying forces that can alter these necessary conditions. Subsequently, a court is asked to resolve the dispute, leading to the next stage in the litigation process: the judicial decision.

Litigation feedback effect on governance

I start with the assumption that through litigation, a court's resolution of societal questions or disputes can lead to the clarification, expansion and creation of rules and procedures that are structures of governance (Shapiro 1981: 35–37). Thus, in any system of governance with an independent judiciary possessing judicial review powers, the judicial decision provides a potential avenue for institutional change. For example, in the case of the American civil rights litigation, activists questioned the constitutionality of school segregation (*Brown v. Board of Education*, see Morris 1984). The US Supreme Court found that racial segregation in schools was unconstitutional, and thus changed what was a lawful practice protected by the US Constitution. In order to understand this

---

[5] See Chapter 3 and Chapter 5 in this book. In the area of EU pregnancy and maternity rights, there are a series of cases involving multiple litigants who share a similar claim (see *Gillespie* ECJ 1996a; *Boyle* ECJ 1998c; *Pedersen* ECJ 1998d). The *Boyle* case for example was organized by a lawyer working within the British Equal Opportunities Commission (EOC) who filed a case against the EOC (a UK governmental agency responsible for implementation and oversight of UK equality policies) on behalf of six of her colleagues. This is an example of women's organized activism from within public and private organizations (e.g. Katzenstein 1998b).

dynamic process of judicial rulemaking, this study adopts an approach that understands the process of rule construction as endogenous to existing governance structures (March and Olsen 1989). That is, a court's rule-making capacity operates within the institutional framework of an existing body of rules and procedures (e.g., a constitution or legislation), yet a court's jurisprudence can subsequently alter these institutions. This approach is not unfamiliar to scholars of judicial politics (Shapiro 1981, 1988; Stone Sweet 2000; Jackson and Tate 1992; Ginsburg 2003).

I refer to this process of institutional change through a court's decisions as *judicial rulemaking*. In the European context, it is well documented elsewhere that these interpretations can significantly alter the original measure in a way that changes what is lawful and unlawful behavior for individuals and public and private bodies operating under EU law (Alter 1998; de la Mare 1999; Mancini 1989; Cichowski 1998, 2004; Stone Sweet 2004). For example, when the ECJ interprets Article 141 of the Treaty of Rome (ex Article 119, the Equal Pay Principle) in a way that now brings maternity pay under the purview of EU equal pay provisions, this creates a new rule (Cichowski 2004). The behavior of public and private bodies must reflect this new rule. And if they do not, individuals now have the ability to claim recourse before national courts.

Stated generally, through litigation and the resolution of a dispute, judicial rulemaking can lead to:
- the construction of new rules and procedures that expand rights
- and, thus, can expand the institutional framework that governs individual and group action (new rights that grant greater access, standing and the judicial obligation to protect).

When might this judicial rulemaking capacity be constrained? This study explores and elaborates the factors arising from the law that may explain a court's decision-making in a given legal system relative to others. Given that judicial rulings can alter governance structures, I now elaborate how this may impact mobilization. In particular, this study focuses on the impact of court rulings on the rules and procedures that are opportunities for social movement action.

Litigation feedback effect on mobilization: opportunities for action

Through the construction of a new rule (expanding the scope, meaning or precision of a right), a court's judicial rulemaking may have general consequences for the balance of power in any political system by providing new opportunities for action (McCann 1994; Epp 1990; 1998; Cichowski 2004, 2006b; Cichowski and Stone Sweet 2003). The ways in which this may provide new opportunity structures for social movement action are twofold. First, sometimes the impact is direct. The extent to which judicial rulings create specific rights of access that provide protection to a class of people or interests that were not previously available, we might expect these formal rights to become the basis for movement development. In particular, we might expect these new rights to provide the foundation for subsequent litigation strategies. For example, legal scholars highlight the significant role that judicial rulings which expanded pay equity rights in the American political system played in "catalyzing" the development of a general pay equity movement (McCann 1994: 13).

Or as Scheingold concluded in his well-known argument of the "politics of rights," it is possible for marginalized groups "to capitalize on the perceptions of entitlement associated with (legal) rights to initiate and nurture political mobilization" (1974: 131).[6] For example, in the European context, the ECJ's *Defrenne II* decision (ECJ 1976a) transformed a treaty provision into an individual right, enabling women throughout the EU to mobilize and utilize litigation strategies to seek protection from sex discrimination, a direct action that was not previously possible under EU law and in many cases, not possible in their own national legal systems (Cichowski 2001). Stated generally, court decisions may have a positive impact on the development and mobilization of social movement activists, the extent to which the decisions create new rights that can enable direct access or be utilized by movement activists to make subsequent claims through litigation.

Second, judicial rulings can also have a more indirect impact on movement activity by changing the rules and procedures in a way that makes the policy process more open to a particular group. This consequence can emerge from the interaction between courts and legislatures. The logic follows. By their very nature of being general and prospective, judicial decisions can have the impact of telling legislatures what to do (Stone Sweet 2000). The ruling produces a legal act that is specific (it binds the two disputants) and retrospective (it applies to a pre-existing dispute). Yet at the same time the ruling can be both general and prospective, by laying down how a similar case may be solved in the future. A court is asked to adapt abstract legal rules to concrete situations, and over time these rulings construct and reconstruct the existing governance structures.

Considerable attention has been given to the limited effect of judicial decisions on policy implementation and change, scholars arguing that courts lack the independence and resources to enforce their decisions on

---

[6] See also McCann (1998); Handler (1978); Olson (1984).

reluctant governments and citizens (Rosenberg 1991; Handler 1978). Nevertheless, others illustrate how courts have played a crucial role in the formation and implementation of policy by legislatures (Lovell 2003; Stone Sweet 2000). Legislatures are able to use these judicial decisions as guides for subsequent legislation, as the court's legal argumentation lays out clearly what is lawful and unlawful behavior. The creation of new legislation and policy statements can subsequently provide the basis for movement action. In the same way that new rights created through judicial rulings can provide the legal basis for new claims, legislation can also lay down the necessary rule for this strategic action.

Stated generally, judicial rulings can alter the rules and procedures that are opportunities for social action. The effects can be:

- direct, by creating new legal rights for an individual or group that enables subsequent legal claims.
- Or they can be indirect, such as by changing the rules and procedures in a way that impacts legislative action and creates a new set of rules that may become the basis for subsequent legal action.

While judicial rulings can have these general effects, this subsequent action is critically linked to the availability of other opportunity structures and the relative capacity of a movement to utilize strategies. We might expect that these judicial rulings will have a greater mobilizing impact the greater the capacity of a mobilized interest to utilize these new opportunities, given other political opportunities and characteristics of the movement. This subsequent action will seek to clarify and utilize the new opportunities created by these rights. At this point, we can see that the litigation dynamic can begin anew – given a necessary rule and strategic action – the court's judicial rulemaking capacity is activated, again enabling the process of institutional change.

In summary, institutionalization can occur through litigation when social activists are empowered by a certain rule or procedure and they bring a legal claim. The courts are subsequently empowered and potentially can expand these rules through the process of judicial rulemaking; and these judicial rulings can impact subsequent activism, both directly through rights creation and indirectly by activating the legislative process whose outputs can expand opportunities for action. In light of this evolving dynamic among institutions, organizations and actors, institutional change can take place through litigation and often in a direction that is not intended. Certain rights are established and through the actions of individuals and organizations these rights are expanded in a direction that leads those governed by these rules down a path that becomes increasingly hard to change (Pierson 2000; North 1990). The judicial rulemaking of a court can expand institutions that over time can empower new actors and legislative action with the consequence of constructing more formal, precise and binding institutions that shape this litigation dynamic in the future. In the next section, mobilization is the focus and I elaborate how institutionalization is also a central product of the mobilization processes.

The mobilization dynamic

In the last section, I illustrated how litigation can serve as a catalyst for further mobilization and legislative action with the overall impact of changing the institutions (rules and procedures) that can provide opportunities for public inclusion and social action. While the processes of litigation and mobilization are interconnected, these two processes are also analytically distinct. Once mobilized, these actors can exert their own impact on governance (rules and procedures) with the effect of changing the general openness or opportunity for civil society inclusion in a given polity. In this section, I ask how mobilization can serve as a catalyst for institutional change (by influencing legislative action and litigation) and how this impacts the rules and procedures that are political opportunities for inclusion and action.

   In the same way that institutional change occurring through the litigation dynamic shaped future litigation, we might expect that rule change evolving from mobilization can condition and shape movement activism (including opportunities for litigation) and public inclusion in the future. Again, social activists can shape political opportunity structures, yet opportunity structures can also guide and impact the development of these movements (Gamson and Meyer 1996: 276; McAdam 1996: 35–37). As argued, the extent to which this action changes over time from discrete and individual to more formally organized and permanent in any given policy arena, we can expect to find institutionalization taking place. It is through this dynamic that institutionalization through mobilization can occur. I elaborate this interaction below.

Necessary conditions for mobilization: political opportunities for action

Political process theorists have long emphasized the significance of the broader political system in structuring opportunities available for social action (Tilly 1978; McAdam 1982; McAdam, McCarthy and Zald 1996). In particular, I am concerned with how formal institutions (rules and procedures) serve as political opportunities for social action and public inclusion within policy processes. I begin with the opportunity structures that activate this mobilization dynamic. In an attempt to explain the key mechanisms which lead to the emergence and involvement of public interest movements within policy processes, scholars have focused on a host of institutional political opportunity structures, such as access to the party system (Rucht 1996) and total number of policy access points (Brockett 1991). Consistently, these scholars and others agree that movement success can be linked to these formal rules, by providing groups with direct access to governing organizations as well as creating a general openness of the polity to a challenging group (see also McAdam 1996; Kriesi et al. 1995; Tarrow 1998). I elaborate this interaction below.

Formal access as opportunity

Rulemaking, through legislative action and litigation, can introduce new political opportunity structures. Social movement scholars argue that policy changes or new legislation can sometimes lead to the creation of new policy access points and mobilizing opportunities for individuals or groups (Tarrow 1998: 42). The converse is also true. These policy changes can also negatively impact mobilization the extent to which opportunities are constricted. These new access points can come in various forms. New legislative innovations often are accompanied by supporting agencies or offices that provide activists with another point of access to the policy arena. In the European context, following the passage of gender equality legislation in the 1970s, the EU began to develop a supporting policy infrastructure, consisting of equality units, parliamentary committees and information services, all of which provided women activists with another point of entry to influence the EU policy process (Hoskyns 1996). A similar dynamic is occurring with the environmental movement worldwide. As national and even international environmental protection agencies are created to help implement environmental standards, environmental non-governmental organizations (NGOs) are increasingly utilizing these organizations as policy access points (Haas 1990, 1993; Keck and Sikkink 1998).

Resources made available through new legislative acts can also change the balance of power in a particular policy arena enabling access. For example, following the passage of the Wagner Act in the 1930s, the American labor movement gained new organizing capabilities, providing the group with a new resource in pursuing their policy objectives *vis-à-vis* the business community. Yet the adoption of the Taft-Hartley Act after the war subsequently minimized this advantage (Goldfield 1989). Further, litigation can sometimes alter the mobilizing impact of these legislative acts. For example, Hattam (1992) illustrates how similar anti-conspiracy statutes in the United States and England led to very different patterns of labor movement mobilization strategies in the end of the nineteenth century largely as a result of intervening state structures that altered these opportunities. In particular, the dominance of US courts over other branches of government in regulating labor policy led to little reward for labor movement strategies that solely pressured for policy change through legislative action. Conversely, the British labor movement was consistently rewarded for their political mobilization in a system in which the Parliament dominated labor policy development rather than the decidedly weaker courts.

As another example, in the European context, in the 1970s the European Commission provided financial support to environmental organizations in Brussels in order to legitimize and develop public support for its new environmental protection policy developments and counterbalance an increasingly powerful European industrial lobby (Barnes and Barnes 1999: 116; Lowe and Goyder 1983; Mazey and Richardson 1992: 120). Finally, as argued earlier, new rights created through litigation as well as legislation can provide individuals and groups with a new access point (enabling enforceable rights claims) to both the courts and the policy process (Cichowski 2006b).

Social space as opportunity

Beyond the formal access to legal and political processes, new policy statements and changes in policy competence can also provide the necessary "social space" to facilitate policy discussions that were not previously possible or available to a particular interest or group (Schneider and Ingram 1997). This is consistent with scholars who argue that public policies can have the affect of creating political opportunities for citizen participation by giving civil society a new voice in the policy process (Walker 1991). The extent to which new policy statements are constructed through litigation or legislative acts, even if they lack concrete policy instruments or enforceability, we might expect increased opportunity for mobilizing action around these issues due to their increased saliency. For example, following the adoption of the United Nations Convention on the Elimination of All Forms of Discrimination Against Women in 1979, women's organizations began mobilizing at the transnational and international level. This general international legal instrument on sex discrimination provided at least some space for women to begin to discuss women's equality as an international issue, a collective debate that would later enable women's groups to alter and expand the discourse in the 1990s to include general protection on 'violence against women' (rape, domestic violence, genital mutilation) (Keck and Sikkink 1998: 166).

Further, policy competence shifts between levels of government can also change this social space. For example, American policy scholars argue that shifts in policy competence from the state to the federal level can create new policy "venues" with the effect of providing new openings for the previously disaffected or disadvantaged (Baumgarner and Jones 1991; 1995). This shift in the venues of political action can bring rapid change in policy participation and ultimately lead to the break-up of "powerful systems of limited participation" (Baumgartner and Jones 1991: 1046). Similarly, in Europe, both environmental and equality legislation adopted at the supranational level has provided national activists with the social space to pressure for policy change and discuss issues that had previously received little public or governmental attention in their national political systems (Cichowski 1998, 2004; Mazey 1998).

In the same way that rules and procedures can *enable* action, these institutions can also *shape* action. The sheer number of rules and procedures that provide opportunities for action is likely to shape movement development. As the numbers of opportunities grow, we might expect a greater number of actors to exploit these opportunities. Over time, for efficiency purposes, we might expect these individual actors to coordinate their action, changing the overall structure of public interest activism to more formal and collective organizations (Olson 1965). Stated generally, formal rules and procedures can provide the necessary political opportunities for public interest action and inclusion. These opportunities include:

- the relative availability and number of formal access points to governing organizations
- and, the relative space or openness of a particular policy arena to a given group's claims.

These can have the following effect:

- The extent to which the institutions that are opportunities for action become increasingly formalized and increase in magnitude (more binding, precise and expanding in scope and number), we might expect the form of social action to shift from individual discrete action to more formalized group action.

I focus on how this variation in political opportunities may have impacted mobilization. Yet we know that once mobilized, these activists can also exert their own impact on existing political opportunity structures.

Mobilization feedback effect on governance

Above I argued that political opportunities can structure action, here I reverse the arrows and ask how this mobilization can shape governance structures that are political opportunities for action. Given that most social movement scholars argue that movement action is a strong influence on societal change, it is surprising that only a handful of studies examine the impact of social movement activism on political structures (Giugni, McAdam and Tilly 1997; Gamson and Meyer 1996). Along with their ability to pressure for specific policy change, we know that social movements may also function to challenge existing rules of access and incorporation that have served to exclude certain citizens or public interests from policy processes (Dalton, Kuechler and Burklin 1990; Giugni, McAdam and Tilly 1997; Button 1989). Further, legal mobilization literature illustrates how once created, rights can be "manipulated by users who are not its makers", and often in ways that are unintended (de Certeau 1984, p. xiii). This scholarship demonstrates that rules can be enabling. They do not merely constrain and dictate behavior, but instead can be actively changed (and often in unforeseen ways) by individual action.

Consistent with this scholarship, I argue that movement activism can be instrumental in altering political and legal processes in a way that influences the construction of new rules and procedures that serve as subsequent political opportunities for action. In this way, social movement activism becomes an integral force in the construction of governance. How can mobilization impact the rulemaking capacity of governing organizations? This action can take various forms.

One such mode of action is legal activism. As discussed earlier, individuals and groups successfully utilize litigation strategies to pursue substantive policy goals and attain group objectives that include greater public inclusion for a particular disadvantaged interest. The litigation strategies of the American civil rights movement and women's movement are exemplary of this strategy (Morris 1984; O'Connor 1980). Costain (1992) and Freeman (1973) illustrate that the political action of the civil rights movement in utilizing rights provided under Title VII of the Civil Rights Act of 1964 subsequently changed the political opportunities for the women's movement. These strategies led to judicial decisions that ultimately changed the existing rules and procedures in a way that abolished exclusionary policies and created new participatory rights. Similarly, movement activists attain substantive policy changes through the courts. The pay equity movement in the United States utilized litigation and the threat of litigation to attain new equal pay regulations enabling new protection from discrimination (McCann 1994). The environmental movement in Europe – in Belgium, Italy and the United Kingdom in particular – utilize legal proceedings against their own national governments in order to strengthen compliance and implementation of EU environmental regulations giving greater rights to environmentalists to bring these claims (Cichowski 1998). In all of these cases, social activists utilize the courts to influence rulemaking and subsequent political opportunities for action.

Social movement activists also utilize lobbying tactics targeted at the policy arena to change the opportunities for inclusion and action. These include tactics that led to reform in both public policy and civic conceptions of nationhood (Giugni, McAdam and Tilly 1997). Button's (1989) examination of the civil rights movement illustrates how movement activists utilized lobbying tactics to change the political structures in American states. Further, other scholars focus on how social movement action can change rules and procedures beyond the production of substantive policy, including procedural change such as state policing methods (della Porta 1995). These studies bring our attention to the direct impact social movements and civil society can have on the rulemaking capacity of governing organizations with the consequence of changing governance structures enabling action in the future.

Similar to the effect of lobbying and direct pressure, scholars observe that activists can influence the general trajectory of policy agendas by utilizing their own expertise and technical knowledge to change policy frames (Mazey and Richardson 2001). Thus, I also explore less formal participation and tactics utilized by public interest movements to change policy frames. Indirect participation can come in the form of informal expert groups, data collection and special reports prepared by groups and policy institutes and the use of informal networks or the media. All of these activities can influence rulemaking by shaping the public policy agendas. Sometimes this takes the form of providing the necessary information for arguments of why an issue should be dealt with at a certain level of government or also through consciousness-raising efforts that change what is and is not perceived as a public policy issue. This argument is consistent with the scholarship on policy frames. Strategic actors operating within movements will act to change policy frames with the impact of changing general policy discourses and mobilizing new members (Snow and Benford 1988). Together these actions can change the overall inclusion of public interests.

As we have seen, social activists will utilize various strategies to pressure governing organizations to adopt rules and procedures that change the political opportunities enabling public access in a given political arena. Stated generally, mobilization can impact governance the extent to which it can successfully shape rulemaking (legislative action and litigation) processes that can lead to new opportunities for action. This strategic activism can take various forms:

- legal activism
- lobbying tactics
- change in policy frames.

It is through this dynamic process of mobilization that institutionalization can occur. I explore how movement form and available political opportunities may explain the relative success of a group to achieve these goals.

I have illustrated that mobilization can lead to the production of new rules and procedures. And just as litigation influenced this mobilization, mobilization can in turn feed back on litigation. Mobilization processes can shape the rules and procedures that subsequently serve as the necessary conditions for litigation. And the cycle begins again. Yet beyond this production of new rules and procedures, we might expect this process of public interest mobilization and subsequent rulemaking to have a direct impact on the overall openness of a given polity to civil society.

Mobilization feedback effect on civil society and public inclusion

We have seen how the extent that political opportunities shape mobilization in a way that enables social movement activists to successfully influence rulemaking by governing organizations, this mobilization may alter subsequent opportunities for action. Over time, the extent to which these opportunity structures (or rules and procedures governing movement access) change in a way that allows greater civil society access and participation, we might expect this institutional change to have a more long-term impact on public inclusion. As these rules and procedures become more formal and precise and larger in number, we might expect a greater presence and permanence of a particular public interest.

Beyond the development of public interest movements, we might expect that over time change in the rules and procedures can affect the overall openness of a given policy arena to public participation. Activists pressure for specific policy goals and objectives and in doing so they can subsequently alter the policy space in a way that promotes greater public access. The activities of the American civil rights movement are a case in point. While activists were fighting for specific rights, such as desegregation in schools, over time these activities expanded the boundaries of politics (Morris 1984). State-sanctioned discriminatory practices were increasingly abolished, changing the rules of access and the rights available to demand this public inclusion.

Further, this consequence is not always intended. For example, in the European context, women throughout the EU have filed lawsuits demanding protection against discrimination in employment. While these cases resolved a specific legal dispute, over time, this body of EU gender equality case law has provided the basis for subsequent EU legislative developments and the creation of a public sphere for women activists in EU politics (Cichowski 2004). This expansion in access to policy making often results for efficiency and legitimacy reasons as policy innovations often parallel a growth in the need for expert knowledge of and public support for complex public issues (Aspinwall and Greenwood 1998: 5). Yet as argued above, once these activists gain some access, their actions can lead to subsequent institutional change that over time can expand public access in a way that was not necessarily intended by the creators of the rule.

Together these arguments suggest the following expectation:

- We might expect that, over time, as public interest movements increasingly become more permanent and the policy process becomes more reliant on their presence, the polity would become increasingly more open to public participation and access.

In this section, I explained how institutionalization can occur through mobilization: how rules and procedures providing formal access and policy space can serve as political opportunities for public interest activism and how this mobilization can subsequently, through legal activism strategies, lobbying and changing policy frames, influence how courts and legislatures create subsequent rules and procedures that govern action. Ultimately, this institutional change can over time structure a given public interest movement and shape the overall openness of a given polity to public participation and inclusion. While scholars focusing on protest action have highlighted the limited activities of reform movements in EU politics, this study brings such conclusions into question by examining the many other strategies, including litigation, that transnational movements have successfully utilized (Imig and Tarrow 2001).

Litigation, mobilization and governance: when cause becomes effect

As we have seen, the interaction between institutions, organizations and actors can over time lead to institutionalization in any given polity. I have focused on how this process of institutionalization can occur through litigation and mobilization and why these two processes are both interconnected and analytically distinct. Figure 1.1 summarizes this dynamic. The black arrows denote the litigation dynamic and in this analysis the process begins with the arrow leading from governance to mobilization. Our discussion began with the necessary conditions that give rise to the litigation: a necessary rule or procedure (governance) embodying at least some implicit or explicit right that can be invoked through mobilization by social activists to bring a legal claim. This legal action can activate a court's judicial rulemaking capacity, a process of institutional change that can alter existing structures of governance. These are the rules and procedures governing a particular polity.

Institutional change can have both a direct and indirect impact on the rules and procedures that are opportunities for social movement action. This process of feedback effect entails both a direct impact on social movement action through rights creation and also a more indirect impact by influencing how legislative action (this involves legislative action by

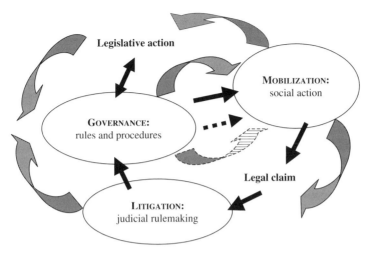

Note: The **BLACK** arrows denote the process by which the *LITIGATION DYNAMIC* proceeds. Beginning with **governance**, a necessary rule provides the opportunity for **mobilization** and this action can lead to a legal claim that activates **litigation** and potentially a court's judicial rulemaking capacity that can change the existing **governance** structures. This institutional change can subsequently affect mobilization both indirectly through legislative action (by lawmakers). Further it is important to note that at this point both executives and legislators can have a direct impact on this dynamic. However, the ruling can also have direct impact on mobilization by creating new rules (rights). Ultimately, these feedback effects denoted by the dashed arrow are not separate but essentially become the cause for subsequent action. The **GRAY** arrows denote the process by which the *MOBILIZATION DYNAMIC* proceeds. Although connected to litigation, it is also analytically distinct. Similar to the litigation dynamic, the process begins with **governance**, the rules and procedures that are opportunities for action. The subsequent **mobilization** can then shape these political opportunity structures through action that includes pressuring for and activating rule change through **litigation** as well as the legislative action. Ultimately, this rulemaking can lead to the expansion of **governance**, which serves as new opportunities for action. Similar to litigation, as denoted by the dashed arrow, this final effect becomes the cause of subsequent mobilization and the process begins again.

Figure 1.1 Conceptualizing the construction of governance through litigation and mobilization

lawmakers) can subsequently alter governance structures in a way that becomes the opportunities for action. This direct impact on mobilization is denoted by a dashed black arrow line in Figure 1.1, as we can see how this effect is not separate from, but essentially becomes the direct cause of subsequent activism. The litigation cycle begins again.

While interconnected, the mobilization dynamic is also analytically distinct. The mobilization dynamic is denoted by the thicker gray arrow and begins with the arrow leading from governance. I elaborated how the rules and procedures (governance) shape mobilization by creating formal access points and social spaces, which serve as political opportunities for action. This mobilization can shape subsequent political opportunities. This stage involves activists utilizing various strategies to influence the rulemaking of governing organizations (legislative action and legal claim leading to litigation). This rulemaking can lead to an expansion in the precision and scope of rules and procedures (governance) that are new opportunities for action. Again, cause becomes effect. Over time this process can shape public interest mobilization, shifting from individual action to the emergence of more formalized collective action, changing the general openness of a given polity to the public and civil society. This process of mobilization and rulemaking subsequently creates the necessary conditions for subsequent litigation. As the rules become more binding and precise, and expand in scope, and social actors increase in both number and permanence in a given polity, we might expect a greater likelihood for subsequent legal claims, an effect that begins the litigation, mobilization and rulemaking dynamic once again.

Explaining supranational governance in the EU: litigation and mobilization

The above discussion provides the general theoretical approach I utilize to explore the emergence of supranational governance in Europe. Litigation and mobilization processes enable us to examine to what degree, how and why supranational governance evolved in the EU. Similarly, the mobilization process, by which activists and groups participate in EU policy formation, is another avenue to study the impact of each of these policy actors on supranational governance.

Two policy areas – social provisions[7] and environmental protection – were chosen to examine how supranational governance might evolve in sectors primarily involved in *positive* integration – the construction of common European policies – as this presents us with a "hard case" (Scharpf 1996; Caporaso 1998). *Negative* integration involves the removal of national barriers to trade, competition and economic concerns, and it remains the driving force and primary explanation behind European integration. Some scholars argue that over time the economic bias in Commission and ECJ rule interpretation has led to the dominance

---

[7] In this study, I refer to this category using the official EU terminology. Despite its label, much of this domain pertains to gender equality. While the sector does include various sub-fields, such as social protection for transport workers or protection for employees when businesses are transferred, and more recently general anti-discrimination law, within the time period of this study the majority of the activity in litigation and mobilization pertain to gender equality and thus will be the focus of the analyses.

of negative over positive integration in EU policy making (Scharpf 1999). Others have argued that domestic commercial and economic motivations were the main force behind national government negotiations to pursue further European integration (Moravcsik 1998).

From the standpoint of the creators of the Treaty of Rome, it is less surprising that policy areas involving negative integration, such as free trade, have become institutionalized at the EU level. Less clear is an explanation for how policy areas involving positive integration, such as the EU regulation of national maternity rights or national bird conservation measures, developed at the supranational level. Further, this study moves beyond substantive policy description by focusing on the processes by which EU rules evolve, and on their potentially mobilizing effects. In doing so, I am able to examine the unintended consequences of EU institutions and organizations and highlight the political implications of economic integration.

Further, the social provisions and environmental policy domains are particularly fruitful for exploring the complex relationships that develop between group mobilization and citizen participation more generally. Both policy domains are characterized by public interest movements, women activists and environmentalists, which are not specific to the EU, but rather are observable in other political systems. Thus, we are able to test whether general characteristics of both the women's movement and environmental movement may influence their mobilizing in the EU setting. The policy domains offer variation in their legal bases: social provisions are traceable to the original treaties, whereas the environment is not. These rules serve as both the necessary conditions for litigation and potential opportunities for mobilization. Thus, by studying two policy domains with varying treaty basis, I can begin to understand the generalizable factors that may influence patterns of litigation and mobilization in the EU.

This study examines how two linked processes – litigation and mobilization – affected the development of these EU policy sectors. Again, it is worth reiterating. The presence of EU institutions in a particular policy area does not presuppose institutionalization. It is the presence and intensity of not only EU rules, but also EU organizations and transnational society in any given policy sector. Supranational litigation and transnational mobilization provide us with an avenue to explore these three elements. It remains an empirical question if, how and to what degree these policy areas became institutionalized at the supranational level. The answer is acutely important to scholars concerned with processes of supranational cooperation, as it may suggest that governance can evolve in directions that are not intended nor preferred by the creators of the process.

Organization of the book

The book will proceed as follows. Chapter 2 provides a quantitative overview of institutionalization through litigation and mobilization in the European Union over thirty-three years (1970–2003), across all fifteen member states during this time period,[8] and across legal domains. Guided by the theoretical approach introduced in this chapter (Chapter 1), I elaborate this model in terms of the European case. I highlight the main tensions characterizing these processes and suggest a set of testable explanations for this evolution.

I then turn to Part I, in which I examine the process of institutionalization through litigation. Chapter 3 focuses on this dynamic in the area of social provisions. I argue that institutionalization through litigation is the product of multiple processes. I explore these in turn. Through quantitative analyses and process tracing, the chapter examines the causes and effects of these processes, including the factors influencing the legal claim, the litigation and subsequently the effects of the ECJ's judicial rulemaking. Chapter 4 serves as a cross-sector comparison. In this chapter, through similar analyses, I test the social provisions findings against litigation processes in the area of environmental protection.

In Part II of the book I examine the process of institutionalization through mobilization. The causes and effects of transnational mobilization in the area of social provisions are the focus of Chapter 5. In particular, I focus on the political opportunities for action and the subsequent impact of this mobilization on public inclusion in the EU. With aggregate data, interviewing and historical documents, I test a set of expectations regarding the historical trajectory of public interest activism in the EU. Chapter 6 examines transnational mobilization in the area of environmental protection. Again, this cross-sector comparison enables us to distinguish generalizable patterns and consequences of public interest mobilization in the EU.

In the final chapter, I discuss the main theoretical and empirical findings of this study by focusing first on the individual processes of litigation and mobilization and then by evaluating these processes in terms of the stability of this institutionalization and implications for democracy in the

---

[8] The European Union today is twenty-five member states, with its most recent ten accession states joining the Community on 1 May 2004. While these new member states may be mentioned in discussion as relevant, the time period of this study limits the analyses to the EU 15.

EU. I end the chapter by discussing a broader set of lessons beyond the European experience. I argue that courts, and the actors they mobilize, are increasingly shaping the direction of domestic and international policy processes – a reality that challenges our current theoretical understandings of comparative and international politics (Cichowski 2006a, 2006b).

2 Overview of institutionalization in the European Union

This chapter offers an overview of the constituent elements of institutionalization in the European Union (EU), focusing on the processes of litigation and mobilization. The chapter is organized around four elements of these processes of institutionalization: the legal claim, litigation, legislative action and transnational mobilization. The legal claim gives rise to the litigation. The litigation activates European Court of Justice (ECJ) decision-making: a process that can lead to institutionalization to the extent to which the Court's judicial rulemaking expands the meaning and scope of EU law. This litigation in turn can alter legislative action at both the EU and national level. Finally, these institutional changes create the political opportunities for transnational mobilization: a process that once initiated can lead to institutionalization to the extent to which these transnational activists become increasingly formalized and expand the public sphere in EU politics.

The legal claim

As argued in Chapter 1, litigation is one process through which rule change can occur. In the EU, an increasing number of legal claims leading to litigation and ECJ decisions have dramatically influenced the shape of the Union. The Court's activism in the 1970s is now widely accepted as having transformed the Treaty of Rome, an international treaty governing nation-state economic cooperation, into a 'supranational constitution' granting rights to individual citizens (Lenaerts 1990; Mancini 1989; Stone Sweet and Brunell 1998a; Weiler 1981, 1991). The effect was dramatic: litigation rates skyrocketed as individuals and national courts were given new powers *vis-à-vis* their own national governments to ask for greater clarity of the rights embodied in EU law. And the ECJ responded, continuing a cycle of litigation that expanded the precision and scope of EU law. Legal claims brought through the Article 234 (ex 177) procedure, or preliminary ruling procedure, were acutely linked to this transformation.

The Article 234 procedure allows (and in some cases requires) national judges to ask the ECJ for a correct interpretation of EU law if it is material to the resolution of a dispute being heard in a national court. This is known as a *preliminary reference*. Thus, individuals are regularly engaging both EU law, and subsequently the EU legal system (if the national judge sends a reference) from their own national courts. This procedure is particularly fruitful for this study as it is the main avenue in which individuals and groups can engage the EU legal system, enabling us to examine the interaction between public interest mobilization and litigation in the EU.[1] Scholars now recognize the importance of this procedure, as it was primarily through the Court's case law pursuant to Article 234 that the Treaty of Rome was "constitutionalized" (Lenaerts 1990; Mancini 1989; Weiler 1981, 1991). Through the construction of the constitutional doctrines of *supremacy* and *direct effect*, the Court's rulings had the impact of expanding supranational governance not only by strengthening the Court's own authority, but by stimulating individual and group legal action that demanded clarification of EU rules (Burley and Mattli 1993; Stone Sweet and Caporaso 1998).

The *supremacy* doctrine (ECJ 1964) requires that national judges give precedent to EU rules over any national law or procedure that comes in conflict with these supranational rules, and *direct effect* (ECJ 1963) gives individuals directly enforceable rights under EU law. Generally, the Court's constitutional doctrine enabled individuals to seek new protection under EU law in their own national courts and provided a basis to bring legal action against their own governments (Alter 2001). Further, national judges were also given a new role by being asked to set aside national law and legal traditions, in order to resolve disputes that presented a conflict between EU and domestic rules (Slaughter, Stone Sweet and Weiler 1998). Following these rulings national governments were no longer the dominant proprietors of EU rule change: national judges, individuals and

---

[1] Article 230 also enables individuals and groups to bring legal proceedings directly before the ECJ. However, the standing requirements for this procedure, that the applicants must show a "direct and individual concern," has historically made it extremely difficult for actual use of this procedure by individuals and groups (Arnull 1995; Granger 2003; Harlow 1992a; Nettesheim 1996; Neuwahl 1996; Rasmussen 1980). The ECJ has interpreted this requirement very narrowly and when denying admissibility of claims has often encouraged organizations to resubmit the claim via their own national court and the Article 234 preliminary ruling procedure (see ECJ 1998c). That said, recent case law by the Court of First Instance in the *Jégo-Quéré* decision (CFI 2002) argued for greater individual access to Community courts to ensure both a better protection of rights and monitoring of Community action. The ECJ did not adopt this approach in a similar case, yet left the issue of standing decidedly ambiguous enough that there may be change in the future (ECJ 2002).

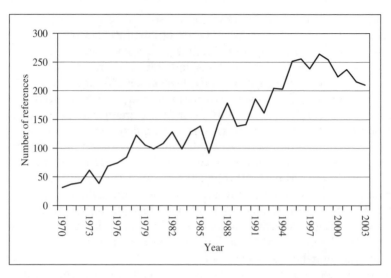

Note: N=4969
Source: Data compiled by the author from European Court of Justice. 2003, *Annual Report
2003, Statistics of Judicial Activity of the Court of Justice*, (p. 230). Luxembourg: Office
for Official Publications of the European Communities.
http://curia.eu.int/en/instit/presentationfr/rapport/stat/st03cr.pdf.

Figure 2.1 Annual number of Article 234 preliminary references sent to
the ECJ, 1970–2003

the ECJ were all given a greater role in EU rulemaking. The consequences
were legendary, with litigation rates skyrocketing: an outcome that could
not have been foreseen by the member states that created the Treaty.

The data in Figure 2.1 illustrate this systematic increase in the number
of legal claims resulting in Article 234 preliminary references. The figure
includes all preliminary references sent to the ECJ between 1970 and
2003 (N = 4969). In 1970, national courts sent only 32 preliminary
references to the ECJ. By the 1980s, this number had doubled, with a
total of 668 references in the 1970s compared to a total of 1253 preliminary references received by the Court during the decade of the 1980s. By
the 1990s, national courts were sending on average over 200 references a
year, a dramatic increase from the annual rate of 66 in the 1970s. Scholars
agree that the Court's constitutional doctrine helps explain this general
trend, as this case law led to the development of rules and procedures that
were opportunities for new legal claims (Stone Sweet and Brunell 1998a).

Further, this general trend is also observed across policy domains.
Figure 2.2 displays the evolution of preliminary references for both the

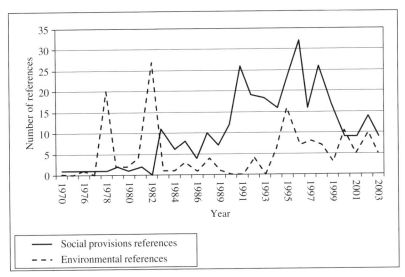

Note: The data begin with the first preliminary reference in each legal domain:
Social provisions references N = 307 (1970–2003)
Environmental references N = 148 (1976–2003)
Source: Data compiled by the author from European Communities. 2004. *CELEX Data Base*. Brussels: Office for Official Publications of the European Communities.

Figure 2.2 Annual number of Article 234 preliminary references by policy domain, 1970–2003

social provisions and environmental protection legal domains. The data begin with the Court's first reference for each domain (1970 for social provisions and 1976 for environmental protection) through 2003. Similar to the general trend these data illustrate that after at least some case law was developed in each area by the 1980s, national courts have on average sent more preliminary references each year. Like the impact of the Court's supremacy and direct effect rulings, the early case law in both of these legal domains provided the basis for subsequent action. The Court's 1970s *Defrenne* rulings (ECJ 1971; ECJ 1976a; ECJ 1978) transformed a distant Treaty provision into a rights provision enabling women throughout Europe to utilize the Equal Pay provision of the Treaty of Rome to bring discrimination claims before national courts (Cichowski 2004). Similarly, some ten years before environmental protection had a constitutional basis in EU law, the ECJ began to develop an environmental jurisprudence that expanded the legal claims available: an effect that enabled legal action, including environmentalists instigating legal proceedings against their own governments for non-compliance (e.g. ECJ 1994a; ECJ 1996b) and individuals and groups who were disadvantaged by national environmental regulations in one member state relative to another (e.g. ECJ 1985a).

Beyond the general trend: the national roots of the litigation

While the general increase in legal claims and subsequent litigation has gained significant attention, far less is known about the variation that characterizes this process (Stone Sweet and Brunell 1999). The cross-national variation is dramatic. Figure 2.3 displays the annual average number of references originating from each of the countries for both policy areas. The numbers are standardized to account for the varying years countries have joined the EU, and thus in which they might possibly be sending references. This comparison presents stark cross-sectoral differences. For example, while British courts are responsible for only 7 percent of environmental protection preliminary references in 30 years of preliminary procedure activity, their social provisions referrals make up

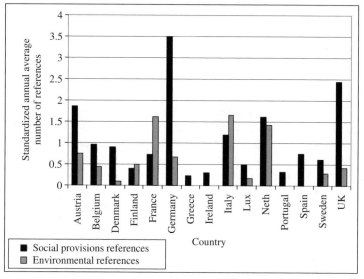

Source: Data compiled by the author from European Communities. 2004. *CELEX Data Base*. Brussels: Office for Official Publications of the European Communities. http://europa.eu.int/celex/htm/celex_en.htm.

Figure 2.3 Standardized average number of Article 234 preliminary references by country, 1970–2003

almost a quarter of all litigation in this area of EU law (20%). Germany exhibits similar patterns with their environmental references representing only 5 percent of the litigation in this area, and German courts leading all other countries in social provisions reference rate (30%). Conversely, Italian preliminary rulings dominate the area of the environment with 56 percent of all references originating from this legal system, yet their social provisions referrals make up a mere 6 percent of the litigation in this policy domain.

These data introduce a host of unanswered questions. Does the fact that over a quarter of all social provisions references originate from German courts suggest that German women face greater discriminatory practices relative to women in other member state countries? I suspect not. Instead, these litigation rates may be linked to the relative organizational capacity and legal resources available to individuals and groups who initiate this litigation. Yet, as previously argued, mobilized interests are clearly not the only essential ingredients for litigation. If they were, we might expect more commensurate rates of environmental litigation between Germany and the Netherlands, both countries with a comparatively strong environmental movement, yet considerable variation in environmental litigation (8 and 40 environmental preliminary references). From what we know about litigation more generally, the rules – both EU and national – invoked in these legal claims may also be a significant factor. Are the policy disparities between national and EU laws creating an opportunity for legal claims to the extent that individuals are disadvantaged by implementation difficulties? Further, do EU rules that construct new rights compared to the claims previously available under national law explain cross-national variation in reference rates?

These data also reveal significant variation across policy domains: 307 preliminary references invoking social provisions and only 148 involving environmental law. Is cross-sector variation a function of the level of ease to which any group or individual can make a rights claim under EU law, rather than the mere strength of an interest? While this study is concerned with explaining cross-national variation in the evolution of litigation in the social provisions and environmental policy domains, these data may give us some insight into general cross-sector differences. When looking at data across 14 domains, similar patterns are evident. Higher levels of preliminary references were found in those legal domains possessing mobilized interests (e.g. business, industry, agriculture, the state) supporting the litigation and whose claims involve fundamental Community rights or significantly legislated areas of Community law (e.g. free trade or agriculture policy). This may be one explanation for the legal domains receiving the highest number of preliminary references across a similar time period, 1958–1998: agriculture (1,008), free movement of goods (832) and Social Security (444).[2]

Explaining preliminary reference rate

In this study, I explore national level factors that give rise to preliminary references. This is important as it suggests how the national context may ultimately frame the ECJ's decision-making. The dynamics of this process continues to be contentious amongst scholars who are concerned with how and to what extent the national context shapes ECJ decision-making decisions (e.g. Garrett et al. 1998; Mattli and Slaughter 1998). I argue that the national context may impact these preliminary reference rates both in terms of the factors giving rise to the legal claims and also a national judge's decision to refer the case to the ECJ.[3]

This later point is important as legal scholars agree that the constitution-alization of the Treaty changed the strategic context facing judges, a shift that has generally been in the same pro-integration direction as EU law (Weiler 1981, 1991, 1994; Stein 1981). National judges acquired, some for the first time, the ability to alter state practices (judicial review) and did so under the protection that they were merely implementing preliminary rulings as required by the Treaty. This judicial empowerment argument has been elaborated by others to understand how this mutually empowering relationship between national judges and the ECJ enabled the integration of national law with EU law to form a new legal order – a consequence that was not necessarily welcomed or expected by member state governments (Burley and Mattli 1993). While this general argument helps us understand why national judges might refer, it does not help us understand the national factors that might inhibit a judge from sending a reference, nor does it help explain the variation noted above.[4] I focus on these latter points.

Mobilized interests

Scholars suggest that the decision to utilize litigation strategies by both individuals and groups can depend on a host of factors – ideas, organization,

---

[2] Data compiled by the author from Stone Sweet and Brunell (2000).

[3] Recognizing the significant challenges associated with identifying the factors that impact judicial preferences generally (e.g. Schubert 1965; Shapiro 1981) and the fact that we cannot systematically account for cases where the national judges have decided not to send a preliminary reference, I focus on measurable factors explaining variation both cross-nationally and across legal domains.

[4] Scholars have raised this question. Stone Sweet (1998) suggests that not all national judges would respond in this pro-integration direction for reasons of other policy opportunities and those who may believe ECJ case law would undermine their own jurisprudence.

economic conditions and political climate – but their findings uniformly confirm the importance of organization (Galanter 1974, 1983: 61; Jenkins 1983: 530; Zemans 1983: 697). Financial resources and foundation support are necessary when groups embark on the expensive road of litigation (Sorauf 1976; Vose 1959). In the European context, legal scholars examining the Article 234 procedure agree that organizational strength and longevity of the group are likely to matter. In the area of social provisions, scholars have found that well-established groups, such as trade unions, have a greater success with litigation strategies (Alter and Vargas 2000). Litigation is an expensive and sometimes last choice option for action, and thus the organizational strength of an interest movement becomes acutely important to not only utilize the national courts, but also possess the knowledge to use EU law (Harlow and Rawlings 1992). These arguments suggest the following general proposition:

- The greater the organizational strength of a national interest movement, relative to those found in other countries, the higher the level of preliminary references.

Legal resources

Beyond the organizational capacity of mobilized interests, the availability of legal resources at the national level for this litigation may help explain cross-national variation. Legal resources can take various forms and have multiple effects. First, legal resources in the form of governmental organizations may matter because they provide the necessary financial and expert resources that a public interest group or individual might lack to carry out litigation. In the area of social provisions, scholars suggest that the presence of governmental organizations, such as equality agencies, which are permeable to these societal interests and are equipped with the legal knowledge and expertise to sustain litigation, may lead to higher levels of Article 234 references from a particular country (Alter and Vargas 2000; Kenney 1992; Cichowski 2001).[5]

Second, legal resources for potential claimants may also come in the form of legal expertise (Vose 1959; Burstein 1991). Training in EU law varies substantially amongst member state countries, and thus we might expect this factor to influence not only the availability of lawyers to assist claimants but also how knowledgeable and thus favorable national judges are to these claims (Tyrrell and Yaqub, eds. 1993). For example, legal scholars observe

---

[5] These studies reveal that the Equal Opportunities Commission, a governmental agency in the United Kingdom, has been very active in generating and supporting litigation pursuant to Article 234.

that German labor court judges possess extensive knowledge and experience in both EU and national equality law, whereas Spanish judges have generally been criticized for lacking the awareness of EU equality law and an interest in resolving issues of gender inequalities (de la Fuente 2000: 98). This may help us understand the considerable variation in social provisions references sent from these two legal systems (68 references originating from German courts and only 5 from their Spanish counterparts).

Finally, I also conceptualize varying national standing rules or access to justice as legal resources that may impact levels of references. In particular, the fact that environmental groups have *locus standi* in Italy, Belgium and France may help explain the greater number of environmental references originating from these legal systems. Access to justice becomes a necessary legal resource, as without this national rule potential mobilized interests can't successfully bring a legal claim. Further, by examining this variation both within and across policy domains, this may bring into question general arguments that other factors such as level of court can explain general cross-national variation in preliminary references (Alter 1996; 2001). The data enable us to test this claim against the following expectation regarding legal resources:

• The greater availability of national level legal resources in a given legal domain, the higher levels of preliminary references from a legal system possessing these resources relative to others.

EU rules
Equally as important as these mobilized interests, the litigation dynamic is reliant on at least some necessary rule. Again, the preliminary ruling procedure involves national courts asking for a clarification or interpretation of EU rules. These EU rules may matter to the litigation in three ways.[6] First, variation in litigation rates may be related to the fit between EU and national policies: that is, the magnitude of the disparity between existing national rules and new EU rules in a given legal domain. Scholars observe that countries possessing greater policy disparities – both leader and laggard countries – are more likely to experience implementation

---

[6] The clarity and precision of EU rules may also matter for Article 234 references, however this is an indirect effect. By this I mean vague EU rules in conjunction with existing national policy priorities can lead to national level implementation problems and disparities. Subsequently, these national policy disparities, as earlier discussed, may be a direct cause of Article 234 litigation rather than the EU law itself. Further, the precision of EU rules is likely to possess greater significance in explaining the second stage of this litigation process: the ECJ preliminary ruling. Scholars suggest that both the precision and clarity of EU rules may impact the ECJ's decision making (e.g. Cichowski 1998; Garrett et al. 1998). I discuss this in the litigation section in relation to the Court's decision-making.

difficulties and delays (Börzel 1999; Knill and Lenschow 1998). Generally, these policy disparities can arise from unanimity voting in the Council, in which policy decisions often result in lowest common denominator positions. Thus, national legal regimes that represent lowest common denominator positions in the Council relative to other member states will disproportionately be the subject of this litigation (Stone Sweet and Caporaso 1998: 124).

Further, member state governments can decide how these policies are implemented into the national legal system, with relative inequalities arising not only from general transposition problems but also from national systems implementing comparatively more or less stringent requirements in line with their national policy priorities.[7] Scholars argue that such comparative inequalities become the basis for legal action (e.g. Stone Sweet and Caporaso 1998; Cichowski 1998).[8] In response to individuals who are either hindered or empowered by this disparity between national and EU rules, the ECJ is asked to provide a remedy to the dispute at hand.

If this expectation is true, it brings into question claims that these policy disparities should negatively impact preliminary references. Drawing from research on the environmental protection case law, Golub (1996) argues that UK judges are generally "loath" to send references, attributing these low reference rates to national judges' decisions to preserve national law that comes in conflict with EU law. If Golub were correct, these policy disparities would diminish reference rates, rather than being the source of higher reference rates as I have suggested. I test this alternate expectation against the following hypothesis:

• The better the fit between national and EU policy, the lower the level of Article 234 references generated from a particular national legal system relative to others.

Second, variation in preliminary references across policy domains may also be a function of the legal basis of the EU rule. In the EU context, individual legal claims are given greater strength against the state or

---

[7] For example, in the environmental case, laggard countries experience more difficulties not only due to substantive policy change, but also procedural questions over which regional or national authority is responsible for implementing this new legislation (Knill and Lenschow 1998). Also, leader countries while experiencing the same substantive policy change difficulties may also inadvertently create disparities by implementing more stringent protective measures (even when allowed under EU law), which may conflict with other EU rights, such as free trade. The Dutch transposition of the Wild Birds Directive is such an example (see Cichowski 1998).

[8] Legal mobilization scholars observe a similar dynamic in domestic court systems, such as disparities between state and federal law in the United States (e.g. McCann 1994). Litigation becomes one way to correct these policy inequalities.

another body when directly effective treaty based rights or general EU principles are invoked. For example, individuals have considerable difficulty making individual rights claims invoking EU environmental law – a legal domain that gained a constitutional basis in the 1980s, much later than other domains, such as free movement of workers or gender equality (e.g. Krämer 1991a). This is true for the following reasons. Member state governments are bound to adhere to general principles when they derogate from a European rule. And national implementations of EU laws are constrained by these principles.[9] As one jurist argues, general principles can directly constrain national legislative actions, even legislation that is solely domestic in origin (Ellis 1998a). Further, litigants are aware that the ECJ can utilize these rights to justify a broad and purposeful interpretation of treaty provisions and secondary legislation (ECJ 1991a).

Finally, the distinction between rights in the Treaty and rights in secondary legislation is crucial, as the nature and scope of the former are relatively immune to change except through litigation. The relative ease of adopting new legislation or making amendments to existing secondary legislation is subject to the voting rules governing that area of law (unanimity versus qualified majority voting) (Craig and de Búrca 1998), whereas treaty amendments require unanimity voting and occur less frequently compared to the production of new legislation (Pollack 1997). Authors have cited this distinction as enhancing the ECJ's power *vis-à-vis* member state governments, by constraining their ability to modify adverse rulings.[10] Further, individuals can invoke treaty provisions that confer directly applicable rights and these rights must be protected. Directives do not provide the same scope of rights as treaty provisions. This is primarily because directives lack horizontal direct effect (they cannot be used in disputes between two private parties), whereas treaty provisions can be invoked in such disputes.

Together these arguments suggest the following expectation:

- Other things equal, we expect more litigation in those policy domains in which treaty based rights are directly effective and in those involving long standing rights derivative of the treaty rather than secondary legislation.

Finally, EU rules, in the form of ECJ precedent, may impact levels of preliminary references to the extent to which these rulings create the opportunity for subsequent legal action. As discussed, the Court's constitutional doctrines of supremacy and direct effect increased the overall opportunity for new legal claims (Stone Sweet and Brunell 1998a; Mattli and Slaughter 1998). Similarly, ECJ rulings that have the effect of

---

[9] The Court has defined this constraint in its case law (ECJ 1989a; ECJ 1994b; ECJ 1996c).
[10] See Pollack (1997; 2003); Garrett et al. (1998: 160–61); Mattli and Slaughter (1998).

invalidating national rules or practices within a particular policy domain may lead to more litigation in that area. Such rulings can empower individuals, who previously may have exhausted all domestic opportunities, by giving them a new avenue to bring legal claims (Cichowski 2001). From what we know generally about political opportunity structures, we would expect individuals and public interest groups to take advantage of these new opportunities created by the Court's rulings (Marks and McAdam 1996). Stated generally:

- The more new rulings create new legal bases for individual claims in a given EU policy domain, the more we expect increasing levels of preliminary references in that domain.

Methodology and data sources

My research problem presents an unusual methodological challenge. I am interested in factors that affect Article 234 reference rates both within and across member states. Further, I must adopt a longitudinal design in order to explain variation over time. To test these hypotheses, I compiled a data set utilizing the European Communities CELEX database[11] and the *European Court Reports*.[12] The data set includes all preliminary references from the sectors of social provisions from the first reference in 1970 to 2003 (N = 307) and environmental protection from the first reference in 1976 to 2003 (N = 148).[13] Each case was coded according to country of origin, file date, level of national court of origin and EU laws invoked in each case. These data are particularly fruitful for my research questions as they allow us to trace over time which countries receive the bulk of legal claims, which level of the judiciary send references and which EU laws are continually the subject of these disputes.

The measures for the individual predictors are compiled from various sources and include all 15 member state countries. In-depth national and EU level interviews with legal experts and EU officials, primary source data collection and public opinion surveys provide the basis for these

[11] The CELEX database contains all Community legal documents until 31 December 2004. The database is located at http://europa.eu.int/celex/htm/celex_en.htm.

[12] This is a compendium published by the Community, including the full text of the case law of the ECJ.

[13] This study utilizes the two categorical subdivisions of Article 234 preliminary references that the Court has labeled "environmental protection" and "social provisions." The former category denotes those cases involving EU environmental regulations and the later category includes cases involving Community social policy: a category that includes equality legislation, protection of employee's social benefits (e.g. working hours) and health and safety standards. It does not include social security measures, which the ECJ labels separately.

measures. For mobilized interests, I examine the organizational strength of groups potentially involved in the litigation by utilizing a general cross-national measure of trade union and environmental group strength.[14] I measure legal resources by coding for the presence of national agencies that support litigation pursuant to Article 234 and the level of training and knowledge in a given area of EU law possessed by the legal community in a given country.[15] To measure the impact of EU rules on reference rate, I constructed a EU/national policy fit variable based on each country's transposition rate for each policy area.[16] Also, through process

---

[14] The question appears in the World Values Survey. The score assigned to each country in each legal domain is the percentage of respondents belonging to the particular organization and represents an average for the four years the survey was given (1981, 1990, 1995, 2001, sample size varies slightly according to country and year, but is generally between 1000–1300). I focus on the two organizations that are most likely to support this litigation: trade unions and environmental organizations. I did not include women's groups, as preliminary research revealed that organized women's groups had little direct involvement in this litigation. Instead, they have served as an indirect effect in terms of legal expertise and disseminating information on sex equality laws (see CEC 2000a; Bretherton and Sperling 1996). The question follows: "Please look carefully at the following list of voluntary organizations and activities and say which if any do you belong to: v.22 Trade Unions v.26 Conservation, the environment, ecology."

[15] In the social provisions sector, countries are coded on a scale of 0–3 depending on the number of legal resources available for EU legal claims in that policy domain. The scale denotes the presence of the 3 main sources of support: an active and accessible (to the public) equality agency, an equality agency that supports this type of litigation, and active community of social provisions legal experts. In the area of environmental protection, countries are coded on a scale from 0–3. The scale denotes the presence of 3 main sources of support: historical legal basis for environmental rights (e.g. Constitutionally protected right), active and accessible (to the public) environmental ministry/agency and network of environmental legal specialists. This coding is derived from extensive primary source documents and interviews to ensure accuracy in this measure. These factors were chosen for their theoretical relevance to litigation pursuant to Article 234. Conceivably each country is home to myriad legal resources that may influence other avenues of litigation in other areas of law. This measure does not attempt to include data on all legal resources that characterize these individual national legal systems. This coding is also policy area specific rather than a general country characteristic. For example, in the area of gender equality the UK is coded 2, as it possesses an active governmental agency and one that can and does support EU legal claims. And in the area of the environment, the UK is coded 0 as it lacks the three requisite legal resources in this policy area.

[16] The average transposition rate for each country in each policy area is the percentage of EU secondary legislation that was applicable to date that has been properly transposed into national law. This is compiled from data collected by the Commission (see *Annual Report on Monitoring the Application of Community Law*, various years, 1985–2003). For example in 1995, Italy had transposed 113 of a total of 133 environmental directives (85%), and thus its transposition rate for that year was 85%. Scholars have brought attention to the limitations of such data in measuring the real national level substantive policy effects of the implementation (Collins and Earnshaw 1992; Macroy 1992). Instead, this measure reveals only when EU legislation is transposed into national law, and leaves unanswered the practical application of these transpositions (e.g. enforcement and monitoring). That said, for the purposes of this study, the measure is theoretically

tracing and case law analysis, I examine the impact of ECJ precedent over time. By reading all the cases in both policy domains, I am able to examine if and how ECJ precedent altered EU rules and procedures at a given point in time and then examine how this influenced opportunities for legislative action and subsequent mobilization in the future.

Litigation and institutionalization

In the previous section I discussed the origins of the litigation: the legal claim. Given that the legal claim leads to litigation that results in a preliminary reference to the ECJ, I now examine how this litigation can impact institutionalization in our policy domains. In particular, I examine the factors shaping the ECJ's decision-making in these cases and ask how this may impact the rules, EU organizations and transnational actors that characterize the policy domains.

Historically, ECJ decision-making has received the vast majority of scholarly attention.[17] This is not surprising as it provides in clear view the Court's reasoning on important questions of European policy and procedure. As previously argued, judicial decisions are important because they can tell the legislature what to do and they also create opportunities for subsequent action. Scholars agree that ECJ rulings have become embedded in EU law and subsequently serve as a benchmark for what constitutes lawful and unlawful practices.[18] In particular, scholars now recognize that over the years the Court's burgeoning body of preliminary rulings was crucial to the expansion of the integration project (Mattli and Slaughter 1998).

The data in Figure 2.4 illustrate a similar increase in preliminary rulings in our two legal domains. This comparison shows dramatic cross-sector differences in total numbers of preliminary rulings. EU social provisions were invoked in ECJ rulings almost four times as often as environmental laws. Further, the general evolution of judicial rulings in

---

relevant and sufficient for an investigation of the causes of legal claims. As earlier argued, transposition problems and inconsistencies, alone, can become the opportunity for legal action.

[17] For a comprehensive overview of political science research on this subject see Mattli and Slaughter (1998); see de la Mare (1999) for legal scholarship.

[18] Burley and Mattli (1993: 67) observe that ECJ rulings establish what is "law" in the EU and this subsequently causes member state governments, national courts and individuals to "shift their expectations" regarding how their behavior in the future should be conducted in accordance with this new rule. Similarly, even early Court watchers observe that the briefs submitted by member states (observations) in Article 234 cases reveal that even national governments who were critical of ECJ rulings, would use these as a basis (or departure) for future argumentation, rather than asking that the ruling be overturned (see Rasmussen 1986: 275–81).

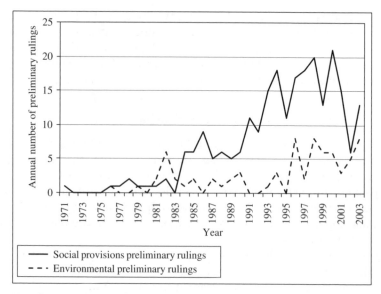

Note: Social provisions rulings N = 240
Environment rulings N = 73
Source: Data compiled by the author from European Communities. 2004. *CELEX Data Base*. Brussels: Office for Official Publications of the European Communities.
http://europa.eu.int/celex/htm/celex_en.htm.

Figure 2.4 Annual number of ECJ rulings pursuant to Article 234 references by policy domain, 1971–2003

these two policy domains is also distinct. ECJ rulings involving environment laws remained relatively low for almost a decade before gaining some momentum in the early 1990s, while the number of cases invoking social provisions has systematically increased since the mid 1980s. The data also reveal some similarities in a general dip in the early 2000s, followed by an upsurge. As discussed, variation in total number may be a product of the relative difficulty experienced by individuals and groups attempting to invoke EU environmental law for individual rights claims. These data also raise questions regarding factors specific to the Court's decision-making. Have judicial rulings in the area of social provisions created more opportunities for subsequent litigation than in the environmental domain, and if so how? Have member state governments been able to constrain the impact of ECJ environmental rulings as a result of rights derived largely from secondary legislation versus treaty based rights? An explanation is important for understanding this process of institutionalization.

General approaches and assumptions

Explanations for the Court's preliminary rulings and jurisprudence more generally have evolved in terms of two opposing approaches: neofunctionalism and intergovernmentalism.[19] In explaining ECJ judicial decision-making, neofunctional explanations privilege the autonomy of the Court in expanding the scope and reach of EU competence and intergovernmentalists maintain that ECJ judicial decisions are largely a function of member state government policy preferences.[20] Despite these opposing explanations, scholars have also come to agree on a set of shared assumptions regarding ECJ decision-making.

First, the ECJ is a strategic actor that is interested in expanding its competence. Although clearly amending an earlier position on the Court's behavior, Garrett et al. assert in no uncertain terms, "the ECJ has a clear institutional interest in extending the scope of Community law and its authority to interpret it" (Garrett et al. 1998: 155). This statement is generally derivative of arguments posited by academic lawyers (Stein 1981; Weiler 1981, 1991, 1994; Mancini 1989). Similarly, it forms the foundations of neofunctional arguments that link legal integration to the Court's interest in promoting "its own prestige and power by raising the visibility, effectiveness, and scope of EU law" (Mattli and Slaughter 1998: 180). Neofunctionalists argue that through the doctrines of direct effect and supremacy, the ECJ extended the reach of the EU legal system deep into national legal systems, enlisting national judges and community citizens in the process of European integration (Stone Sweet and Brunell 1998a; Burley and Mattli 1993).

The second main assumption states that the Court will operate as an independent interpreter of EU law and it is aware that its legitimacy is inherently linked to fulfillment of this obligation. Article 4 of the Treaty of Rome details in what capacity the ECJ was to fulfill this task: (1) by serving as a check on the political authority of EU organizations, such as the Commission and Council of Ministers; (2) by filling in vague aspects of EU laws; and (3) by ruling in cases raised by the Commission or member state governments as a result of member state

---

[19] The utility of these two opposing approaches has received recent criticism (see Mattli and Slaughter 1998: 178–79).

[20] Legal integration scholars writing in the neofunctional tradition include: Burley and Mattli (1993); Stone Sweet and Brunell (1998a); Weiler (1991). For an intergovernmental approach see Garrett (1992, 1995); Moravcsik (1995, 1998). For an overview of this scholarship see Mattli and Slaughter (1998).

non-compliance.[21] In explaining the Court's judicial decision-making, scholars give pride of place to legitimacy as a constraining factor on the Court's behavior. Garrett et al. argue that the ECJ's legitimacy "relies on the support of member state governments and hence its [the ECJ] serving as an impartial interpreter of EU law" (Garrett et al. 1998: 151). Similarly, neofunctionalists argue that the Court is aware of its legitimacy and operates to protect it, especially when making expansive rulings, yet does not yield to the policy positions of national governments in order to do so. Instead, this is achieved through strategies that include the incremental development of doctrine (e.g. Alter 1998; Hartley 1988), strategic use of legal reasoning and precedent (Weiler 1991: 2425; Burley and Mattli 1993; Stone Sweet 2004) and use of the Commission's legal argumentation (Mattli and Slaughter 1998: 181; Burley and Mattli 1993).

Yet these two assumptions leave unanswered many questions regarding important aspects of ECJ decision-making. In particular, do the preferences of member state governments impact the Court's ability to interpret and fill in vague aspects of EU rules? Or is there a larger dynamic driven by the interaction between EU and national legal factors that influence the Court's ability to fulfill its tasks and make judicial decisions independent of national government positions? Equally contested is the Court's behavior in preserving its legitimacy. Is the ECJ's ability to decide against a member state's national practices (an adverse ruling) constrained by potential retaliation and national level political factors or does the Court rely on EU institutions and organizations to protect its legitimacy? While scholars continue to assert very divergent explanations for the Court's judicial decisions, we lack systematic case-by-case empirical tests of these opposing arguments.[22]

---

[21] Although member state governments have voiced concern over unwieldy ECJ activism, these governments continue to strengthen the Court's capacity to fulfill these roles (Alter 1998). In 1986, the Treaty of Rome was amended to include a Court of First Instance to allow greater examination of Commission activities in the area of competition policy. The Treaty on European Union further enhanced the ECJ's power in two ways. First, its capacity to check EU organizational power was extended by providing the European Parliament with the legal opportunity to challenge Council and Commission activities. Second, ECJ judicial decisions were given greater force by enabling the Commission to assess monetary penalties to member states that failed to implement ECJ decisions. A recent ruling by the Court against Greece for a significant monetary penalty illustrates that the Court will not hesitate to assert these new powers (ECJ 2000b).

[22] Scholars have begun to take notice of this deficiency (Mattli and Slaughter 1998; Garrett et al. 1998).

*Explaining litigation: decision-making, rulemaking
and opportunities for action*

In order to test these divergent approaches, I suggest how the Court's rulings pursuant to Article 234 evolved as a dynamic process between the Court's decision-making and rulemaking and individuals and EU organizations seizing these new opportunities to push for greater policy expansion.

Upholding EU interests: allies in the Commission

The fact that the ECJ acts to expand EU competence and that its legitimacy is linked to its role as independent interpreter of EU law presents the Court with a tension. Stated more generally, the Court gains its basic legitimacy from its ability to independently resolve the disputes before it, yet at the same time it acts as an organization of the Community imposing EU rules through its interpretations of the Treaty and secondary legislation. This tension is familiar to scholars of judicial politics who examine the paradox of "judicial independence" (Shapiro 1981). Thus, instead of cowing to the political interests involved in a given dispute – an act that would tarnish the ECJ's image of independence – we might expect the ECJ to act in its own interest by fulfilling its mandated role of clarifying EU rules and creating an effective supranational legal system. In fact, the creators of the Treaty were careful to ensure that the Court was given a significant degree of independence to fulfill this task: judges hold six-year terms and cannot be removed during their tenure, and decisions are made secretly by majority vote.

How does the Court preserve its legitimacy? Scholars suggest that the Commission's position is a far better predictor of how the Court will rule than the policy positions of member state governments (Pescatore 1974; Stein 1981; Burley and Mattli 1993; Mattli and Slaughter 1998; Stone Sweet and Caporaso 1998; Cichowski 1998). Before deciding a case, member state governments and the Commission are able to submit a written brief (known as an *observation*) stating their opinion on how the case should be decided. In this instance, the Court maintains its legitimacy not by yielding to a member state's position that may lead to the threat of member state non-compliance with an adverse ruling, but instead relies on the "advantage of objectivity" as gained from the Commission's argumentation (Pescatore 1974: 80).[23] Similar to the

---

[23] Originally, legal scholars developed this argument (Pescatore 1974; Stein 1981). Today, this proposition plays an integral part in neofunctional theories of legal integration (e.g. Burley and Mattli 1993; Mattli and Slaughter 1998).

Court, the Commission's interests operate to expand the effectiveness of EU competence and thus embody this supranational perspective. As one legal scholar argues, should the Court decide to utilize the Commission's stance, its legitimacy remains intact as this interest is perceived as neutral compared to the individual interests of member governments involved in a given case (Pescatore 1974). Emphasizing the influence of the Commission on ECJ preliminary rulings, this approach suggests the following general expectation:

- All else equal, we would expect Commission positions to predict the final ECJ ruling in any given case more often than the stated policy positions of member state governments.

Clarifying rules

How does the Court's decision-making evolve? As previously mentioned in relation to legal claims, ECJ decision-making evolves in the context of EU laws and national practices that give rise to the dispute. Individuals who are advantaged by EU rules and hindered by national law turn to the Court for third-party dispute resolution (Stone Sweet and Brunell 1998a; Stone Sweet and Caporaso 1998). The Court's ruling provides a resolution to the particular dispute at hand, and is also prospective by signaling how the Court will settle similar disputes in the future. And in fulfilling this demand for an effective supranational legal system, we might expect the Court will act in its own interest by bringing greater clarity to these laws.

Following this argument, we might expect the precision or clarity of EU law to matter in this process of ECJ decision-making. That is, the pre-liminary ruling will, more often than not, function to clarify vague aspects of EU law at the origin of the dispute, rather than systematically serving to preserve national legal practices. For example, EU framework legislation governing waste disposal systems have provided general rather than specific guidelines regarding the definition of waste. The end result has been a patchwork of regulatory systems throughout Europe in which the cost to dispose of a particular material (considered waste in one country and a reusable material in another) varies (Krämer 2000). This economic disadvantage can lead to legal action and the Court is asked to bring clarity to this area of EU law (Cichowski 1998).

This argument stands in stark contrast to scholars who maintain that ECJ decision-making is a product of member state preferences. In parti-cular, Garrett et al. (1998) argue that the ECJ is more likely than not to refrain from making an adverse ruling (a decision that a national practice is in violation of EU law) if there are high domestic costs associated with the ruling and if there are consistently a relatively large number of adverse rulings in the particular area of EU law. Further, opposite of my argument, these scholars assert that the greater the clarity of EU rules invoked in a case the more likely the ECJ will issue an adverse ruling (Garrett et al. 1998: 157). This approach assumes that the Court's legitimacy is compromised not only by member government defiance of rulings that are too costly, but also if the Court deviates from clearly defined EU laws.

The following expectation serves as guide for the analysis and provides an alternate logic by which to test these opposing claims:

- We would expect that disproportionately vague EU laws would be the subjects of Article 234 rulings. Further, in the absence of clear EU policy prescriptions to handle a conflict between EU law and national legal practices, we might expect ECJ rulings to operate to expand and uphold EU rules, rather than preserve the legal practices or policy preferences of member state governments.

Judicial rulemaking, institutionalization and opportunities for action

That said, as the ECJ rulings bring greater clarity to these vague provisions we might expect more litigation rather than less. The logic follows. As earlier argued, through its interpretation of existing law, a court's rulings can lead to the construction of new rules and procedures. Thus, ECJ precedent can provide the opportunity for subsequent rights claims. As the Court's rulings bring greater clarity to an EU rule, defining what is and is not a lawful practice, we might expect individuals to have a more powerful tool to litigate. Quite the opposite of an intergovernmental argument, adverse rulings, while placing a constraint on member state governments (by finding a national practice in violation of EU law), are simultaneously empowering not only the party that won, but also those who might bring a similar claim in the future. Rather than constraining the Court, this adverse ruling instead provides the opportunity for subsequent action, and the process of litigation and judicial rulemaking begins again. Scholars also observe that courts often construct denser arguments to justify adverse rulings, a fact that empowers individuals interested in making a similar claim in the future (Stone Sweet 2000). Further, the increased clarity provided by ECJ rulings can also serve to highlight more gaps between national and EU law, thus increasing the number of possible national practices in question. It is through this process of litigation and judicial rulemaking that institutionalization can occur.

How can we measure this impact of institutionalization? Institutionalization in any policy domain begins by looking at whether the Court's jurisprudence transformed or changed the EU institutions governing activity in this domain. First, I examine the impact of ECJ jurisprudence on EU institutions and ask whether these rules have changed in precision and if they have become more binding and enforceable. As European rules become more precise and non-compliance is met with greater enforceable penalties, we can expect the policy area to become more institutionalized at the EU level. Second, institutionalization can be measured in terms of whether ECJ rulings have changed the scope of EU institutions. As the purview of EU rules expands, one can expect a greater number of actions to be formally governed by EU law. As we move across this continuum of precision, enforceability and scope, we find institutionalization at the EU level taking place. Stated generally:

- The extent to which ECJ rulings expand the scope, precision and enforceability of EU rules relative to the policy objectives of member states, and the extent to which this enables new rights claims *vis-à-vis* existing national rules, we would expect that legal domain to become less intergovernmental.

Judicial rulemaking, institutionalization and EU organizations

This process of rule construction through litigation can also have significant consequences on the relative influence that EU organizations exert on supranational policy outcomes. Scholars assert that through its jurisprudence the ECJ has operated to expand its own competence with the effect of diminishing member government control over integration (e.g. Burley and Mattli 1993; Stone Sweet and Caporaso 1998). It is well-documented in the literature that the Court's constitutional doctrine is an example of the Court enhancing its own power relative to member governments (Mattli and Slaughter 1998). I examine whether the same dynamic may influence the relationship between the Court and the Commission *vis-à-vis* member state governments in controlling the direction of EU policy.

Scholars assert that bureaucracies will operate in an efficient manner. In particular, their behavior will be structured in a way that will facilitate efficient policy making in an environment that is characterized by "limited capabilities and the cost of information" (Downs 1967: 2; see also Mazey and Richardson 2001). The Commission is clearly faced with a tough exercise in procuring less costly information, as it is given the task of policy formulation in an environment where policy proposals are evaluated by 15 national governments with varying policy priorities. The Court's jurisprudence may help to eliminate the uncertainty of policy success in two ways. First, it provides the doctrinal basis and legal argumentation that helps the Commission legitimize its policy proposals. Second, the Court's case law may also provide information on who might support or obstruct a particular policy proposal, giving the Commission a forewarning on potential allies and foes it will encounter with future legislative proposals.[24] EU scholars have taken notice of this symbiotic and empowering relationship (Pollack 1998, 2003; Westlake 1994).

An important aspect of this power relationship between EU organizations and member states relates to the relative ease with which member states can reverse ECJ rulings. Drawing attention to the options available to member state governments, scholars have distinguished between ECJ rulings involving constitutional law (treaty provisions) versus statutory rules (secondary legislation) (Stone Sweet and Caporaso 1998). In order to change or reverse an ECJ decision interpreting the Treaty, member states must reach a unanimous decision to amend the Treaty in a way that would change the meaning or scope of the judicial decision: a relatively difficult act to achieve (e.g. Alter 1998; Stone Sweet and Caporaso 1998). On the other hand, judicial decisions altering the meaning of secondary legislation could be subsequently amended through new secondary legislation: an endeavor that varies in difficulty depending on the policy area (e.g. varying voting and consultation procedures), but is generally easier to attain than Treaty amendments. Thus, we might expect that expansive ECJ rulings involving Treaty provisions will be more likely to enhance the power of EU organizations *vis-à-vis* member state governments than similarly expansive rulings invoking secondary legislation. Together these arguments suggest a second general effect of the ECJ rulings:

- To the extent that ECJ rulings strengthen the relative power of EU organizations *vis-à-vis* members states in shaping a given policy domain, we would expect the domain to become less intergovernmental.

Data sources and methodology

The data utilized in this analysis includes all ECJ rulings pursuant to Article 234 preliminary references in the sectors of social provisions from the first ruling in 1971 to 2003 (N = 240) and environmental protection from the first ruling in 1976 to 1993 (N = 73). I compiled the decisions from the *European Court Reports*, a full text compendium of ECJ decisions. Further, this quantitative data was supplemented by extensive historical documentation collected by the author through personal interviews with legal experts and EU officials in Brussels, Belgium and court

---

[24] The Court's jurisprudence, and especially the written briefs associated with these cases, demonstrates whether national governments and varying national and transnational interests will be opponents or proponents of a given European policy position.

officials in Luxembourg and through the EU Documentation Archive located at the European University Institute in Florence, Italy. This documentation includes official national and EU publications focusing on policy implementation and adoption, as well as those focusing on implementation of ECJ decisions; personal interviews with both current and former EU policymakers and legal advisors; and interviews with legal experts.

Through this systematic and historical examination of ECJ decisions I can determine how and whether the rulings create the opportunity for action. How did the ECJ's jurisprudence impact the Commission's legislative work? And how do member state policy positions impact these rulings? In order to answer these questions, I read all cases, including the decisions, advocate general's statements and the written observations filed in the case. It is only through a systematic examination of the Court's case law that includes all cases in a legal domain over time that we can begin to understand how institutionalization can occur through litigation.

Integral to the Article 234 procedure are 'observations,' which are written briefs filed by the Commission and the member state governments (regardless of whether the case originates in their legal system) stating how they believe the case should be decided (or more generally how the EU law should be interpreted in relation to the national practice). Scholars note that member state governments or EU organizations submitting observations are interested in having their policy position considered, in an attempt to affect the potential policy outcomes of the decisions (de la Mare 1999: 243–44; Granger 2004).

I coded the data in the following manner. The rulings were all coded by country of origin, date of decision, litigants (non-governmental organizations, individuals, multiple parties, etc.) and EU law invoked in the case. The litigant information gives us some idea who is mobilizing the law and whether they are doing it collectively. By examining the EU laws invoked in these cases, I am able to determine how the clarity of EU laws impact the context of the Court's decision-making. Are vague policy positions embodied in framework directives and lowest common denominator decision-making the subject of litigation? Does the Court bring greater clarity to these rules or preserve the member state policy positions they embody? Each ruling was coded into one of two categories:

- **Consistent ruling**: the Court accepted a national rule or practice as consistent with EU law.
- **Adverse ruling**: the national rule was declared to be in violation of EU law.

This measure gives us some idea whether ECJ rulings operate to preserve national legal practices in any systematic way or whether the rulings serve to uphold and expand EU competence. The written observations were also coded into two categories:

- **Successful**: the observation was successful at predicting the ECJ's ruling.
- **Unsuccessful**: the observation was unsuccessful at predicting the ECJ's ruling.

Similarly, this gives us some idea of whether member state policy positions are reflected in ECJ rulings. As an example of how both rulings and observations were coded, consider a case involving the compatibility of a French environmental law with EU law. If the effect of the ECJ judgment is to find French law to be in violation of EU law then this decision would be coded as an adverse ruling. Subsequently, if the British government filed an observation in this case stating that the French law was compatible with EU law, then the British observation would be coded as unsuccessful. The British position, as stated in the written observation, was unsuccessful at predicting the final ECJ ruling.

Further, each case is coded for the total number of member states submitting written observations. The rulings that have larger political or financial impacts (often beyond the particular national legal system in question), often elicit a larger number of member state observations (Granger 2004). This is not surprising, as the rulings can potentially have significant policy impacts in all the member states (often with steep financial costs), and this is an opportunity for national governments to articulate how an important EU policy question should be answered. This measure enables us to test whether the ECJ is at all constrained by the possible high financial costs associated with a potential adverse ruling.

Finally, by reading the case law, I am able to examine the impact of ECJ precedent on subsequent decision-making. Through process tracing, I trace the Court's case law, examining whether the Court's rulings change the precision and scope of EU law and how this may create new rights that are linked to subsequent action and litigation. Further, I examine how this judicial rulemaking may impact EU organizational power, the extent to which member states act to reverse decisions in the future and how this impacts policy development.

Legislative action

The previous sections developed a set of expectations regarding the general pattern of litigation: the national level factors influencing the legal claim and how the litigation can lead to institutionalization through

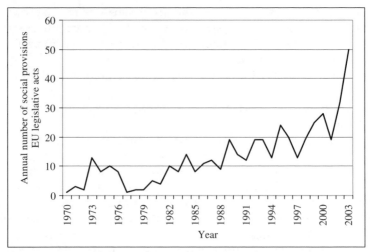

Note: N=457
Source: Data compiled by the author from CEC (2005) and European Communities. 2004.
CELEX Data Base. Brussels: Office for Official Publications of the European
Communities.
http://europa.eu.int/celex/htm/celex_en.htm.

Figure 2.5 Annual number of EU legislative acts in the area of social
provisions, 1970–2003

the court's judicial rulemaking. An explanation of how this litigation
develops is inherently connected to the evolving policy context. As previously argued, legislative action can be both a cause and effect of the
litigation. Further, a similar relationship also exists between this policy
context and mobilization processes; the extent to which these rules and
procedures function as opportunities for transnational mobilization. In
this section, I provide an overview of the evolution of EU legislative action
in both of our policy domains. I contrast the two legal domains highlighting the treaty basis, general developments and policy tensions. By
examining the policy development over time, we are able to examine how
the ECJ judicial rulemaking and public interest mobilization may have
influenced this trajectory.

Expanding EU policy competence: an overview

I begin by looking at the general evolution of our two policy domains
both in terms of total number of legislative acts adopted as well as
supporting policy infrastructure. Figure 2.5 displays the total annual
quantity of secondary legislation adopted in the area of social provisions

between 1970 and 2003. The total number of EU acts adopted increased at a steady rate with 50 pieces of secondary legislation in the 1970s and this doubling to 100 in the 1980s. The legislative output continued to increase with 178 legislative acts passed in the 1990s and 129 acts passed between 2000 and 2003. Although not providing broad social protection, EU policy makers did provide a stronger constitutional basis for EU social policy by the end of this time period through the Social Policy Agreement and the Social Policy Protocol that was introduced in the 1992 Treaty on European Union (although only added to the Annex) and subsequently given full inclusion in the Treaty of Amsterdam in 1997. Despite these legislative advancements, member state governments remain hesitant to allow the EU to legislate in areas such as national social policy, as evidenced by the wide use of unanimity voting (Ellis 1998a).

This expansion in secondary legislation was also complemented by a similar growth in policy infrastructure. For example, during the time period that the Commission was formulating the three equality Directives of the 1970s, it also began constructing specialist policy units within the Commission to advise and oversee this policy development. The creation in 1976 of the Women's Bureau in Directorate General (DG) Employment and Social Affairs and the Women's Information Service in DG Information and Culture are two such examples. These policy units increased in both competence and the opportunities they provided for women activists and lobbyists as EU social policy was expanded and elaborated throughout the subsequent decades. For example, the Women's Bureau in DG Employment and Social Affairs consisted of a 3 person staff in the 1970s and today it is a formal Equality Unit with over 30 persons on staff, overseeing diverse programs and studies from gender mainstreaming to the comparative study of women in the European judiciary (CEC 1998a).

Figure 2.6 displays the annual number of secondary legislation adopted in the area of environmental protection between 1970 and 2003. The amount of environmental legislation stands in contrast to social provisions: 730 pieces of environmental legislation versus 457 social provisions. Even without a formal treaty mandate, Community organizations began developing "incidental" environmental measures as early as 1964, primarily involving the regeneration of oil (Rehbinder and Stewart 1985: 16). Despite a continued lack of a treaty basis, the 1970s marked the beginning of an official EU environmental policy. The two action programs on the environment adopted in 1973 and 1977 served as the foundation for much of the 35 legislative acts passed in the last four years of the decade (CEC 1973a; CEC 1977).

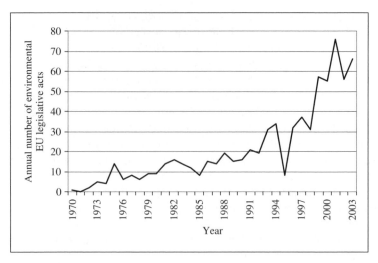

Note: N=730
Source: Data compiled by the author from CEC (2005) and European Communities. 2004.
CELEX Data Base. Brussels: Office for Official Publications of the European
Communities.
http://europa.eu.int/celex/htm/celex_en.htm.

Figure 2.6 Annual number of EU legislative acts in the area of environmental protection, 1970–2003

EU competence in environmental protection continued to grow in the 1980s, both with the continuation of the environmental action programs, but most importantly with the adoption of the Single European Act (SEA, 1986) which gave environmental protection a legal basis in the Treaty (Title VII) and a Directorate General dedicated to environmental issues (DG Environment, Consumer Protection and Nuclear Safety). The impacts of these changes were dramatic. Prior to the SEA, on average 8 legislative acts were adopted each year and following the Treaty this increased to an annual average of 33. EU organizations and environmental organizations were all given a greater opportunity to push for EU environmental policy expansion. Their efforts were realized and EU competence in the area of the environment continued to expand in the 1990s and early 2000s (e.g. amendments in the Treaty on European Union, 1992, had a significant impact on EU environmental policy[25]). A total of 253 environmental legislative acts were

---

[25] For example, the Treaty on European Union amended Article 2 of the Treaty of Rome. It no longer refers to a "continuous and balanced expansion," but "a harmonious and

passed between 2000 and 2003, a number that almost equals the environ-mental legislative outputs of the previous decade (286 in the 1990s). Yet similar to the area of social provisions, unanimity voting has applied to the vast majority of environmental legislation adopted during this time period (Krämer 2000).

These data suggest that legislative action in the EU can vary consid-erably. The data also suggest that while the treaty basis for EU policy expansion is important, the lack thereof does not inhibit subsequent policy expansion. Further, the general increase in legislative action in both EU policy areas illustrates that despite a general hesitancy amongst member state governments, the EU has systematically gained greater competence over sensitive national regulations. In the remainder of this section, I elaborate how this policy expansion occurred. I address each policy domain in turn.

Evolving social competence

Article 141 (ex Article 119)[26] of the Treaty of Rome provides the juridical basis of EU social policy. It provides that member states ensure and maintain the principle that women and men receive equal pay for equal work. The treaty negotiations regarding Article 141 remained strictly focused on fair competition, with the original placement of the principle in the portion of the Treaty dealing with competition distortion not social policy. The intention of Community architects was not based in a con-cern for women's rights. It grew out of a French concern over low paid female labor in the Netherlands, which caused unfair competition for French businesses. However, the provision was ultimately shifted (though the text remained unchanged) to social provisions as an attempt to develop at least some harmonization of social costs within the Treaty.

balanced development of economic activities, sustainable and non-inflationary growth respecting the environment." These treaty amendments also introduced qualified majority voting for matters of environmental policy. This voting rule change enables easier passage of controversial EU environmental regulations as it limits member state veto power.

[26] Article 119 was amended by the Treaty of Amsterdam and is now Article 141. I have included the original text of Article 119, as this is the provision I am referring to in this historical analysis:

"Each Member State shall during the first stage ensure and subsequently maintain the application of the principle that men and women should receive equal pay for equal work.

For the purpose of the Article 'pay' means the ordinary basic or minimum wage or salary and any other consideration, whether in cash or in kind, which the worker receives, directly or indirectly, in respect of his employment from his employer.

Equal Pay without discrimination based on sex means:

a) that pay for the same work at piece rates shall be calculated on the basis of the same unit of measurement;

b) that pay for work at time rates shall be the same for the same job."

Further, and necessary for the development of this policy area, was an ECJ preliminary ruling in 1976 that transformed Article 141 into a rights provision (ECJ 1976a). Following this decision, Article 141 was no longer a distance obligation on member state governments, but instead granted individuals throughout the EU a right that was enforceable in national courts.

Stated generally, Article 141 was inserted into the Treaty for economic reasons, but was placed in the position of having social consequences.[27] This potential dual purpose of the provision has come to embody a set of tensions in the general development of EU social policy:

- the development of EU social policy with broad social and equality protection versus the maintenance of limited employment based protection; and
- the creation of unified Community social justice policy versus preserving national values and standards of social equality and protection.

In sum, the tensions involve competing EU policy priorities – developing broad social justice protection versus narrow employment based standards – and the ultimate location of policy-making competence, either the supranational or national level. Generally, national governments have held the later position on both of these tensions, as illustrated in both the minimal protection provided by, and the limited amount of, EU legislation in this area. Yet EU organizations, such as the Commission and the ECJ, working with national social activists, have used the general right and legal basis provided by the Treaty to pursue policy objectives that attempt to expand this minimal protection (e.g. Cichowski 2001; Hoskyns 1996).

Three pieces of legislation were passed between 1975 and 1979 which clarified the goals set out in Article 141: the Equal Pay Directive, the Equal Treatment in Employment Directive and the Equal Treatment in Social Security Directive.[28] While the function of this equality legislation was to provide greater clarity, and it certainly elaborated a set of equality rights, these general provisions reflected a degree of hesitancy by national governments. The policy debates surrounding these directives were similar to the adoption of Article 141. For example, the Equal Treatment Directive failed to bring clarity between issues of discrimination and general equality. The Directive states that "no

---

[27] Its inclusion laid down a precise legal obligation on member states, yet at the same time it also embodied a general social ideal or instrument (at least indirectly) to harmonize social policy.

[28] Council Directive 75/117/EEC, Council Directive 76/207/EEC, and Council Directive 79/7/EEC.

discrimination whatsoever on grounds of sex" will be allowed under EU law. However, scholars have observed that this general "whatsoever" expression has given ample opportunity to both EU organizations and policy actors to expand the Directive's scope (Ellis 1998).[29] Individuals and women's groups throughout the Union have utilized this general principle of equality to mobilize and pressure for greater inclusion and protection (Mazey 1998).

The passage of the SEA in 1986 did little to alter equality policy as laid out in either the Treaty or legislation. The Council subsequently added only two directives to this policy area in the 1980s,[30] both of which were largely "symbolic" (Hoskyns 1996). Similarly, while the negotiations for the Treaty on European Union (1992) provided explicit equality rights in the Agreement of Social Policy, it was relegated to an annex of the Treaty in order to accommodate the British government's insistence on their opt-out position on further social protection. Six more equality directives were adopted in the 1990s. Three directives introduce new areas of EU equality law: parental leave,[31] pregnancy[32] and burden of proof in discrimination cases.[33] One of the remaining three amends EU rules on equality in social security[34] and the other two extend the parental leave framework agreement and the burden of proof Directive to the UK, as an effect of the Agreement on Social Policy formally being included in the Treaty of Amsterdam.[35] The early 2000s also brought significant revision and expansion to the fundamental principle of equal treatment based on sex as embodied in EU law. The 1976 Equal Treatment in Employment Directive was updated to include revisions that evolved through almost

---

[29] This includes one ECJ decision that found protection for transsexuals against dismissal within the scope of this EU law (ECJ 1996d). Furthermore, the Directive failed to clearly provide a definition for the concept at the heart of the legislation, namely, how is indirect discrimination embodied in general equality? This vague protection would later be at the center of a series of cases heard before the ECJ.

[30] Council Directive 86/378/EEC pertaining to social security and 86/613/EEC on equality for self-employed individuals.

[31] Council Directive 96/34/EC is a framework agreement on parental leave concluded by UNICE, CEEP and the ETUC (three main cross-industry organizations). After previous unsuccessful attempts by the Commission, this framework Directive finally came to fruition in 1996.

[32] Council Directive 92/85/EEC.   [33] Council Directive 97/80/EC.

[34] Council Directive 96/97/EC amends Council Directive 86/378/EEC in order to adapt the provisions which were affected by the *Barber* case-law. The Court's judgment in *Barber* (ECJ 1990a) automatically invalidated parts of the Directive. For a complete list of associated cases see the text of the Directive (OJ L 46, 17.2.1997).

[35] Council Directive 97/75/EC and Council Directive 98/52/EC. The Social Policy Agreement was relegated to an annex of the Treaty on European Union in order to accommodate the British government's insistence on their opt-out position on further EU social protection.

thirty years of ECJ case law resulting in an amended Directive in 2002.[36] And in 2004, a significant departure was made with the adoption of a newly amended general Equal Treatment Directive, which is the first EU equality law to extend protection against sex discrimination outside of the labor market.[37] Generally, as the small amount of adopted legislation and a continued reliance on unanimity voting would suggest, member state governments have been hesitant to let the EU legislate in the area of national social policy.[38]

Constructing European environmental protection

Despite a very different origin and magnitude of legislative action than EU social policy, environmental regulations in the EU are characterized by a similar set of tensions. Even though member state governments share a general enthusiasm for a European-wide environmental protection plan, EU environmental policy poses a challenge to the goals of the single market and varying national environmental goals (Vogel 1993). Because of this consideration, EU environmental protection, similar to social provisions, involves a tension between competing policy priorities and the ultimate location of policy-making competence – either at the supranational or national level. Stated generally:

- the development of EU environmental protection standards versus the preservation of EU free trade policies; and
- the creation of unified Community environmental standards versus preserving a member state government's national environmental standards.

---

[36] Directive 2002/73/EC of the European Parliament and of the Council of 23 September 2002 amending Council Directive 76/207/EEC on the implementation of the principle of equal treatment for men and women as regards access to employment, vocational training and promotion, and working conditions. The Directive brings Community equality legislation in line with ECJ case law, such as the new Article 2, which codifies the ECJ's decisions in *Brown* (ECJ 1998d), *Gillespie* (ECJ 1996a), *Johnston* (ECJ 1986c), *Kreil* (ECJ 2000a) and *Sirdar* (ECJ 1999a).

[37] Council Directive 2004/113/EC of 13 December 2004 implementing the principle of equal treatment between men and women in the access to and supply of goods and services.

[38] Treaty amendments in the late 1990s, such as the Treaty of Amsterdam in 1997, may represent a slightly bolder move by member states than in the past, with the full inclusion of the Agreement on Social Policy and enabling provisions such as Article 13 (which suggests greater protection from discrimination based on a host of factors from sex to sexual orientation). Yet in the area of sex discrimination over time we find the greatest expansion in protection taking place through legislative innovations rather than treaty amendments, much of which serves to play catch up and codify principles and protections already created and extended through ECJ case law (see CEC 2004).

The first tension is typified by conflicts, which arise when the transposition of a EU environmental law, such as one to establish a waste disposal scheme, creates a barrier to those individuals, such as waste collectors, who transport their goods across borders (ECJ 1983). An example of the second tension is the conflict which arises when a member state, such as the Netherlands, implements an EU wildlife protection law in a stronger manner compared to other member states (ECJ 1990b). While the EU law allows such strict national interpretations, ultimately the policy competence is shifted entirely to the supranational level as conflicts arise from these varying national transpositions.

Unlike EU social policies, the origins of EU environmental regulations are not traceable to a rule set out in the Treaty of Rome. EU environmental policy had no basis in the original treaties. The original three treaties lacked any mention of the "environment," an unsurprising fact, as ecological sensibilities were not commonplace in the 1950s. However, with a growing awareness of environmental degradation in the 1970s, member state governments realized there was a need to safeguard the environment at the European level. As a result, through a series of directives and programs, environmental protection emerged as a policy area for the EU despite the absence of a constitutional basis. Environmental activists were an important part of this development. For example, in the 1970s conservation groups throughout Europe began pressuring EU organizations to develop a pan-European plan to protect birds. The outcome of this mobilization was the adoption of the Wild Birds Directive[39] in 1979 (Wils 1994).

Yet the tension between supranational and national policy competence was evident in these initial policy developments. Environmental directives and regulations required unanimous approval in the Council and, as a result, generally included provisions permitting more stringent national policy. As a result, in the early stages, the legal basis for Community environmental protection remained weak and ambiguous. Furthermore, similar to the development of social policy, this environmental protection was conceived in relation to economic priorities, in which the need for EU environmental policy was evaluated in terms of the functioning of the Common Market.

This would begin to change first with an ECJ ruling, then a series of treaty amendments. In a 1985 preliminary ruling, the Court argued that environmental protection was an essential goal of the Union – that could limit the application of free trade provisions (ECJ 1985a). This would

---

[39] Council Directive 79/409/EEC.

later be codified with the adoption of the Single European Act in 1986 that amended the Treaty to include environmental protection.[40] Unlike the resistance to legislate social protection at the EU level, the SEA clearly stated that environmental protection was an essential goal of the Union: national laws and practices must be viewed in light of environmental ramifications and when feasible, member state governments must promote higher levels of environmental protection. Further, dissimilar to the unanimity voting in the area of social provisions, the SEA introduced qualified majority voting pertaining to the harmonization of national laws and established the structure for qualified majority voting within the Environmental Title (XIX). The Treaty on European Union (TEU) in 1992 did not fundamentally change the SEA's environmental provisions, but instead re-emphasized their importance. The TEU directs that environmental concerns "must be integrated into the definition and implementation of the Community's other policies" (Article 174).

The Treaty of Amsterdam in 1997 expanded the scope of EU environmental law by amending the treaties to include the concept of sustainable development: "Environmental protection requirements must be integrated into the definition and implementation of the Community policies and activities referred to in Article 3, in particular with a view to promoting sustainable development" (Article 6 EC Treaty). Soon after the Council and the European Parliament adopted the *Sixth Environmental Action Programme*[41], which introduced a set of ambitious environmental goals to guide EU policymaking in the next ten years – which at the core marks a major shift by stating a commitment to creating an equal balance between economic, social and environmental objectives (CEC 2004). Further, the European Union signing of the United Nations Århus Convention (on *Access to Information, Public Participation in Decision-Making and Access to Justice in Environmental Matters*) in 1998, also led to important changes and adoption of directives in EU environmental policy expanding both the political and legal opportunities of civil society to participate.[42]

---

[40] See Article 174–176 and Article 95 EC Treaty.
[41] Decision 1600/2002/EC of the European Parliament and the Council laying down the *Sixth Community Action Programme*, OJ L 242, September 2002.
[42] See United Nations Economic Commission for Europe (1998) for the full text of the Convention. EU policy consequences included adoption of Directive 2003/4/EC of the European Parliament and the Council of 28 January 2003 on public access to environmental information. This repealed the earlier public access legislation, Council Directive 90/313. Importantly, for both the litigation and mobilization dynamics studied in this book, this Directive gives individuals the right to challenge government institutions if their rights to information are denied and to request that government action or acts are

These treaty amendments have provided a vast array of secondary legislation in the area of the environment, from waste management to wildlife protection.[43] However, similar to the legal basis for social policy, these provisions are relatively vague in prescribing how member state governments can reconcile the tension between environmental protections and "other policies," especially those relating to the internal market. In addition, treaty provisions often lack clarity, such as the following requirement: "Community policy on the environment shall aim at a high level of protection" (Art 74). The Environmental Title illustrates at least some attempt at a comprehensive EU environmental plan, yet at the same time it ultimately preserves national government control over this policy development.[44] Today, the EU has adopted over 700 environmental legislative acts, some of which offer very specific technical regulations, whilst other policies embody vague policy prescriptions. In particular, these later legislative outcomes, often in the form of framework directives, result from indecision over how to balance competing EU policy priorities and to allow for more stringent national environmental standards.[45] Failure to address these tensions in the legislative process only gives the Court the opportunity to resolve these unanswered questions through the litigation process (Cichowski 1998).

Policy tensions and opportunities for action

Today, the EU possesses a complex set of rules governing both social provisions and environmental protection, from regulations on national maternity rights to bird conservation measures. The current shape of these public interest policies were not traceable to the original treaties and could not have been foreseen by treaty architects who were concerned mainly with economic cooperation. Not surprisingly, this evolution has been one of incremental change, with national governments, EU policy makers and public interests struggling to solve the tensions that are

---

reviewed. Directive 2003/35/EC on public access to decision-making on environmental matters was also adopted. And finally, a third directive on access to justice in environmental matters remains at the proposal stage (CEC 2003).

[43] General categories of EU environmental legislation include: sustainable development, waste, noise, air pollution, water, nature, soil protection, civil protection, climate change.

[44] This is evidenced by Article 95 and Article 176.

[45] Framework directives which lay out very general guides for protection are particularly problematic regarding variation in implementation. Not surprisingly, the Waste Framework Directive, Council Directive 74/442/EEC of 1975 has continued to be the subject of litigation and then subsequent amending secondary legislation in light of these disputes and ECJ decisions. The following measures amend this original framework directive: Council Directive 91/156/EEC, Council Directive 91/692/EEC, Commission Decision 96/350/EC and Council Directive 96/59/EC.

inherent in both of these policy areas: competing EU priorities and the ultimate location of policy authority. These have similar manifestations in both policy areas. Although more prevalent in the area of social provisions, both areas possess regulations that introduce general, vague protection but fail to resolve conflicts that arise from disparate national measures or competing EU priorities.

The result has both led to significant implementation disparities in the area of environmental protection (Knill and Lenschow 1998) and enabled individuals to make equality rights claims, without specific EU rules or implementing EU legislation, that would not otherwise be possible in a national legal system (Cichowski 2001). As earlier argued, we might expect these tensions to form the basis of Article 234 references. Disputes arise at the national level, and the ECJ is asked to resolve these unanswered questions. Yet we would also expect this litigation to vary, as the legal basis for and general trajectory of these two policy areas differ. In particular, sex equality law provides a clear treaty (or constitutional) based right, which gives both individuals and the ECJ a powerful tool to argue for and decide the case (Ellis 1998a). While EU environmental law provides a significantly greater quantity of legislation, it lacks a clear individual right to environmental protection.[46] EU legislative developments present individuals and groups with varying opportunities for action both within their own national legal systems and at the supranational level.

Data sources and methodology

I compiled a data set utilizing data from the European Commission's *Directory of Community Legislation in Force and other acts of the Community Institutions* (CEC 2004). The data includes all legislative acts coded by the Commission as secondary legislation (CELEX documentary sector = 3) and other Community acts (CELEX documentary sector = 4) and in two categories created by the Commission: environmental protection and social provisions. The data set includes 1187 legislative acts, composed primarily of decisions, directives and regulations. There are 730 environmental legislative acts (from 1970–2003) and 457 in the area of

---

[46] Technically, there are no Community provisions on access to justice at the EU or national level, in environmental matters. However, individuals and groups have been able to use Article 230(4) if Community measures are directly addressed to them or where they are directly concerned. Also, the Directive on Environmental Impact Assessment (85/337) explicitly gives the public a "right" to express their opinion before a project is commenced (e.g. Krämer 2000, 1991a; Miller 1998; Wyatt 1998). Despite these difficulties, environmental groups have been able to use the Article 234 procedure (see Cichowski 1998).

social provisions (1970–2003). This measure gives us some idea of the evolution of EU legislative action and competence in these two legal domains over time.

This general quantitative data is supplemented by extensive historical documentation collected by the author through personal interviews with EU officials and public interest activists in Brussels and through the EU Documentation Archive located at the European University Institute in Florence, Italy. This documentation includes official EU publications covering policy negotiations, proposals and implementation.

Transnational mobilization and institutionalization

The previous sections lay out how legal claims, litigation and legislative action have evolved in the EU. In particular, I have highlighted how litigation can activate the ECJ's judicial rulemaking capacity with the consequence of expanding EU rules or institutions. These new rules and procedures can serve as opportunities for mobilization, both by shaping the direction of legislative action as well as creating enforceable rights that can be invoked in subsequent litigation. This process of litigation is one way that institutionalization can occur. EU rules become more binding and precise, EU organizations can find new powers *vis-à-vis* member state governments, and individuals are given more powerful legal tools to bring claims against their own governments. As this process of institutionalization occurs we would expect a given legal domain to become less intergovernmental. It is through this process that supranational governance is constructed.

As argued in Chapter 1, while the processes of litigation and mobilization are interconnected, these two processes are also analytically distinct. ECJ rulemaking and expanding EU legislative acts create opportunities for action, yet once mobilized these public interests actors can also exert their own impact on EU rules and organizations and change the shape of transnational society or public space in the EU. Thus, we would expect these political opportunities at the EU level to shape action, but over time we might expect this mobilization to change subsequent political opportunity structures, thus changing the overall development of social movement action at the EU level. As argued, the extent to which we find public interest action changing over time from discrete and individual to more formally organized and permanent at the EU level in both of our legal domains, we may expect institutionalization to be taking place. As these transnational actors are increasingly direct participants in EU policy processes rather than having their interests filtered through national government action, we might expect a policy domain to become less intergovernmental. It is through this dynamic that institutionalization through mobilization can occur in the EU. Similar to litigation, this process can lead to the construction of supranational governance.

A general shift: transnational mobilization and the EU

Historically, scholars have observed a general relationship between new opportunity structures and the locale of mobilization (Tilly 1975; Tarrow 1998). With the emergence of the modern nation-state, policymaking power moved from the local to national and as a result mobilizing actors shifted the locale of their collective activities to target these new governance structures (Tilly 1982). Similarly, social movement scholars are observing increased levels of transnational and international political activism (Dalton and Rohrschneider 1999; Keck and Sikkink 1998; Imig and Tarrow 2001). Today, amongst EU countries, we can see a similar shift taking place from the national to supranational. Scholars have observed that interest groups and lobbying organizations have increasingly become permanent policy actors in Brussels (Mazey and Richardson 1999; Aspinwall and Greenwood 1998). As EU policy competence expands, groups have come to Brussels to have a voice in this policy creation (Mazey and Richardson 2001).

Figure 2.7 displays the annual and cumulative number of organizations involved in social provisions, with particular attention to those involved with gender equality issues, with permanent offices in Brussels by founding year between 1951 and 2003. The data illustrate that women activists have become a noticeable permanent presence in Brussels with only 13 groups operating in the early years of the Union, but 57 by 2003. The annual number of new groups illustrates that the formation of transnational organizations in the area of social provisions has evolved as a set of concentrated formation periods.

The first period coincided with the original Union institution building that took place in the 1950s and 1960s. While eleven groups opened Brussels based offices during this time period, none were dedicated to gender equality issues, but instead were well-established international and national employee organizations. The 1970s possessed a similar number of new groups with 14 new associations becoming a permanent presence in Brussels. The 1980s witnessed the addition of 12 more groups to the Brussels complex. Yet unlike previous decades, the groups established in the 1980s were the first to grow out of the grassroots feminist movement and thus, unlike earlier organizations, possessed policy agendas dedicated to gender equality. Finally, this growth exploded in the early 1990s with the widely publicized "1992 project" (completion of the internal market

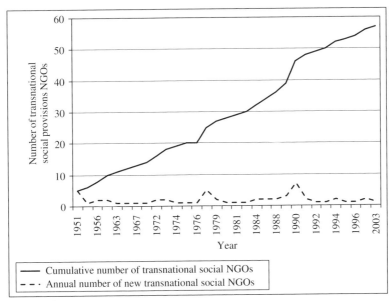

Note: N = 57
Source: Data compiled by author from *Directory of Pressure Groups in the EU*, Philip and Gray
(1996), *Directory of Interest Groups* (Luxembourg: Office for Official Publications of the
European Communities, 1996) and *Consultation, the European Commission and Civil Society*
(European Commission, online database
http://www.europa.eu.int/comm/civil_society/coneccs/start.cfm?CL=en).

Figure 2.7 Evolution of transnational mobilization in the area of social
provisions by cumulative numbers and annual number of new groups,
1951–2003

by 1992) and its manifestation in the amendments passed in the Treaty on
European Union (1992), with seven groups alone setting up offices in the
year 1990 and 17 new groups by the end of 2003 (a 100% increase
between the 1980s and 1990s).

Further, scholars have suggested that the growth of EU interest groups
and associations is best understood in terms of the accumulation of
groups: "once one set of groups begins to exploit incentive and opportunity
structures at the European level, others are bound to follow; they cannot
afford to be left out, whatever the cost" (Mazey and Richardson 2001: 7).
Figure 2.7 also displays the cumulative growth of these public interest
organizations. As national and international interests begin to lobby at the
EU level, other groups, whether competing or even complementary, are
increasingly drawn to pressure EU policy makers or risk having their objectives and claims ignored.

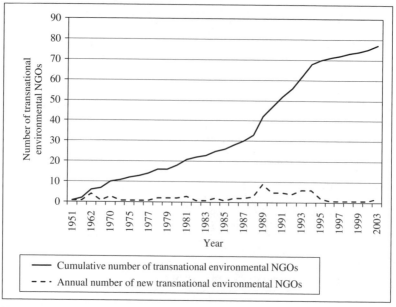

Note: N=77
Source: Data compiled by author from *Directory of Pressure Groups in the EU*, Philip and Gray (1996), *Directory of Interest Groups* (Luxembourg: Office for Official Publications of the European Communities, 1996) and *Consultation, the European Commission and Civil Society* (European Commission, online database http://www.europa.eu.int/comm/civil_society/coneccs/start.cfm?CL=en).

Figure 2.8 Evolution of transnational mobilization in the area of EU environmental policy by cumulative number and annual number of new groups, 1951–2003

How has transnational mobilization around environmental issues developed during this time period? Figure 2.8 displays annual and cumulative number of organizations that are operating in Brussels in the area of the environment between 1951 and 2003. Similar to the pattern of women's activism, environmental activists have become a growing presence in Brussels with only 7 groups in the early years to 77 by 2003. However, the annual number of new groups illustrate that their development has evolved slowly, with its greatest growth period in the 1980s and 1990s. Where women's mobilization experienced relatively similar growth between decades (10–14 new groups in each decade), environmental organizations had much greater variation in growth across decades. There were far fewer new groups in the early years of the 1950s/1960s (7 groups) and the 1970s (9 groups), compared to the growth spurt in the 1980s (26 groups) and 1990s to 2003 (35 groups).

The first period of growth in the 1950s and 1960s involved international organizations with a general interest in waste management and scientific research. Environmental protection was one of many issues of concern to the organization. While an equally small number of organizations established Brussels offices in the 1970s, this decade witnessed the establishment of groups with an exclusive focus on the environment. For example, in 1974 the European Environmental Bureau (EEB), a federation of 130 environmental organizations, opened an office in Brussels and remains a key actor in EU environmental policy development (EEB 1999). The 1980s were particularly important for environmental groups, with over 13 groups establishing Brussels offices in 1989 alone. Finally, the 1990s and into 2000s continued this growth rate with the addition of 35 new groups, 18 of which focused exclusively on general environmental protection.

While these data illustrate clearly that public interest organizations have increasingly become a part of the Brussels complex, we know very little about how they are organizing and what the consequences of their mobilization are. The data raise a host of unanswered questions. How did the political opportunities available at a given point in time shape transnational mobilization? Further, how did this mobilization shape subsequent action in the future? Was this mobilization a catalyst for subsequent EU laws or did it develop as a product of these new policy competences? Further, did the work of individual activists working within more general international organizations, or even on their own in the early years, influence the policy specific collective action that we find in both the social provisions and environmental domains by the early 2000s? The data may also suggest variability in organization across policy domains. Despite a similar rise in the 1970s of both the feminist and environmental movements, there is variation in growth rate between policy domains. Is this a function of the political opportunities available to these different groups or perhaps the characteristics specific to the movement?

Explaining mobilization

These questions remain relatively unexplored by scholars concerned with political action in the European Union.[47] We currently lack any systematic comparative research on what conditions shape transnational public interest mobilization taking place in Europe and more importantly, on what the consequences of this mobilization are on the evolution of

---

[47] For exceptions see Mazey and Richardson (1999) and Tarrow and Imig (2001).

supranational governance. The findings are significant not only for understanding the emergence of supranational governance in the two EU policy areas, but also for the role of mobilization in the emergence of new sites of governance more generally. We have suggested that sometimes the litigation and rulemaking (judicial and legislative) can create the opportunities, and other times mobilization impacts the opportunities for action and ultimately can influence the development of this mobilization.

EU political opportunities as conditions for action

In order to explain the pattern in transnational mobilization in our two legal domains we look to the EU political opportunity structures available to a particular interest. Transnational groups began mobilizing at the EU level in an attempt to exploit all possible avenues of influence. Scholars agree that this is exactly the dynamic that explains the general rise, across all policy sectors, in mobilization of actors and groups at the EU level, into what today is a "highly" developed European interest group system (Richardson 1998: 5; Mazey and Richardson 1999). Scholars point to the increasing power of the ECJ in policy construction (Cichowski 1998, 2001), the general expansion of EU policy competence (Mazey and Richardson 2001; Sidjanski 1970: 402; Hoskyns 1996) and the increasing opportunities for direct structural access for groups and associations in the EU policy making process (Marks and McAdam 1996: 103; Kirchner 1977: 28) as possible opportunity structures.

These arguments highlight the importance of groups having formal access to EU organizations, either through procedures such as the Article 234 litigation process, or even consultation forums supported by the Commission. Specifically, we are concerned with how ECJ litigation and expanding legislative competence may have shaped the development of transnational mobilization. Scholars suggest that beyond direct access or even new rights, expanding EU policy competence often creates the social space to discuss issues at the EU level, providing a new opportunity to discuss and define European problems or issues (Deshmores 1992). Similarly, we might expect that as the saliency of public interest issues changes in the EU, so too will the groups organizing around these issues. For example, in the 1970s there were few transnational organizations dedicated to EU women's issues. Instead mobilization was largely carried out by the commitment of individual feminists, either working from within EU organizations (Hoskyns 1996) or utilizing EU organizations such as the ECJ to press for policy change (Cichowski 2001). By the 1980s and 1990s, the EU possessed a growing set of formal equality rules – including ECJ jurisprudence and legislative acts – and feminist action was also increasingly formalized through such umbrella organizations as the European Women's Lobby. Together these arguments suggest the following expectation:

- We expect that the extent to which EU political opportunities afford greater formal access and create new social spaces for public interests, there will be an increasing amount of transnational mobilization. Also, we expect that generally as these political opportunities increase in formality and magnitude, mobilization will shift from discrete individual action to more formal collective group action.

Mobilization, institutionalization and political opportunities
Once these groups are mobilized, their activism can subsequently alter EU rules and procedures that serve as opportunities for action. As these political opportunities become more formal and precise, institutionalization is taking place and we might expect the legal domain to become less intergovernmental. Transnational groups have utilized various strategies to pressure EU organizations to adopt rules and procedures that change the political opportunities enabling greater public access to European politics. Consistently scholars argue that lobbying strategies are the most successful for transnational groups hoping to gain access to EU organizations and influence policy change (Mazey and Richardson 1999; Aspinwall and Greenwood 1998). Similarly, legal activists have utilized other conventional movement strategies such as litigation as an avenue to change the scope of EU law (Cichowski 1998, 2001). Finally, scholars observe that public interest organizations operating in Brussels have utilized their own expertise and technical knowledge to change policy frames available to Community legislators (Mazey and Richardson 2001). Specifically, these strategies lead groups to influence policy development through work as expert consultants to the Commission and Parliament (Hoskyns 1996) and as legal activists sending test cases to the ECJ (Harlow and Rawlings 1992; Cichowski 1998, 2001).

Further, we might expect there to be differences in how women's groups versus environmental groups influence EU rules and procedures. This variation may be acutely linked to characteristics specific to movement form. For example, scholars observe that the labor movement in European countries experience less success than other movements in lobbying at the EU level, partially on account of its "historically rooted national orientations" that have made "transnational organization immensely difficult to achieve" (Marks and McAdam 1996: 118). On the other hand, the environmental movement has become accustomed to international action on global issues and thus has greater success at adapting these strategies to the EU. Further, unlike the mass member organization and large campaigns characterizing the environmental movement, women's organizing may be more amorphous, with activists working collectively and individually through informal networks. Further, women's groups have historically achieved their biggest successes through litigation strategies rather than large lobbying campaigns (O'Connor 1980). Together these arguments suggest how transnational mobilization may influence EU rules and procedures:

● We expect that transnational activists will be more successful at influencing EU rules and procedures, the extent to which they utilize conventional tactics (lobbying, framing and litigation) and the greater the similarity between these strategies and pre-existing movement strategies.

Mobilization, institutionalization and public inclusion

As we have seen, ECJ litigation and EU rulemaking (judicial and legislative) can create opportunity structures for transnational mobilization. Subsequently, these groups use various tactics to change EU rules and procedures. Yet critical to this process of institutionalization is the increasing permanence of these public interest groups in EU politics. In particular, we might expect that over time the increasing presence of transnational activists in EU politics may impact overall public inclusion in the EU.

For example, expansion in EU equality law in the 1970s provided the basis for collective action in the 1980s by EU level women's organizations such as the Centre for Research on European Women (CREW). These coordinated efforts were critical in creating a general public space at the EU level for discussions that moved beyond equality in employment, but addressed public issues such as sexual harassment and positive action, issues that far surpassed the scope or competence of EU equality law (CREW 1996). Similarly, in the 1990s environmental organizations based in Brussels began a coordinated effort to lobby EU organizations on the issue of general public access to justice (EEB 1999). While the activists were motivated by difficulties experienced by environmental groups bringing claims before the ECJ, their effort led to Community action calling for greater access to justice for the public more broadly (CEC 2000b).

Over time, as EU competence in the area of public interests expands, both as a cause and effect of transnational mobilization, we might expect a similar expansion in public access for efficiency and legitimacy reasons. The Commission often looks to public interest organizations both to fulfill its need for expert knowledge in policy developments, but also to gain public support for complex public policy issues (e.g. Aspinwall and Greenwood 1998: 5). By giving the public direct access to EU politics and a European voice this can change the balance of power: empowering individuals and often EU organizations while diminishing the power of national governments. In the EU, public interest groups may pressure for specific policy objectives, but their action can have the impact of expanding the borders of politics by redefining what is a European public issue and who has access to EU politics. Together these arguments suggest the following expectation:

• The extent that public interest mobilization becomes more permanent in a given EU policy domain and the EU policy process becomes more reliant on this presence, we might expect a general increase in the levels of public inclusion and the domain to become less intergovernmental.

Data sources and methodology

Just as the emergence and development of domestic political action are multidimensional, transnational mobilization can be measured in various ways. I begin by looking at the development of formal public interest organizations in Brussels over time. Since the early 1980s, a group of researchers have compiled a directory of pan-European organizations whose objectives include directly influencing EU policy processes.[48] This compendium includes over 1500 organizations and provides biographical information such as founding date of the organization, principal aims and objectives, organizational structure, activities and EU contacts, amongst other descriptors. I utilize this directory as the main source to compile a data set of Brussels-based organizations that are active in our two EU policy domains.[49] This directory is also supplemented by the European Commission's online database of non-governmental organizations.[50] The data set includes 134 groups established in the 1950s through 2003: 57 transnational groups in the area of social provisions[51] and 77 environmental groups.

---

[48] See Philip and Gray (1996).

[49] There is clearly a methodological bias towards well-established organizations, as the compendium only includes those organizations that were visibly present in Brussels (e.g. a full-time Brussels office) and responded to Philip and Gray's survey (see Philip and Gray 1996: ix). I have verified these organizations against the Commission's own registry of organizations (see CEC 1996) as well as personal interviews and secondary literature.

[50] *Consultation, the European Commission and Civil Society* (European Commission, online database http://www.europa.eu.int/comm/civil_society/coneccs/start.cfm?CL=en).

[51] Similar to the Court's case law and legislative action, while highlighting general activity in social provisions, I focus specifically on gender equality. Thus, I examine those public interest groups that have cited at least some EU level activity in the area of women's rights.

Yet similar to the organizing of public interest activists in both domestic and international policy spaces, we know this mobilization, especially women's activism, can take more discreet and inconspicuous forms (Katzenstein 1998a). Thus, I complement this quantitative data with extensive historical documentation collected by the author through personal interviews with public interest activists in Brussels and through the EU Documentation Archive located at the European University Institute in Florence, Italy. This documentation includes annual reports, studies and newsletters published by transnational public interest organizations and personal interviews carried out in Brussels with both individual activists and organizations. Together, these measures enable a comprehensive examination of the varied patterns of transnational mobilization that have evolved in the two policy domains.

Conclusion

In this chapter, I offered an overview of the constituent elements of institutionalization in the EU. These are the dependent variables at the center of this study. In particular, I explored how the interaction between mobilized interests at the national level and rules at the EU level can lead to legal claims brought through the preliminary ruling procedure. In resolving this litigation, the ECJ's judicial rulemaking can lead to institutionalization by expanding the scope of EU laws and both empowering EU organizations and creating opportunities for public interest activism. Further, I suggested how this judicial rulemaking is both cause and effect of Community legislative action, and how this legislative action can subsequently provide the opportunities for social action. Finally, I explored how this litigation and legislative action can serve as political opportunities for transnational mobilization. I suggested how institutionalization could occur through mobilization, as activists expand EU political opportunities and expand the permanent space for public inclusion. In the next two parts of this book, I test these propositions.

Part I

Institutionalization through litigation

3   The European Court of Justice and the expansion of gender equality rights

In 1958, women's rights were not on the agenda for the newly forming European Economic Community. However, some national governments were concerned with protecting business from unfair competition created by wage disparities, and thus provided that under the Treaty of Rome men and women would receive equal pay for equal work (Article 141). This provision was intended to bestow obligations on national governments and to prevent competition distortion. Today this same social provision bestows a positive right on individuals throughout the member states, a judicially enforceable right that remains the backbone of an expanding net of European gender equality rights: from equal treatment in employment to maternity leave. This dynamic transformation is the focus of this chapter. In particular, I explore the European Court of Justice's (ECJ) social provisions case law pursuant to Article 234 to examine how processes of institutionalization through litigation influenced this policy evolution.

As argued in Chapter 2, the institutionalization of supranational governance through litigation results as a product of multiple processes. I explore these in turn. The first part of the chapter involves quantitative analyses of these processes: factors influencing the legal claim, the litigation and subsequently the effects of the Court's judicial rulemaking. In the second part of the chapter, I supplement this quantitative data with an in-depth case law analysis of a single sub-field of the social provisions policy domain: pregnancy and maternity rights. This provides greater detail to the general patterns highlighted in the quantitative analyses. Through process tracing and case law analysis, I examine how the ECJ's judicial rulemaking impacted subsequent legislative action and whether these rulings created the opportunities for subsequent legal action. The national governments, the Commission and individuals and groups are all participants in this process. I explore whether this process of institutionalization through litigation changed the balance of power between these actors and organizations, ultimately changing the intergovernmental nature of European Union (EU) social provisions.

Legal claims, litigation and opportunities for action

As argued, the litigation dynamic relies on a legal claim reaching a court. As a result of strategic action and at least some necessary rule, the legal claim activates a court's dispute resolution function. In resolving the dispute at hand, a court's ruling can have the effect of expanding both the meaning and precision of the rule in question. Ultimately, this judicial rulemaking can provide new opportunities for action in the future: both legislative action and public interest action. In this section, I first explore the factors that give rise to the legal claim involving EU social provisions: mobilized interests, legal resources and EU rules (EU/national policy fit and ECJ precedent). Second, I explain the subsequent litigation dynamic by examining what factors shape the ECJ's decision-making: does the ECJ act to uphold EU interests by clarifying EU rules or does it operate to preserve the policy positions of member state governments? Ultimately, I ask how this impacts the general trajectory of EU social provisions: are individuals and EU organizations given opportunities for action diminishing member state control over policy development or do member state governments control these outcomes?

Women activists and new legal claims

I argued that certain factors, both national and supranational, are the underlying source of legal claims that ultimately constitute Article 234 preliminary reference rates. The hypotheses posited in Chapter 2 suggest that levels of preliminary references may be rooted in attributes specific to the country, such as the relative organizational strength of national mobilized interests and available legal resources. Further, cases may also arise from factors specific to the EU rules invoked in the legal claim, such as the relative fit between EU and national policy, directly effective treaty-based rights and also the relative amount of ECJ precedent that creates new bases for legal claims in a given policy domain. The following analyses will test the explanatory value of these factors in understanding Article 234 preliminary references cross-nationally and over time.

Mobilized interests

Table 3.1 displays the impact of organizational strength on average rates of Article 234 preliminary references in the area of social provisions.[1] As previously argued, trade unions may be a main organization supporting

---

[1] The dependent variable in this analysis is average rate of preliminary references. The measure utilizes all preliminary references for each member state in the area of social

Table 3.1 *Effect of mobilized interests on average number of Article 234 references in the area of social provisions, 1970–2003*

	B	t-statistic
(model 1) Social provisions mobilized interests	.045 **	3.137

Notes:
** $p < .01$
Entry is unstandardized regression coefficient. For each member state the total number of preliminary references is divided by the number of years in which that country has been making references to the ECJ in this legal domain. Mobilized interests are the percentage of respondents in each member state belonging to trade unions.
Source: Data compiled by the author from European Communities. 2004. *CELEX Data Base*. Brussels: Office for Official Publications of the European Communities and the *World Values Survey* (1981, 1986, 1995, 2000).

litigation in this policy area. Organizational strength is a particularly important feature of successful public interest litigation, and I hypothesized it may have a similar affect on bringing legal claims via the preliminary ruling procedure. The direction of the coefficients displayed in Table 3.1 confirms the expectation that an increase in litigation is linked to the relative strength of national organizations that potentially would support this litigation. In particular, trade unions in the United Kingdom have been strong and active in the area of gender equality litigation (CEC 1993a: 35; CEC 1995a: 32).[2] German trade unions have primarily served indirectly by assisting individuals who are considering filing a legal claim, although they have directly supported some cases including, *Rinner-Kuhn* (ECJ 1989b) (see CEC 1993a: 35). Portuguese courts have not sent any references in the equality sector, a fact that might be partially explained by their comparatively weak trade unions, as well as their limited ability to bring legal action.[3]

Furthermore, the relationship might be stronger if not for certain member states, such as Denmark, which has a strong tradition of trade union strength (45 percent of respondents belonging to unions), yet a comparatively low rate of sending Article 234 references (only 19 in over 20 years,

provisions (from 1970–2003). Each country's average reference rate in each legal domain is calculated by dividing their total number of references in the legal domain by the number of years in this time period that a given country has been making references. By using an average, I am stabilizing the natural total differences that would occur due to varying accession dates for these 15 countries.

[2] Also confirmed in interview with British national legal expert, 26 April 1999, Brussels, Belgium.

[3] This may change in the future as a 1997 Portuguese law (105/97) now gives trade unions the authority to start legal proceedings in discrimination cases (CEC 1999b: 26).

Table 3.2 *Effect of national legal resources on average number of Article 234 references in the area of social provisions, 1970–2003*

	B	t-statistic
(model 1) Social provisions legal resources	.823 ***	4.069

Notes:
*** $p < .001$
Entries are unstandardized regression coefficients. For each member state the total number of preliminary references is divided by the number of years in which that country has been making references to the ECJ in this legal domain. For the legal resources variable each country is coded on a scale from 0–3. The scale denotes the presence of the three main sources of support: an active and accessible (to the public) equality agency (1), an equality agency that supports this type of litigation (1), active community of social provisions legal experts (1).
Source: Data compiled by the author from European Communities. 2004. *CELEX Data Base.* Brussels: Office for Official Publications of the European Communities and various primary source gender equality documents (see Chapter 2 for complete list).

compared to the number of references originating from British courts, 61, in a similar time period). Yet, this low Danish reference rate does not represent minimal trade union involvement in gender equality litigation, instead the unions have been active in equality litigation, but this litigation invokes national laws rather than EU law, as the national legal regime on equality provides greater protection.[4] Ireland represents another case of relatively strong trade unions (11 percent union membership) and low levels of Article 234 references. Irish trade unions are comparatively active in labor law litigation more generally, however, little, if any, of these cases invoke national or EU laws in the area of gender equality.[5]

Legal resources
The interaction between national legal resources and levels of preliminary references is displayed in Table 3.2. The model covers the time period of 1970 to 2003 and explores the impact of national legal resources on Article 234 preliminary references in the area of social provisions. As detailed in Chapter 2, I measure legal resources by coding each country for the presence of national agencies that support Article 234 litigation and the level of expertise in equality law possessed by the legal community.

---

[4] In particular, female dominated unions such as the HKI and the female only union, KAD, pursue litigation strategies (CEC 1995a:32).
[5] See Donnelly, Mullally, and Smith (1999). Also information gathered through interview with EU Commission national legal expert, 8 March 2000, Brussels Belgium.

Both in the strength and the direction of coefficients, the data confirm my expectation. The data illustrate that a point increase in the availability of legal resources produces an almost one case increase in average reference rates.

The United Kingdom, whose average reference rate is 2.44, or almost a quarter of all social provisions references (61 references out of the 307), represents the country with the strongest agency that assists individuals in making legal claims. Scholars have written extensively on the role of the British Equal Opportunities Commission (EOC) in supporting individual litigation (e.g. Kenney 1992: 92–102).[6] And feminist legal scholars and activists were originally critical of the agency for being too conservative and inactive in its earlier years (e.g. Byrne and Lovenduski 1978; Sacks 1987). Yet despite noticeable limitations in terms of litigation potential, in the time period of this analysis, either the EOC or its counterpart in Northern Ireland (NIEOC) funded over 20 references including some of the most significant gender equality cases (CEC 1995a). These include the cases that led to the *Marshall II* decision (ECJ 1993a), that led to the direct effect of the Equal Treatment Directive; the *Barber* decision (ECJ 1990a), which is now legendary for having expanded the equal pay protection provided under Article 141 to include pension benefits despite government opposition; and the *Boyle* decision (ECJ 1998a), a case involving the EOC as both plaintiff and defendant in which a group of EOC employees claimed wrongful discrimination in employment practices relating to maternity leave. Compared to its member state counterparts, this agency goes unparalleled in its support for legal claims that reach the ECJ via Article 234.

Similar to the UK, equality agencies in Ireland, Italy, the Netherlands and Sweden have the authority to litigate and instigate proceedings in their own name. The Irish Employment Equality Agency (EEA) is of similar age to the EOC, yet has exhibited little activity in supporting these legal claims.[7] One reason may be that the EEA lacks the authority to assist claimants beyond the hearings of equality officers and the labor court. The agency is obligated to pass the case on to private lawyers for appeals to the High Court (which is the legal forum for such cases in the Irish legal system) (CEC 1993a: 36–37). This may help explain the low average of social provisions references originating from Irish courts (only 6 cases). Similar to Ireland, the equality advisers within the Italian regional labor

---

[6] The EOC was established in 1975 through the Sex Discrimination Act with the mandate to promote equality between men and women. In terms of litigation, it formally possesses the authority to instigate proceedings against public or private institutions deemed to be engaging in discriminatory practices and may help individual claimants bring cases before national courts.

[7] It was created through the Employment Equality Act of 1977.

commissions have the power to litigate under delegation from an individual claimant or on their own accord: a power they recently acquired in 1991 (CEC 1993a: 37). Further, the Italian Equal Opportunities National Committee does possess considerable expertise on equality issues and has made an impact on the number of legal claims: a fact that may partially explain the medium levels of Italian equality references (13).[8] Lastly, the Swedish Equal Opportunities Ombudsman (EOO) is the only equality agency in Sweden allowed to bring cases before the courts. However, generally the EOO is hampered by its small size and limited resources (CEC 1997a: 11). Again, this may help us understand the comparatively low levels of social provisions references originating from Swedish courts.

Finally, the comparatively high average of references from Dutch courts (34 references out of 307) may be linked to the Dutch Equal Treatment Commission which has played an active role in litigation and just received enhanced powers in 1995. In addition to its "quasi-judicial" function in issuing non-binding recommendations, it now possesses the authority to support litigation on a wide variety of equality issues (CEC 1995a: 31; 1993a: 97). Even equality agencies without authority to litigate might also have an indirect impact on litigation, as those member states possessing active equality agencies (either in disseminating public information on equality or participating in equality legislation formation), such as the Danish Equality Council, were more likely than member states with relatively weak or no equality agencies, e.g. Portugal or Luxembourg, to be involved in legal claims resulting in preliminary references.[9] In Germany, a proliferation of equality agencies at the local and state level are responsible for "enhanced equality consciousness amongst women in recent years", and thus may help explain the high number of German references (CEC 1995a: 29).

Further, in Austria, the work carried out by the Ombudsperson, the Equal Treatment Commission and the Federal Equal Treatment Commission have been effective in impacting the "everyday life" of women in terms of providing an outlet for equality complaints. In 1996, the three bodies combined decided 551 cases that dealt with sex

---

[8] The *Pretore* of Lecce (judgment of 17 November 1997, 13 December 1997, Rivista giuridica del lavoro, No. 3/1998) utilized a recent opinion of the National Equality Adviser supporting the victim in a pregnancy discrimination case (CEC 1999b: 10).

[9] In the time period of this study, Danish courts were responsible for 19 references. While the Portuguese Commission for Equality in Work and Employment (CITE) has the right to intervene in the workplace with opinions on specific equality cases, it does not appear to have taken any action to make use of these opinions through litigation (CEC 1993a: 38–39).

discrimination (CEC 1998b: 10). This may help explain why Austrian courts had comparatively high reference rates despite having just joined the Union in 1995.[10] Finally, one possible reason there is a lack of litigation on equality issues in Luxembourg (1 reference in a 40-year time period), both involving national laws and EU laws, may be associated with the absence of an equality agency or ombudsman[11] Similarly, in Finland the Equality Board (EQ) and Equality Ombudsman possess rather prohibitive procedures regarding individual claims and have not made a significant impact on expanding women's rights. In fact, the only case brought before the EQ in 1996, involved a male nurse receiving less pay than his female counterparts (CEC 1998b: 12).

Beyond the support of government equality agencies, I hypothesized that availability at the national level of legal expertise and legal networks might also serve as a significant legal resource that may impact preliminary reference rates. Germany is a case in point. German legal experts observe informal links between academics and judges over issues of both national and EU equality laws (CEC 1995a: 45). In particular, legal activists operating at the Länder level rather than through the federal labor courts and the Constitutional Court have utilized the possibilities afforded through EU equality law to "circumvent" more restrictive interpretations of German constitutional law (CEC 1993a: 91). It is not surprising that the majority of German equality references are originating from particularly active Länder labor courts, which have been targeted by these activists (CEC 1993a: 91). Overall, German courts are responsible for the greatest number of equality Article 234 references (91 out of 307 or 30%). Further, there is a network of women lawyers that publishes a journal, *Streit*, as a way of circulating updates on equality laws and opportunities, thus disseminating their legal expertise to help support subsequent cases (CEC 1993a: 92).[12]

Belgium exhibits a similar pattern, which may help explain its higher level of social provisions references even without the Council on Equal

---

[10] Austria has the highest number of references (13) in this legal domain out of the 3 newest member states. The average reference rate for Austrian judges was 1.85, which is the third highest reference rate for all the member states included in this study and is clearly much higher than many older member states.

[11] This type of agency would be one way of tackling a legal system – lawyers, judges and even the Council of State – which does not regard sex equality as a real problem, but rather a "marginal issue" (CEC 1999b: 68).

[12] The German Association of Female Lawyers (AFL) has also been active in pressuring for changes in national equality legislation as a result of ECJ decisions. For example, in the *Draehmpaehl* judgment (ECJ 1997a) regarding sanctions for wrongful discrimination, the AFL has suggested that the German legislation should be changed to require employers to hire the victim, rather than just compensation for refusal to hire (CEC 1999b: 11).

Opportunities being able to sponsor litigation.[13] The informal networks of labor law activists, the trade unions and the Ministry of Work, Labor and Equal Opportunities have all actively disseminated information regarding sex discrimination claims (CEC 1993a: 87). This expertise seems to matter. For example, Spanish lower court judges and those on the Spanish Constitutional Court have been criticized for lacking both an awareness of EU equality law and an interest in resolving issues of gender inequalities.[14] Further, national legal systems that lack a supportive equality legal network and also an extensive legal basis and knowledge of the protection for equality claimants may possess low levels of references due to reluctance on behalf of women to bring cases to court.[15] Conversely, countries such as Austria, that provide significant legal support for women, have on average higher levels of preliminary references.[16]

Further, the data illustrate that alternative explanations such as level of national court are less powerful in explaining this variation. Again, Alter (2001) argues that lower courts were more likely to send preliminary references as they gained new powers *vis-à-vis* higher courts and the national executive. Figure 3.1 displays preliminary references in the area of social provisions between 1970–2003 by the level of court referring the case. While lower courts did certainly send more references than the highest constitutional or supreme courts, the overall trend does not suggest lower courts are the main source of these references. Instead, over half the cases originate from either mid appellate courts or high courts (total of 167), whereas lower courts sent 140 references. While the lower courts are certainly active in referring cases, this explanation cannot systematically explain variation in preliminary reference rates.

---

[13] While the Belgian Council on Equal Opportunities cannot directly sponsor litigation it can provide opinions in support of court cases (CEC 1993a: 87).

[14] Personal interview with legal expert from the Commission Legal Experts Group on Equal Treatment of Men and Women, Prof. Dolores de la Fuente. Interview with EU Commission, DG Employment and Social Affairs, national legal expert, 27 April 1999, Brussels, Belgium. However, the Constitutional Court has recently become more favorable and activist in the area of sex equality: in particular, indirect discrimination and burden of proof cases (see discussion below in relation to pregnancy rights).

[15] For example, in Greece women have been reluctant to file claims for fear of victimization and problems of proof (CEC 1999b: 7). Fears of victimization are also prevalent in Spain and Portugal (CEC 1995a: 27). Further, Portuguese legal experts observe a general lack of knowledge in EU equality laws by claimants who often ignore the opportunity to use EU law in challenging national practices and very little domestic gender equality litigation, trade union supported or otherwise (see also Casqueira Cardoso 1999).

[16] Examples of this expert support include the presence of programs supporting test case equality litigation, such as that organized by the Austrian Women's Lawyers and the Vienna Women's Shelter Association (CEC 1999b: 70).

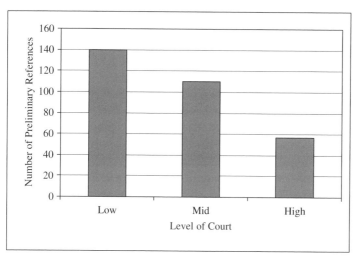

Note: N = 307
The level of court categories denotes the following: low (first instance court), mid (appellate court but whose decision could be appealed to a higher court), and high (court of final appeal).
Source: Data compiled by the author from European Communities. 2004. *CELEX Data Base*. Brussels: Office for Official Publications of the European Communities and World Jurist Association (2002).

Figure 3.1 Total number of Article 234 references in the area of social provisions by level of referring national court, 1970–2003

EU rules

Alongside mobilized interests and legal resources, I hypothesized that preliminary reference rate may also be a function of the EU rules governing a particular legal domain. EU rules may impact litigation by creating the opportunities for action. One way this can occur is through the interaction between these EU rules and pre-existing national policies. I call this EU/national policy fit. Further, I also argued that EU rules in the form of ECJ precedent might also affect subsequent litigation to the extent to which they create new opportunities for action. In the following analyses, I explore these interactions.

EU/National policy fit
The EU/national policy fit measure suggests how the national policy context might matter to Article 234 reference rates. As Table 3.3 illustrates, the less successful a member state is at integrating EU law into the national legal system (or the lower the EU/national policy fit), the higher the levels of Article 234 references originating from those national courts. However, if

Table 3.3 *Effect of EU/national policy fit on average number of Article 234 references in the area of social provisions, 1970–2003*

	B	t-statistic
(model 1) Social provisions EU/national policy fit	−.038*	−2.643

Notes:
* p < .05
Entry is unstandardized regression coefficient. For each member state the total number of preliminary references is divided by the number of years in which that country has been making references to the ECJ in this legal domain. EU/National policy fit is the average transposition rate for each country (the percentage of EU secondary legislation applicable to date that has been properly implemented into national law).
Source: Data compiled by the author from European Communities. 2004. *CELEX Data Base.* Brussels: Office for Official Publications of the European Communities and the *Annual Report on Monitoring the Application of Community Law* (Luxembourg: Office for Official Publications of the European Communities, various years).

we compare countries that exhibit implementation rates that are below average in this policy area, Greece, the Netherlands and the United Kingdom for example, there is still great variation across reference rates. Greece possesses few social provisions preliminary references (2 cases), while courts from the Netherlands and United Kingdom together have sent over a third of all the references in this legal domain (95 out of 307 references). Again, this may illustrate the impact of other factors such as interest group support for these claims. As previously discussed, British trade unions and also government equality agencies have been very active in these cases, while their Spanish and Portuguese counterparts have shown little interest, knowledge or authority to engage in these types of legal claims.[17]

---

[17] Interviews with EU Commission, DG Employment and Social Affairs, national legal expert, 27 April 1999, Brussels, Belgium. Scholars have observed the importance of legal expertise from the British Equal Opportunities Commission (EOC) and also feminist legal experts (e.g. Alter and Vargas 2000; Kenney 1992). Portuguese legal experts observe a general lack of knowledge in EU equality laws by claimants who often ignore the opportunity to use EU law in challenging Portuguese legal practices and very little domestic sex equality litigation, trade union supported or otherwise (see also Casqueira Cardoso 1999). This may change in the future as a 1997 Portuguese law (105/97) now gives trade unions the authority to start legal proceeding in discrimination cases (CEC 1999b: 26). Further, Spanish litigation may be limited as a result of the minimal sex equality rights in Spain. However, the Constitutional Court has recently become more favorable and activist in the area of sex equality: in particular, indirect discrimination and burden of proof cases (see also Arranz, Quintanilla and Velazquez 1999). These factors will be discussed in greater length in the analysis focusing on national legal factors.

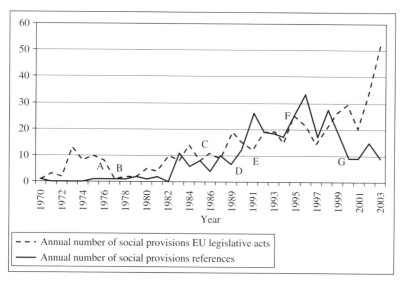

Note: Social provisions references N = 307
Social provisions legislative acts N = 457
The letters denote landmark social provisions ECJ rulings and are labeled as follows: (A)
Direct Effect of Art. 141 (Case 43/75, 1976), (B) Equality is a fundamental EU right
(Case 149/77, 1978), (C) Equal Pay Principle applicable to pensions (Case 170/84, 1986),
(D) *Barber* decision (Case 262/88, 1990), *Dekker* decision, dismissal on grounds of
pregnancy is unlawful (Case 177/88) (E) 'Protective Treatment' (e.g. banning night
work) is unlawful (Case 345/89, 1991), (F) Positive Action (Case 450/93, 1995), (G) Sex
discrimination in military, proportionality of limits (Case 273/97, 1999).
Source: Data compiled by the author from European Communities. 2004. *CELEX Data
Base*. Brussels: Office for Official Publications of the European Communities.

Figure 3.2 Annual number of Article 234 references and EU legislative
acts in the area of social provisions with landmark ECJ decisions,
1970–2003

ECJ precedent

Finally, we turn to the impact of ECJ precedent on levels of Article 234
references. The data in Figure 3.2 illustrate how preliminary references
developed between 1970 and 2003. This figure temporally locates landmark ECJ decisions in the area of social provisions, in order to explore the
effect of ECJ precedent on both legal action and legislative action. The
data suggest that the relationship is mutually constitutive. That is, legislation is both a cause and effect of the preliminary references. Likewise,
past legal claims resulting in ECJ precedent can form the basis for subsequent references and EU legislative acts.

For example, the ECJ's *Defrenne II* decision (ECJ 1976a), establishing
the direct effect of Article 141, and the *Defrenne III* decision (ECJ 1978),

establishing that equal treatment is a fundamental EU principle, provided the legal basis for subsequent gender equality claims and the expansion of EU secondary legislation in the 1970s and 1980s (e.g. Cichowski 2001, 2002; Hoskyns 1996). The growth in social provisions references has been dramatic: an evolution that could not have occurred without the ECJ's *Defrenne II* decision which transformed Article 141 into a positive right enabling women throughout Europe to claim new protection before their own national courts. This general dynamic can be illustrated in numerous sub-fields of EU social provision. For example, the Court's decision in the *Dekker* case[18] (ECJ 1990c) established pregnancy and maternity rights under EU law. Subsequently, this ECJ precedent was codified in Article 10 of the Pregnancy Directive.[19] Further, this judicial decision which led to considerable inconsistencies between EU rules and national pregnancy and maternity regulations, led to subsequent preliminary references asking for a clarification.[20]

A similar dynamic occurred in the area of equal pay and equal treatment in social security. The ECJ first dealt with this issue directly in the *Bilka* decision (ECJ 1986a) which expanded the scope in meaning of pay under Article 141 to include non-contracted pension schemes: a ruling that provided for many women significantly greater protection than national regulations. This decision marked the beginning of a flood of legal claims, the most famous of which was the *Barber* decision (ECJ 1990a) and subsequent legislative action addressing the issue of non-discrimination in pension plans.[21] A similar dynamic has unfolded in the area of equal treatment, as ECJ case law began filling in important details left absent in the original 1976 Equal Treatment Directive, judgments that have today been codified in the newly amended and adopted Equal

---

[18] ECJ 1990c.

[19] Council Directive 92/85/EEC.

[20] E.g. *Habermann* (ECJ 1994c); *Webb* (ECJ 1994d), *Gillespie* (ECJ 1996a), *Larsson* (ECJ 1997b), *Brown* (ECJ 1998d), *Thibault* (ECJ 1998e), *Boyle* (ECJ 1998a), *Pedersen* (ECJ 1998b). See case law analysis below for a thorough discussion of these decisions.

[21] The *Barber* decision (ECR 1990a) which in effect provided the direct effect of Article 141 in the pension sphere (pensions are within the meaning of pay) was met with extreme criticism from member states who realized the costs involved with such a judgment (see in particular, the UK observation in the case which highlighted the potential harm such a ruling would have on the British economy: citing cost increases in the £33–45 billion range). A host of Article 234 litigation followed (ECJ 1993b; ECJ 1993c; ECJ 1993d to name just a few). See the text of Council Directive 96/97/EC for a complete list. And subsequent EU legislative acts included an unprecedented treaty revision (the Barber Protocol) and an amended directive (Council Directive 96/97/EC amending Directive 86/378/EEC).

Treatment Directive.[22] Further, the *Kalanke* decision (ECJ 1995a) regarding positive action provides an example of how ECJ precedent that narrows the protection (rather than expands as in the above cases) provided for women under EU law, can also lead to subsequent litigation and EU legislative action in an attempt to correct or clarify this potentially harmful decision.[23] This interaction between ECJ precedent, Community legislative acts and subsequent legal claims has unmistakably characterized the evolution of EU social provisions.

Explaining litigation: decision-making, rulemaking and opportunities for action

The previous section focused on the factors that give rise to the legal claim and preliminary references. The Court's decision-making played a role in this explanation the extent to which this precedent formed the basis for subsequent legal claims. In this section, I turn our focus exclusively to the factors that shape these ECJ decisions and the subsequent impact on institutionalization of gender equality rights. I explore whether the ECJ acts to uphold EU interests and clarify EU law or whether it operates to preserve national government policy positions. Further, I examine whether these judicial rulings may serve to change the balance of power between national governments, EU organizations and public interest activists.

Upholding EU interests

In order to examine whether the ECJ acts to uphold EU interests or member state policy positions, I begin by exploring the written observations in each case. Again, the member state governments and EU organizations (primarily the Commission) file these written briefs stating how the case should be decided. These legal arguments reveal the policy preferences of member state governments and EU organizations. The data in Table 3.4 include all the written observations submitted in

---

[22] As mentioned in Chapter 2, Directive 2002/73/EC amended Council Directive 76/207/ EEC on Equal Treatment and the new Article 2 codifies the ECJ's decisions in *Brown* (ECJ 1998d), *Gillespie* (ECJ 1996a), *Johnston* (ECJ 1986c), *Kreil* (ECJ 2000a) and *Sirdar* (ECJ 1999a).

[23] The *Kalanke* decision received considerable criticism, from women's groups to legal activists (interview with former General Secretary of the European Women's Lobby, April 1999, Brussels; see also Prechal 1996; Szyszczak 1996). The Commission was also quick to react to this narrow judgment on quota systems by issuing a communication clarifying the decision in a way that did not take such a narrow reading of the compatibility of national quotas regarding women's opportunity and EU law (CEC 1996a). A year later, the ECJ overturned its earlier position in *Kalanke* and adopted the Commission's interpretation in the *Marschall* decision (ECJ 1997c).

Table 3.4 *National government and Commission observations as a predictor of ECJ rulings pursuant to Article 234 references in the area of social provisions by country, 1976–2003*

	Number of rulings	Number of observations	Success rate (%)	Intervention rate (%)
Austria	7	14	67%	8%
Belgium	24	20	63%	5%
Denmark	19	19	63%	6%
Finland	2	11	70%	7%
France	10	40	58%	14%
Germany	59	64	40%	15%
Greece	1	6	40%	2%
Ireland	5	16	47%	5%
Italy	12	15	60%	4%
Luxembourg	0	2	100%	1%
Netherlands	29	48	60%	11%
Portugal	2	7	57%	3%
Spain	7	8	38%	1%
Sweden	5	13	60%	8%
United Kingdom	58	136	58%	44%
Commission		240	84%	100%

Notes:

$N = 240$

Number of rulings column denotes the number of ECJ preliminary rulings originating from the specified country's national courts. Success rate denotes the percentage of cases in which a member state government's written observation (policy position) successfully predicts the final ECJ ruling. Intervention rate denotes the rate at which a given member state intervenes (by submitting an observation) in cases beyond those involving its own legal system. This rate is calculated as the number of observations submitted by a country in cases not directly involving their legal system as a percentage of the total number of rulings not directly involving the country on which they could have filed observations. Intervention rate for the Commission denotes the percentage out of all cases that the Commission submits an observation.

Source: Data compiled by the author from European Communities. 2004. *CELEX Data Base.* Brussels: Office for Official Publications of the European Communities and the *European Court Reports* (Luxembourg: Office for Official Publications of the European Communities, various years).

preliminary rulings in the area of social provisions between 1971 and 2003. The table includes data broken down into various categories for each country: total number of rulings, total number of observations submitted in all cases, rate at which the observation successfully predicted the ECJ decision (success rate) and finally, the rate at which a given member state intervenes in cases beyond those involving its own legal practices (intervention rate). The table also includes data on the Commission. This gives us some idea of how often member states and the Commission are intervening in judicial decision-making and with what impact.

Generally, the findings are consistent with what we know about the Commission's self-decided policy of intervening in preliminary ruling cases. The Commission submitted observations in all cases: an act that reflects this organization's "desire for influence" in EU policy decisions (de la Mare 1999: 244). The data display that whether a country's legal practice is in question does not necessarily determine its general level of participation in submitting observations. The Dutch government intervened in 11% of preliminary rulings that did not directly involve Dutch national practices, compared to less active member states, such as Belgium, which not only did not intervene beyond its own cases, also did not submit observations in 4 of its own cases. Austria and Ireland were also less likely to intervene beyond their own cases, with intervention rates of 8% and 5%. Beyond the German intervention rate, the UK government has been astonishingly active by intervening in 80 out of 181 cases (44%) that did not involve UK legal practices directly. This may suggest that the UK takes seriously the potential policy impact, in all member states, of these preliminary rulings. Thus, in the same way the British government has acted in the Council of Ministers to defend its position that social protection should be dealt with at the national level rather than EU level, the UK takes seriously the opportunity to participate in the policy discussions and decisions that transpire during the preliminary ruling procedure.[24]

How do these member state interventions affect the ECJ's decision-making? The most interesting finding is that the Commission's observations predict ECJ rulings far better than do observations filed by member state governments. The Commission's success rate is approximately 84%: 202 out of 240 observations are successful at predicting the final ECJ decision. The United Kingdom's rate of success is much lower in comparison at 58%. It is interesting to note that while Denmark's success

---

[24] In the time period of this study, the UK government has continually dragged its heels in terms of agreeing to EU social policy. The first real concrete sets of social rights were established through the Social Charter Action Program decided in Strasbourg in 1989. All member states except the UK signed the political declaration. Further, pressure to expand social protection in the negotiations leading up to the Treaty on European Union (TEU) was "met with stubborn resistance on the part of the UK" (Barnard 1999: 485). The EU developed the "Social Chapter" (the Social Policy Agreement and the Social Policy Protocol) as treaty amendments, but they were relegated to an annex of the TEU to secure the UK's opt-out position.

rate is high (63%), in 1 of its observations the Danish Government actually filed an observation stating it believed their national law is in violation with EU law (government preferences in all other cases take a stance to defend or preserve national law) and the ECJ concurred (see ECJ 1996b). In general, the findings presented in Table 3.4 suggest that some member states take seriously the policy-making function of the ECJ preliminary ruling. Further, the findings bring into question claims that the ECJ decisions are systematically influenced by the policy positions of member states. Instead, as the ECJ acts to protect its legitimacy and uphold EU interests, it is not surprising that the Commission's position was much more likely to predict the final outcome of the case.

These conclusions are further illustrated by the data in Figure 3.3 where I test success rates in major cases, or cases with higher political or financial costs. The figure displays the percentage of adverse rulings (rulings in which the ECJ finds a national practice to be in violation of EU law) by four categories denoting the magnitude of the political and financial impact of the case: 1 denotes low impact and 4 is the highest. Generally, a greater number of member states file written observations in cases with potentially high political and financial costs (major cases) (de la Mare 1999; Granger 2004). Thus, the number of member states filing observations in a case becomes a proxy for level of political and financial impact. These data begin to help us understand whether the ECJ is less likely to issue an adverse ruling in major cases. As most national governments submit observations to defend national practices, this also tells us whether member states observations are more or less successful at predicting the final decision in major cases.

The findings are significant. In the social provisions domain, there is some evidence that in cases with a low impact (only 1 member state filing an observation) the ECJ has the highest percentage of issuing adverse rulings (60%). Yet the ECJ is nearly as likely (57%) to issue adverse rulings in cases with the highest political and economic impact (4 or more member states filing observations). What is interesting is that across all types of cases, we find the ECJ not hesitating to declare national practices in violation with EU law, with adverse rulings making up over half of all decisions in each category of cases. Generally, these data bring into question the Garrett et al. (1998) assertion that the ECJ is more likely to withhold adverse rulings, the higher the domestic costs associated with such a ruling.

Clarifying rules

I now turn to the EU rules invoked in the cases: what types of EU laws are continually litigated and which are the subject of adverse rulings? Further, I explore whether the ECJ operates to preserve national practices

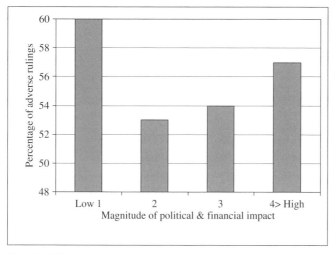

Note: N = 240
Percentage of adverse rulings denotes the total number of rulings in which the ECJ
finds the national law or practice to be in violation of EU law as a percentage of the
total number of social provisions preliminary rulings. Each preliminary ruling is also
categorized has having a low to high financial impact. The categories of magnitude
denote the total number of member state governments filing observations in each case.
These totals serve as a proxy for the magnitude of impact as cases with a larger impact
elicit a greater number of member state governments participating in the case.
Source: Data compiled by the author from European Communities. 2004. *CELEX Data
Base*. Brussels: Office for Official Publications of the European Communities and the
European Court Reports (Luxembourg: Office for Official Publications of the
European Communities, various years).

Figure 3.3 Political and financial impact as a predictor of adverse ECJ
rulings pursuant to Article 234 references in the area of social provisions,
1971–2003

that come in conflict with the EU or clarify these rules in a way that can
dismantle national practices that are in violation. Between 1971 and
2003, the ECJ made 240 social provisions preliminary rulings.
Table 3.5 details the EU laws invoked in these decisions. These data
provide an overview of the pattern of ECJ decisions both as a whole and
also in the individual sub-fields: whether the ruling found the national
practice to be consistent with EU law or in violation of EU law (adverse
ruling). The data suggest that when asked to interpret EU law in light of
national legal practices, the ECJ does not systematically rule in a direction
that preserves national laws. Instead, as we saw above, in over half of the
preliminary rulings in this time period, the Court issued adverse
rulings by finding national practices in violation of EU law (140 out of

Table 3.5 *EU laws invoked in ECJ rulings pursuant to Article 234 in the area of social provisions by judicial outcome, 1971–2003*

	Number of rulings (percentage of all rulings)	Number of adverse rulings (percentage of adverse rulings)
Equality legislation CD 75/117 Equal Pay CD 76/207 Equal Treatment CD 79/7 Social Security CD 86/378 Social Security	86 (36%)	56 (65%)
Equality treaty provision Article 141	61 (25%)	44 (72%)
Health, safety and services Article 117 and Article 92 COMR 66/462 and Article 189 CR 1612/68 and Article 59	18 (8%)	7 (39%)
Transport/Social protection CR 543/69 CR 3820/85 CR 515/72 (amends 543/69) CR 3821/85 CR 2827/77 (amends 543/69)	21 (9%)	5 (24%)
Social protection in transfer of *business ownership* CD 75/129 CD 77/187 CD 80/987 CD 87/164	54 (23%)	28 (52%)
Total rulings	240	140 (58%)

Notes:
Total rulings column denotes the number of cases involving EU laws in a particular sub-field of social provisions. Adverse rulings column denotes the total number of rulings in a particular sub-field in which the national rule was declared to be in violation of EU law.
CD = Council Directive CR = Council Regulation
Source: Data compiled by the author from European Communities. 2004.
CELEX Data Base. Brussels: Office for Official Publications of the European Communities and the *European Court Reports* (Luxembourg: Office for Official Publications of the European Communities, various years).

240, 58%). Further, ECJ rulings upholding national practices were disproportionately in those sub-fields involving clearly defined EU norms.

For example, rulings involving social provisions in the transport sector received the fewest number of adverse rulings (5 out of 21 rulings, 24% of social protection transport rulings). This is not surprising as EU legislation in this area has been issued by way of Council regulations whose policy prescriptions are directly applicable and binding in all member states.[25] The resulting consequence is greater specificity that will ensure direct and uniform application into the legal systems of all member states.[26] The ECJ does not need to bring greater clarity to these laws. On the other hand, directives are binding only to the end to be achieved but leave open to member state governments the form and method of how this will be transposed into the national legal system. In the social provisions domain, many directives possess vague policy prescriptions that resulted from unanimity voting.[27] These lowest common denominator positions embodied in these EU rules illustrate an overall hesitation by member state governments to specify concrete EU rules in the area of equality between men and women (Hoskyns 1996). As the data suggest, when legal questions arose from these vague policy prescriptions, the ECJ did not hesitate to expand both the meaning and scope of these equality directives, often in the face of member state opposition.

Over a third of the social provisions preliminary rulings involved the equality directives alone (86 out of 240 rulings). And in 65 percent of these cases (56 out of 86) the ECJ found national practices to be inconsistent with EU law. This is an astonishing number for a policy area that was intended to remain governed mostly by national measures rather than EU law. Similarly, the ECJ did not hesitate to expand the scope of Article 141, the equal pay provision, when confronted with the possible rights this treaty provision implied.[28] In 61 different rulings, the ECJ was asked to interpret the meaning of Article 141 in relation to national practices: 72 percent (44 out of 61) of these rulings held that national laws were not in conformity with Article 141. While the "adverse ruling" category can give us a general picture of whether the ECJ is in any way systematically

---

[25] For example, Council Regulations 543/69/EEC, 515/72/EEC, 2827/77/EEC, 3820/85/EEC and 3821/85/EEC.

[26] See Craig and de Búrca (1998: Chapter 3) for further discussion of the categories and effects of varying EU legislative instruments.

[27] For example, Council Directive 75/117/EEC, 76/207/EEC and 79/7/EEC.

[28] See the Court's *Defrenne* decisions (ECJ 1971; ECJ 1976a; ECJ 1978) for the Court's initial expansion of the meaning and applicability of Article 141 (Cichowski 2004). These are discussed in greater detail in the case law analysis in this chapter.

preserving national laws when they come into conflict with EU norms, it can sometimes hide the ECJ's most expansive rulings which sometimes come as a side note to the main proceedings.[29] The net effect is that in the particular case a national practice may be upheld, however, the ECJ's expansive interpretation of an EU law provides the basis for subsequent litigation that can provide the basis to overturn national law in the future.[30] Generally, the findings suggest that when the ECJ is asked to clarify vague aspects of EU social provisions it does not hesitate to do. Further, these data suggest in the majority of social provisions rulings the Court does not hesitate to overturn national laws that are incompatible with these interpretations. This would suggest that the Court does not function to preserve national practices compared to EU laws.

Table 3.6 provides a general picture of how the social provisions rulings have evolved cross-nationally and by individual sub-field. The ECJ considered the lawfulness of Dutch practices in 29 rulings, declaring violations in 59% of these decisions. Aggregating results from litigation involving "powerful member state governments" (France, Germany, Italy and the UK), the Court declared violations in 85 of these cases, or 61% of the decisions involving these four countries. These data also give some preliminary indication that those national legal regimes that enshrine the least integrative rules will be asked to upgrade them in conformity with EU law. British laws were the subjects of almost a quarter of all the rulings in this legal domain (58 out of 240). This is not surprising. The UK has continually taken the "opt-out" position to even the thinnest of EU social policy regulations (Pierson and Leibfried 1992). These data confirm the expectation that rulings will disproportionately involve legal disputes arising from legal systems operating to downgrade EU laws.

Further, the findings suggest another explanation for cross-national variation. As previously discussed, Germany and the Netherlands possess a comparatively high degree of legal expertise in the area of gender equality. Thus, while these two legal systems may afford greater legal protection

---

[29] Legal scholars and political scientists recognize this as a common ECJ strategy, of the ECJ specifically and courts more generally, to develop lines of doctrine while avoiding member state opposition to this expansion (see Hartley 1988: 78; Alter 1998: 130–1). The *Costa* decision (ECJ 1964) establishing the supremacy of EU law is a classic example.

[30] The *Defrenne III* decision exemplifies this dynamic (ECJ 1978). The ECJ held that Article 141 did not govern the working conditions in question. However, in its argumentation, the Court gave Article 141 greater legal strength by stating that it embodied a EU right: "there can be no doubt that the elimination of discrimination based on sex forms part of those fundamental rights" (para. 27). Far beyond the intended narrow scope of pay, Article 141 would form the basis for legal claims in the area of pensions (e.g. ECJ 1986a), pregnancy rights (e.g. *Dekker* 1990b) and general indirect discrimination protection (e.g. ECJ 1981a), to name just a few.

Table 3.6 *ECJ rulings pursuant to Article 234 references in the area of social provisions by country and sub-field of EU law, 1971–2003*

	Number of rulings (percentage of adverse rulings)				
	Equality treaty provision and/ or legislation	Health, safety & services	Social protection transport	Social protection transfer ownership	Totals
Austria	4 (25%)		1 (0%)	2 (100%)	7 (43%)
Belgium	10 (40%)	2 (0%)	6 (33%)	6 (50%)	24 (38%)
Denmark	7 (71%)		1 (0%)	11 (36%)	19 (47%)
Finland	1 (100%)			1 (100%)	2 (100%)
France	7 (71%)		1 (0%)	2 (50%)	10 (60%)
Germany	42 (76%)	8 (38%)	3 (33%)	6 (33%)	59 (64%)
Greece	1 (100%)				1 (100%)
Ireland	5 (80%)				5 (80%)
Italy	1 (100%)	2 (50%)		9 (56%)	12 (58%)
Netherlands	22 (73%)		1 (0%)	6 (17%)	29 (59%)
Portugal		2 (50%)			2 (50%)
Spain	1 (100%)	1 (100%)		5 (80%)	7 (86%)
Sweden	2 (100%)		1 (0%)	2 (50%)	5 (60%)
United Kingdom	44 (61%)	3 (33%)	7 (29%)	4 (100%)	58 (57%)
Total rulings	147	18	21	54	240

Notes:
N = 240
Number of rulings denotes the number of judgments in each sub-field for each country.
Percentage of adverse rulings denotes the number of judgments in a particular sub-field involving a particular country finding a violation of EU law as a percentage of the total number of judgments in that sub-field for that country.
Source: Data compiled by the author from European Communities. 2004. *CELEX Data Base.* Brussels: Office for Official Publications of the European Communities and the *European Court Reports* (Luxembourg: Office for Official Publications of the European Communities, various years).

from sex discrimination, compared to other member states, they also possess a degree of equality law expertise that has systematically tested the scope of both EU law and their own national laws by providing real situations for previously vague EU equality laws.[31] This rights

---

[31] Noteworthy German examples are the *Kalanke* ruling that tested whether positive action programs were protected by EU law (ECJ 1995a), the *Bilka* decision which was one of the first cases in which the ECJ dealt directly with issue of pension schemes and the Equal Pay

argumentation and the practical situation of the dispute provides the basis for the ECJ's decision. In an attempt to bring greater clarity to the EU right in question, the Court often dismantles national practices, regardless of member state opposition or in an attempt to preserve national laws. German practices were the subject of preliminary rulings in the equality sub-field almost a third of the time (42 out of 147 rulings). Further, the ECJ declared German practices as inconsistent with EU law in 76 percent of these cases. Similarly, Dutch practices are increasingly the subject of adverse rulings in the area of equality: 73% of Dutch preliminary references in this area ended in the ECJ declaring that the national practice was in violation of EU law. Finally, these data also illustrate that those rulings invoking Article 141, a treaty provision, result in adverse rulings 72% of the time. This is consistent with the argument that fundamental Community rights give the ECJ greater latitude to dismantle national practices and expand EU rules.

The institutionalization of gender equality rights: from pay to pregnancy

These data reinforce predictions arguing that the preferences of powerful member state governments do not generally constrain the Court's judicial outcomes. The pattern of social provisions references and the subsequent judicial rulings reveal the Court's active participation in the integration project. These data give us a general picture of the dynamic driving this litigation. As we have seen, individuals and organizations utilize the rights provided under EU law, such as found in Article 141 or the equality directives, to seek new protection against discriminatory practices in their own legal system. Through the resolution of the dispute, the ECJ has expanded EU social provisions, in a way that can provide new opportunities for legislative action and legal activism. As illustrated, ECJ precedent played a critical role in the development of EU social rights. Following the Court's *Defrenne II* decision, individuals and EU organizations were given new opportunities for action through legislation and case law in a host of social provisions sectors including general equal treatment, social security, pregnancy rights and positive action, to name just a few.

Directive (ECJ 1986a), to name just a few. Similarly, the Dutch courts have sent the preliminary references in decisions such as the *Dekker* decision, which created certain maternity rights in EU law (ECJ 1990c) and also the *Ten Oever* decision which was part of the post *Barber* case law that further clarified the question of EU competence in the area of equality and pension schemes (ECJ 1993c).

To understand more precisely how this litigation dynamic develops and how this changes the balance of power between EU organizations, member state governments and ordinary citizens, I rely on the content of the case law. In the remaining part of the chapter, I examine the case law in a single area of social provisions that exemplifies this general pattern: pregnancy and maternity rights. This case law analysis provides the detail that aggregate data cannot. In particular, I examine the dynamics of judicial rulemaking in the cases to highlight how the Court comes to apply an equal pay provision to the subject of pregnancy rights, despite a lack of any pre-existing EU rights in this area. Further, I examine how individuals, EU organizations and national governments all reacted and participated in this evolving policy expansion.

The necessary conditions for legal claims and litigation

As discussed in Chapter 2, Article 141 provided the legal basis for EU gender equality law and legislative action. Essential to the evolution of the policy sector was, first, a decision by member state governments to include the provision in the Treaty of Rome. As discussed, the origins of Article 141 are embedded in economic rather than social justice concerns. Inclusion of Article 141 in the Treaty was an attempt to protect French businesses from unfair competition created by less stringent equal pay laws possessed by other member state governments. Yet, given this necessary rule, how did individuals come to utilize a treaty provision for their own protection against discriminatory national practices? ECJ precedent is the answer. Thus, the second necessary condition for this activism and litigation was an ECJ decision that transformed this treaty provision into an enforceable rights provision. Together these two factors activated a dynamic of litigation that ultimately brought the creation of a complex set of rules governing gender equality in Europe. Thus, our case law analysis begins with this important landmark decision, the *Defrenne II* decision.

Until the late 1960s, member state governments all but ignored Article 141. Not one national government had undertaken domestic policy changes to implement this equal pay principle. However, Article 141 was far from dead, as it was soon to gain life as a result of the strategic action and activism of a Belgian lawyer. Elaine Vogel-Polsky, who specialized in social and labor law, regarded Article 141 as a stepping-stone to expanding women's labor rights (Hoskyns 1996). Through a series of cases involving Gabrielle Defrenne, a flight attendant with the Belgian national airline, Sabena, Vogel-Polsky was able to work with the ECJ to expand the scope of the article and to begin to provide real situations in which Article 141 was applicable. The Court's *Defrenne* judgments (ECJ 1971; 1976a; 1978), in particular the second case, were critical in transforming Article 141 by establishing its direct effect, and in doing so provided EU citizens with individual rights enforceable under EU law.

The conditions that gave rise to these cases are as follows. Until 1966, Sabena's male flight stewards earned higher wages, were allowed to retire 15 years later, and were entitled to a special pension plan, all benefits that their female counterparts failed to receive. Job responsibilities of stewards and stewardesses were identical. Vogel-Polsky challenged these inequalities. The *Defrenne I* case questioned whether Sabena's pension system contravened the principle of non-discrimination embodied in Article 141. The Court ruled against Defrenne, stating that under EU law the Sabena pension did not constitute direct or indirect payment. However, Advocate General M. Dutheillet de Lamothe raised a critical point not addressed by the Court: did Article 141 provide individuals with direct legal rights that were enforceable in national courts? In his opinion it did:

Although the difficulties of application encountered by certain countries were great and although in particular a conference of member states extended until 31 December 1964 the period initially laid down, it appears to me certain that at least from this date Article 119 [now Article 141] created subjective rights which the workers of the Member States can invoke and respect for which national courts must ensure. (ECJ 1971: 456) [parenthetic numbering added]

Five years later the Court would agree.

The direct effect of Article 141 was central to the *Defrenne II* case. Similar to the first case, Defrenne's claim was dismissed first by the Belgian *Tribunal du Travail*, was appealed before the *Court du Travail*, and finally reached the ECJ by way of a preliminary reference. This case involved the issue of wage inequalities. Vogel-Polsky was again strategic by persisting with the question of direct effect. In order to resolve the dispute, the Belgian court referred two questions. First, does Article 141 introduce the principle of equal pay directly into the national law of member states, and if so from what date? Second, has Article 141 become directly applicable in the internal law of member states by virtue of the Treaty's adoption or is national legislation alone competent in the matter? The consequences of an affirmative answer were legendary.

The Court expanded the scope and purpose of Article 141 by stating that the principle was creative of both enforceable rights in national courts, regardless of national implementing legislation, and that the scope requires further clarification and development. In its reasoning, the Court emphasizes what it sees as the dual function of Article 141:

First, in the light of the different stages of the development of social legislation in the various Member States, the aim of Article 119 [now Article 141] is to avoid a situation in which undertakings established in States which have actually implemented the principle of equal pay suffer a competitive disadvantage in intra-Community competition ... Secondly, this provision forms part of the social objectives of the Community, which is not merely an economic union, but is at the same time intended, by common action, to ensure social progress and seek the constant improvement of the living and working conditions of their peoples ... This double aim, which is at once economic and social, shows that the principle of equal pay forms part of the foundations of the Community. (ECJ 1976a: 470) [parenthetic numbering added]

The argument of Advocate General Trabucchi stated quite clearly that he believed Article 141 was not only an enforceable right, but a fundamental EU right: 'In view of this it seems to me that the prohibition of all discrimination based on sex (particularly on the subject of pay) protects a right which must be regarded as fundamental in the Community legal order as it is elsewhere' (ECJ 1976a: 483).[32]

Not all parties participating in this case concurred with this expansive reading of the Treaty. The governments of both the United Kingdom and of the Irish Republic exercised their right to submit a written observation, stating how they believed the Court should decide the case. In their opinion, Article 141 did not confer rights on individuals, citing the potential "cost of the operation" if the Court was to find the principle directly effective, especially retroactively. Furthermore, their arguments were similar in stating that Article 141 merely implies a commitment to a constitutional principle, but can be effective only when implemented via national legislation (ECJ 1976a: 460). The Commission's observation urged the Court to answer the question of direct effect in the affirmative, yet stated this effect was limited to the relationship between individuals and the state, and did not impose obligations on private employers (ECJ 1976a: 462). The Court's authoritative interpretation of the Treaty developed otherwise.

Not only did the Court's ruling lay down that Article 141 was directly enforceable in national courts, regardless of national implementing legislation, it also suggested who would be protected and obligated by this right. In its judgment, the Court stated:

The principle that men and women should receive equal pay, which is laid down by Article 119 [now Article 141], may be relied on before the national courts. These courts have a duty to ensure the protection of the rights which

---

[32] AG Trabucchi's opinion would be realized in the Court's subsequent *Defrenne III* decision (ECJ 1978).

that provision vests in individuals, in particular in the case of those forms of discrimination which have their origin in legislative provisions or collective labour agreements, as well as where men and women receive unequal pay for equal work which is carried out in the same establishment or service, whether public or private. (ECJ 1976a: 475) [parenthetic numbering added]

Beyond the Commission's argument for 'vertical' direct effect, that is, in relationships involving the state and the individual, the Court's ruling also established the 'horizontal' direct effect of Article 141: granting enforceable rights in contracts between individuals. Article 141 was no longer a distant obligation on member state governments. Following the Court's interpretation of the Treaty, individuals, national courts, and public and private bodies were all bound into a tighter web of legal obligation.

The Court's judicial rulemaking in the *Defrenne II* decision enabled Article 141 to become the site for an expansive rights discourse. As discussed in Chapter 2, Article 141 would become the driving force behind EU gender equality legislation in the 1970s and 1980s. Scholars have described the impact of the Court's jurisprudence as having "opened the way for women within the Commission's own bureaucracy to push for stronger policy" (Hoskyns 1996: 74). The repercussions of these landmark judicial decisions continue today as lawyers, national equality agencies and women's organizations throughout Europe see the ECJ as an access point to influence policymaking (CEC 1998b). Article 141 opened the door to further policy expansion.

The path of institutional evolution: evolving pregnancy rights

The transformation of Article 141 had consequences not only for secondary legislation in the 1970s and 1980s, but also for the litigating environment. The institutional path was paved. Individuals were provided with a new arsenal to demand rights under EU law before national courts. In this section I examine all of the cases involving pregnancy rights referred to the Court through 2003 and explore how this litigation impacted the opportunities for legislative and legal action at both supranational and national level.

Pregnancy, discrimination and judicial rulemaking

This litigation has primarily grown out of rights claimed under Article 141 and the Equal Treatment Directive.[33] There are also a handful of cases towards the end of the time period that invoke the Pregnancy Directive[34], legislation that evolved out of this earlier case law and will

---

[33] Council Directive 76/207/EEC.   [34] Council Directive 92/85/EEC.

be discussed below. The majority of these cases focus on women who have experienced discrimination in terms of either access to or dismissal from employment on the basis of pregnancy. As the Equal Treatment Directive is on its face more relevant to these rights arguments, it lays out "the principle of equal treatment for men and women in regards to access to employment, including promotion, and to vocational training and as regards to general working conditions . . ." Why is Article 141 continually invoked in this litigation?[35] The answer becomes evident from the *Defrenne* decisions. Advocate General Trabucchi's arguments in the *Defrenne II* judgment, which drew largely from the Court's earlier 1970 ruling in *Internationale Handesgesellschaft* (ECJ 1970), emphasized the relationship between Article 141 and this general principle of equal treatment:

If the principle of equal treatment were to apply only to pay in the strict sense of the word or to absolutely identical work, the practical effect of Article 119 [now Article 141] would be rather small. This gives the Member States and the Community institutions enormous scope in taking action to put into effect the principle of non-discrimination laid down in Article 119 without having to rely on its direct applicability. (ECJ 1976a: 491) [parenthetic numbering added]

The Court would later adopt a similar stance in legal argumentation for the *Defrenne III* ruling:

The Court has repeatedly stated that respect for fundamental personal human rights is one of the general principles of Community law, the observance of which it has a duty to ensure. There can be no doubt that the elimination of discrimination based on sex forms part of those fundamental rights. (ECJ 1978: 1365)

As these passages illustrate, the Court's jurisprudence has found this general principle of equal treatment in Article 141 and today it is formally included in the Treaty of Amsterdam.[36] Litigants and their lawyers are acting strategically by invoking this right as they provide the Court with a powerful tool to decide the case. General principles, in theory, do not have the ability to override treaty provisions, yet they have enabled the ECJ to justify a "liberal interpretation of what might otherwise seem to be a narrow rule" (Ellis 1998a: 181). As for the equal treatment principle, the ECJ has utilized it to dismantle both discriminatory administrative decisions and to justify broad interpretations of EC secondary legislation.

---

[35] Furthermore, the Equal Treatment Directive does mention protection for pregnant workers in Article 2. However, this is to prevent a member state's special protection for pregnant workers from being challenged under EU equality law, rather than placing any obligation on a member state to provide such provisions.

[36] See Craig and de Búrca (1998: Ch. 19) and Ellis (1998a: Ch. 3) for an in-depth discussion of the principle of equal treatment.

Article 141 is invoked for these purposes. Even it cases that don't explicitly invoke Article 141 and only involve the Equal Treatment Directive, member states are faced with a more difficult challenge of reversing undesirable rulings that are in line with and elaborate this treaty-based general principle of equal treatment.

The Court first considered the rights of pregnant workers under EU law in the *Dekker* case (ECJ 1990c). The case was brought before the ECJ by a Dutch court in 1988. Mrs Dekker applied for a job with a Dutch company, VJV, and after an interview was found to be the most qualified for the job. She was three-months pregnant at the time and while the hiring committee recommended employment, VJV management decided not to employ Mrs Dekker because its insurer would not cover the necessary maternity pay. Mrs Dekker instigated legal proceedings against VJV, claiming that she had been discriminated against on the basis of her sex. The case was referred to the ECJ for a preliminary ruling on the protection of Mrs Dekker under Article 141 and the Equal Treatment Directive.

In this 1990 ruling, the Court found that discrimination in employment opportunities on the ground of pregnancy could constitute direct sex discrimination, contrary to the Equal Treatment Directive. Scholars observe that the ruling in effect created new European rules by providing explicit protection of pregnant workers under EU law and also created a new interpretation of sex equality for women, emphasizing disadvantage to women rather than comparable treatment with men (McGlynn 1996: 238; Bamforth 1993: 877). Later that same day, the Court made a similar ruling in a case originating from Danish courts, the *Hertz* case (ECJ 1990d), concluding that the dismissal of a pregnant employee also amounts to discrimination under EU law. Together these two rulings established protection under EU law against the dismissal of, or the refusal to employ, pregnant workers.[37]

This question of protection against dismissal was further raised in a case originating from Germany in 1992. *Habermann-Beltermann v. Arbeiterwohlfahrt* (ECJ 1994c) concerned the dismissal of a pregnant woman who had been employed on an indefinite contract to work at night, despite the national law that forbad night work by pregnant women. The Court decided the case by emphasizing that the national

---

[37] Advocate-General Damon in his joint opinion for *Dekker* and *Hertz* stresses that the principles involved in the two cases require the Court to decide what place maternity holds in European society. Prior to these rulings, protection for pregnant workers remained an unelaborated right in the Equal Treatment Directive. Article 2(3) of the directive states: "This Directive shall be without prejudice to provisions concerning the protection of women, particularly as regards to pregnancy and maternity" (ECJ 1990c).

law affected only a limited duration, in contrast to the unlimited nature of the contract, and found that dismissal under these circumstances was contrary to the Equal Treatment Directive. While this clearly represented an expansion in the protection of pregnant women, it also defined the limitation of this protection:

The termination of a contract without a fixed term on account of the woman's pregnancy ... cannot be justified on the ground that a statutory prohibition, imposed because of pregnancy, temporarily prevents the employee from performing night-time work. (ECJ 1994c: 1677)

This ruling begs the question of what protection is provided in EU law for pregnant women with fixed-term employment. The question presents an ambiguity that is the subject of future litigation.

A closer look at these ECJ rulings reveals many unanswered questions regarding pregnancy, maternity and discrimination. In particular, when is pregnancy to be regarded as the determining factor in discriminatory treatment? In a now pivotal case in the development of EU equality law, the British House of Lords referred a set of questions in the *Webb* case (ECJ 1994d) to the ECJ asking for clarification. Mrs Webb, a pregnant woman, had her indefinite employment contract terminated when her employer found out that she would be absent from work during the same period as another pregnant employee whom she was hired to replace. The House of Lords decided that while Mrs Webb had no rights under UK law, she might under EU law and so asked for a preliminary ruling. The ECJ framed the problem thus:

The national court is uncertain whether it was unlawful to dismiss Mrs Webb on the grounds of pregnancy or whether greater weight should be attached to the reasons for which she was recruited. (ECJ 1994d: para. 14)

The Court reaffirmed its early ruling in *Dekker* and found that "dismissal of a pregnant worker on account of pregnancy constitutes direct discrimination on grounds of sex" (para.19). The Court continues to argue that the need for special protection of pregnant workers is embodied in the Equal Treatment Directive and also in the Pregnancy Directive, which had not yet come into force when the case arose: "the Community legislature provided ... for special protection to be given to women, by prohibiting dismissal during the period from the beginning of their pregnancy to the end of their maternity leave" (para. 21). Therefore, the Court concludes, "greater weight" cannot be attached to the reasons for recruitment. The defendant's argument of hardship is viewed not as the reason for dismissal, but as justification for the discriminatory treatment. Under EU law, once direct discrimination is established, it cannot be justified (Boch 1996).

The Court would further clarify this general prohibition on the refusal to hire pregnant workers in two German preliminary references, the *Busch* (ECJ 2003a) and *Mahlburg* (ECJ 2000d) decisions, holding firm on the position that if pregnancy is the reason for refusal, then the employer's action is discriminatory. The *Busch* case was brought by a nurse who had requested, after taking 10 months of her three year maternity leave, to return to work, and upon being granted permission informed her employer she was seven months pregnant and would be commencing maternity leave again upon the birth of her second child. The employer subsequently rescinded the position on "grounds of fraudulent misrepresentation" (ECJ 2003a: paragraph 20) and Mrs Busch appealed by filing a claim with the Arbeitsgericht Lübeck stating that she was not required to declare her pregnancy and would have carried out her duties for which she was reinstated until leave again commenced. Citing its previous case law as detailed above (from *Dekker* to *Webb*), the Court stated that when pregnancy is the reason an employer refuses to reinstate an employee's position while on leave, then this constitutes direct sex discrimination. The *Mahlburg* decision was also brought by a nurse, who was then employed on a fixed-term contract and when applying for a subsequent permanent position, it was found she was pregnant, her employer rejected the application, citing the position would require her to handle dangerous substances. Mrs Mahlburg subsequently appealed, arguing that refusal to give her a permanent contract on grounds of pregnancy amounted to direct sex discrimination. The ECJ not surprisingly concurred.

Scholars have both lauded and criticized the Court's case law on dismissal and refusual to hire on grounds of pregnancy (e.g. Caracciolo di Torella and Masselot 2001). For example, the *Webb* ruling clearly emphasized and expanded the Community's goal of protecting pregnant workers from discriminatory action, despite the harmful costs inflicted on employers and member state governments.[38] Yet the rulings also highlight a significant area of equality law that needs further clarification. The relationship between Article 5 of the Equal Treatment Directive and the Pregnancy Directive remain speculative. In both the *Webb* and *Hertz* decisions and even much later in *Mahlburg*, the Court implied that the Equal Treatment Directive leaves unanswered the question whether pregnant women in fixed-term employment are protected. While the

---

[38] The *Webb* decision helped form the foundation for settlement claims involving pregnant women discharged from the British armed forces. After the dismissal of more than 5,000 women during 1978–90, British courts began awarding settlements in the figures of £33,000–£173,000 per claimant. See Stone Sweet and Caporaso (1998).

Pregnancy Directive is not explicit about unlimited coverage, the Court in the *Larsson* decision (ECJ 1997b) concluded that Article 10 of the Directive in fact offers such blanket protection. Interestingly enough, in this case originating from Danish courts, the Court found that the dismissal of a woman due to pregnancy-related illness was in fact lawful under the Equal Treatment Directive – again, the facts of the case were prior to implementation of the Pregnancy Directive – when the dismissal took place after the end of her maternity leave. The Court's clarification of the Pregnancy Directive and the extension of protection came as a side remark stating that had the Directive been in force the Court would have found the action unlawful.[39]

The Court in two preliminary references that invoked both the Equal Treatment Directive and the Pregnancy Directive would later clear up the issue of fixed terms. In the *Melgar* (ECJ 2001a) and *Tele Danmark* (ECJ 2001b) decisions, the Court rectified early confusions raised in the cases above by declaring that dismissal of or refusal to hire an individual in a fixed-term contract constitutes direct sex discrimination under Community law. The *Melgar* case is one of few preliminary references from Spain in the social provisions area and involved the issue of refusing to renew a fixed-term contract on grounds of pregnancy. In the *Tele Danmark* decision, the claimant was recruited for a six-month contract, and after a month informed her employer she expected to give birth in three months. She was subsequently dismissed. In both cases, the ECJ declared these to be cases of direct discrimination, stating clearly that had the Community legislature intended to leave fixed-term employment beyond the scope of either the Equal Treatment Directive or Pregnancy Directive, it would have done so explicitly (ECJ 2001a: para. 43; ECJ 2001b: para. 33). Serving as an extension of the policymaking process, the ECJ made explicit for future cases what exactly the scope of the directives was.

This pattern of incremental development of the pregnancy and maternity rights is also seen in the Court's *Brown* ruling (ECJ 1998d), a case referred from the British House of Lords. Mrs Brown was absent from work for over six months during her pregnancy for pregnancy-related reasons. All employees at Rentokil Ltd, her employer, were governed by the policy that absences of six months due to sickness justified dismissal. Accordingly, Mrs Brown was dismissed. The Court held, in an explicit

---

[39] The Court remarked: "It is clear from the objective of Article 10 that absence during the protected period, other than for reasons unconnected with the employee's condition, can no longer be taken into account as grounds for subsequent dismissal" (ECJ 1997b: para. 25).

reversal of the *Larsson* decision, that it was contrary to the Equal Treatment Directive to dismiss a woman for pregnancy-related illnesses during her pregnancy.[40] Scholars have rightly argued that this reversal has done little to clarify EU rules in this area, as it contradicted its earlier interpretation of the Equal Treatment Directive (Ellis 1999).[41] However, one could argue that at least the Court has brought past interpretations of EU equality laws – in particular, the Equal Treatment Directive – into conformity with the new norms governing European maternity and pregnancy rights, as established through the Court's expansive reading of the Pregnancy Directive. Furthermore, we are able to see how the Court actively brings national law into conformity with these new rules, even after numerous national courts turned down cases which often reach the ECJ after numerous national level appeals.

The next sets of cases I will discuss demonstrate the Court's further expansion of pregnancy rights in areas other than dismissal and refusal to hire. In particular, these cases involve the clarification of employment rights of pregnant workers. Again, the facts involved in the first case were prior to implementation of the Pregnancy Directive, and thus rely on the rights provided for pregnant workers under the Equal Treatment Directive and also Article 141. Yet both of these cases provide an example of the Court's "parallel" legislating, which in effect provided more stringent requirements than the Directive.

In the *Gillespie* case, the Court was referred a set of questions regarding the applicability of Community law to levels of maternity pay (ECJ 1996a). The referral came by way of a Northern Ireland appeals court after the lower industrial tribunal had dismissed the case of 17 plaintiffs. The plaintiffs had all been on maternity leave from their employment in various offices of the Northern Ireland Health Service during a period in which a proposed back-pay increase was to be given. The maternity leave

---

[40] As in the *Larsson* case, the facts of this case arose before the Pregnancy Directive came into force and so the Equal Treatment Directive was the only instrument available to the litigants.

[41] In particular, the Court's adherence to the rule that where the discriminatory treatment is based on the fact of pregnancy, since only women can become pregnant, this must amount to discrimination based on sex. The *Brown* decision takes this a step further by arguing that pregnancy-related illness is inseparable from the fact of pregnancy and therefore similar treatment as a result of this condition is also discrimination on grounds of sex. Mainly, this is problematic because it again reduces pregnancy to the status of illness; as well, this reliance on illness rather than absence as the cause for dismissal removes the employer's interests from the situation. The European Parliament when reviewing the Council's amendments to the Pregnancy Directive proposal also echoed concerns with the link between pregnancy and sickness. This later logic could dilute the complexity of the situation and thus impede the Court from its job in balancing all the interests in the dispute at hand. See Ellis (1999) for further discussion.

received by Health Service employees consists of a percentage of their given wage. The plaintiffs instigated proceedings on the grounds that they had suffered sex discrimination because they did not receive the full benefit of the back-dated pay raise due to the fact that they were receiving a reduced amount of their wage while on maternity leave. The Court ruled in favor of the plaintiffs and its judgment further clarified how national maternity policies must be interpreted in light of Article 141 and the Equal Pay Directive.

The *Gillespie* ruling also introduced a distinction between different rules that might be applicable to varying types of pay received by women on maternity leave, including bonuses versus minimum payments. The Court would offer a more clear specification of this difference in two subsequent cases. In the *Lewen* case (ECJ 1999b), the Court was asked by way of a preliminary reference from Germany whether a Christmas bonus constituted "pay" within the meaning of Article 141 or the "maintenance of a payment" as laid down by Article 11 of the Pregnancy Directive. Ms Lewen was refused payment of the bonus because she was on maternity and parental leave for a portion of the year in which it was awarded. The Court held that the period in which a woman is on required maternity leave must be considered similar to periods worked, and so payment of the Christmas bonus must be awarded in accordance with her continued employment (under Article 141), rather than be discussed in terms of payments received in relation to maternity leave (making the Pregnancy Directive inapplicable).

In the *Abdoulaye* decision (ECJ 1999c), the Court offers further clarification of the variations in applicable Community rules to remuneration. Mr Abdoulaye and a group of his male colleagues at a Renault factory in France contested the lump sum payment of 7,500 FRF paid to women on maternity and parental leave, a payment that was made in addition to receipt of full wages. The group of men maintained that the lump sum payment constituted discrimination within the scope of Article 141 and the Equal Pay Directive. The Court did not concur, arguing that while the payment did come within the scope of Article 141, the men were not in a comparable situation to women and, thus, the situation was not discriminatory. The Court further agreed with the argument put forth by the Commission, Renault and the United Kingdom government stating such payment is justified to offset the employment disadvantages experienced by women on maternity leave (ECJ 1999c: para. 20). These rulings, while making clear the scope of applicable EU laws to payments received during the commencement of maternity leave, illustrate the increasing complexity of this case law for women's rights – are entitlements paid only to women in connection with parenthood a help or hindrance in promoting equality in the long term in the workplace and society?[42] The Court clearly could have engaged a comparable argument in the *Abdoulaye* case, as both men and women become parents and engage in child care and leave, but instead choose to maintain a non-comparator approach that may have been useful in cases of dismissal (e.g. *Dekker*), but less helpful in dislodging stereotypes of women and childrearing.

The *Thibault* decision (ECJ 1998e) raised the issue of employee rights regarding assessment and evaluation while absent on maternity leave. It is worth mentioning that while the facts of the *Thibault* case took place after the implementation of the Pregnancy Directive, the only instrument which can be relied upon where unfavourable treatment takes a form other than dismissal or refusal to employ is still the Equal Treatment Directive. The case arose when Mrs Thibault registered a complaint with the labor tribunal in Paris against her employer for failing to perform her annual performance evaluation, which is linked to a minimum 2 percent pay rise and promotion, due to the fact she did not fulfill the requisite six months' attendance within the evaluation year. Mrs Thibault was on maternity and pregnancy-related leave for seven months of this time and she argued that her employer's failure to assess her performance based on absences related to maternity leave was discriminatory. Despite the observation submitted by the British government stating that the employer's action did not constitute sex discrimination under EU law, the Court expanded the rights under the Equal Treatment Directive by concluding that it was unlawfully discriminatory to deny a woman the right to possible promotion because of her absence on maternity leave.

The next two cases represent the Court's first opportunity to rule on the Pregnancy Directive, as they came before the earlier discussed *Melgar*, *Tele Danmark* and *Lewen* decisions. The Directive will be discussed in further detail below. In *Boyle* (ECJ 1998a), six female employees of the British Equal Opportunities Commission[43] applied to the industrial tribunal, Manchester, for a declaration that certain conditions of their maternity leave was unenforceable in so far as it discriminated against female employees and was thus contrary to Article 141 of the Treaty and the Equal Pay and Equal Treatment Directives, as well as the Pregnancy Directive.[44] While the Court re-emphasized the provisions in the Pregnancy Directive which afforded national government discretion in

---

[42] See McGlynn (2000) and Caracciolo di Torella and Masselot (2001) for a critical discussion.

[43] This agency was discussed in greater detail in the analysis earlier in the chapter regarding national equality agencies that help support litigation.

[44] Council Directives 75/117/EEC, 76/207/EEC, and 92/85/EEC.

determining when maternity leave commences, it found that a contract prohibiting a woman from taking sick leave during maternity leave without returning to work first was contrary to the Directive. Again, UK laws were the subjects of litigation.

In the month following the *Boyle* ruling, the Court gave its second decision involving the Pregnancy Directive in the *Pedersen* case (ECJ 1998b). By way of a Danish Commerce Court, the four plaintiffs challenged a national law which stated that women who were unfit for work for a reason connected with the pregnancy before the three-month period preceding the birth date were not entitled to full pay. Three women were declared unfit to work while one was only partially unfit to work during this period, and thus their employer ceased to pay them. The four women claimed this law was contrary to the rights given pregnant workers under the same EU laws as invoked in the *Boyle* case. The Court ruled in favor of the plaintiffs, finding that Danish legislation did not aim to protect women's conditions, but rather favored the interests of the employer. This case represented the first time the Court was asked to interpret the rules governing the duties of employers regarding adjusting the workplace to the needs of pregnant workers. The Pregnancy Directive (Articles 4 and 5) requires an employer to introduce temporary adjustments to working conditions and hours in response to risk assessment of the pregnant workers' situation. The Danish employer failed to provide other opportunities to these women. The Court gave breadth to the Directive by defining the scope of this right.

Together the *Boyle* and *Pedersen* rulings represent an extension of the concept of maternity benefits under EU law. The Court has argued that under certain conditions women have the right to receive maternity benefits before maternity leave. Furthermore, scholars have emphasized the importance of the Court's interpretation of Articles 4 and 5 of the Pregnancy Directive in that it imposed duties on the employers, and in doing so the Court recognizes that pregnancy and maternity may require re-organization of the work place (Caracciolo di Torella 1999).

Overall, the case law in this analysis reveals that the Court does not hesitate to shift control over maternity and pregnancy away from national competence even when a decision is costly to member state governments. Furthermore, this is consistent with what we know about the larger body of ECJ litigation involving EU social provisions. As earlier discussed, when we look at the Commission and member state policy positions as stated in their observations in the cases, we find the Commission is much more likely to predict or reflect the final ECJ preliminary ruling. The Commission's success rate is 84 percent, whereas the United Kingdom's rate was much lower at 58 percent. Similarly, German preferences predict

ECJ judicial decisions only 40 percent of the time. These ruling do not go unheard. Looking at national court compliance with rulings between 1970–1992, we find that in 89 percent of the cases the ruling is applied to the case at hand (Cichowski 2001: 130). The Court is not systematically constrained by national governments. Likewise, this litigation has clarified and expanded maternity and pregnancy rights under EU law. The rules have become more precise, binding and enforceable, a process that will continue in the future.[45]

Opportunities for legislative action at the supranational level

Pregnancy and maternity rights have become an integral part of EU social provisions. Strategic action by private litigants and the judicial rulemaking function of the Court has led to the institutionalization of these rights at the European level. What began as a principle governing equal pay has evolved to include a set of rights governing pregnant workers. Through the process of litigation, EU gender equality law has become more binding and precise, and it has expanded in scope. Furthermore, this pregnancy and maternity litigation had distinct legislative policy consequences at the EU level.

The Pregnancy Directive of 1992 developed alongside this litigation.[46] In particular, legal scholarship suggests that Article 10 of the Directive "codifies and amplifies the European Court's decision forbidding discrimination on account of pregnancy in the *Dekker* case" (Ellis 1993: 66; see also Hoskyns 1996; McGlynn 1996; Mancini and O'Leary 1999). It is important to emphasize, however, it was the Court that defined and constructed these rights in *Dekker*, while national governments, the UK in particular, stymied the legislative process that would later develop these rights in the Pregnancy Directive. The political processes that characterized the passage of this Directive, in particular the production of lowest common denominator outcomes, ultimately led to legislation that went little further than the general rights of protection introduced by the Court's earlier rulings. Subsequently, as the previous section of this chapter demonstrated, potential conflicts remained and this led to more litigation seeking a clarification of women's and employers' rights in the this area of EU law.

The text of the Directive is based on Article 138 (ex 118a) of the Treaty, which governs policy on the health and safety of workers. Directives adopted under this article permit the Council to act in the field of qualified

---

[45] Beyond the time period of this study, there are already four more cases clarifying the Pregnancy Directive: ECJ 2004a; ECJ 2004b; ECJ 2004c; ECJ 2005.

[46] Council Directive 92/85/EEC.

majority voting. While the principle of majority voting suggests the potential for passage of legislation that not all member states agree to, the legislative history of the Pregnancy Directive illustrates why this is not necessarily true in practice. The text proposed by the Equality Unit in DG Employment and Social Affairs offered broad protection. This original proposal provided for 16 weeks of paid maternity leave, replacement services for self-employed women, paternity leave and a reversal of the burden of proof in cases arising out of these rights. However, the final proposal adopted by the Commission in September 1990 was considerably weaker; it reduced the minimum leave to 14 weeks and omitted references to paternity leave and replacement services. Furthermore, the burden of proof issue was removed and instead member states were instructed to review their legal rules in this area (CEC 1990a). The proposal elicited varying reactions. The UK government protested that the Directive was too far-reaching. In particular, the British Employment Secretary, Michael Howard, at the Social Affairs Council in June 1991 argued that only the aspects of the draft concerning issues regarding exposure to harmful substances fell under Article 118, and thus only this portion should be governed by majority vote, with all other aspects utilizing unanimity. The Commission threatened to withdraw the proposal for fear of fragmentation. Ultimately, a common position was arrived at in December 1991.

However, both the United Kingdom and Italy abstained from this position, the latter on the grounds that the proposal was now too thin to be effective.[47] The proposal experienced considerable "last-minute political horse trading" between the more stringent amendments proposed by the European Parliament and the UK's reluctance to accept such expensive changes (Ellis 1993: 65). Finally, on 19 October 1992, the Directive was passed, with abstentions from both the UK and Italy, in a form that largely reflected the minimalist ambitions of the UK. Furthermore, while the UK abstained from the vote, it was not able to prevent the Directive's adoption. In codifying the Court's *Dekker* decision, the Council's adoption of the Pregnancy Directive gave pregnant workers greater legitimacy and protection under EU law. Yet, ultimately the Directive did little to clarify the complexity of rules that the Court had begun to create forbidding discrimination based on pregnancy or involving maternity rights. Both before and after national transpositions of the Directive, the Court continued to expand EU rules in this area. These rulings had distinct implications for national policy.

---

[47] Unanimity was necessary at this point under Article 149(1) because the Council was amending the Commission's proposal, yet unanimity does not preclude abstentions under Article 148(3).

Opportunities for action at the national level

The ECJ rulings regarding pregnancy and maternity rights – as embodied in the Pregnancy Directive and subsequent judgments clarifying protection – resulted in significant national policy changes. These new rights introduced numerous conflicts with existing policies and levels of protection provided by many member states (CEC 1999c). The conflicts are highlighted in three ways. First, they are evident from the significant implementation errors characterizing almost all member state transpositions of the Pregnancy Directive. Second, these conflicts are the subject of national policy changes required by ECJ and national court rulings that subsequently clarified levels of protection. Finally, national level legal disputes highlight areas of EU law and national regulations that remain unclear and that continue to be the subject of litigation. The main areas of potential conflict surround the issues of night work, maternity leave pay, general discrimination protection and fixed-term contract employment.

Implementation of the Pregnancy Directive

Generally, all member state governments provided some protection for pregnant workers before the adoption of the Directive. In Italy, the Netherlands and France protection was higher than required, whereas in other member states, primarily Sweden and Portugal, implementation of the Directive had the effect of increasing the health and safety protection and the employment rights of pregnant workers. In the UK, qualifying periods of maternity leave were reduced. Ireland experienced considerable improvements, in particular the possibility of "health and safety" leave if a woman's work could not be altered in order to avoid an identified risk to the pregnancy. Finally, paid time off for ante-natal exams was introduced in Belgium, Austria, Denmark, Ireland and Finland (CEC 1999c).

National governments have experienced various difficulties with implementing the Directive. This is illustrated by the fact that the Commission instigated infringement proceedings with a majority of the member states on the basis of incorrect implementation (CEC 1999c). British and Irish national laws were found to be contrary to Article 4 of the Directive for failing to provide adequate assessment of the risk of exposure to pregnant workers of various agents and conditions as laid out in the Directive. French and Spanish laws were found to contravene the protection provided in Article 5 of the Directive as they did not insure that once a work-related risk was identified, the affected pregnant woman was first provided with alternative work opportunity if possible (e.g. change in shift or re-assignment) or in the end granted leave. Despite having generous maternity allowances that provide for nearly all women to be on leave after birth, Swedish and Finnish practices were found to be inconsistent with the Directive for not actually implementing legislation that mandated a compulsory minimum of a two-week maternity leave (Article 8).

The issue of night work is another such conflict. Article 7 of the Directive states that member states shall ensure that workers are "not obliged to perform night work during their pregnancy and for a period following childbirth." Pregnant workers are provided special treatment by not being required to work at night. As a result of national government opposition, this Article fails to solve the real issue at the heart of night work, that is, balancing non-discrimination with a concern for the health and safety of workers. It has been the subject of national government contention since 1991, when the ECJ ruled that a French provision which banned night work by women, when no such ban existed for men, was contrary to the Equal Treatment Directive (*Stoekel*, ECJ 1991b). The ruling led to subsequent infringement proceedings against Belgium, Greece, Italy, Portugal and France. These proceedings culminated in two judgments in 1997 involving France and Italy (ECJ 1997d; ECJ 1997e).[48] Italy finally amended its national legislation in 1999 to reflect the inadmissibility of a blanket ban on night work by women.[49] France's continual opposition to this EU position on night work has since led to Commission action against France under Article 228: a letter of formal notice on 20 January 1998, a reasoned opinion on 29 July 1998 and finally a formal announcement on 23 April 1999 to ask for the ECJ to impose a daily fine of 142,425 euros on France for non-compliance (CEC 1999c).

This issue of night work is reintroduced in relation to pregnant workers, as many national transpositions of the Pregnancy Directive go further than required, and ban pregnant women and women who have just given birth from working at night. The Commission has since initiated infringement proceedings on this point with Austria, Italy, Luxembourg and the UK, and German provisions are currently under scrutiny for possible infringement (CEC 1999c). National governments have resisted having the issue of night work dealt with at the Community level. This resistance was voiced in the debates surrounding the adoption of the Directive (Ellis 1993: 65). However, over time, we can also see how the Court has shifted this issue to the European level despite this continual opposition, as evidenced by disputes arising from member state non-compliance or problems with transpositions.

---

[48] The Commission has since initiated legal proceedings against both of these countries for failing to implement these 1997 rulings (CEC 1999c: 41).

[49] Act 25/1999 passed by the Italian Parliament on 27 January 1999. The ban now applies only to working mothers in the first year of their child's life.

Despite the initial difficulties highlighted by these infringement proceedings, most member states implemented the Directive without too much national legislative change (CEC 1999c). Luxembourg was the noticeable exception, as correct implementation was only recently achieved in 1998 and only after the Commission referred the matter to the ECJ under Article 226.[50] However, there were differing national reactions to both these transpositions and previous ECJ rulings that clarified the protection provided by the Directive in the early years following national implementation.

National litigation and new legal claims

In Portugal, women were able to bring actions before the national court relying on the Pregnancy Directive, which at the time had not yet been transposed into national law (CEC 1997a 16). This judgment was especially significant as Community law is rarely invoked in the Portuguese courts or applied by them, as most gender equality claims rely on the constitutional prohibition of discrimination (CEC 1997a: 16). In Ireland, there was a significant national reaction to this new set of rights. The 1995 Annual Report of the Irish Employment Equality Agency states there were 1,747 queries involving the Maternity and Adoptive Leave Legislation, which implemented the Pregnancy Directive. The Irish government was asked to change a policy area that was deeply embedded in existing employment structures (CEC 1997a: 41). Implementation of the Directive by the Spanish government has also received attention. Legal experts have observed that its transposition has been "far from sufficient," particularly in the area of protecting workers from health risks (CEC 1997a: 43–44).

Maternity benefits and pay had been a major concern of the UK throughout negotiations of the Directive and it remained contentious in the British legal system (see Ellis 1993: 63–65). It was at the heart of the *Gillespie* case, discussed above. Far more than the individual back-pay amounts allotted to the plaintiffs, the ruling had a more general financial impact on UK maternity pay policies. Almost two years after the transposition of the Pregnancy Directive into national law, this 1996 ruling created the very maternity pay requirements which the UK government was careful to remove from the Directive. The Court concluded that neither Article 141 nor the Equal Pay Directive lays down a criterion to determine the amount of pay required, however EU law does guarantee a minimum level: "The amount payable could not be so low as to

---

[50] Case C-409/97 *Commission v. Luxembourg*, was dismissed following Luxembourg's adoption of new measures to transpose the Pregnancy Directive on 7 July 1998 (CEC 1999c: 77).

undermine the purpose of maternity leave, namely the protection of women before and after giving birth" (ECJ 1996a: para. 20).

Prior to this ruling, the UK's statutory maternity pay system was calculated on the basis of length of employment and weekly hours worked prior to commencement of the maternity leave, and was figured in terms of relevant statutory sick pay. In practice, the UK laws left some pregnant workers in a position of receiving no maternity pay during their leave. Those numerous part-time employees who do not earn more than the National Insurance threshold do not qualify for UK statutory sick pay. Therefore, they do not qualify for maternity pay. Maternity leave without any pay may induce an employee to return earlier to work, and thus undermine the real "purpose" in the 14-week leave period. The UK's lowest common denominator position, as embodied in the Directive, was ultimately shifted upwards by the Court.

ECJ rulings have also impacted national maternity and pregnancy benefits that were originally thought to be in conformity with the Pregnancy Directive. In Denmark, the national follow-up to the *Pedersen* ruling (in which the ECJ had expanded the maternity benefits required by the Directive) led to a 1999 amendment of the Danish Salaried Employees Act. The ruling and subsequent amendment enable women, who in the past received a compensation benefit rather than full pay for absences involving pregnancy related illness, to now claim back pay. Not surprisingly, the Danish court system has received numerous cases in which women are demanding back pay.[51] As the *Pedersen* ruling did not limit the time effect of the decision, this initial reaction from claimants in the Danish legal system might suggest the possibility of a Community wide reaction in the near future, similar to the post *Barber* case law and subsequent Treaty provision.

The Directive's general discrimination protection, in particular its prohibition of dismissal from employment, has also been the subject of

---

[51] The High Court's (Vestre Landsret) decision on 16 March 2000 allowed a woman to claim back pay for the period of September through November 1996 (Case B-0836-98, *FM Maskiner Aps v HK acting for Else Knudsen*). Further, in another recent judgment in a case involving the Danish Women's Workers Union and an employer's organization (10 February 2000), an industrial arbitration tribunal granted back pay amounts. The ruling in effect constructed an exception to an established Danish labor law tradition that limits a tribunal's judicial interpretation to only take effect from the date of the judgment (e.g. the new protection provided by the 1998 *Pedersen* ruling, should only have been applied to subsequent infringements, but instead was applied to practices in the past). The Court justified this ruling by arguing that this derogation was allowable in cases where the interpretation involves mandatory legislation (e.g. implementation of EU rules) (CEC 2001). Also, personal communication between the author and Danish Legal Expert in the Commission sponsored Network of Legal Experts, October 2000.

national legal disputes. The Court's case law in this area (e.g. *Dekker, Hertz, Habermann,* and *Webb* decisions) and its subsequent codification in the Directive prohibits discrimination in access to and dismissal from employment on the basis of pregnancy. However, not all member states have duly recognized or enforced this prohibition on discrimination and the scope of who is protected remains a question before numerous national courts. While the Spanish transposition of the Pregnancy Directive has been criticized for the inadequate protection it provides, national courts have exhibited a mixed reaction to enforcement: some maintaining this low level of protection, while others have utilized ECJ rulings to expand the protection (CEC 1997a: 15). A recent decision of the High Court of Justice of Catalonia is an example of the former.[52] The court accepted the necessity to dismiss a pregnant woman without subjecting the employer's reason for dismissal to strict scrutiny, an act that is at odds with the requirements of the Directive.

Further, another case that was first heard in a lower court, and then on appeal to the High Court of Justice of Andalucia, led to a decision that found that "although the dismissal of the claimant was unfair and should have been declared null and void, they found that there was not a sufficient link between the pregnancy and the termination of the employment relationship and, therefore there was no presumption of discrimination" (CEC 1998b: 13). Legal experts concur that such cases are obvious instances of pregnancy discrimination, yet the national courts continue to hand down judgments that are inconsistent with the Directive and also earlier rulings of the Constitutional Court (see below): decisions that some criticize as seeming "almost absurd" (CEC 1998b: 13).

A ruling from the Spanish Constitutional Court (SCC) and a series of subsequent lower-court rulings exemplify that some national courts have acted to uphold higher standards of protection than afforded by national transpositions. In a case concerning the dismissal of a pregnant woman, the SCC arrived at an important shift in the burden of proof applied in these cases.[53] This was particularly significant, as the burden-of-proof clause had been removed from an earlier version of the Pregnancy Directive due to national government opposition. It was now up to the employer to prove that the real cause of dismissal was unrelated to discrimination on grounds of sex. Furthermore, the SCC based its ruling on the above-mentioned ECJ judgments, as clarifying the Pregnancy Directive. This ruling led to subsequent lower-court decisions; interestingly enough, no reference to

[52] Judgment of 9 April 1996.   [53] Judgment of 23 July 1996.

EU law is made in these latter cases.[54] These judgments are significant because we are able to see how the acceptance or enforcement of EU law by national judges in effect forced compliance with EU rules where the national government action had failed to do so.

Other national court rulings have questioned exactly who can seek protection under the Directive. In a British case, *Iske v. P&O (European) Ferries*, a claimant argued that the British transposition of the Pregnancy Directive had not adequately addressed the situation of seafarers. Rather than being given alternative work, per the requirements of the Directive, the then pregnant Ms Iske was forced to go on maternity leave (CEC 1997a: 43). In Spain, the Superior Court of Justice of Catalonia ruled that the maternity leave provided by national law (as mandated by the Directive) could not be extended to men, even in the given case in which the mother had died during childbirth.[55] The court referred to the ECJ's pregnancy case law (*Dekker, Hertz, Habermann, Webb* and *Brown*) but held that they were not relevant to the given case. Conversely, a recent legislative amendment to Belgian regulations pertaining to leave in the federal civil service, maintains that maternity leave can be transferred to the father when the mother dies or must remain in the hospital.[56] This is just one example of the variation in protection that can arise from differing national interpretations of EU law.

In Denmark, the follow-up to the *Larsson* decision is an interesting example of how national courts have reacted to the ECJ's clarifications of the protection provided for pregnant workers by EU law. As earlier discussed, the facts of the *Larsson* case transpired before the required national transposition of the Pregnancy Directive. Thus, the questions referred by the Danish court involved whether a Danish law, that allowed the time period during pregnancy and before the commencement of the maternity leave to be utilized in calculating total absences from work and subsequently utilized for grounds for dismissal, was contrary to the Equal Treatment Directive. The ECJ held that the Danish practice was not contrary to the Equal Treatment Directive, but went on to argue that had the Pregnancy Directive been in force, the practice would have been unlawful under EU law (a finding that the Court later made in the *Brown* decision). Instead of handing down the 29 May 1997 *Larsson* decision, the Danish Maritime and Commercial Court put the case on hold and waited until the ECJ had given a judgment on a similar pending

---

[54] For example Tribunal Superior de Justicia of Málaga, judgment of 1 February 1996 and Tribunal Superior de Justicia of Pais Vasco, judgment of 19 March 1996.
[55] Judgment of 20 January 1998.
[56] Royal Decree of 19 November 1998, *Moniteur Belge* of 28 November 1998.

preliminary reference from the UK (regarding Mary Brown). The ECJ's *Brown* decision departed from the *Larsson* decision in a way that made the Danish practice inadmissible under EU law. Thus, over a year later, in a 22 September 1998 judgment, the Danish Court subsequently disregarded the preliminary answers it had received, and it applied the *Brown* decision instead. Ms Larsson was consequently awarded compensation for unfair dismissal (CEC 1999b: 75). This case illustrates the substantive policy difference that a well-informed national judiciary can make in applying the evolving EU rules that govern the area of EU pregnancy and maternity rights.

Finally, the lack of clarity in EU law – both the Pregnancy Directive and ECJ rulings – on the issue of protection granted to pregnant workers in fixed-term employment, has led to various conflicts and inconsistencies in national legal systems and it is not surprising that it has led to more case law at the EU level as well as the national level. In a case that came before the British Employee Appeal Tribunal (EAT), *Caruana* v. *Manchester Airport*,[57] an employer argued that the ECJ's *Webb* decision suggested that employees under fixed-term contracts were possibly exempt from the prohibition of dismissal on grounds of pregnancy. The plaintiff in the case, who had been working on a series of fixed-term contracts, was dismissed on grounds of pregnancy. The EAT found in favor of Ms Caruana, however the tribunal based its judgment on the fact that the employee in reality was working on a continuous basis. Similar problems in definition and thus protection of pregnant workers in fixed-term employment, is evidenced in Finland. Finnish equality experts report that nurses, who are often employed under fixed-term contracts, find that their employment contracts are not renewed when they are found to be pregnant. No legal action has been brought in these instances: an outcome that has been linked to fears of victimization and women who do not want to be labeled as "troublemakers" (CEC 1997a: 41). These two cases illustrate an area of EU pregnancy and maternity law that is likely to continue to be the subject of litigation.

By the mid 2000s, all member states possessed "flawless" implementations of the Pregnancy Directive (CEC 2005b: 7). Variations exist along protection that extends beyond EU law. For example, Germany and France allow paid time off for post-natal medical examinations and Ireland even includes attendance in ante-natal classes in this coverage. Some member states also go further in extending a right for fathers to take paid paternity leave, although more limited than maternity leave; such is

[57] (1996) IRLR 378.

the case in Denmark and the United Kingdom (CEC 2005b: 24, 77). And the ECJ's case law on pregnancy and maternity was directly influential on the national implementations of the Directive and amendments to national legislation in this area.[58] Yet as the above analysis illuminates, while member states currently may be in compliance with the Pregnancy Directive, this remains a relatively new area of labor law in most member states, and just as before we would expect new disputes to arise from the areas that lack clarity, such as mentioned on fixed-term employment and even issues of dismissal while on leave (CEC 2005b: 8).

Generally, this case law analysis reveals that maternity policy is an evolving area of EU law that has followed a trajectory that was not necessarily welcomed by member state governments. The ECJ's judicial rule-making capacity has led to the development of pregnancy and maternity rights that protect women throughout the EU. These rulings have led to both supranational policy changes – in the form of the Pregnancy Directive – and also subsequent national policy changes. Litigants are given new arsenal to bring claims before their national courts demanding improved protection under national law. The analysis revealed that ECJ rulings have empowered national court judges to make rulings that in effect clarify and change levels of protection that are provided to pregnant workers in national law. Furthermore, the findings illustrate that those legal systems that pose minimal protection or problematic transpositions are continually the subject of litigation. ECJ rulings have come to define the existing rights granted to pregnant workers in the EU, and I would expect that both the ECJ and national courts would continue to play an important role at solving the many conflicts that still characterize this area of EU law.

Conclusions

The EU today governs what has historically been a protected national legal domain, social policy, of which pregnancy and maternity rights are an integral part. The analysis demonstrates that the creators of the Treaty may not have foreseen this process of institutionalization and the policy implications have not all been welcomed by member state governments. Despite the belief of certain scholars, the relative power of national governments cannot explain the expansive logic that characterizes the Court's jurisprudence.

---

[58] For example, in Denmark, the Sickness and Maternity Benefit Act was amended after transposing the Pregnancy Directive, and the amendment also refers to the ECJ's 1998 *Boyle* decision (CEC 2005b: 24).

This chapter emphasizes the mechanisms of institutionalization through litigation in the area of social provisions. Trade unions and individual activists utilized available legal resources and EU rules to bring legal claims before their national courts. Operating to uphold EU interests and bring greater clarity to EU law, the ECJ resolved these disputes, and in doing so expanded the meaning and scope of EU social provisions. This judicial rulemaking created the opportunities for action both through EU legislative action and subsequent legal claims. In particular, we saw how institutional evolution began with the activation of the EU legal system by a Belgian stewardess and her lawyer in the *Defrenne* cases. This led to the ECJ transforming Article 141, a treaty provision governing equal pay and fair competition, into a positive right enforceable in national courts. Transformation into a positive right conferred on individuals the opportunity to bring claims before national courts, and the provision no longer simply placed duties on member state governments. The consequences have required national governments to construct or change national policies to protect these rights. Positive integration has ensued, as the Court's judicial rulemaking provided the framework and the necessity – given the opportunity, litigants were able to claim that national practices were in conflict with their EU rights – to develop a common European policy on gender equality.

In Chapter 4, I explore this dynamic process of institutionalization through litigation in the area of environmental protection. Important questions will be answered. Does the lack of a treaty basis make environmental legal claims more difficult than gender equality claims, which are firmly grounded in treaty-based rights? How has this variation in legal basis for the policy domain impacted the ECJ's judicial rulemaking capacity and the relative ease to which member state governments can retaliate against adverse rulings? Further, how might this variation influence the role of litigation in creating opportunities for action?

4 Environmental protection, non-compliance and judicial politics

The origins of European Union (EU) environmental protection are not traceable to the Treaty of Rome. The original three treaties lacked any mention of the "environment," an unsurprising fact as ecological sensibilities were not commonplace in 1957. Today, environmental protection possesses a formal constitutional basis under EU law. Beyond technical measures to ensure proper waste disposal systems, the Treaty calls for integrating environmental protection and sustainable development into all EU policies. Further, EU environmental measures were developed by national governments as a result of their concern over unfair competition created by varying national environmental regulations. Yet today environmental activists are able to use these same EU laws against the very governments who created them in order to pressure for higher environmental standards.

This institutional evolution is the focus of this chapter. In particular, similar to Chapter 3, I explore the European Court of Justice's (ECJ) environmental case law pursuant to Article 234 to examine how processes of institutionalization through litigation influenced this policy development. Through similar analyses as Chapter 3, I examine institutionalization through litigation as a set of interrelated processes and examine how national level activists, EU organizations and national governments play a part in this evolution. The analyses in this chapter serve to test our expectation of these processes in the area of environmental protection and in doing so, enable us to understand the considerable cross-sector variation that exists in litigation.

Legal claims, litigation and opportunities for action

I first explore the factors that give rise to the legal claim involving EU environmental protection law: mobilized interests, legal resources and EU rules (EU/national policy fit and ECJ precedent). Second, I attempt to explain the subsequent litigation dynamic by examining what factors shape the ECJ's decision-making: does the ECJ act to uphold EU interests by clarifying EU rules or does it operate to preserve the policy positions of member state governments? Ultimately, I ask how this impacts the general trajectory of EU environmental protection: are environmentalists and EU organizations given opportunities for action diminishing member state control over policy development or do member state governments control these outcomes?

Environmental activists and new legal claims

In Chapter 3, I found that while mobilized interests were crucial to these legal claims, cross-national variation in social provisions references was mainly attributable to the presence of legal resources such as governmental organizations, like the British Equal Opportunities Commission. Further, characteristics specific to the EU rules were also an essential ingredient for these legal claims. While the fit between EU rules and national policy did have a positive impact on reference rates, the fact that EU social provisions embody a treaty-based right, and that ECJ precedent continued to expand this right, was a strong determinant of the consistently growing number of preliminary references in this policy domain. In this chapter, I explore how these factors impact environmental claims.

Mobilized interests

As argued above, organizational strength is a particularly important feature of successful public interest litigation, and I hypothesized it may have a similar affect on legal claims involved in preliminary references. Similar to the social provisions analysis in Chapter 3, I utilize average rates of environmental preliminary references and a general cross-national measure of environmental group strength to examine this relationship.[1] The direction of the coefficients displayed in Table 4.1 confirms the expectation that an increase in litigation is linked to the relative strength of environmental groups who may bring these claims. However, the strength of the coefficient is not as strong as in the area of social provisions. This may be a product of the greater difficulties faced by environmental groups in making these claims before a national court. Thus, in terms of mobilized interests,

---

[1] The dependent variable in this analysis is average rate of preliminary references. The measure utilizes all preliminary references for each member state in the area of the environment (from 1976–2003). Each country's average reference rate in each legal domain is calculated by dividing their total number of references in the legal domain by the number of years in this time period that a given country has been making references. The data sources and methodology for the independent variables are detailed in Chapter 2.

Table 4.1 *Effect of mobilized interests on average number of Article 234 references in the area of environmental protection, 1976–2003*

	B	t-statistic
(model 1) Environmental protection mobilized interests	.052*	2.340

Notes:
*p < .05

Entry is unstandardized regression coefficient. For each member state the total number of preliminary references is divided by the number of years in which that country has been making references to the ECJ in this legal domain. Mobilized interests are the percentage of respondents in each member state belonging to environmental organizations.
Source: Data compiled by the author from European Communities. 2004. *CELEX Data Base.* Brussels: Office for Official Publications of the European Communities and the *World Values Survey* (1981, 1986, 1995, 2000).

other interests such as business, who are defending their practices in light of environmental regulations, may influence Article 234 reference rates.[2] The difficulties are twofold. First, unlike the gender equality claims, individuals and environmental groups experience greater difficulty in making environmental claims before national courts as it is hard to claim an individual right to the environment versus a right to equal treatment (e.g. Krämer 2000). The cases that directly involve environmental groups as the litigant (a total of 13 or 18% of all cases in this legal domain) have invoked such EU laws as wildlife protection[3] and water quality[4] laws, but have not done so by claiming environmental rights (e.g. ECJ 1987a, ECJ 1994a, ECJ 1996e, ECJ 1996f, and ECJ 1996b). Instead, these groups target national laws with minimal standards relative to other member states and question the compatibility of these laws with the greater protection provided by EU environmental laws. They also bring into question compliance problems.

Second, the groups are limited by the national legal rules regarding *locus standi*; thus, it is unsurprising that group sponsored cases have primarily originated from Italian, French and British courts, legal systems

---

[2] For example, a group of French oil recyclers questioning a competitor's practice (e.g. ECJ 1983) and individual waste disposal operators defending their practices (e.g. ECJ 1990e; ECJ 1990f). Yet there is significant evidence that environmental groups are also active in supporting this litigation and may in the future potentially be more prominent (see Cichowski 1998; Krämer 1996:1).
[3] Council Directive 79/409/EEC.   [4] Council Directive 78/659/EEC.

allowing non-governmental organizations access to the courts.[5] Studies
have shown that there are "wide empirical disparities" on access to justice
for non-governmental organizations (NGOs) in environmental matters
throughout the EU member states, suggesting that beyond standing
rules, socio-economic and cultural factors might also be at play in determining cases brought by environmental NGOs (CEC 2002a: 3). Yet,
overall strength of environmental organizations may still go some distance in explaining why there are no environmental references originating
from Ireland, with only 2.8 percent of respondents belonging to ecology
groups compared to the Netherlands whose national courts sent 40
environmental preliminary references or 27 percent of all cases in this
legal domain.

It is also worth noting that in Spain and in Italy, where environmental
mobilization is relatively low, NGOs have been active in specific areas of
EU environmental law. For example, Spanish NGOs (Greenpeace,
AEDENAT and CODA) have actively mobilized to pressure for proper
implementation of the EU Access to Environmental Information
Directive.[6] Further, there are several successful lawsuits filed by NGOs
in Spanish courts over this Directive, yet neither led to preliminary
references, reflecting a general trend exhibited by national judges to not
send preliminary references.[7] In Italy, NGOs have been generally active
in the area of EU waste laws and have also supported two preliminary
references questioning the Italian transpositions of EU nature conservation laws.[8]

---

[5] For example, in the UK *locus standi* for groups is a relatively new rule (1992) yet British
conservation groups were quick to use the greater protection provided by EU law against
national laws. The Royal Society for the Protection of Birds (RSPB) supported a test case
(ECJ 1996f) that questioned the British government's decision to develop a portion of a
nature preserve (a derogation that was vaguely defined under the Birds Directive). The
national court stayed the proceedings and asked the ECJ for clarification. The ECJ
concurred with the RSPB, an outcome that had a far-reaching impact, both in terms of
successful group litigation and also a rare occasion in which the ECJ expanded EU
environmental protection in the face of economic policy priorities. Other member states
have standing such has Portugal. The Portuguese Constitution (Article 52) also gives
individuals and associations the right to go to court in order to prevent or end actions that
infringe on their right to the environment. Despite this legal basis, there is little use of this
opportunity by environmental groups (CEC 1993c: 58).

[6] Council Directive 90/313/EEC. Greenpeace Spain lodged two complaints to the
Commission for improper implementation in 1993 and 1994. The Spanish government
responded by introducing a new law and it was transposed in 1995. Greenpeace lodged
another complaint in 1996 arguing that the Spanish law fell short of the rights to access
outlined in the EU law (see Sanchis Moreno 1996).

[7] See Sanchis Moreno (1996); Arranz, Quintanilla and Velazquez 1999; also interview with
national legal expert, Dolores de la Fuente, November 2000.

[8] See ECJ (1996e).

Table 4.2 *Effect of national legal resources on average number of Article 234 references in the area of environmental protection, 1976–2003*

	B	t-statistic
(model 1) Environmental protection legal resources	.53**	3.252

Notes:
**p < .01
Entries are unstandardized regression coefficients. For each member state the total number of Article 234 preliminary references is divided by the number of years in which that country has been making references to the ECJ in this legal domain. For the legal resources variable each country is coded on a scale from 0–3. The scale denotes the presence of three main sources of legal resources: historical legal basis for environmental rights (e.g. Constitutionally protected right) (1), active and accessible (to the public) environmental ministry/agency (1) and network of environmental legal specialists (1).
Source: Data compiled by the author from European Communities. 2004. *CELEX Data Base.* Brussels: Office for Official Publications of the European Communities and various primary source environmental documents (see Chapter 2 for complete list).

Legal resources

The interaction between national legal resources and levels of preliminary references is our next interest. The model in Table 4.2 covers the time period of 1976 to 2003 and explores the impact of legal resources on environmental preliminary references. Similar to Chapter 3, I measure legal resources by coding for the presence of either active EU law networks or national environmental agencies that may provide support for this litigation.[9] Table 4.2 displays the relationship by illustrating that the presence of legal resources has a positive impact on litigation rates. Both in the strength and the direction of coefficients, the equation confirms my expectations. Yet again, this relationship is weaker than the interaction revealed by the social provisions litigation.

This is not altogether surprising given the limitations regarding rights claims and access to justice in the area of the environment, and thus the kinds of resources that would aid these legal claims. Further, in terms of supporting claims, there are no comparable environmental national governmental organizations, similar to the British Equal Opportunities Commission, with this mandate. Yet despite no direct involvement in the litigation, governmental organizations have had some impact to the extent to which they have provided a wide dissemination of information on environmental rights and law and have served as mediating organizations for environmental groups to lodge complaints that alert the local

[9] See Chapter 2 for coding details.

authorities to possible environmental violations. For example, in 1993 the Italian environmental organization, Lega Ambiente, lodged a complaint with the Ministry of the Environment bringing attention to the inconsistency between the new Italian Decree Law on Recyclable Waste (DL 443) and EU waste laws. This inconsistency provided a loophole that would allow industrial enterprises to treat hazardous waste as a recyclable waste and thus avoid more stringent regulatory measures (Guttieres and Bayley 1994: 8).[10] Both the group's vigilance in the area of waste management, but more importantly the opportunity to report possible violations afforded them through the Ministry of Environment, may help explain the subsequent prosecution of numerous Italian individuals involved with waste disposal and transport.

Similar to the equality claims, national level legal expertise also serves as a resource for legal claims. Such legal expertise and institutional legal networks are generally most prevalent in countries where there is first a well-established and protected legal basis for environmental rights claims. In some member states this takes the form of explicit environmental rights in a written constitution such as the Netherlands, Germany and Belgium.[11] While others, such as Italy, possess general constitutional rights, such as the protection of national heritage and the protection of health, that national courts over time have interpreted to include a "healthy environment" (Francioni and Montini 1996: 246).[12]

In Italy, there are now environmental law firms in Rome and Milan specializing in EU environmental law,[13] non-profit organizations specializing in EU and international environmental law, such as the International Juridical Organization for Environment and Development[14] in Rome, and the University of Padova, which is renowned for its environmental

---

[10] The decree law was issued as an interim measure until the EU waste directives (Council Directive 91/156/EEC and Council Directive 91/689/EEC) were transposed into national law.

[11] Other member states such as Finland, Portugal, Greece and Spain also include the environment in their constitutions. However, generally these countries lack a well-developed public environmental movement, that in effect brings life to these "constitutional" rights (Seerden and Heldeweg 1996: 427).

[12] Article 9 of the Italian Constitution states "the republic protects the landscape and cultural and artistic heritage of the nation." The other main provision giving legal basis for environmental regulations is Article 32. This provision states that "the republic protects and guarantees health as a fundamental right of an individual and an interest of the community." In 1979, the Italian Constitutional Court expanded the scope of Article 32 to include a specific right to a healthy environment (see judgment n. 5172 of 1979).

[13] Examples of such law firms are Cappelli e de Caterini Avvocati Associati and Gianni, Origoni & Partners in Rome and Studio Legale Cutrera in Milan (Tyrrell and Yaqub 1993).

[14] This organization provides thorough legal updates and information on changes in Italian environmental law.

law program, was one of 5 member state universities selected to host a Commission sponsored research unit providing training in EU environmental law (CEC 1997b: 10). These national legal resources may help explain the high number of references originating from Italian courts. As earlier mentioned, most of these references involved criminal proceedings in the area of waste management. This reference rate may be explained by the conflicts between Italian law and EU law in this area; however, it was also reliant on Italian judges and the defendant's lawyers to be significantly familiar with EU waste laws to persistently question the inconsistencies between these two regulatory regimes.[15]

The Netherlands also possesses an extensive network of lawyers trained in EU and international environmental law, both of which are integral to the general "active environmental diplomacy" which characterizes the Dutch approach to EU environmental policy (Liefferink and Andersen 1998: 72). This legal expertise in EU law and openness to the EU legal system may impact the litigation in two ways. First, in terms of judges who possess extensive training in EU environmental law and thus can identify possible inconsistency between EU and Dutch law, and thus are more likely to send preliminary references.[16] And second, this prevalence of expertise in EU environmental law has provided environmental groups with the knowledge of how to successfully adopt litigation strategies.[17] This latter point is also observable in Spain, where the NGO AEDENAT in cooperation with a Dutch NGO, Stichting Natuur en Milieu produced a users guide to filing complaints and appeals against improper implementation of the EU Access to Environmental Information Directive.[18]

Further, similar to the analysis in Chapter 3, these data illustrate that alternative explanations such as level of national court are less powerful in explaining this variation. Figure 4.1 displays preliminary references in the area of environmental protection between 1976–2003 by the level of court referring the case. Again, the data do not confirm that lower courts

---

[15] Interview with Head of Waste Management Unit, DG Environment, Brussels, April 1999.

[16] For example, the Dutch judge responsible for the preliminary reference originating from the Raad van Staat in *Dusseldorp BV* (ECJ 1998f) was formerly a law professor trained in EU environmental law and has alone been responsible for at least 5 Dutch preliminary references.

[17] Furthermore, one Dutch environmental organization, Stichting Natuur en Milieu in Utrecht has produced a brochure detailing how environmental NGOs can effectively use a litigation strategy. (Interview with Head of Waste Management, DG Environment, Brussels, April 1999).

[18] Council Directive 90/313/EEC. See Sanchis Moreno (1996).

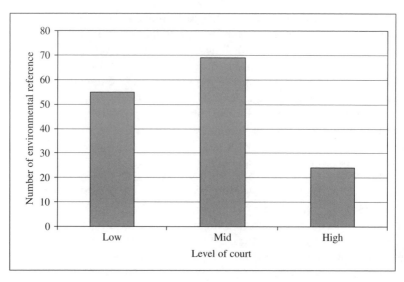

Note: N = 148
The level of court categories denotes the following: low (first instance court), mid (appellate court but whose decision could be appealed to a higher court), and high (court of final appeal).
Source: Data compiled by the author from European Communities. 2004. *CELEX Data Base*. Brussels: Office for Official Publications of the European Communities and World Jurist Association (2002).

Figure 4.1 Total number of Article 234 references in the area of environmental protection by level of referring national court, 1976–2003

are the main source of preliminary references in this legal domain (Alter 2001), yet do show that the highest courts send much fewer references (24 out of 148). Mid appellate courts were clearly responsible for the bulk of preliminary references in this legal domain (69 references), while lower courts sent 55 references or 37% of all environmental protection cases.

EU rules

Alongside mobilized interests and legal resources, I hypothesized that preliminary reference rate may also be a function of the EU rules governing a particular legal domain. As argued, EU rules may impact litigation by creating the opportunities for action. One way this can occur is through the interaction between these EU rules and pre-existing national policies. Similar to Chapter 3, I explore how the EU/national policy fit affects levels of preliminary references. Further, I examine the impact of ECJ precedent on subsequent environmental claims.

Table 4.3 *Effect of EU/national policy fit on average number of Article 234 references in the area of environmental protection, 1976–2003*

	B	t-statistic
(model 1) Environmental protection EU/national policy fit	−.035*	−2.347

Notes:
*p < .05
Entry is unstandardized regression coefficient. For each member state the total number of preliminary references is divided by the number of years in which that country has been making references to the ECJ in this legal domain. EU/National policy fit is the average transposition rate for each country (the percentage of EU secondary legislation applicable to date that has been properly implemented into national law).
Source: Data compiled by the author from European Communities. 2004. *CELEX Data Base.* Brussels: Office for Official Publications of the European Communities and the *Annual Report on Monitoring the Application of Community Law* (Luxembourg: Office for Official Publications of the European Communities, various years).

EU/National policy fit
Our next analysis examines the effect of the relative fit between EU and national policies on average preliminary reference rate. The variables in Table 4.3 display the impact of implementation rates (the ease to which a country transposes EU law) on litigation rates. These data suggest that the less successful a member state is at integrating EU law into the national legal system (or the lower the EU/national policy fit), the higher the levels of preliminary references originating from those national courts. Both Denmark and Austria have experienced few transposition problems (average rate at successfully implementing directives at 87 and 95 percent compared with Greece's low at 69 percent), and both countries possess little litigation in this legal domain (2 cases from Denmark and 3 cases from Austria).[19] Referring back to Chapter 3, these countries also exhibited a similar pattern in the area of social provisions with policy fit scores at 74 percent for Denmark and 93 percent for Austria. In fact, the correlation between average EU/national policy fit in the two legal domains is also quite high and significant ($r = .78$) suggesting that each of these countries may be generally more or less successful at transposing EU directives across all domains. These findings confirm the claim that national

---

[19] These policy fit findings are consistent with what we know about general patterns of EU environmental policy implementation in Austria and Denmark (see Liefferink and Andersen 1998). Both countries have had few problems integrating EU environmental laws into their already extensive national conservation legal frameworks.

policy traditions and institutions may create general patterns of transposition problems across member states (e.g. Knill and Lenschow 1998).

Subsequently, the laggards in policy fit have been increasingly the targets of litigation. Almost a quarter of all environmental preliminary references originated from Italian national courts. The vast majority of these Italian cases involved EU waste directives – cases where the Italian government's delinquency and accuracy in implementing EU waste regulations was in question.[20] Further, these data also highlight the significant conflicts embedded in the Italian transpositions over enforcement and implementation responsibilities (federal versus regional authorities).[21] Claimants asked for a clarification that was currently lacking in both the EU waste directives and the Italian interpretations of these laws. Similarly, France has experienced difficulties in national transpositions that arise from regional variation in implementation of EU waste and nature conservancy measures.[22] These data remind us that while policy misfits may function as a cause of the legal claim, mobilized interests are equally important in explaining reference rates. For example, in Spain, scholars have observed a noticeable absence of mobilized environmental groups providing the "pull" for proper and effective national transpositions of EU environmental laws; the lack of environmental references from Spain may also be attributed to this factor (e.g. Börzel 1998; 2001).[23]

---

[20] One of the main contentions arising from this litigation is the differing definitions of "waste" under Community versus Italian law. In particular, the Court was asked whether reusable, recyclable or recoverable items are considered waste under EU law. In 1990, the ECJ argued in the *Zanetti* case (ECJ 1990f) that wastes that are recoverable and recyclable were not excluded from the Community definition of waste. Despite this judgment and others (e.g. ECJ 1995b), Italian legislators proceeded to adopt waste decree laws that distinguish between "wastes" and "residues" (previous decree laws, such as Decree n. 443 were confirmed by Law n. 575 of 1996). Residues that are defined as secondary raw material are then exempt from the Italian waste legislation – an action that is inconsistent with EU waste laws (Guttieres and Bayley 1994: 8; Krämer 2000). This inconsistency was at the center of subsequent preliminary references (e.g. ECJ 1997f) from Italy.

[21] Scholars have observed that problems associated with the implementation and enforcement of Italian environmental laws often arise from a "lack of co-ordination between the state and regional level" (Francioni and Montini 1996: 252). In the area of waste management, regional authorities are responsible for permitting and authorizing waste disposal.

[22] In particular, the French regulations on hunting are handled at the regional level and have created regional disparities with enforcement of the Birds Directive (79/409/EEC) (Krämer 1991b: 25; see also ECJ 1996g and ECJ 1994a). In the area of waste, varying regional waste disposal systems (transpositions of the EU Waste Directive 75/439/EEC) have been at the center of four preliminary references (e.g. ECJ 1983, ECJ 1984a, ECJ 1985a, ECJ 1993e).

[23] Börzel does argue that this "pull" of mobilized societal actors in the Spanish implementation process does vary within EU environmental policy areas. For instance, Spanish NGOs have been very active in the implementation process for the Access to Information Directive (90/313/EEC), but were not active in similarly problematic national transpositions of the Drinking Water Directive (80/778/EEC).

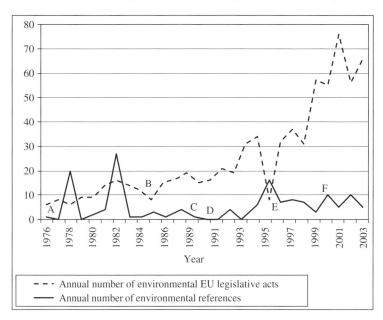

Note: Environmental references N = 148
Environmental EU legislative acts N = 780
The letters denote landmark environmental decisions and are labeled as follows: (A) Expansion of Jurisdiction in Pollution Cases (Case 21/76, 1976), (B) Environmental Protection is a Fundamental EU Objective (Case 240/83, 1985), (C) Environment can Obstruct Free Trade (Case 302/86, 1989) (D) Expansion of the Definition of Waste (Case 206/88, 1990), Introduced Environmental Standing (Case 361/88, 1990), (E) *Lappel Banks* – Habitat Protection (Case 44/95, 1996) and (F) Imposed Payment Penalty on Failure to Comply (Case 387/97, 2000).
Source: Data compiled by the author from European Communities. 2004. *CELEX Data Base*. Brussels: Office for Official Publications of the European Communities.

Figure 4.2 Annual numbers of Article 234 references and EU legislative acts in the area of environmental protection with landmark ECJ decisions, 1976–2003

ECJ precedent
How does ECJ precedent impact subsequent legislative and legal action? The data in Figure 4.2 display this relationship. Comparing these data to the social provisions sector, a number of similarities and differences stand out. First, the most significant difference is the dynamic between the two variables. Although the development of both environmental litigation and legislative acts is in the predicted direction, the relationship between the two is significantly weaker ($r = .27$) than that in the social provisions sector ($r = .50$). The findings in Chapter 3 illustrated a close mutually reinforcing relationship between ECJ precedent, legislative action and

future legal claims in the area of social provisions. Conversely, EU environmental claims and EU legislative acts have developed on generally separate, albeit parallel, trajectories.

Despite the initial lack of a treaty basis for environmental protection, the EU possesses an extensive body of legislative environmental acts, far exceeding that of the social provisions sector.[24] While EU environmental legislation has developed with comparative ease at the EU level, there remains a very large disjuncture between these laws and the ultimate adoption of similar norms in the national legal systems (see Chalmers 1999: 655–59; Sbragia 1996: 235). As was explored earlier, improper implementations often led to legal claims, when there is significant national level awareness and knowledge amongst those affected by the regulation, be it environmental groups or waste disposal unions. However, the extensive body of EU environmental law alone does not necessarily provide an increased opportunity for legal claims, as often these laws provide weak national legal norms or remain lost in the gap between federal and regional administrations.[25] Thus, the steady increase in EU environmental legislative acts since 1981 may have more to do with non-litigation related factors such as the official incorporation of environmental protection into a Directorate General, coupled with the Commission's investment of resources into protecting the environment. Further, the sudden increase in environmental references in the 1990s may have more to do with ECJ precedent and national level policy disparities than Community legislative action.

Second, Figure 4.2 illustrates that ECJ precedent has a similar, albeit not as dramatic, impact on environmental legal claims as it did in the area of social provisions. The area of waste management is one example. The *ADBHU* preliminary ruling (ECJ 1985a) involving a waste disposal system in France led to the now legendary decision that established

---

[24] See data in Chapter 2. By the end of 2003 there were 730 pieces of environmental secondary legislation compared to only 457 social provisions.

[25] For instance, circulars (or administrative measures) rather than national legislation are widely used to transpose EU environmental laws: a practice that in effect provides a weak legal norm as circulars are easily amended and changed leading to public uncertainty over the protection provided. The ECJ and the Commission have repeatedly criticized this practice, in cases where the Directive confers rights or imposes obligations on private individuals (see ECJ 1991c, ECJ 1991d). Further, in terms of implementation gaps, in the area of nature conservation, the gap between what federal executives agree to in the Council of Ministers and the subsequent implementation of these EU environmental laws is particularly acute in member states that delegate regulation to regional administrations, such as in Belgium, Germany, Italy and Spain (see Krämer 1991b: 25). Similarly, the disjuncture is even experienced in relatively unitary states, such as the UK, France and the Netherlands, in such areas as pollution control which is administered by local authorities (see CEC 1998d).

environmental protection as a fundamental objective of the EU that could limit the free movement of goods: a decision that pre-empted Community legislators who added environmental protection to EU goals in the Single European Act. A waste directive[26] was at the center of this case. The *Danish Bottles* decision (ECJ 1988a) (which upheld a Danish recycling program that was deemed in conflict with free trade norms) cited this earlier judgment and reaffirmed the argument that national environmental protection measures could in certain instances remain in place despite obstructing free trade. The Court constructed a balance between environmental protection and free trade norms: a balance that was then lacking in EU law. These rulings provided the basis for subsequent ECJ decisions.[27]

The waste directives continued to be the subject of legal claims both over this conflict in free trade and environmental norms, as well as its vague definition of waste, which led to considerable variation in national implementation. Litigants demanded clarification, a point that is illustrated by the fact that almost a third of the ECJ's environmental preliminary rulings (24 out of 73) pertain to the original EU waste directives (including a framework directive): 75/442/EEC, 75/439/EEC. This litigation highlighted the need for greater clarity in EU waste regulations. Subsequently, amended waste legislation was issued to begin to address these issues: Council Directives 91/156/EEC, 91/689/EEC, 91/692/EEC and Council Regulation 259/93/EEC. The newly amended Waste Framework Directive 91/156/EEC adopted the Court's expansive definition of waste (Cichowski 1998). While the materials that now fall under EU regulation were expanded, the original "waste" versus a "good" difference persisted. This Directive was subsequently the subject of 13 new ECJ decisions pursuant to preliminary references with the time period of this study: a dynamic of litigation that many argue will persist until vague EU waste laws are clarified (Cheyne and Purdue 1998; Cichowski 1998).

Explaining litigation: decision-making, rulemaking and opportunities for action

The previous section focused on the factors that give rise to the legal claim and preliminary references. The Court's decision-making played a role in

---

[26] Council Directive 75/439/EEC.
[27] The *ADBHU* decision was cited in 11 subsequent ECJ decisions and the *Danish Bottles* case appeared in 14 subsequent decisions. The author compiled this information from the *OJCD* compendium of ECJ case law.

this explanation to the extent to which this precedent formed the basis for subsequent legal claims. In this section, I turn our focus exclusively to the factors that shape these ECJ decisions and the subsequent impact on institutionalization of environmental protection. The findings from Chapter 3 illustrate that even in the face of member state opposition the ECJ operated to uphold EU interests. This is illustrated clearly as the Commission's argumentation is a much stronger predictor of ECJ rulings than member state positions. Further, the ECJ consistently operates to clarify EU law rather than preserve the national practices, despite the potential costs involved with the rulings. In this section, I explore how this dynamic interaction has evolved in the area of environmental protection. Have ECJ rulings served to change the balance of power between national governments, EU organizations and public interest activists? Unlike the treaty based rights involved in the social provisions case law, environmental litigation has disproportionately involved secondary legislation (especially laws governed by qualified majority voting). As argued, we might expect this to provide member state governments greater ease in reversing or adopting subsequent legislation to alter adverse rulings. Thus, member state governments may retain greater control over the policy trajectory.

Upholding EU interests

How do national government policy positions impact ECJ decision-making? Table 4.4 explores how the written observations (briefs) of member state governments and the EU organizations impacts ECJ decision-making. These data include all the written observations submitted in preliminary rulings in the area of environmental protection between 1976 and 2003. Similar to Chapter 3, the table includes data broken down into various categories of observations for each country: number of rulings, number of observations submitted, and of these observations, percentage of observations that successfully predict the ECJ ruling (success rate), and finally the rate at which a given member state intervenes in cases beyond those involving its own legal practices (intervention rate). Again, the data reveal the Commission's active participation by submitting written observations in all cases.

Compared to the social provisions cases, there were a greater number of member states that actively participated and then also conversely a greater number with considerably low intervention rates. This later category was indicative of a much smaller number of member states having preliminary references originate from their national courts (Greece, Ireland, Portugal, Spain all had no rulings, with a handful of others only receiving 2, Sweden, Denmark, Finland). Interestingly, all of the

Table 4.4 *National government and Commission observations as a predictor of ECJ rulings pursuant to Article 234 references in the area of environmental protection by country, 1976–2003*

	Number of rulings	Number of observations	Success rate (%)	Intervention rate (%)
Austria	3	15	100%	28%
Belgium	4	4	25%	1%
Denmark	2	11	50%	13%
Finland	2	7	20%	11%
France	15	34	55%	33%
Germany	5	16	64%	18%
Greece	0	1	0%	1%
Ireland	0	1	100%	1%
Italy	16	17	75%	9%
Netherlands	15	27	44%	22%
Portugal	0	1	0%	2%
Spain	0	2	100%	3%
Sweden	2	2	100%	4%
United Kingdom	8	24	59%	26%
Commission		73	85%	100%

Notes:
N = 73
Number of rulings column denotes the number of ECJ preliminary rulings originating from the specified country's national courts. Success rate denotes the percentage of cases in which a member state government's written observation (policy position) successfully predicts the final ECJ ruling. Intervention rate denotes the rate at which a given member state intervenes (by submitting an observation) in cases beyond those involving its own legal system. This rate is calculated as the number of observations submitted by a country in cases not directly involving their legal system as a percentage of the total number of rulings not directly involving the country on which they could have filed observations. Intervention rate for the Commission denotes the percentage out of all cases that the Commission submits an observation.
Source: Data compiled by the author from European Communities. 2004. *CELEX Data Base.* Brussels: Office for Official Publications of the European Communities and the *European Court Reports* (Luxembourg: Office for Official Publications of the European Communities, various years).

countries that possessed no preliminary rulings in this policy domain were still active in submitting observations. France and Austria possessed comparatively high participation rates (33% and 28% respectively); the UK and the Netherlands were also very active in submitting observations in this legal domain (26% and 22%). Generally, these patterns suggest that member states will be more likely to intervene in legal domains that are of particular importance to their own policy priorities, be it promoting a high level of environmental protection or minimizing the economic impacts of the policy.[28] Further, it might also suggest that some member states are generally more active in intervening in the preliminary ruling procedure, as evidenced from the UK's high participation rate in both legal domains, suggesting a general concern with how the Court might impact national regulations in all domains.

How have these interventions affected the ECJ's decision-making? Similar to the area of social provisions, Table 4.4 reveals that the Commission's observations predicted ECJ rulings far better on a consistent basis than did observations filed by member state governments (excluding those with 100% success rate but who had few observations, e.g. Sweden and Spain). The Commission's success rate is approximately 85%: 62 out of 73 observations are successful at predicting the final ruling. French observations predict ECJ decisions 55% of the time and Austria, despite being a comparatively new member state, had a 100% success rate in the 15 observations it filed. It is interesting to note that while Italy's success rate is high (75%), in 2 of its observations the Italian Government actually filed an observation which stated it believed their national law was in violation of EU law (government preferences in all other cases take a stance to defend or preserve national law) and the ECJ concurred. In general, the findings presented in Table 4.4 suggest that member states take seriously the policymaking effect of ECJ decisions. Further, the findings bring into question claims that the ECJ preliminary rulings are systematically influenced by the policy positions of member states. Instead, like the social provisions domain, the ECJ acts to uphold EU interests, and thus the Commission's position was much more likely to predict the final outcome of the case.

These conclusions are further illustrated by the data in Figure 4.3. The figure displays the percentage of adverse rulings (rulings in which the ECJ finds a national practice to be in violation of a EU law) in each legal domain by four categories that denote the magnitude of the impact of the case: 1 denotes low impact and 4 is the highest. As earlier discussed, we would expect a greater number of member states to file written observations in the cases in which there are potentially high political and financial costs if the ECJ hands down an adverse ruling. The number of member states filing observations in a case becomes a proxy for level of political and financial impact. This gives us some idea whether high financial costs associated with a ruling prevent the ECJ from making an adverse ruling.

---

[28] This is consistent with de la Mare's argument, "each member state's patterns of intervention are records of the importance attached to participating in debate" (de la Mare 1999: 244).

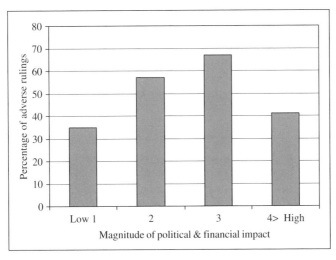

Note: N = 73
Percentage of adverse rulings denotes the total number of rulings in which the ECJ
finds the national law or practice to be in violation of EU law as a percentage of the
total number of social provisions preliminary rulings. Each preliminary ruling is also
categorized as having a low to high financial impact. The categories of magnitude
denote the total number of member state governments filing observations in each case.
These totals serve as a proxy for the magnitude of impact as cases with a larger impact
elicit a greater number of member state governments participating in the case.
Source: Data compiled by the author from European Communities. 2004. *CELEX Data
Base*. Brussels: Office for Official Publications of the European Communities and the
European Court Reports (Luxembourg: Office for Official Publications of the
European Communities, various years).

Figure 4.3 Political and financial impact as a predictor of adverse ECJ
rulings pursuant to Article 234 references in the area of environmental
protection, 1976–2003

Similar to the social provisions rulings, the environmental domain brings
into question the relationship between high political and financial costs
and adverse rulings.

Figure 4.3 illustrates that those cases with a magnitude of 1 were the
least likely to have adverse decisions (35% of rulings in this category
found violations), whereas those with a magnitude of 2 or 3 received
adverse rulings well over half the time (57% and 67% of the time). Yet the
data does show that in cases where 4 or more member states filed
observations, the ECJ found slightly fewer violations (41% of decisions).
In both sectors, half if not more of cases receive a magnitude of 2 or more:
a total of 118 rulings in the social provisions sector and 43 in the environment. And throughout these categories we find the ECJ issuing adverse

decisions at least half the time, sometimes much more (67% environment category 3) with the one exception of the environment category 4 cases (41% are adverse rulings). Again, despite the claims that the ECJ will withhold an adverse ruling with potentially high financial costs (Garrett et al 1998) or with a negative political impact (Golub 1996), these data suggest that generally the ECJ does not hesitate to make an adverse ruling even in the face of member state opposition.

Clarifying rules

What EU rules are invoked in these cases and has the ECJ operated to preserve the national practices that come in conflict with supranational law? Between 1976 and 2003, the ECJ made 73 environmental preliminary rulings. Table 4.5 details the EU environmental laws invoked in preliminary rulings. The pattern of litigation is not surprising. The majority of cases involve EU laws with comparatively general rather than specific policy prescriptions. These include the waste directives, interim fishing measures and the nature protection directive. The litigants demanded clarification of EU rules and the ECJ fulfilled this task. Further, these data suggest that the Court is not systematically constrained by member state policy positions. The data illustrate that the Court does not hesitate to dismantle national laws that come in violation with EU law, but did so to a lesser degree than the social provisions sector: in 47 percent of the cases the ECJ found national practices in violation of EU law (35 out of 73 rulings).

The types of EU laws invoked in this litigation are similar to the social provisions sector. Like the equality directives, the Waste Framework Directive offered a general rather than specific definition of waste (the results of unanimity voting), which led to inconsistent transpositions and introduced uneven burdens on competition (37% of environmental preliminary rulings pertain to EU waste laws). The fishing measures introduce a similar dynamic. These rules were adopted to safeguard marine resources until the EU could construct a common fisheries policy. However, there was considerable delay in implementing this common policy, and the measures did little to prevent a patchwork of national regulations causing considerable comparative disadvantages as illustrated in the case law.[29] Similarly, the Birds Directive (Council Directive

---

[29] All 10 of these rulings involve criminal proceedings brought against various fishing operations, for being in violation of French, Dutch or British fishing regulations. The ECJ is asked to bring clarification to these vague rules. For example, in ECJ (1981b), a Dutch court stayed criminal proceedings against a Dutch fishing vessel, which exceeded the catch limit established by national law, to ask the ECJ for a correct interpretation of the interim Community fishery measures. The defendant in the case argued that the

Table 4.5 *EU laws invoked in ECJ rulings pursuant to Article 234 in the area of environmental protection by judicial outcome, 1976–2003*

EU environmental laws	Number of rulings (percentage of all rulings)	Number of adverse rulings (percentage of adverse rulings)
Dangerous substances CD 67/548 CD 79/831 CD 79/117 & Free Trade (Articles 30–36)	5 (7%)	2 (40%)
Nature conservation CD 79/409	17 (23%)	7 (41%)
Waste CD 75/442 CD 75/439 CD 78/319 & Free Trade (Articles 30–36)	27 (37%)	15 (56%)
Water CD 78/659 CD 80/778	7 (10%)	3 (43%)
Conservation of fishery Article 102 (Act of Accession) CR 554/81 CR 1569/81 CR 272/81 CR 1719/80 CR 2527/80 CR 3305/80 CR 2897/79 CR 101/76 CR 1177/79 CR 541/80	10 (14%)	2 (20%)
Public access to information CD 90/313	7 (10%)	6 (86%)
Total rulings	73	35 (47%)

Notes:
Number of rulings column denotes the number of cases involving EU laws in a particular sub-field of environmental protection. Adverse rulings column denotes the total number of rulings in a particular sub-field in which the national rule was declared to be in violation of EU law. CD = Council Directive CR = Council Regulation
Source: Data compiled by the author from European Communities. 2004. *CELEX Data Base.* Brussels: Office for Official Publications of the European Communities and the *European Court Reports* (Luxembourg: Office for Official Publications of the European Communities, various years).

79/409/EEC) specifies general provisions for bird protection and also allows considerable leeway for member states to implement more stringent regulations. This provision subsequently led to varying national implementations either due to implementation errors or more stringent protection that obstructed free trade.[30]

Table 4.6 provides a general picture of how the environmental protection preliminary rulings have evolved cross-nationally and by individual sub-field. The ECJ considered the lawfulness of French practices in 15 rulings, declaring violations 40 percent of the time. Aggregating results from litigation involving "powerful member state governments" (France, Italy, Germany and the UK), the Court declared violations in 39% of the decisions (17 out of 44), suggesting that in the area of environmental protection the ECJ found fewer violations amongst these member states. Again, these data also give some preliminary indication that those national practices that enshrine least integrative rules will disproportionately be the subject of these legal disputes.

Together France and Italy received 42 percent of all the litigation in this policy sector. This is not surprising. France has historically favored inter-governmental cooperation rather than an integrative EU policy on the environment and thus its administrative practices embody this non-integrative position (Demiray 1994). Similarly, while Italy tends to agree to rather strict EU measures in the Council, they do so with the intention that they will not have to fully implement the EU laws (Rehbiner and Stewart 1985). This pattern also holds when looking at legal systems that possess stricter environmental laws. Almost one quarter of the references attacked Dutch laws as a result of strict environmental codes compared to other member states. These can sometimes cause obstructions to free trade (ECJ 1989c). These data confirm the hypothesis that disputes will arise around national practices that function as hindrances to free trade. Also, to the extent that a member state possesses least integrative environmental norms (weaker or stronger implementations of EU laws), I find that these legal systems are the subject of litigation.

The data in Table 4.6 also give us some idea of how the Court decides when confronted with conflicts between areas of EU law. The conflict

Council of Ministers' failure to construct a fisheries policy, in accordance with the proposed policy laid out by the 1972 Act of Accession and subsequently in Council Regulation 101/76/EEC, had created a "legal vacuum" that the interim measures and national regulations failed to fill (para. 5 of the decision). The ECJ did not hesitate to fill this void.

[30] Example cases include ECJ 1994a, 1996b, 1996f, 1996g, 1996h. Interestingly, environmental groups have exploited the Directive's general provisions to force more stringent protection in legal systems that possess weak interpretations of the Directive.

Table 4.6 *ECJ rulings pursuant to Article 234 references in the area of environmental protection by country and sub-field of EU law, 1976–2003*

	Number of rulings (percentage of adverse rulings)						
	Dangerous substances	Nature	Waste	Water	Conservation fishery	Public access	Totals
Austria		1 (0%)	1 (0%)			1 (0%)	3 (0%)
Belgium		1 (100%)	2 (50%)		1 (100%)		4 (75%)
Denmark			1 (100%)		1 (0%)		2 (50%)
Finland			2 (100%)				2 (100%)
France		6 (50%)	5 (60%)		4 (0%)		15 (40%)
Germany	1 (100%)	1 (0%)	1 (100%)			2 (100%)	5 (80%)
Italy	3 (33%)	1 (100%)	8 (13%)	3 (33%)		1 (100%)	16 (31%)
Luxembourg						1 (100%)	1 (100%)
Netherlands	1 (0%)	2 (50%)	5 (100%)	3 (67%)	2 (0%)	2 (100%)	15 (67%)
Sweden		1 (0%)	1 (100%)				2 (50%)
United Kingdom		4 (25%)	1 (0%)	1 (0%)	2 (50%)		8 (25%)
Total rulings	5	17	27	7	10	7	73

Notes:
N = 73
Number of rulings denotes the number of judgments in each sub-field for each country. Percentage of adverse rulings denotes the number of judgments in a particular sub-field involving a particular country finding a violation of EU law as a percentage of the total number of judgments in that sub-field for that country.
Source: Data compiled by the author from European Communities. 2004. *CELEX Data Base.* Brussels: Office for Official Publications of the European Communities and the *European Court Reports* (Luxembourg: Office for Official Publications of the European Communities, various years).

between free trade and environmental protection is a well-established tension in EU environmental law and member states have failed to construct rules to balance these two interests (Cichowski 1998). In the absence of EU measures to decide on a given dispute, does the Court defer to national level practices, or does the ECJ construct new EU norms in order to decide the case? The Court was asked in five cases to decide between national environmental regulations (that were implementations of EU law) and free trade norms, and in three of these cases the Court held the national practice to be in violation of EU free trade norms and the ruling upheld free trade laws over environmental protection. The ECJ operates to clarify EU rules and in doing so can expand both their meaning as well as limit their ability to override other rules.

The institutionalization of environmental protection: birds and beyond

These data reinforce predictions arguing that the preferences of powerful member state governments do not generally constrain the Court's judicial outcomes. Much like the pattern of social provisions references, environmental litigation reveals the Court's active participation in the integration project. These data give us a general picture of the dynamic driving this litigation. As we have seen, individuals and organizations that are disadvantaged by incomplete implementation or member state non-compliance are able to bring legal claims against their own national governments to correct these national practices. While individuals have a greater difficulty claiming direct rights under environmental law compared to the area of social provisions, environmental groups have succeeded at utilizing EU law to dismantle comparatively weak national environmental regulations. Through the resolution of these disputes, the ECJ has expanded EU environmental laws, in a way that can provide new opportunities for legislative action and legal activism. As illustrated, the Court operates to clarify EU rules, and in doing so this ECJ precedent can create the opportunity for subsequent legal action and at times legislative action. Again, we expect the connection between litigation and legislative action to be less strong in the area of the environment than social provisions, due to the comparatively weak treaty basis. However, we have seen how ECJ precedent has played a powerful role in initiating subsequent action through legislative action and new legal claims in a host of environmental sectors, including the EU's general objective of environmental protection, waste management and nature conservation and in creating a balance between EU free trade norms and environmental protection.

To understand more precisely how this litigation dynamic develops and how this changes the balance of power between EU organizations, member state governments and ordinary citizens, I rely on the content of the case law. Similar to Chapter 3, in the remaining part of this chapter I examine this general pattern in a sub-field of the policy domain: nature conservation. This case law analysis provides the detail that aggregate data cannot. In particular, I examine the legal argumentation in the cases to highlight how the Court comes to expand EU nature conservation rules despite member state opposition. Further, I examine how individuals, EU organizations and national governments all reacted and participated in this evolving policy expansion.

The necessary conditions for legal claims and litigation

Council Directive 79/409/EEC (the Birds Directive) constituted the first binding legal instrument for EU-wide nature conservation programs.[31] By the end of the time period of this study, two more nature conservation EU laws were adopted, the Habitats Directive[32] and the Protection in Trade of Species of Wild Flora and Fauna Regulation.[33] They appear in only four of our preliminary ruling cases, but will be discussed below, in particular how the Habitats Directive grew out of this earlier Bird Directive litigation. Essential to the ECJ's role in the evolution of EU natural conservation measures was first a decision by member states to develop at least some natural habitat protection measures as embodied in the Birds Directive.

The origins of the EU nature protection measures are traceable to the activism and influence of environmental NGOs in the early 1970s. After considerable negotiations the Birds Directive was adopted in 1979 despite the fact that such a measure surpassed the EU's powers as granted by the EEC Treaty.[34] Thus, the Council justified adoption of the Directive under Article 308 (ex 235) of the Treaty and was careful to explicitly link the need for a European-wide nature protection measure to the functioning of the Common Market.[35] Despite this link to economic objectives, the Birds Directive introduced at the EU level for the first time

---

[31] Scholars observe that until the late 1980s most member state governments were under the impression that nature conservation was under their "exclusive competence" despite the existence of Community obligations since 1981 under the Birds Directive (Krämer 2000: 131). The Community officially gained an explicit competence in the area of nature protection with the addition of Article 175 (ex 130s) in the Single European Act (see general overview of EU environmental policy in Chapter 2). However, relinquishing national control over nature conservation has been very slow: mainly for the reason of overlapping with sensitive national issues such as land-use planning and the structural weaknesses (in terms of enforceability) of both national and EU nature conservation measures (CEC 1999d).

[32] Council Directive 92/43/EEC on habitat protection.

[33] Council Regulation 338/97/EEC on the protection of species of wild fauna and flora by regulating trade. This regulation was adopted to transpose provisions of CITES (Convention on International Trade in Endangered Species).

[34] Prior to the Single European Act (SEA) in 1986, the EC Treaty made no mention of environmental protection. Thus, prior to the SEA the legal basis for nature conservation was Article 308 (ex 235).

[35] The Directive states: "Effective bird protection is typically a trans-frontier environmental problem entailing common responsibilities ... (and) the conservation of the species of wild birds naturally occurring in the European territory of member states is necessary to attain, within the operation of the common market, ... the Community's objectives regarding the improvement of living conditions, a harmonious development of economic activities throughout the Community and a continuous and balanced expansion" (Council Directive 79/409/EEC).

that nature protection, albeit with very specific linkages to particular birds and their habitats, could at times override national economic priorities.[36] However, the real commitment to shift control over national natural habitat protection to Community legislators was not entirely clear. The Directive introduced general rather than specific requirements for protection that have resulted in significant national level conflicts over various portions of the provision: from hunting regulations (Article 7 and 8) to the allowable national derogations (Article 9).[37]

Yet, given this necessary rule, how did individuals come to utilize a piece of secondary legislation that did not grant individual rights to bring legal actions against their own national governments? The second necessary condition for this activism and litigation was the strategic action on the part of environmental NGOs to file complaints with the Commission, leading to infringement proceedings (pursuant to Article 226) that ultimately resulted in an ECJ case law developing EU habitat protection law. Together these two factors activated a dynamic of litigation that ultimately brought the creation of a complex set of rules governing nature conservation in Europe. Thus, the case law analysis begins with this ECJ precedent that served as the roots for subsequent action.

Until the mid 1980s member states had all but ignored their obligations under the Birds Directive. While all member states possessed national legislation on the protection of birds by the implementation date (6 April 1981), many national regulations did not fully implement or were in conflict with provisions of the Directive.[38] In general, national implementation of this Directive has been fraught with errors: in 1991 and again in 1998 the Commission announced that only Denmark was in full compliance with the Directive, nearly 20 years after the Directive's adoption (CEC 1991: 220; CEC 1998d: 21).[39] Yet this lack of commitment on the part of member state governments provided NGOs with the opportunity to participate in EU policy expansion, even without an explicit "right" to individual action for environmental protection.

---

[36] Article 2 of the Directive states: "Member states shall take the requisite measures to maintain the population of the species referred to in Article 1 at a level which corresponds in particular to ecological, scientific and cultural requirements, while taking account of economic and recreational requirements, or to adapt the population of these species to that level" (Council Directive 79/409/EEC). Scholars agree this passage places economic and recreational considerations second to habitat protection (see Nollkaemper 1997: 276; Wils 1994: 226).

[37] See Krämer (2000: 65 and 1991b: 25–6) for a further discussion of this tension.

[38] One general problem was that in a number of member states, this legislation was hunting legislation rather than bird conservation (see CEC 1993c).

[39] Even Denmark's compliance rate is questioned by some scholars (e.g. Pagh 1999).

National and transnational environmental NGOs' use of the Commission's complaint procedure has provided detailed compliance information that was otherwise extremely difficult for the Commission to collect (CEC 1993c: 113). Subsequently, these complaints have activated the ECJ via the Article 226 procedure making the Birds Directive the most litigated piece of EU environmental law (Wils 1994). In 1990 alone, the Commission received 129 complaints in the area of nature compared to only 32 pertaining to air quality or even 104 in water quality (CEC 1990b.). It is this litigation pursuant to Article 226 that marks the beginning of the Court's judicial rulemaking in the area of nature conservation and provided the legal precedent that would later be essential for Article 234 rulings involving direct action before national courts.

The significance of this case law is twofold. First, it has enabled the ECJ to begin to bring further clarity and precision to the real protection provided by the Directive and thus expanded the claims possible before national courts. In its case law, the Court has re-emphasized the general scope of the protection provided by Articles 1 and 2 of the Directive. For example, ECJ rulings clarified the Directive as applying to "the European territory of member states as a whole", which led to the correction of national legislation in Belgium and France that limited protection to their own territory (ECJ 1987b: para. 18–23; ECJ 1988b: para. 13–16). Further, in its very first judgments (ECJ 1987b; ECJ 1988b: para. 8) on the Directive and also in a later judgments (ECJ 1991e),[40] the Court has interpreted Article 2 as providing a general philosophy rather than providing a general principle that could restrict other provisions of the Directive (a principle that would have empowered national governments to derogate from protective measures for economic reasons). On this later point, member states have not arrived at a similar opinion, with both Italy and Belgium arguing that the economic and recreational requirements mentioned in Article 2 enable them to implement national legislation that restrict the protection provided by other Articles of the Directive.[41] Further, the Court has expanded the protection provided against the

---

[40] While interpreting Article 4 (4) (the requirements for Special Protection Areas (SPAs) and in particular the allowable factors that can be given priority over SPA designation), the Court has argued that the "interests referred to in Art 2 of the Directive, namely economic and recreational requirements, do not enter into consideration". The Court further held that this argument applied to Article 4 (1) and (2) in ECJ (1993f: paras. 16–19) and in relation to the interpretation of Article 7 (hunting provisions) in ECJ (1994a: paras. 19 and 20).

[41] Written observations from ECJ (1987b) and ECJ (1987c).

hunting of birds (ECJ 1991f), and has restricted the general derogations originally allowed in member state transpositions (Article 9).[42]

Second, this case law has implications for the direct effect of the Birds Directive. Yet this is different than in the area of social provisions. The Court's decisions regarding the Birds Directive have not expanded the provision in a way that confers new rights on individuals. That is, an individual cannot claim an individual right to nature conservation, whereas, following the ECJ's *Dekker* decision, individuals could demand a right to equal treatment before a national court on the basis of the Equal Treatment Directive – an important difference when an individual or association is faced with questions of *locus standi* before national courts. Instead, the Court's litigation pursuant to Article 226 has provided greater clarity and precision to the Birds Directive so that it might be successfully utilized before national courts. The logic follows.

Article 249 (ex 189) of the Treaty gives the impression that individuals and environmental organizations cannot directly rely on the Directive, instead they must rely on the national legislation transposing the measure. However, following the Court's doctrine of direct effect, a Directive can be directly applicable given that it is "unconditional and sufficiently precise" and "in so far as the provisions define rights which individuals are able to assert against the State" (*Becker* decision, ECJ 1982a).[43] The Birds Directive's failure to meet these criteria (especially, providing individual rights) has led some scholars to argue that this provision does not have direct effect – in that it is not fully capable of

---

[42] Article 9 originally authorized wide derogations from the general system of protection as laid down in Articles 5–8. The Court's case law in effect has expanded the scope of reasons that *do not* allow member state derogations: this includes agricultural, forestry or fishing purposes in general (ECJ 1987d: para. 25), historical and cultural traditions (ECJ 1987e: paras. 20 to 23) and as previously mentioned that Article 2 does not allow for reasons not specifically mentioned in Article 9 (ECJ 1987b and ECJ 1991f). Article 9 (1) (c) has been particularly controversial. This provision "permit(s), under strictly supervised conditions and on a selective basis the capture, keeping or other judicial use of certain birds in small numbers." The Court has held that the "small numbers" refers not to an absolute criterion, but refers to the overall maintenance of the species (ECJ 1988b). This case had involved the capture of several hundred thousand thrushes and skylarks by certain French departments who had argued this was a "very small percentage", and thus was consistent with the Directive despite the Court and Commission's opposite conclusion. Interestingly, the ECJ had no other choice but to declare the case as unfounded because the Commission hadn't explicitly contested the French interpretation of "small numbers" and in Article 226 cases the burden of proof lies entirely on the Commission's side (see para. 30 of the decision). Despite this seemingly non-adverse ruling (the French practice remained in place), the ECJ judgment provided a precedent that argued for a higher standard of protection and would be utilized in subsequent cases.

[43] This case built on the Court's earlier jurisprudence establishing the main tenets of the direct effect doctrine especially in relation to directives (ECJ 1963; ECJ 1974; ECJ 1979).

individual action before national courts (Miller 1998: 35; Geddes 1992: 38).[44] Despite this lack of a clear right to individual action before national courts, over time legal scholars and national judges have come to agree on the direct effect of Articles 5 through 9 of the Directive, and parts of Article 4.[45] The litigation pursuant to Article 226 was crucial to this acceptance, as the ECJ rulings gave greater precision and clarity to the Directive, providing national courts with guidance on how the Directive must be interpreted, which ultimately enabled applicants to invoke this EU law before some national courts.[46]

How have individuals been able to bring legal action before national courts to force national compliance *without* an explicit "right to action" in EU law? In the case of the Birds Directive, individuals and environmental associations are often given some national level administrative or legal recourse against state authorities that fail to comply with their duties as established in national law. If the national or regional authority

---

[44] In addressing the issue of direct effect, Miller concludes that if the Birds Directive does not recognize the rights of individuals and "if the protection of the rights or interests of human individuals is a sine qua non of direct effect, then the Birds Directive (and its cognates) cannot have this property" (1998: 35). Further, Geddes points to the difficulties with EU environmental law and the challenge to gain access to national courts: "There are many provisions of Community environmental law which have direct effect but where it cannot be said that those provisions were intended to protect the welfare of individuals as to create 'Community rights' which a national court must uphold" (1992: 38).

[45] The high courts of France, the Netherlands and Belgium have recognized the direct effect of Articles 5–9 of the Directive. Cases include: France, Conseil d'Etat, Case 41.971, 7 December 1984; The Netherlands, Afdeling Rectspraak Raad van State, Case A-1.0511, 6 March 1986; Belgium, Conseil d'Etat, Case 31.573, 9 December 1988. It is interesting to note that in a 1991 ruling, Case 100 27 February 1991, the highest administrative court in Italy, Consiglio di Stato, denied direct effect to the Birds Directive. Scholars have criticized this judgment as being in error (see Wils 1994: 239 note 126). Further, scholars suggest that the Court's rulings on Article 4 (designation of protection areas) have further clarified why the requirements of portions of this Article (paras. 1 and 2 in particular) are clear and unconditional and therefore, directly effective (Krämer 1991b: 46).

[46] For example, following a series of ECJ rulings clarifying the hunting provisions of the Directive (ECJ 1991f and ECJ 1991g), a number of Italian national courts utilized these rulings to uphold claims made against the local authorities for allowing the hunting of birds that were protected by the Directive, but remained unprotected by Italian law (Regional Administrative Tribunal of Umbria, 4 March 1992, no. 70, Riv. giur. amb. (1993), 310; Reg. Adm. Tri of Lombardy, sec. II, 10 Sept. 1992, no. 603; Pretore of Terni, 24 Sept, 1992, Kir. Com. Sc. Internaz. (1993), 381; Court of Cassation (criminal, joined section, 28 Dec. 1994, No. 25, Cassazione penale (1995), 892; Consitutional Court, 22 July 1996, No. 272, Const. St. (1996), II, 1239.) However, prior to these ECJ rulings numerous Italian courts maintained that the Directive did not have direct effect, and thus individual claims were not admissible (e.g. Reg. Adm. Tr. Of Marche, 10 April 1985, No. 116, Foro amm. (1985), 1978; Reg. Adm. Tr. of Sicily, 30 May 1986, I Tar (1986), I, 2557; Consiglio di Stato, sec. IV, 27 Feb. 1991, No. 100, Riv. it. dir. pubbli. com. (1992), 506).

responsible to implement a certain prohibition as required by the Directive has failed to enforce established law (e.g. ban on hunting certain birds), national law usually provides some avenue for groups and individuals to initiate administrative procedures (complaints, or possibly legal action) to ensure the law is enforced. Thus, legal resources such as national rules on *locus standi* for environmental groups become the main criterion that has to be fulfilled, rather than the actual rights embodied in the EU provision.

Birds and beyond: evolving EU nature laws

The Birds Directive, together with the ECJ's case law pursuant to Article 226, has in effect given individuals and environmental organizations the ability to bring legal action before national courts without a "right of action" (Krämer 1991b: 52). The legal norm was not designed to give rights to individuals or associations. However, this Directive has enabled legal action before national courts. In this section I examine all of the cases involving nature conservation referred to the Court through 2003 and explore how this litigation impacted the opportunities for legislative and legal action at both the supranational and national level.

This case law analysis provides a comparison to the Court's pregnancy litigation, as examined in Chapter 3, on a number of important points. First, similar to the gender equality area, nature protection was not a priority for the Community and the ability of individuals and associations to bring claims before national courts, that in effect force national compliance, was certainly not foreseen. I explore the dynamic interaction between national mobilized interests, national courts and the ECJ's judicial rulemaking function as an explanation for this similar outcome. Second, the variation in the legal basis between gender equality law and environmental law (treaty versus secondary legislation) enables us to explore how this may affect the ability of member state governments to change, reverse or amend undesirable ECJ rulings that involve these varying EU laws.

Birds, environmental activists and judicial rulemaking

This litigation has primarily grown out of legal claims under the Birds Directive. Although, towards the very end of the time period of this study, two cases involved the Habitats Directive and two involved the Flora and Fauna Regulation. The majority of cases involve environmental associations bringing legal action against a public authority for wrongful implementation of the Directive. Not surprisingly, these have arisen in national legal systems that allow standing for environmental organizations: Belgium, France, Italy, Germany and the United Kingdom.

The remaining cases involve criminal proceedings in which the defendant has been charged with violating national environmental regulations in which the questions referred ask whether or not these regulations are in conformity with the Directive. Unlike the area of gender equality law, litigants do not have the strength of a directly applicable treaty-based right to back their environmental claims.[47] Theoretically, we might also expect the ECJ to have a diminished basis to make expansive rulings without the strength of a treaty provision. However, this helps explain why the Court's prior case law pursuant to Article 226 plays an important role in the development of the ECJ's preliminary rulings in this area. Even in the absence of a clearly defined EU environmental right, this case law has enabled the Court to respond to the legal claims brought by individuals and environmental groups in a way that often changes national laws. The following case law analysis illustrates this dynamic.

The first time the ECJ had the opportunity to rule on a case in which an individual invoked EU nature conservation laws before a national court was by way of a preliminary reference from the Netherlands, in the *Gourmetterie Van den Burg* case (ECJ 1990b). This case involved Article 14 of the Birds Directive that allows member states to adopt more stringent nature protection measures. The reference originated from a Dutch appellate court in which the plaintiff was appealing the charge that he had wrongfully imported a bird species, which was protected by the Dutch law implementing the Directive. The plaintiff argued that the Dutch interpretation of the EU law presented an obstruction to the free movement of goods. Since Article 14 of the Directive permits stricter implementation, the legal question revolved more particularly

---

[47] Article 2 of the EC Treaty (as amended by the SEA in 1986) incorporated the environment as one of the Community's objectives: "... a high level of protection and improvement of the quality of the environment." This general objective is further elaborated under Articles 6, 95 (ex 100a), 161 (ex 130d), 175 and 176 (ex 130s and 130t). Scholars have made persuasive arguments as to why Article 174 (ex 130r) should be able to be relied on by individuals in national courts (Doyle and Carney 1999). Yet the ECJ has yet to rule on the direct effect of EU environmental treaty provisions, and has only twice explicitly addressed the direct effect of environmental directives. The Court held in ECJ (1991h) that directives that fix quality standards (the case dealt specifically with Council Directive 80/779/EEC) also confer rights on individuals: "whenever the exceeding of the limit values could endanger human health, the persons concerned must be in a position to rely upon mandatory rules in order to be able to assert their rights" (p. 2601). Surprisingly, this clear statement of rights has not led to further legal action in national courts. Finally, the Court was also asked in a preliminary reference from Italy whether Article 4 of Directive 75/442/EEC on waste confers rights on individuals. The Court answered in the negative (ECJ 1994e: para. 14–15).

around whether the Netherlands' preventing the importation and consumption of a wild bird, a red grouse lawfully hunted in the United Kingdom, was simply too strict.

The ECJ cited its prior case law and argued that while the Directive aimed at a high level of protection for bird species specifically listed in Annex I, the Dutch law went beyond this protection.[48] In short, the ECJ held that a member state government could not extend its laws to protect species falling outside the concerns of the Directive and particularly when that species fell within another member's territory. While Article 14 of the Directive originally allowed for the implementation of more stringent nature conservation measures, the ECJ does not hesitate to restrict this right, especially when it infringes too deeply on Community free trade norms.

Four years later the Court would have the opportunity to rule on another preliminary reference involving the Birds Directive. The case originated from a French administrative court and resulted from six actions brought by environmental associations against a local authority, questioning the compatibility of a decision to fix hunting dates with the regulations laid out in Article 7 of the Directive (ECJ 1994a). Again, the ECJ referred to its prior case law to reaffirm first, its earlier interpretation that Article 7 provides a system of complete protection (para. 9) (ECJ 1991f), and second, that it does not allow a member state to fix closing dates for hunting season that vary by species (paras. 20–22) (ECJ 1987b; ECJ 1987c).

All parties did not agree with this interpretation of the Directive. Both the French government and the French hunting association involved in the case argued that the Court's past case law (ECJ 1991f and ECJ 1987c) provided that staggering of closing dates *was* compatible with Article 7. The Court did not concur. Following the Court's interpretation of Article 7 (4), local authorities were given less discretion over hunting regulations and were now required to give greater protection to nature conservation. This issue would arise again in a similar case brought in 2003 by three French environmental groups, the League for the Protection of Birds, the Association for the Protection of Wild Animals and the Anti-Hunting Union (ECJ 2003c). The Conseil d'Etat sent the preliminary reference after a question arose over the compatibility of French provisions regulating the hunting of migratory birds with the Birds Directive. The Conseil d'Etat had already annulled a portion of the law and the preliminary ruling provided the further clarifications

---

[48] The Court refers to its judgment in ECJ (1988b), which makes a general statement of the importance of EU nature conservation measures.

needed for member states to apply coherently the derogations and requirements laid out in Article 9 regarding hunting.

National hunting provisions were the subject of another preliminary reference originating from Italy in 1994. *WWF Italia* (ECJ 1996e) concerned Article 9 of the Directive and specifically the question of how far national governments were allowed to derogate (Article 9) from the hunting prohibitions outlined in the Directive (Articles 5 and 7). The case involved seven Italian environmental organizations[49] that instigated legal proceedings against the Region Veneto for the annulment of a measure that fixed the hunting calendar. The groups argued that this law, Italian Law No 157 of 11 February 1992 (which transposed the Birds Directive), was in violation of the principles laid down in the Directive by allowing the hunting of certain protected bird species.[50] The defendants in the case, the Italian authorities (Region Veneto) in cooperation with a hunting federation, argued that the hunting regulations in question did not involve the Birds Directive but instead should focus on the national law in question. While the national court generally agreed with this argument, the judge decided to suspend the proceedings to ask the ECJ for an interpretation of Article 9.

The ECJ did not agree with the defendants in the case. This 1996 ruling was of particular significance as the Court made a clear argument why individuals should be able to invoke the Birds Directive before national courts. More importantly, the Court articulated why national courts were obligated to respond. The ECJ emphasized its earlier judgments which took a very narrow view of the derogations allowed by the Directive and thus, subsequently declared that the Italian practices were inconsistent with the objectives of the Directive.[51] This case clearly

---

[49] Associazione Italiana per il World Wildlife Fund, Ente Nazionale per la Protezione Animali, Lega Ambiente, Comitato Regionale, Lega Anti Vivisezione – Delegazione Regionale, Lega per l' Abolizione della Caccia, Federnatura Veneto, Italia Nostra – Sezione di Venezia.

[50] The Italian law is described in the judgment: "Under Article 1(3) on the protection of warm-blooded wild fauna and on hunting (GURI No 46 of 25 February 1992, supplement, p. 3, "Law No 157"), ordinary regions (regioni a statuto ordinario) are to adopt regulations governing the management and protection of all species of wild fauna in accordance with Law No 157, international conventions and EU directives. Article 1(4) of Law No 157 wholly transposes and implements Council Directive 79/409/EEC in the manner and within the time-limits prescribed by that Law" (ECJ 1996e, para. 7).

[51] The Court cites its previous case law stating that derogations must be implemented in a clear and concise way and refer to specific national provisions (ECJ 1988b; 1987c; 1987b; ECJ 1990f). Further, the national legislation that in principle limits hunting, but then doesn't remain vigilant to regional rules that are in violation, is incompatible (ECJ 1991f).

marks the successful use of the Directive by environmental associations before national courts and also the Court's judicial rulemaking that in effect narrows the derogations that were originally allowable under Community law.

The following two 1996 preliminary rulings resulted from criminal proceedings and illustrate the Court's expansion and re-emphasis of the general protection provided by the Directive (Articles 1 and 2) and when this can be extended in light of stricter national measures (Article 14). In the *Vergy* case (ECJ 1996g), a man was charged with having offered for sale and sold a live bird that was protected by French conservation legislation. The species in question was a dwarf Black Canadian goose and it was born and raised in captivity. The defendant argued that the French legislation did not apply to such species, and if it did, it was contrary to the Birds Directive. The French court stayed the proceedings and asked the ECJ for an interpretation. In response, the ECJ held that the Directive does allow for the prohibition of trade/sale of species not listed in Annex III, but only those species that are naturally occurring in the wild state of the European territory. Further, birds that are born and bred in captivity are not within the scope of the Directive. Finally, the Court again cited ECJ (1988b) to argue that member states are required to provide "complete protection," to the species listed in the Directive, regardless of whether their natural habitat is in the member state in question. This ruling provided greater clarity and precision to the real protection provided by the Directive. Furthermore, it illustrates that the Court is at times willing to uphold national conservation legislation even when it restricts trade: a ruling that is counter to the ECJ's earlier decision in *Van den Burg*.

The *Van der Feersten* case (ECJ 1996h), a preliminary reference from the Netherlands, gave the ECJ another opportunity to decide on the scope of protection, and in particular the compatibility of more stringent national measures. Mr Van der Feersten was charged with possessing a bird that was imported from Denmark where it received no conservation protection, but that was protected by Dutch law. Further, the sub-species of the bird did not occur in the wild in Netherlands or within the European territory. The species however did occur within the European territory. In order to decide the case, the Dutch court asked whether the Directive protected such non-European sub-species and whether this measure was considered a strict national measure that was allowable under Article 14 of the Directive, and whether it was allowable even when the bird was not protected in Denmark. The Court upheld the Dutch law by answering the first question in the affirmative (making the subsequent questions redundant).

The ruling expanded the scope and meaning of the Directive. In effect, the ruling extended the Court's earlier judgments of wide protection, but went one step further by suggesting situations in which certain non-European birds could receive protection (despite the Directive's clear limitations to only "... the species of wild birds naturally occurring in the European territory of the member states").

While the previous preliminary rulings dealt with the Directive's hunting provisions, allowable national measures and general protection, it wasn't until a preliminary reference from the United Kingdom, in the *Lappel Bank* case (ECJ 1996f), that environmental groups were able to bring up the issue of the Special Protection Areas (SPAs) provided for in the Birds Directive (Article 4) and also the Habitats Directive. The case concerns the relative freedom member states have to take into account economic reasons when designating SPAs. The Royal Society for the Protection of Birds (RSPB) initiated the legal action in order to quash a decision by the Secretary of the State of the Environment to exclude a portion of the Medway Estuary and Marshes, the Lappel Bank area, from SPA designation. The Estuary and Marshes are home to various water fowl and serve as an important area for breeding and migration. The Secretary of State's decision to exclude this 22 hectare mudflat at Lappel Bank was made for economic reasons.

The Secretary of State argued that this decision was consistent with Article 2 of the Directive which stated: "member states shall take the requisite measures to maintain the population of the species referred to in Art 1 at a level which corresponds in particular to ecological, scientific and cultural requirements, while taking account of *economic* and recreational requirements."[52] The RSPB argued that Directive did not allow for economic considerations to be regarded when classifying an SPA. A lower court and then an appellate court upheld the government's decision. As a final resort, the RSPB appealed to the House of Lords. In order to decide the case, the House of Lords asked the ECJ for a correct interpretation of Article 4. In particular, the high court asked whether economic reasons could be taken in consideration in the designation of SPAs. The ECJ's negative answer was legendary.

The Court again cited its past case law and stated quite clearly that economic interests *could not* override ecological objectives when constructing SPAs.[53] This ruling flew in the face of the written briefs submitted by the UK and French governments. They both argued that

---

[52] Article 2, Council Directive 79/409/EEC, emphasis added.
[53] The ruling cited two important decisions on the aim of special protection (see ECJ 1994a: para. 20; and see ECJ 1993f: para. 17, 18).

member states were obligated, when designating SPAs, to "take account of all the criteria mentioned in Article 2 of the Birds Directive, which is general in scope, and, therefore, inter alia, of economic requirements" (para. 21). The ECJ's response came in one sentence: "Those arguments cannot be upheld" (para. 22). Further, the ECJ clarified its previous case law which had allowed for exceptions in the case of a general interest: "in the context of Article 4 of that Directive, considered as a whole, economic requirements cannot on any view correspond to a general interest superior to that represented by the ecological objective of the directive" (ECJ 1996f: para. 30).[54]

The *Lappel Bank* decision has far-reaching consequences. The significance is twofold. First, it illustrates that the Court will not hesitate to dismantle economic arguments posited by member state governments in favor of Community nature conservation measures. This ruling further develops the Court's case law, which places environmental protection as one of the "Community's essential objectives:" a finding the Court made in 1985 before Community decision-makers decided to do so a year later in the Single European Act (ECJ 1985a). Second, this ruling illustrates very clearly how Community environmental law can provide national environmental organizations with another opportunity for legal action when they have exhausted domestic legal routes, and that the ECJ will be favorable to such claims (e.g. Cichowski 1998).

Thus, it comes as little surprise that the ECJ's next decision involving the Habitats Directive held firm on this new interpretation of Article 4 and the limitations that nature conservation can place on economic activities. The *FCS* case (ECJ 2000c) was brought by the British Secretary of State on behalf of the First Corporate Shipping Company, who was demanding judicial review of a decision to list the Severn Estuary as an SAC under the Habitats Directive, and raised again the question of whether economic requirements could be taken into consideration when designating these sites. Again, the ECJ answered with a resounding, no, upholding the *Lappel Bank* decision. And similar to the earlier case, the *FCS* case also included two environmental NGOs, WWF and Avon Wildlife Trust, as formal interveners.

Another case involving NGO activism introduced the question of how far member states can derogate from protective measures for the purposes of recreational criteria – in particular, the capture and breeding of wild

---

[54] The two governments cited the Court's *Leybucht Dyke* decision (ECJ 1991e) that stated exceptions to Article 4 were possible for reasons of general interest, yet these were specifically related to reasons of public health and safety. The Case involved work within an SPA that was necessary to protect a fishing village at risk of flooding.

birds by bird fanciers. The preliminary reference arose in an action brought by two Belgian bird groups (ECJ 1996b) against the Belgian Regional Government of Wallonia (ECJ 1996b). The historical and legal background to this 1996 ruling is of particular significance as it illustrates the NGO–national court–ECJ relationship that can develop with the consequence of forcing member states to comply with EU regulations.

As outlined in the facts and background to the case, the national practice in question involves *tenderie*, the act of capturing small birds, especially finches, for the purposes of breeding and display. This activity has long been a pastime in the Belgian Region of Wallonia. It was this national practice that led the Belgium government in the late 1970s to submit a reservation regarding allowable national derogations to both the Bern Convention on the conservation of European wildlife and habitats in 1979 and also the Birds Directive.[55] Upon the entry into force of the Directive, the Wallonia regional government adopted an Order that allowed the regional authority to determine annually the number of species that could be captured. Subsequently, this regional law was the subject of Article 226 infringement proceedings, and in a 1987 decision the ECJ declared the law inadmissible under EU law (ECJ 1987b). In an attempt to correct the regulation, the Wallonia government adopted another Order in 1990 that provided greater specification of fixed numbers of wild birds that bird breeders could capture.[56]

Throughout this period, national authorities and environmental groups continued to scrutinize the regional authority, even without pressure from the EU to do so, and in 1991 the Belgian Conseil d'Etat annulled this regional law on the grounds that it infringed European obligations laid out in the Birds Directive.[57] A similar fate awaited three more legislative attempts by the regional government between 1991–1994.[58] This NGO–national court activism illustrates how litigants

---

[55] The Belgium government argued that "the capture of birds for recreational purposes . . . will continue in the Walloon region," albeit ostensibly "without prejudice to the Community provisions" (See Advocate General Fennelly's opinion, ECJ 1996b: 6775).

[56] On 13 September 1990, the Walloon Regional Executive adopted an Order on restocking by bird breeders permitting the capturing of fixed numbers of wild birds of each of 13 species, totalling 40, 580 specimens.

[57] This Order was annulled by the Conseil d'Etat by a judgment of 11 June 1991, several months after the capturing season was over.

[58] A similar fate awaited the restocking Orders of 26 September 1991 and 8 October 1992, (11) both annulled by judgments of 4 November 1994. In each case, the Conseil d'Etat held that the capture of the birds in question was prohibited under the Directive, that the Walloon region was obliged to prove that there was no other satisfactory solution, and that it had failed to do so. In particular, the Conseil d'Etat did not consider that capture in the wild was justified pending the outcome of studies on the feasibility of breeding which the Walloon Regional Executive had ordered. Similarly, the regional government

cooperating with national courts can attempt to force compliance with EU laws, despite the lack of national government action to do so.

Yet resolution of this ongoing litigation–legislation conflict came to a halt in 1994 when the Conseil d'Etat drew the ECJ back into the circle. Again, two bird groups were responsible for bringing the legal action against the regional authorities, and in this case the question focused very specifically on whether capture of wild birds for the purpose of breeding and reproduction in captivity constituted an "other satisfactory solution" within the allowable derogations of the Directive (Article 9), for the purposes of the bird fancier to replenish its breeding population. In its legal argumentation before the Court, the Belgian government argued that Article 9 of the Directive *did* authorize the capture of protected bird species to enable bird fanciers to stock their aviaries, where breeding and reproduction of the species in captivity is possible but not yet feasible on a large scale. The ECJ did not concur.

In line with the observations of both the Commission and the plaintiffs (the Belgian bird groups), the Court argued that while Article 9 of the Birds Directive and the previous case law (ECJ 1987c) clearly allow for the capture and sale of wild birds for recreational purposes in fairs and markets, this has limitations. Member states may derogate from the prohibition on killing or capturing protected species laid down in Article 5 "only if there is no other satisfactory solution," in which the Court has previously held that breeding and reproduction constitute such a solution (ECJ 1987b: para. 41). However, the Court argued that the capture of birds to replace captive bird populations that could successfully be bred in captivity, if it were not for limited facilities, could not be authorized by the Directive. Despite continued opposition by both the Belgian national and regional governments to have this practice regulated by EU law, the ECJ, activated by environmental activists and the willingness of a national court to engage the EU legal system, was able to shift the competence over this area of nature protection to the supranational level.

The final two cases are the only ones in the time period to ask the ECJ for an interpretation of Council Regulation 338/97/EEC, the Community rules implementing the Convention on International Trade in Endangered Species (CITES) requirements on regulating trade of protected species. Both cases involve criminal proceedings brought against individuals

adopted another Order on 14 July 1994, which was subsequently annulled by the Conseil d'Etat on 7 October 1994. The government persisted by adopting a new Order on 13 October 1994 authorizing the capture of the same quantities and species of birds as those covered by Annex XIII to the first Order (in the light of the need to supply bird breeders in order to accelerate the development of breeding). The Conseil d'Etat was quick to react and by judgment of 14 October 1994, ordered that implementation of this second Order be suspended immediately.

either buying or selling protected species. The *Nilsson* case (ECJ 2003b) originated from Swedish courts and the *Tridon* case (ECJ 2001c) was a preliminary reference from France. There are a variety of approaches that states can take to ensure the level of protection required, be it a complete ban on trade of protected species or differentiation based on whether the species is found in the wild versus those bred in captivity. Legal disputes result from these disparities. The *Tridon* case made clear that member states can prohibit the commercial exchange of all species, including those bred in captivity, included in Appendix I or Annex A. Similarly, in the *Nilsson* decision, the Court widened the scope of both the type of animals protected and also the process by which they are acquired, to include stuffed animals for display as well as such animals that might have been purchased more than fifty years ago. Yet the Court has left unanswered a key tension, between environmental protection and trade, as the *Tridon* decision leaves open that a total ban on commercial use of captive-born species can be limited in so far as it pertains to species imported from another member state, if there are other measures available that are less restrictive of trade and equally effective at species protection, a ruling and proportionality test that places trade in the favored position, much to the dislike of environmentalists striving to attain a global ban on trade in endangered species (Slot 2003: 175).

Opportunities for legislative action at the supranational level
I now turn to the policy impact of these rulings. As earlier suggested, unlike the area of social provisions, we might expect that the extent to which the Court's rulings expanded the scope of secondary legislation rather than a treaty provision, there is a greater possibility that member state governments can limit or reverse the impact of these rulings. Member states that are dissatisfied with the direction of the Court's rulings are able to change this outcome through secondary legislation alone, rather than attempting to revise the Court's interpretation of the Treaty. Even though both Treaty amendments and much of EU environmental legislation is subject to unanimity voting, the latter poses less of a difficulty to member state governments The following sections explore this dynamic by examining the impact of the ECJ's nature conservation litigation at both the EU and national level. I will focus on the main piece of nature conservation legislation in this time period, showing a connection to this earlier case law.

The Habitats Directive of 1992 was shaped by ECJ litigation.[59] In particular, its specifications and requirements for habitat protection

---

[59] Directive 92/43/EEC. See also Holder (1997) and Baldock (1992).

resulted from the significant difficulties member state governments experienced in implementing similar provisions of the Birds Directive. And even after the Habitats Directive was adopted we saw how the ECJ's rulings continued to clarify this legislation. Yet unlike the social provisions case law, member states have wielded greater power over the general trajectory of this policy development. In the social provisions case law analysis, we saw how the ECJ's interpretation of Article 141 empowered both the Commission and ordinary citizens by expanding the available rights discourse. The Court found a general principle of equality in Article 141 and over time, this treaty provision provided protection to a number of individuals and situations including pregnant workers and maternity leave.

The ECJ and the Commission have not wielded the same amount of policy power in the area of nature protection. While the Court's rulings pursuant to both Article 226 (infringement proceedings) and Article 234 (preliminary ruling procedure) have clearly expanded the scope of the EU competence in the area of nature conservation, member state governments have successfully constrained the impact of these rulings and ultimately retained control over the direction of the policy area. This outcome is traceable to the EU rule that is the subject of ECJ interpretation. Again, member states have only to pass subsequent legislation to correct or change an ECJ ruling that expanded the meaning and scope of the Birds Directive. Thus, it is not surprising that in the face of costly rulings that began to encroach on national government control over land use and habitat protection, member states acted.

The Habitats Directive was the target of this member state action. This piece of secondary legislation had been on the negotiating table for some time and was developed with the purpose of creating a "coherent European network of special areas of conservation" (Natura 2000).[60] The aim of the Directive is far-reaching and broadens the scope of nature conservation beyond the protection of birds and their habitats as provided by the Birds Directive: "to maintain or restore, at favorable conservation status, natural habitats and species of wild flora and fauna of Community interest" (Art 2 (2)). As the legislative proposal required member states to designate special areas of conservation far surpassing earlier regulations regarding bird habitat, the degree of member state control over

---

[60] The Commission proposed the Directive in 1988 and it received considerable negotiating from Environmental ministers in the Council until its passage in 1992 (CEC 1988). The Habitats Directive draws from the Convention on the Conservation of European Wildlife and Natural Habitats, Bern 1979, UKTS 56 (1982). The Directive is generally duplicative of this international agreement, yet provides for greater enforcement capabilities as a piece of binding EU law.

designation of special protection areas remained contentious throughout the negotiations (Wils 1994). In particular, the *Leybucht Dyke* decision involving the Birds Directive would eventually lead member states to amend the proposal in a direction that both changed the Directive and provided greater national level control over decisions to designate and alter protected habitat in the future (ECJ 1991e).

In this 1991 decision, the Court held that Article 4 (4) of the Birds Directive provides protection, regardless of national economic interests/costs, in designated habitats. At issue was the legality of a dyke that was being built in Germany in an area that had been designated as bird habitat. This decision diverged greatly from the argumentation of member state governments. In their argumentation before the Court, both the British and German governments argued that Article 4 must be interpreted to mean that the national authorities are to be given wide latitude in "weighing different interests", including social and economic concerns when deciding on potential changes to a designated area.[61] The Court did not concur. In particular, the ECJ was clear to state that the arguments put forth in the case regarding the economic interests of fisherman were "in principle incompatible with the requirement of the provision" (para. 24). This ruling represented the culmination of ECJ precedent that had slowly diminished the ability of member state governments to place economic priorities over nature conservation.[62] The message was heard loud and clear.

Member state retaliation came in the form of Article 7 of the Habitats Directive. In late 1991, following this ruling, certain member states, including the UK, proposed an amendment to the Commission's proposal for the Habitats Directive. In particular, Article 7 of this new Directive would bring the Birds Directive in line with the less restrictive exceptions that were proposed to be added to the text of Article 6(4) of the Habitats Directive (namely, that economic and social reasons could justify national government derogations from protection).[63] Scholars observe that these amendments effectively reversed the *Leybucht Dyke*

---

[61] See the decision at para. 13–15 for the UK argument. And para. 12 for the German argument.

[62] The Court took a similar position in various other judgments: ECJ (1987b) and ECJ (1987c).

[63] In its original version, Article 4 (4) of the Birds Directive read: "member states shall take appropriate steps to avoid pollution or deterioration of habitats or any disturbances affecting the birds, in so far as these would be significant having regard to the objectives of this Article." Article 7 of the Habitats Directive replaces the obligations arising from Article 4 (4) by the criteria laid out in Article 6(2), (3), and (4) of this new Directive. In particular, Article 6(4) states: "If, in spite of a negative assessment of the implications for the site and in the absence of alternative solutions, a plan or project must nevertheless be

decision (Baldock 1992: 144; Holder 1997: 1479).[64] Following the passage of the Directive in 1992, member states were given greater latitude to authorize development in special protection areas as laid down by both the Habitats Directive and also in reference to habitats and species still requiring special protection under the Birds Directive. Scholars have argued that as environmental law, the Habitats Directive is a "poor piece of legislation," to the extent that it creates large loopholes allowing development in protected areas (Nollkaemper 1997: 286). This legislative act shifts the control over national conservation measures back into the hands of member states.

Opportunities for action at the national level

How have these ECJ rulings and subsequent secondary legislation impacted nature conservation claims in the national legal systems? The Community's nature protection laws have consistently received inadequate attention and improper implementation at the national level (CEC 1993c). This is illustrated by the Court's extensive case law involving the Birds Directive. Yet even though this litigation has given the ECJ an opportunity to expand the scope of EU competence in this area, the Habitats Directive is an example of how member states can limit this impact. In the following two sections I explore the impact of the Habitats Directive on national policy change and the national litigating environment.

Implementation of the Habitats Directive

The Habitats Directive entered into force on June 1994. However, much like the Community's other nature conservation measure (the Birds Directive), member states were not fulfilling their obligations, even with the safeguard of greater national control over protected sites. The Commission published a report in 1998 citing that "a number of member states had not notified the Commission of all, or in some cases, any of the measures required to implement the Directive" (CEC 1999d: 22). The Commission continues to receive a large number of complaints concerning unsatisfactory implementation (of both the Birds Directive and now

---

carried out for imperative reasons of overriding public interest, including those of a social or economic nature . . . ." The second sub-paragraph of Article 6(4) does exclude "priority" habitat and species from this exception stating that loss can only be justified on grounds of "human health or public safety" (essentially the *Leybucht* criteria, see following footnote).

[64] Although it is interesting to note that the Habitats Directive also in effect codified the Court's *Leybucht* criteria in the case of priority habitats and species (e.g. endangered versus those habitats and species receiving general protection). This is evident in Article 6 (4) of the Directive justifying loss to these endangered habitats only in the case of human health and public safety.

the Habitats Directive). Beyond general failures to report national implementing measures, the main issues of contention remain the designation of protected areas and authorization of infrastructure projects in designated sites (Article 6 and Articles 12 to 16) (CEC 1999d: 22, 25).

Infringement proceedings have abounded as evidenced from a 1997 Commission report surveying the implementation of EU nature provisions (CEC 1998d). In a June 1997 ruling, the ECJ found that Greece had not fulfilled its obligations by failing to notify the Commission of implementing measures (ECJ 1997g). Similarly, Germany was the subject of Article 226 proceedings that resulted in a 1997 ECJ ruling (ECJ 1997h). Two cases involving Italy and Portugal were also referred to the Court, but were discontinued when the national governments implemented sufficient measures (CEC 1998d). Beyond these general failures to report, infringement proceedings continue against France for failure to implement Article 6 and against Finland for problems with the protection of areas in the Åland islands (CEC 1998d). Proceedings were also opened against Spain for failure to comply with Article 16 of the Habitats Directive. Problems have also involved the protection of species, as well as sites. The Commission has decided to bring infringement proceedings against Greece for endangerment to the loggerhead turtle, which is afforded protection under the Habitats Directive (CEC 1999d).

What national policy change that has evolved, has done so slowly and commenced in reaction to infringement proceedings (CEC 1999d). Following the earlier-mentioned 1997 ruling, Germany adopted new legislation in 1998. Further, Spain issued a new Royal Decree in June 1998 that attempted to bring national legislation in line with Article 16 on conditions for derogating from the obligations to protect certain species. Finland passed a decree in November 1998 with the intent of bringing national legislation in line with both the Birds Directive and the Habitats Directive, yet the Commission is still reviewing whether it protects the province that was earlier in question. However, some member states such as Greece have taken further cajoling from both the Commission and the Court to implement these measures: the ECJ's earlier ruling fell on deaf ears, and the Commission has since pursued the implementation of the ruling with Greek authorities on the basis of Article 228 (ex 171) of the Treaty (CEC 1999d: 22).

Another issue that has received considerable member state implementation error is the requirement to submit the lists of special protection areas. All member states failed to meet the June 1995 deadline. This failure is somewhat unsurprising given the fact that member states are still experiencing difficulties with the designation of special protection areas required by the Birds Directive, despite it being in force for almost twenty years (see CEC 1999d: 21).[65] It is also important to note that the designation of protected habitat under the Habitats Directive is still quite legally distinct from the Birds Directive and presents a greater challenge. Designation of SPAs under the Birds Directive is effectively a national-level decision whereas the Habitats Directive introduces a step-by-step approach involving both national authorities and the Commission with the aim of constructing a Community-wide nature protection network (Natura 2000). The initial designation of sites begins with a list compiled by member states that is then reviewed and approved by the Commission with the ultimate aim of creating Community-wide management plans (possibly even contractually binding ones) to protect a wide variety of both habitats and species (CEC 1998d). Failure to comply fully with this process has led the Commission to initiate infringement proceedings with almost all member state governments on this matter (CEC 1998d: 63; CEC 1999d: 22–23).

Generally, member states have been slow to implement the Habitats Directive. Failure to submit lists of proposed SPAs effectively stops the forward movement of the Natura 2000 network laid down by Directive 92/43/EEC (CEC 1999d: 25). The Commission, working with the ECJ, has valiantly pushed forward to try to rectify this situation (as illustrated through the infringement proceedings). Further, the Commission has also begun to maintain a very strict policy regarding the grant of Community funding for conservation of sites in light of these violations (CEC 1999d: 25). As we have seen with both the Birds Directive and subsequently the Habitats Directive, member states are hesitant to let the EU regulate certain aspects of nature conservation (in particular, designation of protected areas) and they have been successful at retaliating against EU organizations that have reduced member state control over these decisions (e.g. the ECJ's *Leybucht Dyke* decision and subsequently the amended exceptions allowable under the Habitats Directive). In the next section, we will explore another avenue of national level impact: that

---

[65] Article 4 of the Birds Directive pertaining to the designation of SPAs was the subject of five infringement proceedings in 1998 alone. The Commission continues with Article 228 proceedings against Spain to secure full implementation of the Court's earlier Santoña Marshes decision. Proceedings against France in connection with the Seine estuary continue (ECJ 1999d) and the Commission has referred two more cases against France involving the Marais Poitevin (ECJ 1999e) and the Basses Corbiès/Vingrau (ECJ 2000e). Further, proceedings continuing against France in connection with the Baie de Canche and the Plaitier d'Oye, the Plaine des Maures and the Basse Vallée de l'Aude. Finally, the Commission has also brought an action against the Netherlands in connection with the Waddenzee area (Case C-63/98, but it did not end in a judgment) (CEC 1999d: 23).

is, how national courts and individuals are accepting or rejecting these new claims.

National litigation and new legal claims

While the Habitats Directive clearly represents an expansion in the scope of EU nature laws (from birds to all species of flora and fauna and habitats deemed worthy of protection) and perhaps an attempt at Community control over the future direction of conservation – the real national policy effect of the Directive has been the expansion in member state control over opting out of conservation regulations (e.g. exemptions laid out in Article 6(4), economic and social reasons). However, while national policy makers retain control over how they want to implement a directive into the national legal system, individuals acting through national courts and ultimately the ECJ can subsequently alter the meaning and scope of these national laws. For example, in the area of social provisions, Spanish courts expanded the protection provided for pregnant workers by interpreting minimalist national legislation (that had transposed the Pregnancy Directive) in line with more expansive ECJ pregnancy case law and even beyond the original scope or meaning of the Pregnancy Directive.[66] Similarly, in the area of nature protection we saw how the ECJ in coordination with national courts and national environmental organizations was able to expand both the meaning and scope of the Birds Directive and subsequently upgrade national laws that were not in conformity.[67]

Although not the main focus of the case, the earlier discussed *Lappel Bank* decision had implications for how the British courts applied the Habitats Directive to national law. Again, the controversy arose when the Royal Society for the Protection Birds (RSPB) contested the decision by the British Secretary of State of the Environment to authorize the exclusion of Lappel Bank (an area containing species and habitat qualifying for protection) from SPA designation for the purposes of development. In its argumentation before the ECJ, the British government stated that Article 6 (4) of the Habitats Directive must be interpreted as allowing economic considerations to be a part of the initial classification decisions, as well as the stage of derogation since "to hold otherwise would be to impose an unnecessary administrative burden on a member state" (Holder 1997: 1471). The ECJ did not concur. Instead, the Court argued that while Article 6(4) clearly justified development in protected areas for economic reason, this exception did not extend to the original

---

[66] See discussion in Chapter 3. [67] See discussion earlier in the chapter.

classification of the designated land. The ECJ's interpretation of the Habitats Directive essentially means that even though a member state might plan to develop an area for economic reasons permitted by the Directive, it must *first* designate the site as an SPA if it meets certain ornithological criteria, linking it to the European network of protected areas (Natura 2000).

This interpretation was radically different than the position taken by both the British government and the judges in two British courts that heard the case before it finally reached the House of Lords on final appeal (and subsequently reached the ECJ by way of a preliminary reference).[68] Prior to this ruling, national courts and local authorities agreed that economic considerations could play a role in designating sites. Unfortunately, the Lappel Bank area could not be saved despite this decision (due to development going forward while the case was on appeal). However, authorization of developments in the UK would in the future take place in the shadow of this ruling (Harte 1997: 178). Yet from a comparative perspective, the ECJ ruling is not so radically different than practices found in other member states. The ECJ's *Lappel Bank* decision is largely in line with the logic German courts apply when assessing planning decisions (Winter 1997: 179). The ECJ's ruling in this case in effect upgraded the British courts' minimalist interpretation of the Habitats Directive.

However, other cases remain untouched by the arm of the European legal system, and thus illustrate how both member states and national courts can retain control over the application of EU nature laws in the national legal system. In a similar case in 1999, a British Court of Session held that the stage of designating Special Areas of Conservation (SACs), as required by the Habitats Directive, could involve taking into account pre-existing recreation areas in limiting the boundaries of the

---

[68] The RSPB had originally filed for an application for judicial review with the Divisional Court, Queen's Bench Division on 8 July 1994. This was refused. The Court of Appeal similarly rejected the appeal against this judgment on 18 August 1994. On final appeal, the House of Lords referred a set of questions to the ECJ regarding the interpretation of both the Birds Directive and the Habitats Directive so that it might resolve the dispute (ECJ 1996f: para. 8, Advocate General Fennelly's opinion). The RSPB's involvement with the Lappel Bank area actually preceded these cases, as the group in 1990 had made a request for judicial review regarding an environmental impact assessment carried out by the government for the area (*R v Swale*, Queen's Bench Division, 5 February 1990). The group claimed the granting of planning permission to the Medway Ports Authority to develop Lappel Bank was in violation of the Town and Country Planning Regulation 1988 (which implemented Council Directive 85/337/EEC on environmental impact assessments). The court did not concur and further, the national judge's decision only gave side reference to the Community law behind the national law in question.

designated area.[69] The issue at hand involved the development of a funicular railway at Caingorm, Britian's largest ski area. The applicants in the case, the environmental groups WWF and RSPB, along with disputing the required consultation for the development, also argued that the initial boundaries of the SAC had been inaccurate by taking account of the skiing facilities (in particular, economic and recreational criteria): an act that was incompatible with the Directive. The Court of Session did not agree. Instead, the British court held that while the boundaries of an SAC must be based on ornithological criteria, in its view, such criteria could involve taking account of the impact of a pre-existing ski area on the habitats in the designation decision. Clearly, this national court ruling is in complete disregard of the ECJ's *Lappel Bank* decision: a ruling that interpreted the Habitats Directive in a way that made economic and social reasons inadmissible in the criteria utilized to designate protected areas. However, as the *Lappel Bank* case also illustrates, the tenacity of national environmental organizations may prove to ultimately change the outcome of this national court decision.

The recent development of the A20 Motorway (Baltic Sea Motorway) in Germany provides another illustration of how EU nature laws are engaged at the national level. The project at issue involved the construction of a motorway of approximately 300 km that will create an east–west link connecting the Baltic Seat ports of Rostock and Stralslund. This project is part of a larger transportation plan (involving 17 projects) and has been given priority by the German government for the reasons of boosting the economy in the Meklenbur – Western Pomerania (CEC 1996b: para 1.3). The proposed A20 motorway would transverse two protected areas in Germany: the Trebel and Recknitz Valley and the Valley of the River Peene. Both areas were home to many rare and endangered birds and had previously been designated as protected areas under both the Birds Directive and subsequently the Habitats Directive. In order to build the proposed motorway, Germany invoked Article 6 (4) of the Directive and fulfilled the three conditions that would allow the plan to move forward despite the protected designation. First, Germany found that no other alternative measures existed; second, they had planned adequate compensatory measures and finally, they submitted a request to the Commission for an opinion on the compatibility of the projects with the Habitats Directive.

The Commission's ultimate decision to approve the development through both protected valleys reportedly did not come without some

---

[69] *Re the Petition of WWF-UK & the Royal Society for the Protection of Birds* (1999) 1 CMLR 1021.

conflict (CEC 1995b).[70] Yet the logic behind the Commission's opinions seemed to suggest that Community nature laws could be balanced
against, and ultimately deemed secondary to, "imperative reasons of
overriding public interest," of which high unemployment was included
(CEC 1995b: para. 4.2–4.6; CEC 1996b: para. 4.2). This was the practical application of the exemption that member states had been careful to
insert into the Habitats Directive: a reaction to the ECJ's extensive case
law that had consistently expanded EU nature protection in spite of
conflicting national economic and recreational interests. Yet the question
of whether Article 6 (4) requires member states to balance economic and
ecological interests remains unanswered, as it still remains sufficiently
unclear whether a "reason of overriding public interest" must be considered apart from or in connection with the magnitude of the effects on the
ecosystem.[71] Much like the vague provisions included in the Birds
Directive, this question will no doubt be the subject of future national
and ECJ litigation.

Further, it is interesting to explore the impact of these EU nature laws
in member states that have comparatively strong nature conservation
regulations. Have they implemented EU law in line with more expansive
ECJ interpretations? Or are these national practices similarly the subject
of derogations from a high standard of protection? Generally, the Danish
government has stood out as a leader in timely and complete implementation of EU environmental laws. Indeed, public debate in Denmark
over the last few decades has criticized EU regulations as presenting a
threat to the potentially high-level of protection embodied in national
legislation.[72] Further, the near absence of both national and ECJ case
law (either Article 234 or Article 226) questioning Danish environmental
law for failing to meet the requirements of EU law, would suggest there
have been few implementation errors.[73] Despite this comparatively
strong record, Denmark does not have a perfect level of compliance in

---

[70] The Commission originally did not approve the proposed plan through the Peene Valley,
but ultimately authorized the project on 12 December 1995 after Germany revised the
plans. See also "Spat over Motorway Construction Programme in East Germany"
European Report, 22 April 1995.

[71] See Nollkaemper (1997) for an in-depth discussion of the limitation and legal ambiguities of balancing economic interests in the Habitats Directive.

[72] This issue was often at the center of public discussions surrounding the Danish referenda
of 1986, 1992, 1993 and 1998 (see Pagh 1999: 301).

[73] As discussed ealier in the chapter, there were no preliminary references from Denmark
before 1998. One case involving EU waste laws has since been filed (Case 209/98
Contractors Association, Waste Section v City Council of Copenhagen). Further, there have
been few ECJ rulings pursuant to Article 226 involving Denmark, other than those
pertaining to conflicts arising between more protective Danish environmental regulations
and EU free trade rules (e.g. *Danish Bottles* case).

the area of nature conservation, especially on the issue of special protection areas.

Despite the 1981 deadline for the full implementation of the Birds Directive (including Article 4 on SPAs), designation of an SPA was not made legally binding in Danish law until 1994. Prior to this, Danish authorities were given considerable latitude in allowing development in previously designated areas and even did so despite Community officials' awareness of the violations.[74] Further, without a legally binding instrument, national environmental groups systematically encountered difficulties in filing claims before national courts.[75] Finally in 1994, following considerable public outcry and complaints arising from a bridge project involving two major bird areas, national implementation improved (Pagh 1999: 309). Designation of SPAs became legally binding through a Statutory Order (No 407, 1994) and the Danish government implemented a very strict procedure for intervention in SPAs. While this may bode well for future projects, Denmark's implementation record continues to be less than perfect. Danish authorities have since wrongfully interpreted Article 6(4) of the Habitats Directive to justify approval of multiple projects that encroach protected areas (for economic reasons), without engaging the Commission in the consultation and approval procedure (as mentioned in the German case above) that is mandated by the Habitats Directive.[76]

[74] One example involves the Danish authorities original attempts to comply with the Birds Directive. In 1983, (already two years past the deadline), the Danish government submitted a list of preliminary designation of SPAs to the Commission. In 1985, the Commission informed Denmark that this was insufficient to implement the Directive because it lacked a legally binding instrument and only provided general guidance to local authorities. The Danish government responded arguing that a final designation would be submitted, but one that only included minor revisions. However, no final designation was adopted. And in the following years, the Danish Nature Appeal Board authorized numerous construction projects in certain SPAs for economic and recreational reasons (Pagh 1999: 309). This decision was based on the exceptions laid out in Article 2 of the Birds Directive, but was clearly inconsistent with the ECJ's interpretation of this provision (e.g. *Santoña Marshes* ECJ 1993f and *Lappel Bank* ECJ 1996f).

[75] Environmental organizations had attempted to bring legal proceedings invoking the Birds Directive against a decision by local authorities to approve a bridge project that would span two protected areas, the Öresunds Bridge. The Eastern High Court dismissed the case in 1994 on the grounds that the allegations were political and not judicial (e.g. not sufficiently precise). See discussion in Pagh (1999: 310).

[76] This includes a 1995 decision to authorize a shipping company to route a high speed ferry through an SPA. Also, in 1997, the Danish Environmental Protection Agency (EPA) approved the expansion of the Tune Airport despite close proximity to two SPAs. However, following a complaint to the Commission, the Danish EPA agreed to re-evaluate the decision on the Tune Airport after admitting that it had forgotten to take into account the procedures laid out in the Habitats Directive (CEC 1999d).

Conclusions

The analyses in this chapter illustrate that nature conservation is an evolving area of EU law. National environmental organizations, national courts, member state governments and EU organizations have all contributed to what today is an expanding set of EU rules governing national environmental regulations. Institutional evolution in this area began with the activism of national and transnational environmental groups demanding European-wide solutions to deteriorating national wildlife and habitats. Responding to this political pressure, member state governments began to develop at least some European-wide protective measures to address these concerns. Despite this attempt at Community regulation, the pervasive non-compliance that ensued reflected the true intention of national authorities to maintain control over this sensitive and sometimes costly national issue. The judicial rulemaking of the ECJ would begin to change this.

Activated by environmental groups utilizing both the Commission's complaint procedure and legal action in national courts, the ECJ over time has come to expand the precision, scope and enforceability of EU environmental law. Yet these rulings have been met with national government opposition and retaliation. Due to the fact that these rulings involved secondary legislation, member state governments exercised a greater ability to reverse costly decisions by adopting subsequent secondary legislation (e.g. the Habitats Directive). The immediate national consequence has been to weaken Community control over national conservation decisions.

Comparing these findings to the analyses in Chapter 3, the impact of the Court's judicial rulemaking suggests a generalizable pattern. First, EU rulings can provide litigants with new opportunities before national courts to pressure for and achieve national policy change to secure compliance with EU laws. For example, in the area of social provisions, pregnant workers in Spain were able to use national courts to secure protection that was not currently provided in Spanish legislation (a minimalist transposition of the Pregnancy Directive). Similarly, national environmental organizations in Italy utilized national courts to bring legal action against local authorities with the consequence of dismantling national hunting practices that were not in conformity with the Birds Directive. Second, the extent to which these disputes involve vague aspects of EU law in which the Court subsequently provides clarity, these rulings can expand the precision, scope and enforceability of EU law. The ECJ's case law in the area of both pregnancy rights and nature conservation had this effect.

Third, the subsequent supranational and national policy impact of these decisions is acutely linked to the legal basis of the ruling. While both legal domains illustrate how expansive ECJ rulings can provide the opportunities for subsequent legislative action, the legal domains varied in the relative power of member state governments to control the trajectory of these policy developments. In the area of gender equality, ECJ rulings that involved treaty based principles enhanced the power of EU organizations *vis-à-vis* member state governments in subsequent policy evolution. Despite the costly impact of numerous rulings in this legal domain, there was a higher degree of difficulty associated with reversing such a decision. On the other hand, in the area of nature conservation where rulings involved the interpretation of secondary legislation, member state governments were quick to retaliate against a particularly expansive ECJ ruling by altering a subsequent legislative proposal to reverse the decision.

Finally, the enforcement and utilization of ECJ rulings by national courts and a willingness of national courts to engage the EU legal system highlights how this policy trajectory can change despite member state opposition. As evidenced in both policy domains, ECJ rulings can enhance the power of national courts in their own legal system *vis-à-vis* the executive and legislative branches by providing the opportunity for review of national legislation. It is this action that ultimately can change the direction of both national and EU policy, despite the original intentions of national governments. The Court's preliminary rulings involving the Birds Directive are a case in point.

It is through this dynamic process that member states have discovered that over time EU rules have expanded in precision, scope and enforceability. EU social provisions have become less intergovernmental as policy decisions are shifted away from national government executives. Certain treaty provisions are established and through the actions of individuals and organizations these rights are expanded in a direction that leads those governed by these rules down a path that becomes increasingly hard to change (see Pierson 1996). On the other hand, in the area of nature protection, member state governments have diminished or at least delayed the impact of expansive rulings. While such intervention has minimized the immediate policy consequences of these rulings and perhaps slowed the process of institutionalization, the general trajectory is not easily reversed once the rules are created that are opportunities for action. The cycle begins again. Through the action of litigants, national courts and the ECJ, these EU rules can be changed leading to subsequent action.

As argued, litigation can be the opportunity for action, yet once mobilized these individuals and groups can exert their own impact on these opportunity structures. In the next two chapters, I switch focus and examine mobilization as the starting point of the analysis. How does institutionalization take place through mobilization?

Part II

Institutionalization through mobilization

5   Women's rights activists: informal to formal organizing

"Europe, an opportunity for women; women, an opportunity for Europe."[1]

Transnational activists have become an integral part of European policy making. Public interest advocates were not direct participants in the making of the European Union (EU) in the 1950s and public interest policies were not on the agenda. As we have seen from the previous chapters, today this same supranational space possesses jurisdiction over an ever-expanding array of public policies. The EU possesses a growing net of rules governing national social provisions and environmental protection. In Chapters 3 and 4, I illustrated how this process of institutionalization could occur through litigation and how the rules over time have become more binding, precise and expanded in scope. Yet equally important to this policy evolution is the fact that today national executives are no longer alone in this space. Instead, public interests – as represented by non-governmental organizations (NGOs), legal consultancy firms and individual activists, to name just a few – are equally present in EU policy processes. As this litigation and legislative action provided new political opportunities for action, individuals and groups answered the call, shifting their mobilization to this newly forming supranational space.

The causes and effects of this transnational mobilization are the focus of this chapter and Chapter 6. In particular, I focus on how institutionalization can take place through mobilization. As argued in Chapter 2, we might expect this activism to follow a generalizable pattern. As these EU political opportunities afford greater formal access and create new social spaces for public interests, we might expect a general growth in the number of groups and activists in EU policy processes. Further, I hypothesized that as these political opportunities increase in formality and magnitude, we might expect this transnational mobilization to over

---

[1] A phrase that gained widespread usage by women's organizations both at the national and EU level in the 1990s (CEC 1992: 5).

time shift from discrete individual action to more formal collective group action.

Yet once mobilized, activists can subsequently alter these opportunities. In particular, we might expect activists to be more successful at changing these EU rules and procedures, to the extent to which they utilize more conventional tactics (lobbying, framing and litigation) and the greater the similarity between these strategies and pre-existing movement strategies. It is through this process that institutionalization can occur. As public interest mobilization becomes more permanent in a given EU policy domain and the EU policy process becomes more reliant on this presence, we might expect increasing levels of public inclusion and that over time the EU policy domain will become less intergovernmental.

In the following analysis, I examine the development of transnational mobilization in the area of social provisions, focusing on the mobilization of women activists. The chapter provides a historical analysis of this transnational mobilization focusing on the interaction between EU political opportunities and activists in three time periods: the 1970s and before, the 1980s and the 1990s through 2003. By tracing this development over time, we are able to examine how legal and political opportunities might shape this action, and also how this action may have led to the expansion of EU rules and procedures that subsequently were opportunities for greater inclusion and mobilization in the future.

The 1970s and before: the early years of mobilization

In the 1950s, 1960s and 1970s the EU policy arena was in its infancy. Following the signing of the Treaty of Rome in 1957, domestic pressure groups would begin to look upward to an increasingly important set of EU institutions and organizations. Yet at this stage, this unprecedented form of supranational governance was primarily an economic agreement, with social issues remaining a distant necessity. At the same time, this time period witnessed the global rise of the feminist movement and as a result women's rights were becoming an increasingly salient issue in domestic policymaking (Katzenstein and Mueller 1987). This domestic activism would soon begin to find a home in this newly forming supranational space.

Litigation and legislative action as political opportunities for mobilization

We begin by examining the available opportunities for transnational mobilization in this time period. As discussed, the European Court of

Justice (ECJ) had just issued its first equality ruling in the 1970s, the *Defrenne I* decision (ECJ 1971). While the 1970s elicited the fewest number of preliminary rulings in this policy domain compared to other decades, the litigation in this time period was legendary. The landmark *Defrenne* decisions were directly attributable to the tenacity and dedication of a feminist activist, Belgian labor lawyer, Elaine Vogel-Polsky, who in the late 1960s saw Article 141 (ex Art 119) as a stepping stone to advancing women's rights.[2] As discussed in Chapter 3, the *Defrenne II* decision in 1976 created the direct effect of Article 141 enabling women throughout Europe to bring discrimination claims before national courts and subsequently the third decision in 1978 developed a doctrine stating equality was a fundamental EU right (*Defrenne II*, ECJ 1976a; *Defrenne III* ECJ 1978).[3]

These rulings provided an important opportunity structure for women throughout the Union by creating new rights that effectively gave them an opportunity to not only change national policies but to begin to play a role in the Court's subsequent expansion of EU equality law (Cichowski 2004). Prior to these rulings, Article 141 remained the only legal instrument or opportunity for equality claims. Further, the Treaty provision merely placed duties on member state governments: a general requirement to apply the principle of equal pay that all member states had failed to implement by the December 1962 deadline (CEC 1963: 58). Both the Commission and subsequently the member state governments attempted to give some application to Article 141 in the early 1960s by clarifying the principle of equal pay and establishing precise targets and deadlines.[4]

---

[2] In 1967, Vogel-Polsky published an article in a Belgian legal journal suggesting that individuals should be able to utilize Article 141 before national courts against member states who had failed to implement the principle into national law (L/Article 119 du traité de Rome – peut-il ê considéré comme self-executing? *Journal des Tribunaux*, 15 April 1967). Vogel-Polsky began looking for a test case and with little interest from the trade unions, ultimately found her case in the private sector: a stewardess, Gabrielle Defrenne, employed by Sabena Airlines (interview as cited in Hoskyns 1996: 68).

[3] For a more detailed discussion of this case law see Chapter 3 and Cichowski (2004).

[4] The Commission issued a Recommendation in July 1960 that offered an interpretation of the principle of equal pay that was in line with the International Labor Convention 100. That is, it surpassed the "minimalist" interpretation of Article 141 being favored by some member states, and instead focused on the various forms of direct discrimination in pay, such as in collective agreements and administrative instruments (CEC 1960: 46–7). The Commission Recommendation asked for notification of implementing measures by July 1961. Not a single member state met the deadline. The Council subsequently issued a Resolution, at the insistence of France who refused to move forward to the second stage of the common market unless some action on equal pay was taken (again, France felt its own equal pay regulations would cause unfair competition to their business sector if other member states did not possess similar provisions) (CEC 1962: 8–10). The Resolution set a 1964 deadline.

However, these attempts proved futile, with Article 141 appearing to lack an enforceable right and with little incentive for effective implementation.[5]

The Court's rulings of the 1970s would begin to change this. By creating a new set of EU equality rights, these judicial decisions provided women with a new supranational political opportunity structure to demand protection from discrimination. Further, these new political opportunity structures were particularly compatible with the litigation strategies already being pursued by women's organizations and activists (O'Connor 1980; Harlow and Rawlings 1992). Vogel-Polsky's strategic activism in the *Defrenne* cases is an example of this and also the subsequent Article 234 equality cases that were supported by national equality agencies, such as the British Equal Opportunities Commission (EOC) or Danish trade unions.[6]

The data illustrate this trend clearly, as the 1970s was not a period in which associations or NGOs or even groups of litigants were bringing claims. Table 5.1 includes data on the type of litigants in social provisions preliminary rulings between 1971 and 2003. During the 1970s, the ECJ decisions pursuant to preliminary references each involved only a single litigant. That said, it is important to note that this category can be misleading, in that behind this single litigant there may be strategic mobilization by an individual or a group to use the Court to pressure for policy reform. Interviews and historical documents reveal this information and I have included it throughout this book as available. The three *Defrenne* decisions of the 1970s are an example, as again these were test cases brought by an activist Belgian labor lawyer. This begins to change by the next decade, with 42 percent of the cases either involving women who joined together to bring a similar claim or an association directly involved in the case (these were all social protection non-governmental organizations). As illustrated by the data, the number of decisions skyrocketed with 193 preliminary rulings in the final time period, yet the

---

[5] The Council Resolution stated that implementation of the equal pay principle would be carried out in three stages: that wage differences of more than 15 percent would be decreased to that figure by 30 June 1962, that more than 10 percent would be corrected by 30 June 1963 and that "all discrimination would be abolished by 31 December 1964" (CEC 1963: 58). Subsequent Commission reports revealed the difficulties that all member states experienced in complying with this timetable (CEC 1963: 53). Despite some national level action, by the mid sixties there was a waning "political will" to harmonize social policy. Scholars observe that even France was less active on the issue of equal pay, as the threat of competition distortion paled in comparison to the newly realized profits realized by French industry in a liberalized market (Hoskyns 1996: 64).

[6] See discussion in Chapter 3. For example, the pregnancy case law including the *Boyle* decision (ECJ 1998a) and the *Pedersen* decision (1998b).

Table 5.1 *Social provisions Article 234 preliminary rulings by type of litigant bringing the case, 1971–2003*

	Number of cases (as a percentage)			
	1 litigant	2 or more litigants	Association/NGO litigants	Total cases
1970–1979	6 (100%)	0	0	6
1980–1989	24 (58%)	8 (20%)	9 (22%)	41
1990–2003	133 (69%)	51 (26%)	9 (5%)	193
Total cases	163 (68%)	59 (25%)	18 (8%)	240

Note:
The Association/NGO litigant category included NGOs, trade unions and equality agencies. The cases in this last category came from the following countries Denmark, France, Germany, Netherlands, Spain, Sweden and the UK, with 10 out of the 18 cases alone involving associations/NGOs from Denmark.
Source: Data compiled by the author from European Communities. 2003. *CELEX Data Base.* Brussels: Office for Official Publications of the European Communities. http://europa.eu.int/celex/htm/celex_en.htm.

number of multiple litigants and associations did slightly shrink from the previous decade (26% multiple litigants and 5% association litigants). Interestingly however, this later category now expanded beyond NGOs to include labor unions and also national equality agencies (such as the EOC in the United Kingdom and the Equality Ombudsman in Sweden, who were bringing claims against their own governments).

At the same time, the 1970s marked the beginning of EU legislative action in this area, and a Brussels-based infrastructure to support this policy expansion. As we have seen, the Court's rulings and these legislative advancements were linked and together they began to develop a strong net of political opportunities for women at the EU level. The Court's *Defrenne I* judgment in 1971 made a clear argument why Union policymakers needed to expand the scope of Article 141 in order to achieve its objectives. A few years later the Commission presented a series of legislative proposals that attempted to achieve these ends. These proposals formed part of the first Social Action Program that was adopted in 1974. While the program served more as a "public relations exercise" to lift waning public support for the Union, the program emphasized the importance of equality and gave the Commission the opportunity to present its proposals on women's rights (Vallance and Davies 1986: 75). Subsequently, while member state governments were negotiating and adopting the Equal Pay Directive (1975)[7] and the Equal Treatment Directive (1976),[8] the *Defrenne II* case was working its way through the Belgian court system. The Court's *Defrenne II* decision (1976) paralleled these legislative advancements by giving further meaning to EC equality law, yet as discussed in Chapter 3 this ruling far surpassed member state intentions by creating directly enforceable rights: an EU political opportunity structure that would soon be utilized by women against their own governments.

The Social Security Directive (1979)[9] was also influenced by the Court's jurisprudence. The *Defrenne I* decision argued that statutory social security schemes were outside the scope of Article 141, yet suggested that occupational schemes were not. The Commission regarded this as untenable and thus included social security in the initial drafts of equality legislation (Hoskyns 1996: 99). Together, these legislative advancements in the 1970s created a body of European equality law that in theory provided a comprehensive ban on sex discrimination in the workplace. Through ECJ precedent and EU legislative action, the rules and procedures that served as opportunities for sex discrimination claims increased in both formality and magnitude.

The Commission also began developing specific policy units in Brussels during this time period in order to support these new legislative developments. In 1976, the Commission established the Women's Information Service as part of DG Information and Culture. This office was a progressive step for its time, as it represented the first official organization housing an office specifically targeting women and promoting information exchange between national women's organizations and EU organizations (Deshormes 1992). It gave women's organizations formal access to an EU organization. In the same year, DG Employment and Social Affairs created a Women's Bureau, a policymaking unit that was a direct product of the women civil servants and employment experts that were brought together to negotiate and develop the Equal Treatment Directive. Although this office did not offer as much access to women's groups as the Women's Information Service, many of the inhabitants of this space, although staff members, were themselves feminist activists.[10]

Finally, the 1979 election for the European Parliament (EP) also represented a significant development in new opportunities. This marked the

---

[7] Council Directive 75/117/EEC.   [8] Council Directive 76/207/EEC.
[9] Council Directive 79/7/EEC.
[10] The Bureau was headed by Jacqueline Nonon and had a very small staff. Its main functions were to oversee the implementation of the Equal Treatment Directive, monitor the European Social Fund and develop future equality initiatives. Interview with former Head of the Equality Unit in DG Employment and Social Affairs, Brussels, March 2000.

first open elections and the percentage of women elected as Members of the European Parliament (MEPs) jumped from 5.5 percent in the preceding delegation to 16 percent.[11] The mere increase in the number of women parliamentarians does not necessarily presume a greater emphasis on women's issues. However, there is sufficient evidence in the case of the European Parliament that the women elected in 1979 would prove instrumental in keeping women's issues on the EU agenda. For example, almost immediately following the election an *ad hoc* Women's Committee was created and its research and statistical reports on the situation of women would be essential to future legislative action.[12] Further, greater attention was given to women's issues through parliamentary questions and resolutions: the number of questions raised in the EP relating to women's issues went from 12 in 1978 to 45 in 1979 (Vallance and Davies 1986: 137). The women elected during this time period would begin creating a new European social space for women by keeping equality issues on the policy agenda.

Mobilization, institutionalization and political opportunities for public inclusion

In response to the growing number of EU political opportunities in the area of social provisions, transnational social interests began knocking on doors in Brussels. In the late 1950s and 1960s, thirteen groups became permanent actors in the newly forming European policy community. Over half the groups were trade unions, with the remaining few representing particular political or regional interests. Table 5.2 displays each of these organizations along with their founding dates and type of organization. Unsurprisingly, given the time period and the lack of EU political opportunities for women before the 1970s, these organizations had little involvement with women's issues during their founding years (the European Union of Women (EUW), established in 1953 is a noticeable exception). However, all of these organizations have over time become involved with EU women's policy in some capacity and have utilized EU opportunity structures to promote their policy agendas. For example, the European

---

[11] CEC (1979). Beyond record percentages of women MEPs, these numbers were also significant, as all member states send a greater proportion of women to the European Parliament than to their national parliaments. This trend continued, as in 1984 Denmark had 25 percent women in the Folkering and 37 percent women MEPs; the UK has 3 percent in the House of Commons and 15 percent in the European Parliament, and even Greece which elected comparatively few women MEPs, 8 percent, still exceeds its numbers in the national parliament, 4 percent. See Vallance and Davies (1986) for further discussion of women in the European Parliament.

[12] Examples of these reports are *Reports of Enquiry, European Parliament Working Documents* (EP 1984) and the *Maij-Weggen Report* (EP 1981).

Table 5.2 *Transnational organizations in the area of social provisions by organizational type and founding date, 1950–1969*

Organization	Founding date
Trade unions	
PSI/ISP	1951
SETA-UITA	1956
EFA	1958
EEBWW	1958
COPA	1958
IPTT	1967
Regional/Local authorities	
CEMR (IULA)	1951
EFCT	1963
Women's rights/Family/Social welfare/Human rights	
ICSW	1928
FIDH	1922
EUW	1953
Religious	
OCIPE	1956
Development	
FORUM	1964

Source: Data compiled by author from *Directory of Pressure Groups in the EU*, Philip and Gray (1996), *Directory of Interest Groups* (Luxembourg: Office for Official Publications of the European Communities, 1996) and *Consultation, the European Commission and Civil Society* (European Commission, online database http://www.europa.eu.int/comm/civil_society/coneccs/start.cfm?CL=en).

Committee of Food, Catering and Allied Workers' Union (SETA-UITA) and the European Federation of Agricultural Workers' Union (EFA) engage in lobbying DG Employment and Social Affairs on the equal rights of workers or participating in the Social Affairs Committee of the European Parliament. Further, often this participation resulted in the creation of new opportunity structures. For example, the women's committee of the Committee of Agricultural Organizations in the EU (COPA) was instrumental in the adoption of the 1986 Directive on equal treatment for the self-employed, which created a new set of EU rights for workers.[13]

[13] Council Directive 86/613/EEC. The women's committee of COPA has been strong since the mid 1970s (CEC 1978: 16). They held a European seminar in 1982 from which they produced a report entitled "The Legal and Social Position of Women in Agriculture"

Further, it is interesting to note how well-established international organizations shifted their focus to the European level, as the EU became a noticeable supranational actor. For example, Public Service International (PSI) which is a large and influential international organization (its membership boasts 20 million workers, from 436 unions in 128 countries) has a women's committee and while its policy activities are clearly wider than the EU, it cites itself as "an important player" in EU policy processes (PSI 1996: 435). Similarly, the Council of European Municipalities and Regions (CEMR) was established in 1951 as the European regional section of a larger international union, the International Union of Local Authorities (IULA) as a result of a need for more concentrated cooperation amongst European national sections. The CEMR contains five specialist committees, one of which deals with women elected representatives of local and regional authorities. Both of these organizations strengthened their presence in Brussels, as the EU provided new access points to influence policy outcomes (CEMR 1996; IULA 1996).

Finally, this time period did see the foundation of one transnational women's organization: the European Union of Women. This group is composed of women in elected positions (members of parliament, local councils, etc.) from the Christian Democratic and Conservative political parties. While pursuing the aim to "encourage women to take their place in the decision-making process as elected representatives," the Christian "spiritual and moral values" underlying this endeavor for equal opportunities were measurably different than the claims made by the women's organizations of the 1970s (EUW 1996: 348). Instead, their policy objectives were concerned generally with the "conservation of human dignity and freedom" and in particular, increasing the political representation of women (EUW 1996: 348).

The mid to late 1970s represented another growth period in the founding of transnational organizations. The data in Table 5.3 illustrate that between 1971 and 1979, fourteen new groups began focusing their lobbying efforts at the supranational level. The growth rate doubled from the previous two decades. The policy-making capacity and competence of EU organizations was expanding and these groups heard the message loud and clear. Similar to the previous decades, these groups were primarily trade unions and religious organizations. However, the groups in this period placed a higher priority on their direct commitment and involvement in the promotion of general equality rights for women. As the political opportunities for women's issues in EU politics increased in both formality and

(May 1983). This would later serve as a lobbying platform that would eventually be included in the Directive as a set of EU rights protecting self-employed workers (CREW 1983: 5).

Table 5.3 *Transnational organizations in the area of social provisions by organizational type and founding date, 1970–1979*

Organization	Founding date
Trade unions	
FEM	1971
EURO-FIET	1972
ETUC	1973
ETUCE	1975
ETUI	1978
JOC	1978
EPSU	1978
Human rights	
HRW	1978
Religious	
EECCS	1973
CSC	1974
QCEA	1979
Development	
Int'l Movement ATD 4th World	1972
Other voluntary orgs.	
ILGA (lesbian and gay rights)	1978
COFACE (family)	1979

Source: Data compiled by author from *Directory of Pressure Groups in the EU*, Philip and Gray (1996), *Directory of Interest Groups* (Luxembourg: Office for Official Publications of the European Communities, 1996) and *Consultation, the European Commission and Civil Society* (European Commission, online database http://www.europa.eu.int/comm/civil_society/coneccs/start.cfm?CL=en).

magnitude, as seen through ECJ precedent, equality legislation and Commission offices such as the Women's Information Service, we can see a shift in mobilization. Further, the growing presence of women activists within these EU organizations was crucial in making EU politics more accessible to both NGOs and trade unions involved with women's issues (CREW 1991: 9).

Examples of these organizations include both the European Trade Union Confederation (ETUC) and the European Metalworker's Federation (FEM). They are trade union organizations and while they are committed to a variety of labor issues, they also were actively involved with the Commission's Advisory Committee on Equal Opportunities for Men and Women, as well as the Women's Committee of the European

Parliament. Further, when EU reports in the 1960s and early 1970s were issued revealing the failure of member states to comply with equal pay regulations, trade unions were active in pressuring the Commission to develop equal pay legislation.[14] Thus, while the groups established in this decade were not explicitly women's organizations, they marked the beginning of organizations that illustrated a high level of commitment to expanding the rights of women in EU policy.

In terms of formal organizations, this early time period was characterized by organizations that held only a distant, if any, commitment to women's rights and was limited to issues of formal equality (e.g. equal representation). While these organizations began establishing a permanent presence in EU policy processes during this time period, it would be misleading to say the advancement of women's rights was in anyway a main objective of these organizations. Instead, this time period generally marked the beginning of organized labor becoming part of the policy dialogue in Europe: they focused on general employment rights that later would expand to issues of equality. And lobbying successes were largely attributable to the discrete action of individual activists within these organizations. Further, despite, the long history of trade-union involvement in EU policy processes and their increasingly active participation on European employment issues, these groups have remained comparatively weak in promoting women's issues.[15] This may be attributable to movement characteristics. The labor movement has experienced comparative difficulty with transnational cooperation at the EU level due to its focus on employment issues, such as equal pay, which remains entrenched in national wage systems and workplace practices (Marks and McAdam 1996; Hoskyns 1996: 64).

Yet focusing on formal organizations only reveals one part of the transnational mobilization dynamic that was occurring during the 1960s and 1970s. Informal organizing and individual activism from *within* EU organizations would prove equally if not more powerful in the area of social provisions. By the mid 1970s, the women's movement was becoming a common presence in national politics throughout Western Europe and

---

[14] A 1961 report issued by the European Parliament highlighted the difficulties associated with both national structures and cultures in member states when applying equal pay regulations (EP 1961). Further, the Commission held similar findings a decade later in its report (CEC 1973b).

[15] See Cockburn (1996) for a critique of the current status of women representatives and women's interests in European trade unions. Braithwaite and Byrne (1995) also illustrate the noticeable absence of women representatives from trade unions involved at the European level.

political parties could no longer ignore their policy demands. These activists would soon establish their presence both around and within EU politics.

One example of informal organizing of feminist activists is the Women's Organization for Equality (WOE), which formed in 1971.[16] The group originally formed as a consciousness-raising group, an increasingly common manifestation of the feminist movement at this time (Katzenstein and Mueller 1987), and consisted of English-speaking women of various nationalities who happened to be living in Brussels during this time period. By the end of the 1970s, the group had a membership of 100 and regularly published a newsletter. As the EU increasingly became active in the area of social provisions, both through the ECJ's jurisprudence and the legislative developments stemming from the Commission's action on women, WOE decided to create a special sub-group in 1978 that was specifically dedicated to "finding out how the European institutions work, what they do (and don't do) for women, and how women get into politics" (Hoskyns 1996). This group was know as the Women's European Action Group (WEAG) and would become increasing formalized and powerful in the 1980s.

In terms of feminist activism from within EU organizations, the Commission's use of French sociologist Evelyne Sullerot's research is one example. Sullerot published widely in the 1960s and 1970s on the role of women in society and argued for more in-depth studies on the real situation of women in both society and the labor markets of Europe.[17] Further, she was involved in the work of international organizations such as the OECD and the Council of Europe and together it was these research interests and involvement that would bring her to the attention of European officials. In 1968, she was asked by DG Employment and Social Affairs to prepare a cross-national study on women's employment in member states.[18] The impact of the overall trends and assessments contained in the final report were far-reaching, influencing subsequent

---

[16]   This group does not appear in Philip and Gray's (1996) compendium of pressure groups in the EU. This information was gathered from the *Women of Europe* newsletter (CEC 1978).

[17]   Her 1970 study, *Women, Society and Change* focused on women's changing position, both in terms of demographics and increased participation in the labor market. An earlier study, *Historie et sociologie du travail feminine*, 1968, brought to the forefront the need to understand the real work of women (both paid and unpaid labor).

[18]   Evelyne Sullerot, *L'emploi des femmes et ses problèmes dans les états membres de la Communauté Européene*, CEC, 1970, English Summary, 1973. The study was particularly pathbreaking for its time by emphasizing the structural disadvantage of women (pp. 44–45). Her general conclusions urged for the broadening of EU policy beyond equal pay and that women must attain wider participation in all sectors and levels of the economy.

Commission recommendations and ultimately the Equal Pay Directive.[19] Further, the study was not only important by providing much needed cross-national data for subsequent legislative developments, it also provided a new feminist consciousness at the European level of the real structural disadvantages experienced by women. As one scholar observes: "For the first time a study concerning women was written by someone with expertise who cared about the subject" (Hoskyns 1996: 84). Sullerot's influence provided the foundation that would be necessary for further policy action and activism in the 1980s. Thus, in many ways the Commission created the opportunity for Sullerot's involvement, and subsequently her own activism created the subsequent opportunity structure by changing the policy frame for EU women's policy.

At the same time, women working in other Directorate Generals of the Commission were beginning to carve out a European space, beyond legislative developments, for the concerns and issues facing women throughout the member states. The work of Fausta Deshormes in DG Information and Culture is such an example. Following the 1975 International Women's Year, the Commission began receiving a growing number of requests from national women's groups and the women's press. In response, Fausta Deshormes was asked to set up the Women's Information Service in the following year. In the beginning, the service was meant to provide information to women's organizations throughout the member states: the news bulletin *Women of Europe* (first published in 1976) was to fulfill this task along with helping to organize conferences and activities at the national level.[20] Reflecting on her intentions behind the publication, Deshormes stated:

I wanted *Women of Europe* to show that the EC's activities were not abstract, but held real importance for our daily lives. We also intended to expose discrimination against women and to highlight everything that concerned women's situations. (Deshormes 1992: 51)

The newsletter quickly took on a significant role in the development of transnational activism and networking, as women throughout Europe began contributing information: from the changing role of women in political parties and trade unions to EU law and women. In particular,

---

[19] CEC (1973b). The report, consistent with Sullerot's findings, emphasized the need for a "new Community instrument" to make effective Article 141 (p. 44–5). This would subsequently be instrumental in the development of the Equal Pay Directive.

[20] For example, the Information Service sponsored a conference in Athens following Greece's accession to the EU in 1981. The conference was intended to provide information on EC policy on women, as well as an opportunity to gather information on the status of women's issues in Greek politics and society.

in the 1970s the newsletter was the main avenue in which the ECJ judgments achieved widespread dissemination to women's organizations throughout the member states (Deshormes 1992). Reflecting on the newsletter and the changing role of women in Europe, Deshormes stated:

Women of Europe has tried to reflect and to participate in these changes by providing information: thus, a real network has built up across national boundaries. Thanks to *Women of Europe*, we have seen how information can stir people into action and how it can contribute to the launching of joint actions. Discussion and debate have reached previously unattained levels. (Deshormes 1992: 52)

Deshormes' commitment as realized in the activities of the Women's Information Service was integral both in developing a space for the discussion of women's issues at the EU level, but more importantly, by constructing the transnational links between national activists. Once created, these transnational links would eventually evolve into permanent coordination at the EU level that would lobby for and achieve EU policy change.[21]

In general, the early decades of the EU witnessed the development of an initial foundation for transnational mobilization around women's issues. Through the Court's equality rulings in the 1970s and a similar expansion of EU legislative action, political opportunities for transnational activists began to increase in number and formality. Yet when compared with the business sector, opportunities for public interests were comparatively small. Thus, it was not surprising that the mobilization around women's issues during this time period was overwhelmingly traceable to discrete individual action rather than highly organized collective action. This was exemplified by the work of legal activists such as Vogel-Polsky or Deshormes in the Commission. Further, the tactics pursued by these activists seemed to show similarities to domestic patterns, both through their success with litigation strategies and the organizing through informal networks. Although the lobbying strategies of trade unions were less successful at impacting EU politics, the individual activism of individuals such as Vogel-Polsky and Sullerot impacted the EU organizations in a way that shaped subsequent litigation and legislative action. These rules and procedures would form the basis for further action in the following decade.

---

[21] Supplement 27, *Women of Europe: 10 Years* includes an analysis by Janine Mossuz-Lavau of the issues and subjects covered in the news bulletin over its first 10 years. The general conclusion illustrated that the publication has been important both for reporting on change, but equally important for facilitating change (Mossuz-Lavau 1988). The transnational exchange of information and collaboration that the Women's Information Service provided, would later serve as the basis for coordinated efforts at the EU level.

The 1980s: mobilization and institutionalization in a hostile environment

The blanket expansion in political opportunities for social interests at the EU level would not continue in the next decade. With a recession at home, and with the initial enthusiasm for at least some harmonization of social costs waning, member states began dragging their heels on EU advancements in the area of social policy. Yet this general slowing of member state action at the beginning of the decade in this area (and thus, decreasing legislative action), would stand in stark contrast to the innovations in ECJ equality case law and an increasingly organized community of Brussels based activists.

Litigation and legislative action as political opportunities for mobilization

Litigation in the area of social provisions skyrocketed in the 1980s. This pattern stands in stark contrast to the general "slowing" of integration as member states returned their focus to domestic issues in light of the global economic recession. Referring back to the data in Chapter 2, we saw that in 1983 alone, the Court received a quantity of social provisions preliminary references that exceeded the total amount for the entire time period since it received its first reference in 1970 (11 references). The mobilizing effect of the Court's second *Defrenne* decision is clear. The direct effect of Article 141 gave women throughout member states the ability to bring claims under EU equality law against discriminatory national practices before their own national courts: an action that was not possible prior to this ruling. As we saw in the previous section, activists helped ensure the widespread knowledge of this litigation, through their contributions to publications such as *Women of Europe*.

The subsequent case law that came from these diverse claims enabled the ECJ to clarify the rights of women under EU law. Again, the ECJ's *Defrenne* rulings created the political opportunity for further action, yet individuals and legal activists created the subsequent opportunity for the ECJ to further expand and elaborate these rights. The decisions expanded EU law both in substantive scope and included further procedural innovations granting individual's protection against the state. Highlighting some of the cases from this decade, they include: the expansion of EU equality law to include pensions (*Worringham* decision, ECJ 1981c; *Bilka* decision, ECJ 1986a) and working conditions (*Garland* decision, ECJ 1982b), to protect claimants from *indirect* discrimination (*Jenkins* decision, ECJ 1981a), to allow equal pay claims using a hypothetical male comparator (*Macarthy* decision, ECJ 1980); the Court's case law which demanded that national legal systems make the necessary changes to provide "real and effective judicial protection" for claimants (*Von Colson* decision, ECJ 1986b); a shift in the burden of proof (*Danfoss* decision, ECJ 1989d); and finally, a widely criticized ruling that refused to extend EU equality law to men in relation to maternity benefits (*Hoffman* decision, ECJ 1984b). EU equality rights were clarified and more importantly, women were given significant new legal instruments to demand effective remedies against discrimination. Developments in women's transnational activism were linked both to the national level proceedings that gave rise to these ECJ decisions, as well as the subsequent mobilizing effects of these rulings. Litigation continued to be a successful tactic for individuals who wanted to pressure for greater equality rights.

Unlike this trend in equality litigation, EU legislative advancements on women's issues were "ghettoized" in the early 1980s (Hoskyns 1992: 23). That is, there was little proof of a general concern within the Council of Ministers or the Commission (beyond the Women's Bureau) to further legislate at the EU level on women's issues. Generally, as the 1992 Programme and the Single European Act (SEA) were proposed and negotiated in the 1980s, little if any attention was given to the issue of women's rights (Hoskyns 1992; 1996). Further, social policy in general was clearly a back-burner issue around these initial negotiations (Moravcsik 1991). The Single European Act (1986) was a first step at amendments to facilitate the necessary expansion for 1992, yet expansion in the area of social policy was minimal: the most notable social provision was the introduction of the "social partners" that developed an EU-level dialogue between management and workers.[22] This series of meetings, which became known as the "Social Dialogue," clearly represents a formal access point for social interests in EU politics. However, during this time period, this political opportunity provided access to a process that did not want to move forward on social issues, thus minimizing the potential impact.

This hostile environment would somewhat change by the end of the decade through the work of Jacques Delors, a moderate socialist and former French finance minister, who was appointed as President of the European Commission in 1985 with the main objective of seeing the completion of the internal market through fruition. In the area of social policy, he was instrumental in the drafting and passage of the Social

---

[22] This formalized series of meetings between management and trade unions became known as the "Social Dialogue."

Charter (1989) (despite vehement British opposition that ultimately resulted in the British opt-out position on the Charter). The Social Charter gave the Commission the competence to propose further legislation on social policy issues.

The failure to attain substantial equality legislative outcomes during this time period was not due to a lack of effort by EU organizations and individuals. In 1981, the Commission's Women's Bureau proposed the *First Action Programme on Equal Opportunities* (1982–1985), which was adopted by Council Resolution in July 1982 (CEC 1981, 1982). It introduced a two-pronged framework for EU equality advancements that would continue into the future: first, by establishing legal rights through law (equal treatment) and second, by the development of programs, research and outreach projects with the purpose of implementing equal opportunities in practice (special treatment). Although the action program had few legislative successes,[23] the internal and national-level project developments would prove essential by providing both the horizontal and vertical links that were necessary to keep advancing women's issues at the EU level, despite a lack of member-state enthusiasm to do so. These political opportunity structures were acutely linked to the mobilization that would occur throughout this decade as discussed below.

Mobilization, institutionalization and political opportunities for public inclusion

In terms of total growth, the 1980s paralleled the previous decades with twelve new groups developing permanent offices in Brussels. Table 5.4 displays the transnational organizations involved in EU social provisions that were founded between 1980–1989. However, politically, these organizations were very different than previous decades. In the early 1980s, grassroots women's organizations became part of the political landscape in Brussels, such as the Centre for Research on European Women (CREW) and the European Network of Women (ENOW). These were women working for women, and whose political objectives and claims moved far beyond formal equality, but began forging the path for substantive equality measures: positive action programs that included vocational training and education opportunities for women. Further,

---

[23] Council Directive 86/378/EEC and Council Directive 86/613/EEC are two such successes (these were considerably weaker than the original proposals). Numerous other proposals from parental leave to positive action programs (e.g. vocational programs and the special needs of immigrant women in employment and training, Action 14) were shelved due to member state resistance. For an in-depth discussion on the failure of the Parental Leave Directive see Hoskyns (1996: 146).

Table 5.4 *Transnational organizations in the area of social provisions by organizational type and founding date, 1980–1989*

Organization	Founding date
Trade unions	
EFCGU	1988
Regional/Local authorities	
RETI	1984
ECTARC	1988
Women's rights/Social welfare	
CREW	1980
ENOW	1983
EWMD	1984
WIDE	1985
YMCA	1989
Religious	
KE	1989
Other voluntary orgs.	
EUROLINK (elderly)	1981
AI-EU Association (human rights)	1985
FEANTSA (homeless)	1989

Source: Data compiled by author from *Directory of Pressure Groups in the EU*, Philip and Gray (1996), *Directory of Interest Groups* (Luxembourg: Office for Official Publications of the European Communities, 1996) and *Consultation, the European Commission and Civil Society* (European Commission, online database http://www.europa.eu.int/comm/civil_society/coneccs/start.cfm?CL=en).

these groups illustrate that women's mobilizing was becoming more formalized in collective organizations.

Following the adoption of the Single European Act in 1986, and the extension of EU social policy competences, there was another growth spurt with four groups forming in a two-year time period. Unlike previous decades, the groups forming in the 1980s were less likely to be trade unions (EFCGU is the only employee organization founded compared to the five in the 1950s–60s and six in the 1970s) and more likely to be either dedicated explicitly to women's issues (CREW, ENOW and EWMD), or other non-employment-related social issues with a secondary emphasis on women's rights, such as the elderly (EUROLINK), human rights (AI-EU) and the homeless (FEANTSA). The women's organizations founded during this period were crucial to sustaining the advancements that had begun in the early years. Further, the links between the ECJ's equality case law, EU legislative developments and this transnational activism were becoming clearer. The Centre for Research on European Women (CREW) exemplifies this relationship. This organization was established in 1980 and grew out of the earlier discussed WEAG, which was the European sub-group of an informal feminist organization operating in Brussels. The group remained consistent with the philosophy of WEAG by adopting a "feminist approach" but it placed a more formalized commitment to closing the "information gap" by examining and disseminating information on "issues of gender, employment and training at the European level" (CREW 1996: 141; 1994).

This non-profit research institute employs 11 full-time staff members and disposes of an annual income of 966,000 euros million that is raised through sales of publications and consultancy services. Throughout the 1980s, the Commission consulted the group on white and green papers as it attempted to develop social legislation (CREW 1993). Similar to the impact of Sullerot's research in the 1970s, the research provided by CREW served to change the policy frames that characterized the EU social policy agenda. Further, the group was important for creating a new social space for women at the European level. CREW provided not only the physical space that women could come to receive information about their rights, the group also served as a transnational site to exchange information and collaboration between national organizations.

The *CREW Reports*, a monthly publication, would prove decisive in fulfilling these actions. The Reports were published between 1985 and 1995 in both French and English and "provided a source of information and a focus for networking among feminist and grassroots women's organizations" (Hoskyns 1996: 130). Further, these reports became a key reference point for up-to-date information on ECJ case law and national legal action taking place in the area of sex equality.[24] The effect was a transnational dissemination of information that ensured a wide audience for the real effects of the ECJ rulings and suggested how these new rulings and EU equality laws could be used for future legal action. For example, the adverse publicity that followed the Court's 1984 *Hoffman* ruling, in which the Court refused to extend the Equal Treatment Directive to the position of fathers in German national maternity programs, was widely publicized and discussed in the Report and served to help mobilize women both at the national level and those

---

[24] Each *CREW Report* has a section that is specifically dedicated to ECJ case law and then subsequent national level equality cases (the column "The Verdict").

working at the EU level to pressure for a parental leave Directive.[25] The transnational exchange of information facilitated by groups like CREW again would prove decisive for publicizing ECJ rulings, which impacted further mobilization. In this case, the negative ruling did not empower women *per se*, but instead mobilized them to act for fear EU equality rights were moving in a less progressive direction.

Another grassroots organization that was gaining an increasing presence in EU politics during this time period was the European Network of Women (ENOW). The creation of ENOW in 1983 was the direct manifestation of CREW's efforts (and a grant from the Women's Bureau in DG Employment and Social Affairs) to set up a coordinated organization of European women's groups. Significant disagreement surrounded the issue of how and on what issues a European women's lobby should act. This lack of consensus resulted in the establishment of a group by CREW, rather than coordination that might have included a broader base of women's interest groups.[26] Instead, it remained as a "loose association of grassroots, autonomous women's organizations" and a formal lobby wouldn't materialize for another decade. The group describes its aims as "to improve the position of women in Europe. ENOW represents grassroots women's organizations, which feel that directives adopted by the EU are not always positive for women. It lobbies on behalf of women in political, economic, cultural and social contexts" (ENOW 1996: 249).

An example of the group's efforts were seen in its widely distributed 1985 report assessing the Commission's *First Action Programme on Equal Opportunities* (ENOW 1985). While it is unclear whether the Commission really considered the points raised in the report, the organization's real aim of informing national and transnational feminist groups of the

---

[25] See CREW (1985). In 1986, the German government would amend the *Mutterschutzgesetz* (maternity leave program) to provide a parental leave program that was equally available to mother and father. This outcome has been attributed both to the significant adverse publicity from the *Hoffman* ruling, as well as a newly appointed "progressive" woman Minister for Youth, Family, Women and Health. The Parental Leave Directive was proposed in November 1983 and, as mentioned above, ultimately failed during this time period due to member state opposition. The Directive would finally be adopted in 1996 (Council Directive 96/34/EC).

[26] In May 1982, the Commission's Women's Information Service in conjunction with the German Women's Council (*Deutshcer Frauenrat*) organized a meeting of European women's organizations in Bonn. The majority of invited groups were traditional women's organizations, such as UK groups the National Council of Women and the Federation of Business and Professional Women. However, some feminist groups were included along with CREW and the women's committee from the ETUC (trade union). These later groups would stand in disagreement with the more traditional women's organizations over the issue of a single EU women's interest organization. And so, CREW subsequently established ENOW which brought together grass roots groups and represented the feminist project. See Hoskyns (1996) for a further discussion of ENOW.

strategies and policies being pursued by the EU was met (Hoskyns 1996: 147). The difficulties experienced by women activists in forming a collective lobbying organization versus their comparative success at informal networking, use of litigation and individual expertise at changing policy frames, may be indicative of the movement more generally. A single lobbying organization is generally incompatible in style with grassroots women's organizations, which are generally characterized by non-hierarchical, loosely organized, consensus-based structures. Emulating such a structure and operation at the EU level proved difficult, not least for the reason of accommodating various nationally embedded beliefs on equality, but also the variation in feminist agendas from conservative to more progressive.[27]

Similar to the previous decade, transnational organizing was also taking place both around and through EU organizations. In many ways an extension of the activists working in EU organizations in the 1970s, these more or less frequent transnational meetings brought together national specialists and activists working on gender equality issues. One example of this type of organizing is DG Employment and Affairs' Advisory Committee on Equal Opportunities for Men and Women. By the early 1980s, some national equality agencies, such as the British Equal Opportunities Commission (EOC) and the French Comité Travail Feminin (CTF), had become increasingly active in implementing EU equality law and sponsoring national legal proceedings invoking EU law. As a result these agencies began to form close links with the Women's Bureau in DG Employment and through these interactions the idea for a European-wide conference on women's issues materialized and was convened in Manchester in May 1980.[28] Although primarily representing individuals from national equality units, conference participants presented proposals for the future direction of EU equality policy: from positive action programs to childcare facilities.

Following the conference, the Commission brought together various national equality representatives and formed the Standing Liaison Group which was ultimately institutionalized in 1982 as the formally constituted Advisory Committee on Equal Opportunities for Men and Women. Its mandate was "to advise the Commission on the formulation and implementation of policy and to ensure the continuous exchange of information."[29] One of the first concrete contributions of this Committee was the

---

[27] Interview with former CREW member, Brussels, March 2000.
[28] *Equality for Women, Assessment – Problems – Perspectives, a European Project*, EOC, Manchester 1980.
[29] Commission Decision 82/43/EEC.

proposal that eventually became the Commission's *First Action Programme on Equal Opportunities*. Many of the more progressive programs on positive action that grew out of the Manchester conference, and subsequently were included in early drafts of the action program, would later fall on deaf ears in the Council of Ministers. However, this transnational exchange of information from women within national equality agencies to EU officials would prove vital to sustaining the momentum of feminist activists in the 1970s and equally important, would continue to provide a network of expertise for future legislative proposals. Again, while the EU created the original opportunity for inclusion, activists pushed to expand the opportunities provided for women in the future.

A final example of transnational mobilization in this time period was the development of DG Employment's Legal Experts Network On the Application of the Equality Directives. This network of national experts drawn from the legal profession, academics and trade unions provided in-depth national updates on the implementation of EU equality laws, detailed national legal and legislative developments in equality policy and provided suggestions on new directions for EU policy. The publications from this group would prove essential in providing a transnational exchange of information on ECJ decisions, subsequent national court decisions, and ultimately, national legislative change and compliance.[30] In particular, the regular reports of the Experts Network pointed to the comparative advantages and disadvantages facing potential claimants who hoped to utilize Article 234 preliminary ruling procedure to bring claims before national courts.[31] Alongside these regular updates, experts affiliated with the Network have prepared in-depth special reports for the Commission that include subjects such as the analysis of legal redress in member states for equality claims and the use of litigation strategy in national legal systems.[32] In this case, the Commission created the opportunity for transnational coordination, but when given the space, these legal activists have facilitated the subsequent expansion of EU law through legal proceedings before national courts.

The ECJ rulings would remain an important thread in the development of transnational networks of legal activists. And alongside the reports issued by the Commission sponsored Network of Legal Experts, the Commission also issued a series of *Women of Europe* Supplements on "Community Law and Women" throughout the 1980s, that served to

---

[30] Personal communication between the author and the Network coordinator, April 1999.

[31] *First Report of the Network Experts*, V/564/84-EN, Commission of the European Communities, 1984.

[32] For example, CEC (1984) and more recently, see CEC (1993a) and CEC (1995a).

provide up-to-date information on the Court's rulings for subsequent discrimination claims (CEC 1983, 1985, 1987a). These publications served as "major reference works" on EU equality law, were widely read throughout the EU and subsequently fostered collaboration and cooperation between national legal experts (Deshormes 1992: 51). As earlier mentioned, the *CREW Reports* also continued to serve as an outlet for ECJ judgments.[33] Again, the wide dissemination of information on ECJ precedent enabled subsequent action. As illustrated, this happened not only from the growing formality of transnational networks developing to exchange this information, but more importantly the subsequent action involved legal claims that required the ECJ to decide on important questions of EU social law and often the rulings in effect expanded the rules and procedures enabling greater protection in the future.

By the end of the 1980s, the presence of a public interest on behalf of women had become a coordinated and organized part of the European landscape. Not only was this a continuation of individual action by women pushing for formal equality from within EU organizations and within trade unions as seen in the 1970s, this mobilization had become more collective. Permanent offices and networks dedicated solely to the promotion of more progressive EU women's policy were established in Brussels. However, much of this action did not lead to legislative outcomes, as a result of blockages in the Council by less enthusiastic member state governments.

On the other hand, the advancements made by both women activists and the Commission did provide a growing base of research, expert networks and formal organizations for these public interests. These efforts provided a growing European social space for women's interests, a space that wasn't necessarily readily available at the national level. Thus, even when national governments were hesitant to legislate, women activists continued to pressure for more expansive EU social provisions and their increasingly permanent and formal presence in Brussels helped to shape Commission proposals. While this mobilization may not have accomplished major legislative advancements, this transnational action helps to prevent slippage. These public interests had come to Brussels to stay. Further, ECJ rulings continued to serve as new political opportunities as they expanded EU equality law despite member state opposition: decisions that were both a cause and effect of the extensive mobilizing taking place around the use of EU litigation strategies to fight discrimination. While these policy-framing and litigation

---

[33] For example, particularly significant ECJ rulings, such as the *Hoffman* and *Danfoss* decisions, received extensive attention in the *Reports* (CREW 1985; CREW 1989).

strategies continued to be successful avenues for action in the 1980s, women activists continued to experience difficulty forming a formal lobbying organization: a structure that seemed incompatible with the informal, consensus building activities of these activists.

The 1990s and early 2000s: institutionalized solidarity and a united presence

Once the path was paved, the subsequent developments in the 1990s and early 2000s, including a formal women's lobby and an expansion in EU policy to include a wider scope of gender discrimination, was almost inevitable. The advancements made by the Court and the Commission in the previous decades helped sustain and expand EU social provisions, despite member state hesitation to adopt legislation. Further, the efforts of women activists operating through increasingly formal transnational organizations and networks were both cause and effect of these EU developments. Their efforts would prove crucial to expanding the space needed for greater inclusion of women's interests in EU politics in the 1990s and into the new millennium.

Litigation and legislative action as political opportunities for mobilization

Within the 1990s alone, the ECJ had already received four times as many preliminary references as the previous decade (a total of 206 social provisions references). Increasingly, EU law served as a political opportunity structure for women throughout Europe who were now enabled to seek protection from discriminatory national practices. Likewise, as we saw in Chapter 3, national judges who were often exerting newly realized powers of statutory review were increasingly engaging the EU legal system by sending preliminary references. Further, the diversity of claims continued to expand as information regarding the opportunities afforded through EU law spread through transnational networks to legal experts, trade unions and women activists at the national level. As a result of this subsequent litigation, the ECJ was asked to give EU equality laws greater applicability and clarity. If the 1970s litigation established general formal equality rights, and the 1980s represented clarification and elaboration of these rights, the case law from 1990–2003 saw an unparalleled expansion in diverse situations in which these general equality rights were applicable: from protection of pregnant workers to discrimination against transsexuals.

The case law in this time period served as political opportunities for mobilization by eliciting effects both in terms of legislative action by EU organizations and also political and legal action by women activists. One example is the 1990 *Barber* decision (ECJ 1990a), which created the direct effect of Article 141 in occupational pensions. The potential costs associated with the ruling and an extension in individual rights resulted in a member state attempt to narrow the scope of the ruling (a treaty amendment: the Barber Protocol) while at the same time individuals continued to flood national courts with claims based on this newly created right.[34] The Court's *Kalanke* decision (ECJ 1995a) on positive action would result in a similar effect: except the highly criticized ruling would limit rather than expand EU rights, illustrating that both "good" and "bad" decisions can result in mobilization. As illustrated in Chapter 3, this time period also included the Court's pregnancy and maternity case law beginning with the *Dekker* decision (ECJ 1990c), which developed in tandem with EU legislative action in this area.[35] Further, the case law in this time period delved into issues of sexual orientation and discrimination including the Court's *Grant* decision (ECJ 1998g) involving same-sex partners and the *P v. S* decision (ECJ 1996d) extending equal treatment protection to transsexuals. Member state sovereignty over military organization was also impacted with a series of important cases, the *Sirdar* decision (ECJ 1999a) and the *Kreil* decision (ECJ 2000a), on discrimination and women in military posts. Similar to the general trend in the previous decade, this case law was both cause and effect of the transnational mobilization that was increasingly present and institutionalized at the EU level. Building on the momentum generated for the 1992 project (completion of the internal market) early in the decade, the 1990s alone experienced record growth in terms of annual social provisions legislative outputs: on average 18 EU legislative acts were adopted each year during the 1990s, whereas the average for the previous decade was 10. Further, the beginning of the next decade seemed even stronger with an average of 32 social provisions being

---

[34] The *Barber* decision which in effect provided the direct effect of Article 141 in the pension sphere (pensions are within the meaning of pay) was met with extreme criticism from member states who realized the costs involved with such a judgment (see in particular, the UK observation in the case which highlighted the potential harm such a ruling would have on the British economy: citing cost increases in the £33–45 billion range). A host of Article 234 litigation followed (e.g. *Moroni* ECJ 1993b; *Ten Oever* ECJ 1993c; *Neath* 1993d, to name just a few). See the text of Council Directive 96/97/EC for a complete list. And subsequent EU legislative acts included an unprecedented Treaty revision (the Barber Protocol) and an amended Directive, (Council Directive 96/97/EC amending Directive 86/378/EEC).

[35] The Pregnancy Directive, Council Directive 92/85/EEC.

adopted annually from 2000 to 2003. Although the area of women's policy specifically reflected a similar hesitancy on the part of national governments as seen in the 1980s, the adoption of the Maastricht Treaty in 1992 did strengthen the social advancements made by Delors at the end of the 1980s.

The Social Charter was affirmed and strengthened through the Treaty's Protocol on Social Policy (although the protocol remained an annex to the Treaty due to British opposition).[36] This gave greater strength to the Commission's 1990 Action Programme which proposed a series of legislative initiatives that attempted to make concrete some of the social commitments introduced in the Charter: these included draft directives on working hours, protection of pregnant workers and atypical work. The Commission's *Third Action Programme on Equal Opportunities* was also adopted in 1990 and provided further funding and support for transnational expert networks (CEC 1990c).[37] The program developed the objective of "gender mainstreaming" which would later serve as a new opportunity for mobilization. This policy action promoted the idea of "integrating equality into general mainstream policy" (CEC, 1990c: 3).

This requirement provided a new European social space to begin discussing the diversity of women's rights. Women activists mobilizing in Brussels utilized the idea of "gender mainstreaming" to bring attention to and greater awareness of gender in a wide scope of EU policy areas (Cockburn 1997: 463). Further, the Commission's 1994 White Paper on Social policy was an attempt to move beyond the conditions of workers and introduce the need for social protection for individuals as European citizens (CEC 1995c). And finally, these new innovations were laid out more formally in the Commission's Communication on Gender Mainstreaming, which was adopted in 1996 (CEC 1996e). Thus, EU social provisions were attempting to provide the platform for greater public inclusion in the net of EU politics. The Union was no longer simply about workers, but in fact pertained to general public interests.

This expansion is clearly illustrated in other Community actions during this time period. Notably, the *Community Framework Strategy on Gender Equality* was adopted in 2000 and set out important developments for the first half of the new decade (CEC 2000d). The issue of democracy and inclusion is made explicit:

---

[36] With the election of Tony Blair, the United Kingdom Government finally signed the Charter in 1998.

[37] A total of nine networks were established covering issues that ranged from childcare to positive action in enterprise.

Democracy is a fundamental value of the European Union, Member States, EEA States and applicant countries ... Its full realization requires the participation of all citizens women and men alike to participate and be represented equally in the economy, decision-making and in social, cultural and civil life. (CEC 2000d: 2)

Importantly, the Commission calls for an extension of this equality beyond employment, which foreshadows key legislative innovations, such as the Equality in Goods and Services Directive of 2004.[38] This Commission document is also important as it lays out exactly how the EU will operationalize and put into action the gender mainstreaming goals and objectives that were introduced in 1996.

While these EU policy agendas and programs provided the opportunity for mobilization and discussion on new areas of EU social policy, the Treaty amendments also provided greater space for public inclusion not only by strengthening the gender equality Treaty basis[39] as seen in the 1997 Treaty of Amsterdam and also through the strengthened role of the European Parliament (EP) in the policymaking process as seen most significantly in the Treaty on European Union (1992). This enhanced role of the EP, in particular its Women's Committee, continued to be very supportive of both NGO activities and the promotion of women's issues through conferences and studies during this time period. Thus, a strengthening of the policymaking power of the Parliament *vis-à-vis* other EU organizations represented greater political opportunity and space for the policy objectives of women's public interests. Further, the Parliament took very seriously its role as most powerful defender of European public interests, especially in the area of women's rights. So much so, that as the European Women's Lobby became increasingly powerful and autonomous in the late 1990s, an animosity began growing between this organization and the Parliament.[40] Finally, the Convention on the Future of Europe (2002–2003) and the draft constitution it created marked an important step forward both proposing to codify a set of civil, political, economic and social rights (the Charter of Fundamental Rights) into the Treaty on European Union as well as the unprecedented inclusion of non-governmental organizations and civil society into this treating drafting process.[41]

---

[38] Council Directive 2004/113/EC of 13 December 2004 implementing the principle of equal treatment between men and women in the access to and supply of goods and services.

[39] See Article 2, Article 3, Article 13 and Article 141 of the Treaty of Amsterdam.

[40] Interview with General Secretary of the European Women's Lobby, Brussels, March 2000.

[41] The draft EU Constitutional Treaty was signed by all member state governments on 29 October 2004. However, the ratification process came to a stop in 2005 when public referenda in France and the Netherlands ended in a No vote. The future of the EU Constitutional Treaty continues to be discussed at the present time.

Table 5.5 *Transnational organizations in the area of social provisions by organizational type and founding date, 1990–2003*

Organization	Founding date
Trade unions	
CESI	1990
EFFAT	2001
Regional/Local authorities	
IULA-CEMR	1990
EUROCITIES	1992
Women's rights	
EWL	1990
Religious	
APRODEV	1990
Misc voluntary orgs.	
EAPN (anti-poverty)	1990
ECAS (citizen rights)	1990
EUROSTEP (equal participation)	1990
ESAN (social action)	1991
EU Migrant Forum	1991
ECRE (refugees and exiles)	1994
CENPO (non-profits)	1994
EFC (foundations)	1993
Platform of Euro. Soc. NGOs	1995
ILGA (lesbian & gay rights)	1996
CIAD (HR & development)	2001

Source: Data compiled by author from *Directory of Pressure Groups in the EU*, Philip and Gray (1996), *Directory of Interest Groups* (Luxembourg: Office for Official Publications of the European Communities, 1996) and *Consultation, the European Commission and Civil Society* (European Commission, online database http://www.europa.eu.int/comm/civil_society/coneccs/start.cfm?CL=en).

Mobilization, institutionalization and political opportunities for public inclusion

Building on this momentum and that of the political events of the 1992 project, the EU experienced an unprecedented growth in transnational mobilization in the 1990s and into 2003. Table 5.5 illustrates that 7 new organizations were founded in the year 1990 alone and a total of 17 were established between 1990 and 2003. Further, building on the policy objectives and activities of previous EU women's groups, this decade marked the establishment of a formal grassroots women's lobby in

Brussels. The European Women's Lobby (EWL) (established in 1990) is an umbrella organization representing over 4000 grassroots women's organizations that is a regular participant in EU policy arenas and lobbies on a range of women's issues from domestic violence to trafficking in women.[42] Similar to a trend in the previous decade, the organizations forming in this time period again were more likely to represent an expansion in the voluntary organization sector, than trade unions. As illustrated in Table 5.5, 11 out of the 17 groups founded in this decade were voluntary organizations. Although, women's issues were not necessarily their only policy aim, these organizations continued to place a high priority on the promotion of women's rights at the EU level.

An example of this type of organization is the European Anti-Poverty Network (EAPN), established in 1990 and today representing over 20 organizations from all EU member states, 3 of which have an explicit focus on women's issues.[43] These organizations decided to form a European federation of groups "to put the fight against poverty and social exclusion on the political agenda of European institutions" (EAPN 1996: 156). The general social policy developments of the early 1990s created the EU opportunity structures to begin introducing the issue of poverty at the European level. A women's committee of the EAPN was established in 1991, after a group of women in the organization demanded greater representation in decision-making and greater attention to issues confronting women in poverty, such as racism and domestic violence (Cohen 1998: 369–72). Another social organization, Europeans for the Equal Participation of People (EUROSTEP), was also important for changing policy frames and raising new issues of women's rights at the EU level. In particular, EUROSTEP was instrumental in developing preparatory documents on gender equality for the official EU contribution to the 1995 Bejing Women's Conference (EUROSTEP 1996: 162). Finally, such groups as the European Union Migrant Forum, whose establishment in 1991 is traceable to a Parliament initiative, were also very active in developing transnational networks and conferences on issues specific to women immigrants.[44]

---

[42] Interview with policy coordinator from the European Women's Lobby, Brussels, April 1999.

[43] These include European Network of Women (ENOW), Grass Roots Organizations Operating Together in Sisterhood (GROOTS) and the International Voluntary Women's Group Education and Development (VIDES).

[44] For example, in 1994 the Forum sponsored a conference in Athens, Greece entitled "European Migrant Women Conference" and brought together participants from throughout EU countries (EU Migrant Forum 1996: 157).

The Platform of European Social NGOs is another example of formal transnational mobilizing that took place during this decade and represents a "peak" or federation organization. The Platform was established in 1995 and includes over 38 European NGOs, federations and networks. The organization's policy aims range from specific social issues such as social exclusion and public health, to the needs of specific groups of individuals, such as women, migrants or older people. The organization cites its origins to the Commission's 1993 Green Paper which emphasized not only the importance of social policy in the European agenda but also the need for greater inclusion of NGOs in future policy development. Again, this illustrates how over time the social provisions area has provided both EU organizations and transnational activists the platform to expand EU politics and policies to a greater European public. What began as an informal meeting between various social NGOs to discuss the Green Paper in April 1994, led to continued cooperation and a common position on subsequent EU proposals such as the *European Social Policy Forum* and *the Social Action Programme 1995–1997* and ultimately the decision to formalize this NGO cooperation by establishing the Platform in 1995 (Platform of European Social NGOs 1998: 1).

The Platform has continued to be integral for the formal inclusion of NGOs in EU activities, through its involvement and organization of the European Social Policy Forums, first in 1996 and again in 1998. These events were seen as crucial by the Commission in developing a "civil dialogue" and were organized in close coordination with both the Platform and social partners (the European trade unions, such as ETUC, CEEP and UNICE).[45] Further, these Forums were merely one manifestation of a series of EU actions between 1996 and 1998 that sought to formally include NGOs in EU policymaking.[46] In his opening speech before the 1998 Forum, then Commission President Jacques

---

[45]   CEC (1999e: 5). While these dialogues between NGOs, the Commission and Parliament have produced substantial policy suggestions and agreement, they do not always lead to policy outcomes. For example, such collaboration in preparations for the 1996–97 Intergovernmental Conference led to substantial policy suggestions, such as a Treaty basis to the civil dialogue with NGOs. Yet ultimately, the Treaty of Amsterdam did not include these suggested changes (p. 8).

[46]   This formal inclusion of voluntary organizations grew out of the 1992 Maastricht Treaty (Declaration 23, annexed in the Treaty) and the Commission's 1993 Green Paper on social policy, which first introduced the idea of a "civil dialogue" between EU policymakers and social NGOs. This was elaborated in the Commission's 1997 *Communication On Promoting the Role of Voluntary Organizations* (CEC 1997c) which proposed a series of actions to create a space for social NGOs in EU politics, one of which created a Commission budget heading [B3–4101] for "cooperation with charitable associations and with NGOs" (CEC 1999e).

Santer emphasized the importance of social NGOs in the integration process:

You make Europe a tangible reality. Your projects give form and substance to the Social Europe that I have been discussing and which we want to create. They are a key element of the civil dialogue and deserve to be encouraged on more than one ground ... Europe has been built on the idea of partnership: between nations, between institutions, between political actors and the representatives of civil society. And I expect of this Forum that it will create conditions conducive to this exchange and encourage you to submit proposals to us in order to advance matters in an area which is of great concern to us. (Santer in CEC 1999e: 12)

Thus, the Commission clearly saw itself as creating the political opportunities to help facilitate mobilization and inclusion of public interests in EU politics. And these groups responded. These efforts were duplicated in the Platform's participation in the Convention on the Future of Europe (2002–2003), in which they pressed for not only a stronger basis for social policies in the new constitution, but for greater "civil dialogue and participatory democracy" (Platform of Social NGOs 2003: 3). The Social Platform also exemplified the formal and collective action that was increasingly visible amongst transnational activists in the 1990s through early 2000s. Mobilization efforts were increasingly being carried out by highly organized peak organizations, rather than the individual activism characterizing the 1970s.

The European Women's Lobby (EWL) is another example of this type of mobilization. As mentioned, this is an umbrella organization representing over 4000 women's organizations throughout the member states.[47] After over a decade of debate, a European level women's lobby was finally formed in 1990.[48] However, these origins in contention and cooperation between traditional women's organizations (such as national women's work councils) and those representing more marginalized women's issues (such as domestic violence and migrant women) would continue to characterize the general operation and policy activities of the EWL. One senior member of the General Secretariat of EWL stated that reaching consensus on certain issues such as abortion and prostitution had proved impossible, with many meetings ending with some members walking out of the room, while on other issues, such as positive action, after years of debate, members were able to reach agreement and put forth a concrete policy agenda and action plan.[49] Ultimately, the member organizations were keenly aware that cooperation and consensus was important or they would risk

---

[47] European Women's Lobby website: http://www.womenlobby.org/
[48] See discussion regarding CREW and ENOW in previous 1980s section.
[49] Interview with General Secretary of the EWL, Brussels March 2000.

having women's issues left out of European politics altogether. Speaking on behalf of the EWL, Jacqueline de Groote emphasized the need for women's participation in EU politics:

Women's organizations are now ready to intervene effectively to defend their rights in the political sphere. Furthermore, women cannot fight for equality in a society built by men only – women's views are an essential part in the construction of any new society. The European Community is a new society in the making. It is essential that women should be able to say now, how they propose to make it a democratic society that protects individual rights and emphasizes solidarity. (de Groot 1992: 49)

This statement illustrates that the EWL saw their lobbying efforts as essential to creating a space and opportunity for women's issues in EU politics. This continued on into the 2000s, when the EWL played an aggressive role pressuring for a strong basis for gender equality in the new European Constitution (EWL 2005).

The EWL would come to be the main formal organization representing women's interests in EU policymaking: an outcome that was as much driven by the organization's constant attempt to represent diverse interests, as well as the Commission's influence by discouraging women's groups from operating autonomously from the EWL.[50] Thus, while this transnational mobilization helped to shape political opportunities, the Commission clearly maintained control over which groups subsequently utilized these formal access points.

At the same time, formal Commission sponsored networks remained an important form of transnational mobilization as seen in the last decade. In 1990, the *Third Action Program for Equal Opportunities* introduced a total of nine new networks: ranging from issues such as women in decision-making, broadcasting and childcare. These complemented the original two networks of Legal Experts (established in 1982) and Women in the Labor Market (1983), which continued to be invaluable for the transnational exchange of information regarding ECJ equality case law and the status of EU equality law in national legal systems. Together these informal networks created a pan-European network that bound together national women's NGOs, national equality units, women activists and lawyers in developing a European space for women. Generally, these networks consisted of representatives from each member state, a

---

[50] European Women's Management and Development (EWMD) had attempted to participate in Commission consultation processes (e.g. through the Platform of Social NGOs) but were denied independent access and were told to coordinate their efforts through the EWL (of which they are now a member) (personal communication between the author and policy coordinator of EWMD, March 1999).

general coordinator, received funding from the Commission and convened an annual meeting. However, by the end of the action program in 1995, the funding for such networks came under scrutiny, and as a result only the original two networks continued to receive funding in the subsequent *Fourth Action Programme.*[51] Yet even when the formal organizations disappeared, the transnational connections and activism remained. Transnational collaboration and coordination amongst former network members remained commonplace over such EU policy issues as childcare and women in decision-making.[52]

Similar to the previous decade, ECJ decisions continued to be an important part of an expanding net of EU equality laws enabling women to bring claims against their own governments and seek newly found protection from discriminatory behavior. Transnational legal activists – operating through the Network of Legal Experts, CREW and even consultancy firms such as ENGENDER[53] – were an important element in ensuring widespread knowledge of the ECJ decisions that were essential for subsequent legal action and mobilization. The legal action via the ECJ developed alongside transnational lobbying efforts, and rather than directly impacting this activism, was seen as a parallel effort to expand the rights of women at the EU level.[54] In 1996, this would change.

Following the Court's *Kalanke* decision (ECJ 1995a), the ECJ would take on a new role to women's organizations operating in Brussels. The ruling stated that the Equal Treatment Directive must be interpreted strictly in terms of allowable positive action programs: the decision in effect condemned a German law providing that where job candidates were equally qualified for a particular position, women must be given

---

[51] In May 1998, the ECJ issued a ruling (ECJ 1998h) brought by the UK government against the Commission arguing that the Commission had overstepped its competence by funding 86 projects focusing on social exclusion, under budget heading B3–4103. The Court concurred and the Commission was asked to review a number of budget headings to ensure they met the criteria of the Court's ruling, including the need for both a EU budget entry and a legal basis (e.g. a Regulation, Directive or Decision). A number of projects directly related to social networks were involved including: "cooperation with charitable associations (B3–4101)," "cooperation with NGOs and associations formed by the socially-excluded and the elderly (B3–4116)," "measures in the social economy sector (B5–321)," and "subsidies for certain activities of organizations pursuing human rights objectives (B7–70400)" (CEC 1999e: 10).

[52] Interview with a former Head of the Equality Unit, DG Employment and Social Affairs, Brussels, June 2001.

[53] ENGENDER was established in Brussels in 1996 and is a group of ten individuals working on common projects in the area of "equality and participation." The group of consultants have performed both individual and collaborative research projects for the Commission on such subjects as the "Structural Funds and Equal Opportunities" and "Women in the Judiciary." Interview with ENGENDER member, Brussels, June 2001.

[54] Interview with General Secretary of the EWL, Brussels, March 2000.

priority if they are underrepresented in that particular profession. From the perspective of women's groups, the ECJ was no longer the reliable ally paralleling their effort in expanding European equality politics. The ruling instigated a flood of criticism from a wide spectrum of women activists: academics, lawyers and women's organizations alike.[55] The European Women's Lobby was quick to mobilize in opposition to the decision and as a result of their pressure the Commission subsequently issued a communication offering an interpretation of the ruling (CEC 1996a).[56] The Commission's communication stated that all positive action programs must not be viewed as inconsistent with EU law, despite the ruling, and suggested a list of compatible programs. The Commission's action would shape subsequent rulings. A year later, the ECJ would adopt a similar position in the *Marschall* decision (ECJ 1997c)[57]: a decision that ultimately narrowed the potential scope of the *Kalanke* ruling.

This adverse ruling had a direct impact on mobilizing transnational activists, whose subsequent pressure helped to reverse the effect of the decision and ultimately preserve a space for women both in national and European politics. The positive action programs that were the focus of the ruling are one avenue to help create a space for women, and these groups acted quickly to preserve their previous attempts to make positive action a priority in EU politics.

By the 1990s and early 2000s transnational mobilization in the area of social provisions was characterized by formal collective action, as exemplified by groups such as the EWL and the Social Platform. While women's organizations had exhibited considerable difficulties in establishing a formal lobbying organization, the political opportunities afforded them through both the Commission and the support of the Women's Committee in the Parliament would finally help facilitate such an organization. Further, these organizations realized that if they did not organize collectively they might risk losing the access that the Commission extended to formal lobbies. Yet even more than the work of the EWL, activists working through Commission sponsored networks and those utilizing legal strategies continued to alter the shape of EU social provisions by altering policy frames and through litigation.

---

[55] For example, see Prechal (1996).

[56] Positive Action had long been a policy focus for the EWL and thus this ruling came in stark contrast to the policy agenda they had hoped would develop at the European level. EWL (1996) and interview with General Secretary of EWL, Brussels, March 2000.

[57] Similar to the *Kalanke* case, the preliminary reference originated from a German court and involved a male job candidate disputing the decision to hire a female for the position.

When comparing the mobilization in the 1950s/60s to that taking place by 2003, the policy priorities of these groups had also evolved. While the earlier groups were largely trade unions with only a secondary focus on women's issues, by the this later time period the majority of groups were voluntary organizations with a primary focus on broad issues of social protection from women's equality to poverty. These groups were concerned with carving out a larger space in EU politics for public interests. And EU organizations responded. As discussed, this was evident from various programs and actions adopted during the 1990s and into the early 2000s, such as the Commission's activities to preserve positive action programs and also the move to develop greater access for all NGOs to EU politics as exemplified through the Convention on the Future of Europe process.

Conclusions

This historical analysis illustrates that the tenacity of women activists, operating within and in coordination with EU organizations, has enabled EU politics today to possess an institutionalized public sphere for women. As EU political opportunities, such as ECJ precedent and Commission sponsored networks, allowed greater formal access, created new social spaces and increased in number we have seen an incremental increase in permanent Brussels based social organizations. Further, what began as discrete forms of transnational mobilization, such as the legal activism of Elaine Vogel-Polsky or the work of feminists such as Deshormes in the Commission, have today manifested themselves in the form of formal collective organizations, such as the EWL.

The analysis also illustrated that the relative success at mobilization strategies may be related to characteristics specific to the movement. Equality agencies and legal experts exhibited considerable success at utilizing litigation strategies to pressure for greater equality rights, a pattern found more generally amongst the women's movement. Further, organizing through informal networks to change policy frames rather than through collective lobbying to attain these same ends achieved greater success, as exemplified by the difficulties with the formation of the EWL.

Together these factors have shaped the direction of EU social provisions. EU political opportunities can empower transnational activists, but over time this mobilization has altered the rules and procedures governing this policy domain. Even when national governments were hesitant to expand the area of social provisions, the action of EU organizations and transnational activists sustained and expanded these rules and procedures. As we have seen, this process of institutionalization can expand both the meaning and scope of EU rules and empower EU organizations and transnational organizations *vis-à-vis* national governments. Over time, the policy area becomes less intergovernmental as individuals and groups attain greater direct access to EU policy processes and are enabled to bring claims against their own national governments.

Beyond the expansion of social policy, this process of institutionalization has implications for public inclusion in EU politics. Although not necessarily intended by their action, over time, we saw how transnational mobilization expanded what is a European issue, shifting from employment concerns to broader social protection to now a more general concern with including public interests. In Chapter 6, I explore this dynamic in the area of environmental protection. This comparative analysis will enable us to test whether the patterns revealed in this chapter are indicative of other EU public interests.

6 Collective activism for the environment

In this chapter, I explore how institutionalization has taken place through mobilization in the area of environmental protection. In particular, I examine how litigation and legislative action functioned as political opportunity structures for transnational environmental organizations. Similar to Chapter 5, we might expect as these European Union (EU) level opportunities increase in formality and magnitude a shift in transnational activism from individual to more collective mobilization. Although this general pattern may hold across policy domains, we might expect the strategies and tactics of these groups to vary. As we have seen, women's organizations had relative ease at utilizing litigation strategies but were less successful at forming a single lobbying organization, an outcome that is consistent with the patterns of women's mobilizing more generally.

Here, I explore the relative success of different strategies the environmental movement utilizes to shape EU rules and procedures. It is through this action that we might expect to find institutionalization taking place. Further, as these rules and procedures provide new opportunities for action and greater inclusion, we might expect that over time this public interest will increasingly become more permanent actors in EU politics. As the civil society gains greater direct access to EU politics we might expect a shift away from intergovernmental politics. As earlier discussed, this analysis will provide comparisons with Chapter 5, in order to highlight the variation and similarities we might expect to find across public interest sectors.

The 1970s and before: transnational European environmentalism in its infancy

In the 1950s, 1960s and 1970s the EU policy arena was in its infancy. And at this time, environmental protection was a distant concern of EU policymakers. However, this was not due to a lack of action on behalf of environmental organizations. Conservation groups throughout Europe had been organizing since the late 1800s and their activities increasingly promoted a European-wide solution to environmental conservation and protection (Bowman 1999; Dalton 1994). Yet their presence was noticeably absent from EU politics. This would begin to change as this new supranational policy arena began to develop political opportunities that gave environmental groups access to this increasingly important new policy venue.

Litigation and legislative action as political opportunities for mobilization

How did the European Court of Justice's (ECJ) rulings and EU legislative expansion impact this mobilization? The ECJ issued its first environmental protection ruling in 1976 (ECJ 1976b). However, similar to the patterns of litigation in the social provisions domain, there were few environmental preliminary references in these initial years. Further, although small in number, the case law in both legal domains was foundational with potentially expansive policy and mobilization implications. Yet there were also noticeable differences. The ECJ decisions in the *Defrenne* equality cases created a new set of equality rights that both became the backbone of legislative developments in the 1970s and opened a floodgate of subsequent litigation, as women were given a new opportunity to bring discrimination claims before national courts. The environmental case, *Handelskwekerij* decision (ECJ 1976b), although exhibiting a similar mobilizing potential, did not have the same effect (Cichowski 1998; Sands 1990).

By way of an Article 234 reference from the Appellate Court of the Hague, the ECJ was asked in the *Handelskwekerij* case to interpret the "where the harmful event occurred" clause of the 1968 Brussels Convention. The defendant in the case allegedly discharged 10,000 tons of chloride for consecutive twenty-four hour periods into the River Rhine. The ECJ ruled that Article 5(3) "must be understood as being intended to cover both the place where the damage occurred and the place of the event giving rise to it" (para. 24). This progressive interpretation of Article 5(3) not only reversed the original Dutch court decision, it expanded the jurisdiction intended by the Brussels Convention. The ruling had in theory enabled victims of transboundary pollution to choose the jurisdiction in which they want to bring tort; either in the country in which the damage was suffered or the country in which the event giving rise to the damage occurred. As member states possess varying rules regarding *locus standi*, environmental protection, legal costs and time delays, legal scholars argue that this ECJ ruling allowed the possibility of forum shopping for environmental groups wishing to bring proceedings against polluters (Sands 1990).[1] However, in reality few individuals and environmental groups have been able to utilize this opportunity.

One component of this, and a crucial difference between the sex equality and environmental case law in this time period, was the direct effect of EU laws: the *Defrenne II* ruling stated that Article 141 of the Treaty was directly effective, providing women an individual EU right that could be utilized before a national court. The direct effect of EU environmental law remains a contentious issue.[2] Further, and more generally, as elaborated in Chapter 4, claiming direct harm in environmental cases, even when there are more favorable standing rules for environmental organizations, remains difficult in legal systems across the EU (see Führ and Roller 1991). Thus, the limited impact of this potentially empowering ruling becomes evident. Thus not surprisingly, legal action has long been a comparatively useful and successful tactic for women activists for these reasons, as individual rights and proof of individual harm are significantly easier to claim in equality cases than in environmental protection litigation (O'Connor 1980). Despite the potential empowering effects of ECJ rulings in both domains, characteristics specific to the movements, which are traceable to feasible political strategies, help explain this variation.

Interestingly, this cross-sectoral variation may play a larger role at explaining disparity in total number of cases brought than individual level non-governmental organization (NGO) direct involvement in cases. Table 6.1 includes data on the type of litigants in environmental protection preliminary rulings between 1976 and 2003. Similar to the area of social provisions, there were no associations directly involved in litigation in the 1970 time period, but again there were also very few environmental cases in the 1970s (only two decisions). The next decade produced similar trends across both policy sectors regarding multiple litigants as the environmental ruling in this category amounted to 22 percent of cases. Only one case during this time period involved an NGO, compared to 22 percent of social provisions cases in the similar time. However, the most interesting find comes in the last time period. Again, we would expect *locus standi* issues to be easier to surmount in the social provisions area given the challenge of making environmental claims, yet between the two domains, in this last time period, environmental NGOs continued to expand the number of cases they supported

---

[1] The ECJ has since clarified its interpretation of eligibility on long-arm jurisdiction stating that it is only available to victims of direct harm (Sands 1990).
[2] See Krämer 1991a: 51; Miller 1998: 30–32; Geddes 1992. Also see discussion in Chapter 4.

Table 6.1 *Environmental protection Article 234 preliminary rulings by type of litigant bringing the case, 1976–2003*

	Number of cases (as a percentage)			
	1 litigant	2 or more litigants	Association/NGO litigants	Total cases
1976–1979	1 (50%)	1 (50%)	0	2
1980–1989	13 (72%)	4 (22%)	1 (6%)	18
1990–2003	29 (55%)	12 (23%)	12 (23%)	53
Total cases	43 (59%)	17 (23%)	13 (18%)	73

Note:
The cases in the Association/NGO category of litigants were references originating in the following countries: Belgium, France, Germany, Italy and United Kingdom.
Source: Data compiled by the author from European Communities. 2003. *CELEX Data Base.* Brussels: Office for Official Publications of the European Communities.
http://europa.eu.int/celex/htm/celex_en.htm.

(23% of environmental cases directly involved environmental associations compared to 5% in the similar time period for social provisions). This increase in environmental NGO participation is not altogether surprising given their comparatively strong transnational mobilization and successful utilization of EU-level opportunities (as discussed in the following analysis), traits that were not immediately forthcoming to women's organizations. Furthermore, by the end of the 1990s and into 2000, the demand for improved access to justice for environmental organizations and environmental concerns remained a salient topic with real policy reforms.[3]

EU legislative action in the area of the environment during the 1960s would exhibit similar limitations for mobilization, as did this review of litigation. Different from the area of social provisions, there was no treaty basis for EU environmental protection measures, making environmental claims comparatively challenging.[4] However, EU policymakers did develop at least some competence over national environmental

[3] See discussion in Chapter 2 and in the following section on the 1990s and 2000s. In particular, Directive 2003/4/EC on public access to environmental information, Directive 2003/35/EC on public access to decision-making on environmental matters and the Commission proposal for an access to justice in environmental matters directive (CEC 2003).

[4] Environmental measures were based on either Article 94 (ex 100) which enables the Council to unanimously adopt measures "for the approximation of such provisions laid down by law, regulation or administrative action in member states and directly affect the establishment or functioning of the common market" or on Article 308 (ex 235) which is

regulations as early as the 1960s. Generally, legislation produced during this time was related to the objective of harmonizing laws to abolish trade barriers, and involved such issues as automobile pollution and product packaging.[5] Scholars have referred to the environmental policy developed during this early EU building stage as "pragmatic" and "incidental" rather than "real," primarily for the focus on economic harmonization rather than a concern for real protection of the natural environment (Hildebrand 1992: 15). Despite a continued lack of a formal legal basis for EU environmental protection, this policy trend would begin to change following the 1972 Paris Summit. This shift was both cause and effect of the environmental group mobilization.

This 1972 intergovernmental conference concluded with all member states agreeing on the need for at least some concrete European environmental policy and charged the Commission with producing an official framework by 31 July 1973 (CEC 1972). This decision to act grew out of both environmental activism that fostered public awareness of environmental destruction and also a growing concern amongst national governments of the trade distortions that were resulting from uncoordinated national environmental regulations (Hildebrand 1992: 20; Rehbinder and Stewart 1985: 409). By the end of 1973, the Council had adopted the Commission's proposal, the *First Community Action Programme on the Environment* (CEC 1973a). This marked a significant new opportunity to expand EU competence in the area of environmental protection and create a supranational space for environment concerns. As stated by the Commission, it "added a new dimension to the construction of Europe." In particular, it focused on pollution control, coordination of actions with international organizations active in environmental issues and measures that were associated with common policies, such as the Common Agriculture Policy (CAP) and regional policy. These were significant accomplishments given the lack of a treaty basis for such programs.

A second program was adopted in 1977 and expanded the EU's environmental aims focusing on preventive policy, including the management of space, the environment and natural resources (CEC 1977). Yet adoption of this second program was a function of a momentum nurtured by the Commission, rather than a growing commitment on the part of

---

also based on unanimity and it enables the Council to adopt "appropriate measures" to "attain, in the course of operation of the common market, one of the objectives of the Community" where the "Treaty has not provided the necessary powers" to do so.

[5] Council Directive (Dir.) 70/220/EEC on pollutant emission of motor vehicles and Dir. 67/548/EEC on the classification, labeling and packaging of dangerous substances. Other directives adopted before the *First Community Action Programme on the Environment* in 1973 included: Council Directive 70/157/EEC on noise levels, Council Directive 72/306/EEC diesel automobile emissions.

member state governments to expand EU competence over national environmental regulation. In reality, following the passage of the first program, member states exhibited a general reluctance to put these general declarations into practice, a reaction not altogether different from the initial reaction to EU gender equality policies. However, as illustrated in Chapter 4, this member state non-compliance in the 1970s would in turn create the opportunity for litigation in the 1980s. Environmentalists were able to force recalcitrant member states into compliance, often giving the ECJ the opportunity to further expand the scope and precision of EU law enabling further action in the future.

Further, the internal administrative resources for the environment were comparatively limited. During this time period, environmental issues were tasked to a 20-person strong unit on Environment and Consumer Service, rather than incorporating this into the administrative structure of a directorate general. Some scholars have observed that the "under-staffing and under-budgeting" of the Environmental and Consumer unit was a direct attempt by national governments to "temper" the Commission's environmental ambitions (Rehbinder and Stewart 1985: 409). Despite this attempt, the Commission continued to pursue and expand EU environmental competence as exemplified by the two action programs. Further, the Commission felt public support was crucial, and thus began to reach out to environmental groups to help support this agenda. The Commission's financial support for the development of the European Environmental Bureau in 1974 is a clear example. I discuss this in further detail below.

Finally, the construction of the European Parliament's (EP) Environmental Committee in 1972 is a noteworthy development during this time period. While some scholars have highlighted the EP's limited role in the EU policy process (e.g. Rucht 2001), the Parliament's Environmental Committee has garnered a considerable history of successes in the initiation, amendment and implementation of EU environmental measures (e.g. Judge 1992). Observers describe an almost zealous commitment to environmentalism by the committee, "the Environmental Committee is different from most other committees, it sees itself as a crusader, at the cutting edge of one of the most important policy areas of our time ... Occasionally you get the impression that some of its members feel that they are predestined to save the earth."[6] It is this commitment that has made the committee very hospitable to the concerns of environmental NGOs, even at this early stage of EU development. For example, as discussed in Chapter 4, the

---

[6] Interview with Committee member, as quoted in Judge (1992: 209).

origins of EU nature protection policy (the Wild Birds Directive, 1979) was traceable to NGOs' transnational activism that targeted the Environmental Committee which led to subsequent parliamentary questions, adoption of an EP resolution and ultimately the formulation and adoption of the Directive.[7] The EP Environmental Committee was a key link in this chain. The significance of this political ally and opportunity for both the Commission and NGOs would develop in subsequent decades.

Mobilization, institutionalization and political opportunities for public inclusion

How were transnational interests organizing around European environmental issues at this time and what was the interaction between these political opportunities and this mobilization? The evolution of European environmental organizations in many ways exhibited a parallel, and certainly interconnected, development with EU environmental initiatives, with the early decades possessing little if any groups with a primary commitment to environmental protection (instead an overriding concern with economic priorities) and a more visible environmental presence developing by the end of the 1970s. In the 1950s and 1960s, seven groups became permanent actors in the newly forming European policy community. Table 6.2 contains each of these organizations by their founding date and organization type. With over half the groups forming in 1962, clearly the growing visibility and importance of the EU, signified by expansive EU policy developments during this time such as the Common Agriculture Policy (CAP) in 1962, highlighted the importance of this new supranational political arena.

Further, these groups represented diverse issues, such as consumer rights, regional interests, health issues and scientific research. Only one group was explicitly dedicated to environmental protection, the Western European Institute for Wood Preservation (WEI) established in 1951, and this was a specific rather than general environmental interest. Similar to the area of social provisions and a lack of an explicit concern for women's issues at this early stage, few of these organizations had much involvement in EU environmental issues during their early founding years: not unsurprising given the lack of any EU environmental measures before the 1960s. However, this would change over time, illustrating the diversity of non-environmental organizations that would become active in promoting EU environmental policy.

---

[7] See Chapter 4.

Table 6.2 *Transnational organizations in the area of environmental protection by organizational type and founding date, 1950–1969*

Organization	Founding date
Environmental/Natural resouces	
WEI	1951
Consumer rights	
BEUC	1962
EURO COOP	1962
Regional/Local authorities	
CLRAE	1957
AEIAR	1966
Health	
EORTC	1962
Scientific research	
CONCAWE	1962

Source: Data compiled by author from *Directory of Pressure Groups in the EU*, Philip and Gray (1996), *Directory of Interest Groups* (Luxembourg: Office for Official Publications of the European Communities, 1996) and the database for *Consultation, the European Commission and Civil Society (CONECCS)* (European Commission, online database http://europa.eu.int/comm/civil_society/coneccs/.

For example, the European Bureau of Consumer Unions (BEUC) established a Brussels office in 1962 with the aim to "lobby at the European level for consumer protection" (BEUC 1996: 46). While the organization's concerns span a wide spectrum of consumer rights issues, the group remains active in lobbying DG Environment and also liaises regularly with the Parliament's Environmental Committee. Further, it coordinates on environmental issues with other European-level consumer groups such as the European Community of Consumer Cooperatives (EURO COOP) which was also established during this time period (EURO COOP 1996: 316). Along with consumer interests, other groups with a less public concern for the environment also opened their doors during this time period. The Oil Companies' European Organization for Environment, Health and Safety (CONCAWE) is a research institute that "conducts studies on environmental issues related to the oil refining industry" including "air and water pollution, health and occupational aspects, and soil pollution" (CONCAWE 1996: 135). While the institute conducts valuable scientific studies on European environmental issues that may have influenced the early EU focus on

Table 6.3 *Transnational organizations in the area of environmental protection by organizational type and founding date, 1970–1979*

Organization	Founding date
Environmental/Natural resources	
EEB	1974
IEEP	1976
Waste management/Recycling	
BIR	1970
EFR	1970
EUROMETREC	1970
EUREAU	1975
Health	
AIA/EAC	1978
Scientific research	
ECETOC	1978
Development	
ESED	1977

Source: Data compiled by author from *Directory of Pressure Groups in the EU*, Philip and Gray (1996), *Directory of Interest Groups* (Luxembourg: Office for Official Publications of the European Communities, 1996) and the database for *Consultation, the European Commission and Civil Society (CONECCS)* (European Commission, online database http://europa.eu.int/comm/civil_society/coneccs/.

environmental issues such as the regeneration of oil, its ties to the oil industry illustrate the considerable influence economic interests played at this early stage of EU environmental policy.[8]

The early and late 1970s represented another growth period in transnational organizations in the area of EU environmental policy. As illustrated in Table 6.3, between 1970 and 1979, nine new groups began focusing their lobbying efforts at the supranational level. These groups

---

[8] The disposal of used oil was the subject of the EU's first environmental policy developments (Council Directive 75/439/EEC on the disposal of waste oils) and continues to be a contested EU issue today (see ECJ case law discussed in Chapter 4; also Krämer 2000: 258). Although this Directive stated that member states must give priority to the recycling of waste oil, they were given considerable room for exceptions: "where technical, economic and organizational constraints so allow." While this clause may very well be attributable to the growing strength of the oil industry's European lobby during the 1960s and 1970s, it has only led to subsequent legal difficulties for many companies in the associated industries of waste oil disposal and manufacturers of oil stoves and heaters (for example, see ECJ 1983, ECJ 1985a and ECJ 1990e).

would be considerably "greener" than their previous counterparts. Similar to the dynamic between the rise of the feminist movement in domestic politics and subsequent mobilization at the EU level in the 1970s, as the environmental movement gained strength in domestic arenas, it too began to utilize the increasing number of political opportunities provided by expanding EU competence. Yet the organizations established during this decade were still disproportionately associations with environment as a secondary focus, with 75 % of the groups representing other interests, such as waste management, health, scientific research and development issues. This trend is generally consistent with mobilization patterns in the area of social provisions. Yet the interaction between litigation, legislative action and mobilization would be quite different during this time period.

For example, even during this early period of EU development, feminist activists were quick to utilize ECJ precedent to further expand women's rights under EU law, both through subsequent discrimination litigation and by pushing for policy expansion within the Commission. While women activists utilized the opportunity structures provided by both the Commission and European Parliament, the ECJ rulings were equally important for this mobilization. This pattern is attributable to the pre-existing political strategies of the women's movement, as litigation was proving a successful tactic to advance women's rights claims. As earlier discussed, the relative difficulty experienced by environmental groups making legal claims may help explain the minimal impact ECJ precedent had on mobilization in this time period. Instead, transnational mobilization developed more as a function of the political opportunities created by both the Commission and the Parliament. These included legislative action that highlighted the conflicts between national environmental regulation and EU free-trade laws, action programs that provided funding for NGOs, as well as action by both the EP's Environmental Committee and the Commission that fostered a European policy debate on the environment. Together, these opportunities created a social space for new policy demands as well as formal access points to EU politics.

For example, the waste management/recycling industry began making a clear presence in Brussels in 1970 as the potential conflicts between national waste disposal and recycling regulations and the increasingly powerful EU free-trade norms began being debated by EU policymakers. The Bureau of International Recycling (BIR) established a Brussels office in 1970 with the aim to "promote recycling, thereby conserving natural resources, protecting the environment and facilitating free trade and movement of recovered materials" (BIR 1996: 51). With the same founding date in 1970, the European Ferrous Recovery and Recycling Federation (EFR) and the European Metal Trade and Recycling

Federation (EUROMETREC), came to Brussels with similar political objectives.[9] Simultaneously, EU legislators were showing a similar concern, as waste management played a significant part of EU environmental policy from the beginning (Krämer 2000: 236). A Commission declaration in 1972 mentioned the importance of waste recovery[10], the *First Community Action Programme on the Environment* (1973) emphasized the need for the harmonization of national waste management legislation (CEC 1973a) and finally in 1975 the Waste Framework Directive was adopted.[11] These advancements did not take place in isolation of the waste management lobby that was increasingly important on an international scale and whose European lobby engaged in highly organized networking during this time period, and would continue to grow in the next decade.[12] Thus, even at this early stage the political opportunities created by EU organizations were both cause and effect of transnational mobilization.

The 1970s also witnessed the development of European organizations dedicated exclusively to the protection of nature and the environment. These groups developed as the EU began to exhibit a concrete commitment to legislating in the area of the environment protection in the early 1970s. The Institute for European Environmental Policy (IEEP) was set up in 1976 by the European Cultural Foundation with the aim of "advancing environmental policy in Europe" and has done so through publications and conferences on a wide range of EU environmental topics (IEEP 1996: 420). This international research network has carried out research commissioned by national governments and DG Environment and states that this research "guides and informs policy-makers at the EU level and national levels, NGOs, researchers, professional bodies and

---

[9] EFR operates mainly through BIR, but focuses specifically on the "commercial, legal, environmental and technical problems concerning the European ferrous metals industry" (EFR 1996: 228). EUROMETREC also collaborates with EFR and BIR, yet has also liaised with the Commission on its own right in the area of non-ferrous metals by providing statistics for the Commission's annual *Panorama of EU Industry* (EUROMETREC 1996: 332)

[10] [1972] O.J. C52/1.   [11] Council Directive 75/442/EEC on waste.

[12] BIR alone, as an international federation, represents more than fifty countries. It estimates that the industry employed more than 1.5 million people worldwide at this time. Further, BIR would have an annual general assembly that included the other "European supranational sister federations" EFR and EUROMETREC. This cooperation also took the form of joint lobbying efforts, as BIR would sometimes act as a representative of these organizations in promoting waste and recycling issues to DG XI (Environment) and in monitoring the EP's Environmental Committee. This waste management lobby cites the adoption by the EU of their "three-tiered system of categorization of waste and secondary raw materials" as proof of the effectiveness and success of their involvement in EU policymaking (BIR 1996: 51).

industry" (IEEP 1996: 420). Again, these groups mobilize around the new space created for European environmental issues, but their action subsequently can impact new legislative action, that over time expands EU competence and creates subsequent opportunities for action.

Similarly, in 1974, national environmental NGOs developed a European "voice" by establishing the European Environmental Bureau (EEB) (Commission 2000b: 6).[13] The umbrella organization represents NGOs from EU and European Free Trade Association (EFTA) member states with a current total of 140 member organizations from 31 countries.[14] The founding of this organization was aided by financial support provided by the Commission. The idea behind the opportunity was to provide greater formal access to EU politics for this environmental public interest in order to support the Commission's environmental agenda and offset an increasingly powerful Brussels based industrial lobby (Barnes and Barnes 1999: 116; Mazey and Richardson 1992: 120). As discussed in Chapter 5, a similar outreach attempt by the Commission's Women's Bureau had failed in this early time period (and would not succeed until 1990), due to the considerable disagreement within the feminist movement over the issues, objectives and exclusivity of a single European organization.[15] Conversely, the environmental groups and conservation organizations that comprise the EEB's membership were more easily able to utilize this EU opportunity as they were already successfully engaging in international and transnational cooperation on nature conservation issues, through groups such as the World Wide Fund for Nature (WWF) and on European issues such as wild bird protection.[16]

Today, the EEB's political activities are widespread.[17] The Commission has given the group formal access to policy development. For

---

[13] In the Commission newsletter, *Environment for Europeans*, they referred to the EEB as the "voice of the environmental movement in Brussels" (CEC 2000b: 6). See also Lowe and Goyder (1983) on the EEB.

[14] EEB website: http://www.eeb.org/.   [15] See Chapter 5.

[16] See Chapter 4 on the role of national environmental NGOs in the development of EU nature protection policy. In particular, these conservation groups have an extensive history of political influence on wildlife protection measures in Western European countries and also international conventions in this field. Historically, European conservation NGOs are characterized by their affluent membership base and also their greater degree of political power and influence than their general ecology counterparts (see Dalton 1994). Both national organizations such as the Royal Society for the Protection of Birds in the UK and international associations, such as the International Council for Bird Preservation (ICBP or Birdlife International as it is now called), have been lobbying for habitat protection since the early 1920s.

[17] This includes monitoring EU institutions' respect for the principles of the European Treaty, issuing position papers on EU environmental policy concerning issues from pollution control to tourism, and public outreach through publications, seminars and workshops (EEB 1999: 2–3).

example, in 1998 the Commission asked the EEB to evaluate the policy developments resulting from the *Fifth Environmental Action Programme* (1993). The Commission utilized this assessment to develop a Communication proposing new priorities for EU environmental policy (EEB 1998: 3). Thus, once given access, this activism can also play a part in shaping new opportunity structures through EU policy development and by keeping issues of public concern on the European agenda. This exemplifies the group's use of strategic framing, in order to affect what was introduced and remained an EU issue. Another example is the EEB's action in the Greening the Treaty Campaign (1990) that pressured for increased use of the qualified majority voting rule for environmental policy, a change that was subsequently adopted in the 1992 Maastricht Treaty (WWF, EEB and FOEE 1990). Further, the EEB has gained formal access to policy development through the Commission sponsored "structured dialogue." This policy dialogue enables environmental NGOs to directly participate through working groups and committees on the development of EU environmental policy proposals in such areas as eco-labeling and air quality (CEC 2000b: 6). Again these examples illustrate that these NGOs were actively engaged in both lobbying strategies as well as framing.

Far from having no policy impact, some observers have cited a concern by the European industrial lobby that environmentalists possess a monopoly on access to and influence on DG Environment's policy proposals (Mazey and Richardson 1992: 122). While the EEB lacks the resources and staff of other European policy sectors, such as the agriculture or industrial lobby, its policy presence and agenda-setting power is far from negligible as certain observers persist (Rucht 2001: 133; Ruzza 1996). Recently, it played a critical role in consultation and development of the Constitutional Treaty (despite the Treaty's current on-hold status) with six out of its ten policy objectives being adopted – importantly, one being the goal of greater participatory democracy and transparency in the EU (EEB 2004).

Despite the lack of an initial Treaty basis for environmental claims, we have seen that in the early stages of EU development, protection for natural resources and wildlife emerged as an EU policy objective. At this first stage, EU environmental opportunity structures were fairly limited due to a lack of formal environmental provisions, and thus the requirement to link legislative actions to the objectives of economic and community harmonization. Not surprisingly, there were few transnational environmental organizations mobilized during this period, most of which exhibited a secondary concern for environmental protection related to their industry and mainly with the relationship between national environmental regulations and the free movement of goods.

This trend in mobilization would begin to change in the 1970s as both a cause and an effect of the EU opportunities evolving during this time period. The Commission and the Parliament reached out to NGOs and provided both the formal access and social space to develop a permanent public voice for the European environment. The national environmental organizations exhibited little difficulty developing a European lobbying organization, an achievement that was harder for women's groups to attain. Generally, environmental groups exhibited little difficulty acting collectively at the EU level, even at this early stage, a fact that is attributable to a pattern of international collaboration amongst environmental groups. Further, once mobilized these transnational activists began leaving their mark on EU politics, through organized lobbying campaigns and by shaping EU policy frames. Litigation tactics posed a greater challenge for environmental groups. Despite the Court's expansive *Handelskwekerij* ruling (ECJ 1976b), environmental activists were confronted with the challenges of making legal claims for the environment, leaving lobbying and framing strategies much more successful.

The 1980s: the institutionalization of a European environment

Different from the area of social provisions, the 1980s witnessed an expansion in environmental legislative action. Along with a growing body of environmental legislation, environmental protection attained a legal basis in the treaty following the adoption of the Single European Act (1986). Environmental litigation would also incrementally increase as member states experienced considerable difficulty implementing EU environmental law. Together, this expansion in both legislative action and litigation would provide new opportunities for an equally growing European environmental lobby.

Litigation and legislative action as political opportunities for mobilization

Environmental litigation doubled in the 1980s (46 preliminary references). Further, similar to the dynamic in social provisions litigation, the Court adopted potentially expansive and far-reaching rulings during this decade that often pre-empted subsequent legislative advancements of EU decision makers. For example, the Court's *ADBHU* decision (ECJ 1985a) held that the protection of the environment was "one of the Community's essential objectives" which may justify certain limitation of the free movement of goods provisions of the Treaty (para. 13 of the decision). This ruling effectively constructed a legal basis for EU environmental objectives before member state governments agreed to do so through amendments to the Treaty in the Single European Act (Cichowski 1998: 399–400). Yet unlike the social provisions case law, those individuals empowered by a new legal basis for environmental claims still faced the barrier of standing rules and the general difficulties claiming environmental rights before national courts. Thus, there was not the same powerful impact on subsequent direct legal claims through Article 234 as seen in the social provisions domain; however, the ruling did create the opportunity for another type of mobilization. The decision became the subject of a campaign by a growing network of transnational environmental lawyers who criticized the EU for lacking a legal basis for environmental protection. Further, the ruling strengthened EU environmental priorities, a policy objective that the Commission was simultaneously attempting to achieve, and in doing so gave individuals and the Commission greater power to hold member states accountable for non-compliance. And thus, the dramatic increase in litigation pursuant to Article 226 was partially attributable to this ruling (Krämer 2000).

As discussed in Chapter 4, the Court's environmental preliminary rulings in the 1980s arose in large part from the growing number of national and transnational actors who were experiencing an increasing number of conflicts over varying national implementations and preexisting EU free-trade laws. These decisions arose from conflicts, such as those between fishermen in various member states (e.g. *Van Dam & Zonen* decision[18]), individuals disadvantaged by comparatively weak or incomplete implementations of EU water quality laws (e.g. *Angler's Association* decision, ECJ 1987f), and between transnational businesses who experienced relative disadvantages caused by ambiguities between EU environmental regulations and free trade laws (e.g. *Nijman* decision, ECJ 1989c, *Danish Bottles* decision, ECJ 1988a and *Inter-Huiles* decision, ECJ 1983). Ultimately, these rulings highlighted the problems that were beginning to arise due to the lack of a constitutional basis for EU environmental regulations that was unconnected with economic harmonization. This created a social space to discuss this problem at the European level. Environmental lawyers throughout the EU, some working within public bodies, others through NGOs, began to take note and subsequently utilize these rulings to push for more stringent and concrete EU

---

[18] ECJ (1981b). Almost half the cases (10) during this time period involved fishing disputes arising from French, Dutch and British courts. See Chapter 4 for a full list of the cases.

environmental policy. This growing network of environmental lawyers would prove instrumental in the subsequent litigation as well as the expansion of EU environmental policy. I will discuss this in greater detail in the mobilization section below.

Further, unlike social provisions, the environmental advancements made by the Court in the 1980s would be accompanied by an even greater expansion in the EU's legislative competence and policy infrastructure in this area. Beyond quantity, the quality or scope of EU environmental policy also underwent a distinct change. In the early 1980s, public outcry over the expansion of nuclear capabilities and forest destruction due to acid rain provided the spark for EU action. Diverging from the past trend to develop EU environmental policy from a fear of trade distortions, the 1983 Stuttgart European Council and subsequently the *Third Environmental Action Programme* (1983) introduced an "integrated approach" that recognized environmental protection as a fundamental part of other EU policies, such as economic, industrial, agricultural and social provisions. In particular, environmental destruction must be addressed in its own right at the EU level alongside the harmonization of other policies, due to the noticeable adverse environmental impact of economic integration.[19]

While clearly the EU was expanding the scope of EU environmental policy, it was largely "reactive" rather than proactive in the early 1980s and continued to be comparatively weak due to the lack of a constitutional basis for EU environmental law. The adoption of the SEA in 1986 would change this in two fundamental ways: (1) it introduced majority voting and the cooperation procedure; (2) and it established the Environmental Title in the Treaty providing provisions that define EU environmental policy. These institutional changes enabled the EU organizations to take considerable strides towards developing and expanding a supranational space for environmental concerns.

The first change not only diminished member state government veto power over EU environmental initiatives, but also more importantly gave the European Parliament, and its increasingly active Environmental

---

[19] Examples of legislation that was adopted following this change include: three air quality directives (Council Directive 80/779/EEC on smoke and sulfur dioxide, Council Directive 82/884/EEC on lead and Council Directive 85/203/EEC on nitrogen dioxide); a waste directive (Council Directive 84/631/EEC on toxic waste and the transfrontier shipment of waste); vehicle emissions directives (Council Directive 83/351/EEC on vehicle emissions and Council Directive 84/360 on emissions from industrial plants); and also the Major Accidents Directive (Council Directive 82/501/EEC regarding the accidental spillage of toxic substances).

Committee[20], a greater hand in policy development.[21] Thus, it is not surprising that the EP was proactive and instrumental in securing the environmental provisions in the SEA.[22] This had both a general and specific impact on new opportunities for public inclusion. As the EP is directly elected, and has traditionally been both the voice and advocate of the European public, the SEA in effect strengthened this voice in the policy process. More specifically, new environmental policy developments by the EP provided formal procedures and opportunities for direct citizen participation. One example is the 1985 Environmental Impact Assessment (EIA) Directive that in theory provided citizens with a right to be informed and an opportunity to state a position on developments covered by the Directive.[23] The national level structures that were created to implement this assessment procedure would begin to construct not only a formal access point, but also a social space that empowered citizens against their own national governments (Chalmers 1999: 673).

The second change, which introduced a concrete treaty basis for environmental protection, gave the Commission greater power to expand EU environmental protection programs.[24] At the same time the Commission had already begun to experience an increasingly powerful autonomy over

---

[20] Notable legislative successes of the Committee's pressure during the 1980s included: directives on seal pups, disposal of waste batteries, small cars and environmental impact assessment.

[21] Qualified majority voting (QMV) was not a new provision to the Treaty *per se* (as laid down previously in Article 148 EEC). However, it was new that under Article 100a it was possible to use it for environmental policy and thus the co-operation procedure (which gave two readings to the Parliament) would also then be utilized for environmental measures at this time. This is different than pre-SEA environmental legislation that was based on Article 100 or 235 (both unanimity) and also post-SEA Article 130s, which also requires unanimity for certain environmental measures. Significant disagreement often existed between the Commission and the EP on one side and the Council on the other over the new choice between Article 100a (QMV) or Article 130s (unanimity) for environmental measures. For a further discussion of these changes see Hildebrand (1992). The considerable power given to EU organizations and the public *vis-à-vis* member state governments with Article 100a, was underlying this conflict. The ECJ would intervene in this matter in the subsequent decade. See discussion below of the *Titanium Dioxide* decision (ECJ 1991).

[22] As Juliet Lodge states, "without the constant pressure from the EP it is doubtful that the SEA would have seen daylight" (1989: 68). Also, Haigh and Baldock (1989: 20) note the importance of the EP for inclusion of specific environmental concerns in the SEA.

[23] The Directive had been significantly weakened through the negotiation process due to member state opposition, in particular Denmark and the United Kingdom (Chalmers 1999: 670). Subsequently, many of these weakened or loosely drafted provisions led to delinquency and difficulty with national transpositions (see CEC 1998d). These conflicts would have a direct impact on both litigation and transnational mobilization in the 1990s (see discussion below).

[24] The Commission's *Fourth Environmental Action Programme* (EAP) (CEC 1987b) reflected this change. For example, the Commission strengthened the framework for

environmental protection, with organizational changes that included the upgrading in 1983 of the environmental and consumer protection service to Directorate General status (DG Environment, Consumer Protection and Nuclear Safety). By the late 1980s, observers have noted that DG Environment had developed a "strong counterculture" enabled by a disproportionate hiring of external "green activists" rather than the usual career EU personnel.[25] This created a series of formal access points for both individuals and environmental groups.

For example, in the mid 1980s the Commission began encouraging citizen participation in monitoring the implementation of EU environmental law. In particular, citizens were encouraged to report possible national level transposition problems through the Commission's complaint procedure, a formal process which had originally been established in the 1960s as a way for the EU to obtain information on possible free-trade infringements.[26] Another example was the creation of the Coordination of Information on the Environment (CORINE) program. This network was established in 1985 and enabled DG Environment to collect cross-national data on the current state of the environment in all member states.[27] The impact on policy development and mobilization was direct; DG Environment became known as a policy entrepreneur developing innovative EU environmental policy and drawing in a network of actors from NGOs to scientists to support its activities (Chalmers 1999: 660). New political opportunities were created and the activists began to come and likewise, these activists began working within EU organizations in a way that began changing the scope of EU environmental innovations.

Mobilization, institutionalization and political opportunities for public inclusion

This expanding net of EU level political opportunities was instrumental to the transnational mobilization of environmental organizations that would radically increase during the 1980s. Unlike the pattern of mobilization around EU women's issues that expanded equally each decade

subsequent legislative developments by formalizing and completing earlier statements or notions of EU environmental policy. Further, this EAP introduced new policy directions such as environmental educational efforts and a focus on gene-technology.

[25] Jean-Charles Leygues, member of Delors Cabinet, responsible for personnel matters, is quoted as saying, "60 percent of DG XI people are external appointments, off the usual EU career line, and they are overwhelmingly Green activists" (quoted in G. Ross (1995: 301).

[26] [1987] OJ C328/1, 9.   [27] Council Decision 85/338/EEC [1985] OJ L 176/1.

Table 6.4 *Transnational organizations involved in the area of environmental protection by organizational type and founding date, 1980–1989*

Organization	Founding date
Environmental/Natural resources	
EUROGROUP	1980
EFG	1980
EWA	1981
YEE	1983
IoH	1984
FOEE	1986
EURONATURE	1987
EFEDAH	1987
EDRC	1988
CNE	1989
EBCD	1989
GLOBE EU	1989
GREENPEACE- Europe	1988
SAR	1989
T&E	1989
WWF International	1989
STEM	1989
EAZA	1988
Waste management/Recycling/Energy/Packaging	
EWPCA	1981
FEAD	1981
EPIA	1985
APEAL	1986
EUROPIA	1989
ERRA	1989
Regional/Local authorities	
RETI	1984
Development	
CARE International	1982

Source: Data compiled by author from *Directory of Pressure Groups in the EU*, Philip and Gray (1996), *Directory of Interest Groups* (Luxembourg: Office for Official Publications of the European Communities, 1996) and the database for *Consultation, the European Commission and Civil Society (CONECCS)* (European Commission, online database http://europa.eu.int/comm/civil_society/coneccs/.

until the 1990s, environmental activists turned to Europe in force in the 1980s. Similar to the women's mobilizing, the 1980s illustrated that environmental groups continued to become more collective and coordinated with their campaigns. Table 6.4 displays the transnational organizations involved in EU environmental policy founded between 1980 and 1989. In terms of total growth, more organizations opened their doors in Brussels during this decade than in the time since the founding of the EU (total of 26 groups added to the existing 16). The waste management sector, which established 3 groups, was still making its presence known as the EU continued to define and expand this area of EU environmental policy.[28] But most noteworthy, 70 percent of these new organizations were dedicated explicitly to nature protection and ecological concerns, an unprecedented number compared to previous decades.

The change in character of these groups, being rooted more in grass-roots citizen politics than long-established professional or business organizations, paralleled the rise of feminist organizations at the EU level also taking place at this time. However, both the number and the activities of these two public interests were remarkably different. The three women's organizations established at this time (CREW, EWMD and ENOW) were not mass member organizations, with ENOW being the only association actually representing grassroots women's organizations. Further, their European activities concentrated on research, outreach to specific groups of women (e.g. EWMD's focus on women in management positions), dissemination of information on EU equality law and policy and informal networking. The expanding net of equality law both from legislation and ECJ rulings was an integral part of the European space these groups were beginning to carve out for women (CREW, in particular, through its outreach and publications). Yet the majority of this action took place through informal lobbying and legal action, with little formal coordination of efforts during this time period. Beyond the considerably larger number of environmental associations, this pattern of action would only vaguely resemble the formalized public environmental advocacy that was beginning to take shape in this same European space.

The green public sphere that was evolving involved two types of activism. First, a community of European lawyers began to emerge as a

---

[28] The European Water Pollution Control Association (EWPCA) cited a "good relationship" with the Commission over its role in providing comparative reports on national implementation of the Urban Waste Water Directive (91/271/EEC) (EWPCA 1996: 353). Both the European Federation of Waste Management (FEAD) and European Recovery and Recycling Association (ERRA) were involved in the collaborative Packaging Chain Forum in order to "influence the packaging waste directive" (ERRA 1996: 260; FEAD 1996: 359). It is hard to trace the cause and effect of this growing waste management lobby, but the Commission continued to expand this area of regulation, first through the *Fourth Environmental Action Programme*, and subsequently with the introduction of the need for a concrete waste management strategy (CEC 1987b: para. 5.3), and then in a 1989 Commission communication that fixed a strategic guideline for waste management (CEC 1989).

substantial force in shaping the direction of EU environmental law. The ECJ's environmental decisions provided the basis for their action and discussion; this in turn influenced EU agenda setting. Preliminary rulings such as the earlier discussed *ADBHU* and *Inter-Huiles* decisions and an increasing number of environmental rulings pursuant to Article 226 infringement proceedings would begin to get the attention of lawyers throughout Europe.[29] Again, many of these disputes were traceable to conflicts involving environmental regulations (both national and EU) that were infringing on EU free-trade principles, as well as non-compliance problems with environmental directives (Cichowski 1998).

By the mid 1980s, public law scholars and practitioners, all of whom were working from within either national environmental agencies or DG Environment, began to review and write critically about this emerging area of supranational law.[30] The most important effect of this legal community was a voice in unison criticizing the lack of a constitutional basis for EU environmental policy and the need to separate environmental protection from economic harmonization objectives. It was this mobilization that would be crucial to the development and ultimate addition of the Environmental Title in the Single European Act (Chalmers 1999: 665). ECJ decisions created the space to mobilize by highlighting the conflicts; subsequently the legal community began to develop a public voice and European space for critical discussion of these tensions in current EU policies, and ultimately this influenced the creation of a formalized basis for EU environmental competence. This new environmental opportunity structure, a constitutional basis in the SEA, would subsequently be one factor motivating the second type of green activism: NGO mobilization.

Unlike the individual action of this legal community, the environmental NGOs opening Brussels based offices during the late 1980s were highly organized and coordinated associations. Three of these groups, Friends of the Earth Europe (FOEE), World Wide Fund for Nature (WWF) and Greenpeace represented European offshoots of larger international environmental organizations. FOEE is the European policy

---

[29] Chalmers (1999: 665). Prior to 1990, there were twenty Article 226 actions in the area of the environment (*European Court Reports*, various years).

[30] The first three systematic accounts of EU environmental law were published by Nigel Haigh (*EEC Environmental Law and Britain*, ENDS, 1984) who worked for the British Department of the Environment; Ludwig Krämer (*EEC Treaty and Environmental Protection* (Sweet & Maxwell, 1990) who was the top law officer for DG Environment at the time and today is the head of the Waste Unit, and finally S. Johnson and G. Corcelle *The Environmental Policy of the European Communities* (Graham and Trotman, 1989). For a further discussion of the activities of this environmental law community see Chalmers (1999).

office of the organization Friends of the Earth International (FOEI).[31] In 1985, the European members of this international organization decided to form FOEE as a "response to the increasing need for coordination and cooperation throughout Europe" (FOEE 1999: 3). Further, some of FOE members had originally been excluded from the European Environmental Bureau, necessitating their own Brussels based office.[32] Indeed, the group's activities – from GMO campaigns to monitoring the accession process for Eastern enlargement – are guided by the aim to create a European space where policy advancements are made in a way that respects "global environmental limits."[33] Along with membership dues and funding, the group receives 25 percent of its annual budget from the EU (FOEE 1996: 399). Thus, EU legislative action created not only the social space to pressure for EU environmental policy, but also enabled formal access to this European space by providing these groups with financial support to sustain a Brussels based office.

Similarly, WWF, whose global network represents some 4.7 million supporters, opened a European Policy Office (EPO) in 1989 as a result of the increasing amount of European environmental legislation and their interest in being a part of this coordinated effort.[34] WWF also receives Commission funding, although it explicitly caps this amount at less than 15 percent.[35] Finally, Greenpeace, which organizes some 3 million supporters worldwide with approximately 2 million residing in EU member states, opened a European Unit (EU) in 1989. It stands out most noticeably from the other groups for its confrontational tactics and its refusal to accept any funding from the Commission.[36] That said, Greenpeace EU has also accepted that in order to be successful in EU politics the group

---

[31] FOEI is a worldwide federation with members from 59 national environmental organizations, whereas, FOEE represents 30 associations from 29 European countries with over 3,000 local chapters (FOEE 1999).

[32] Greenpeace had a similar experience.

[33] Interview with policy coordinator for FOEE, Brussels, March 2000.

[34] Tony Long, Director of the EPO, states: "Decisions taken in Brussels matter ... It has been estimated that four out of five environmental laws in European Union countries originate in Brussels. To influence that legislation, it is clearly important to be active in the committees and corridors of power where decisions are taken. That is why WWF decided to open its European Policy Office" (*Into the Millennium* WWF European Policy Office, 2000).

[35] Interview with representative from WWF, Brussels, March 2000. In 1999, WWF received 8 percent of its income from the Commission, 45 percent from WWF national organizations, 28 percent from WWF International and 19 percent from foundations and other sources.

[36] Funding for Greenpeace EU comes from membership dues and merchandise sales. Interview with representative from Greenpeace, Brussels, March 2000.

has had to adopt more conventional tactics to achieve its policy goals. Hans Wolters, Director of the EU Greenpeace office states:

Climbing chimneys attracts media attention and stimulates discussion, which is very important. But at the same time we work with hard facts and concrete proposals, because that is the only way to convince industry and politicians.[37]

By the end of the decade, these three internationally based European groups, along with the earlier established European Environmental Bureau, would form the "G4" and begin a formal coordination of their EU policy campaigns that would expand in membership and in importance in the next decade (Stetter 2001: 151). This marked a distinct shift to even more formal collective collaboration between these already mass member organizations.

Besides environmental groups with international origins, the 1980s also witnessed the establishment of transnational mobilization that was European in origin. The European Federation for Transport and Environment (T&E) was established in 1989 and consists of 35 member NGOs working in the area of transport and environment from 20 European countries. With a growing number of transportation decisions that influence the environment being taken at the EU level (e.g. air quality standards and emission limits), member organizations decided to take advantage to this new policy arena: "Europe offers a great opportunity to work to higher standards of environmental protection."[38] Further, the founders of T&E recognized the differences between the EU and national lobbying climate, stating the Commission relies much more heavily on outside organizations than national ministries (T&E 1998: 3). They decided to utilize this access point. Finally, Climate Network Europe, established in 1989, is another noteworthy European umbrella organization representing 78 NGOs on climate-related issues. Drawing the public into the issue of climate change both at the EU and national level is a major priority of the organization (CEC 2000b: 6). Thus, the group has actively lobbied the Commission in order to change how the EU addresses issues of climate change. As climate change involves various issues, they actively target not only DG Environment, but also the Energy, Transport and Agriculture Directorate Generals.

By the end of the 1980s, a green public sphere was undeniably becoming instrumental to the integration project. National public outcry in the early 1980s over an increasing number of environmental disasters, such as widespread forest destruction and the waste spill in Seveso, Italy, led to

[37] Wolters quoted in CEC (2000b: 6).
[38] Interview with representative from T&E, Brussels, March 2000.

reactive, yet expansive, EU environmental policy. At the same time, national level conflict between environmental regulations and EU free-trade rules would lead to a series of ECJ decisions that began to provide solutions to these tensions, but more importantly broadcast loudly the problems inherent in an EC policy area that lacked a constitutional basis. This message in turn became the mantra of a growing network of environmental legal activists throughout the EU, who utilized the social space created by these rulings and the tensions they displayed to argue and press for a Treaty amendment that would give environmental protection a formal constitutional basis. In 1986, this activism would prove instrumental to the decision to include an Environmental Chapter in the Single European Act. This new constitutional basis was a watershed in the greening of EU politics.

The Single European Act gave the Commission and the Parliament renewed power to introduce and develop EU competency over environmental protection. And so they did. The *Fourth Environmental Action Programme* introduced both new policy directions, such as environmental education programs, as well as formalizing earlier policy notions to integrate the environment into other EU policy sectors. International and national environmental NGOs realized the importance of the formal access and European social space created by these developments and set up Brussels based offices. This mobilization was increasingly collective as mass member environmental groups, such as the EEB, WWF, FOEE and Greenpeace, began collaborating on their EU lobbying campaigns.

The 1990s and early 2000s: institutionalization of a green public sphere

Once the opportunity was created, the mobilization of groups in the 1980s would begin to plant the seeds for greater coordination in the future: an action that led to the institutionalization of a green public sphere in the 1990s and a European public space that far surpassed this initial opening. EU legislative action would continue to support these efforts and increasingly ECJ litigation would come to play a more influential role in this evolution.

Litigation and legislative action as political opportunities for mobilization

The 1990s through 2003 experienced a distinct increase in environmental Article 234 litigation. The Court again doubled its caseload of environmental preliminary references from the previous decade (total of 81 references). While the caseload increased, many of the cases dealt with a familiar conflict. Over half the cases involved EU waste laws, and the problems that arise between improper national implementations, as well as conflicts with EU free-trade laws.[39] This problem also arose in the area of EU nature law (e.g. *Gourmetterie Van den Burg* decision, ECJ 1990b) and with environmental impact assessment procedures (*Kraaijeveld* decision, ECJ 1996i). Yet similar to the area of social provisions, these often expansive rulings not only clarified EU law through the jurisprudence, but also often impacted subsequent legislative amendments, and in a particularly important infringement ruling, re-emphasized the need for the Parliament's power in EU environmental policy development.[40]

Further, by the 1990s, with a growing body of ECJ environmental jurisprudence and an increasingly active network of transnational environmental lawyers, the Court's decisions would begin to resonate amongst environmental associations, especially over the issue of nature protection. Similar to the legal action taking place since the late 1970s on behalf of women by legal activists, unions and national equality units, national environmental organizations began utilizing EU law to dismantle national administrative practices. A total of twelve preliminary rulings in this time period involved cases brought by environmental associations before courts in the United Kingdom, France, Belgium and Italy and one case from Germany. Yet this comparatively small number of cases reflected the old hurdles: standing rules for environmental associations and difficulties making individual environmental claims under national or EU law. And even beyond difficulties at the national level, throughout the 1990s environmental associations have attempted to bring legal

---

[39] Examples of Waste cases that arose in the early part of the decade include: *Vessosso and Zanetti* decision (ECJ 1990e) and *Zanetti* decision (ECJ 1990f). Italian courts continued to be the main source of these preliminary references with cases such as the *Tombesi* decision (ECJ 1997f). See discussion in Cichowski (1998).

[40] For example, scholars have noted that the Court's wide interpretation of Council Directive 85/337/EEC in the *Kraaijeveld* decision may have influenced the substantial amendments to the environmental impact assessment (EIA) procedure that were included in a revised EIA Directive in 1997 (Council Directive 97/11/EC) (see Krämer 2000: 113). Further, as examined in Chapter 5, the Court's jurisprudence involving the Wild Birds Directive ultimately led to member state retaliation in the form of the Habitats Directive. Finally, in the *Titanium Dioxide* decision (ECJ 1991i), the Court attempted to bring some clarity to the controversy over which legal basis and decision rule to utilize for EU environmental policy (Article 100a or Article 130s). The Court's ruling makes a clear preference for Article 100a, which supports majority voting; an act that potentially empowers both the Commission and Parliament *vis-à-vis* member state governments in the legislative process.

proceedings directly to the ECJ via Article 230 and have been even less successful (e.g. *Greenpeace* cases).[41]

Although these rulings certainly highlight the unresolved problems regarding issues of access to justice in the area of the environment, it would be wrong to conclude that the ECJ is inhospitable to environmental rights claims. Instead, ECJ rulings in this decade began to develop a jurisprudence that empowered environmental organizations and explicitly encouraged the use of national courts (and the Article 234 procedure) to make these legal claims.[42] Further, this ECJ precedent highlighted the general problems with access to justice for environmentalists and in doing so created the space to begin talking about this as a national problem that needed a collective European solution.[43] By the end of this time period legal opportunities were being expanded, as the Community adopted two directives with the explicit right of access to justice in matters of public access to environmental information and on public participation in environmental decision-making.[44] And a third directive that is dedicated solely to access to justice in environmental matters remains at the proposal stage (CEC 2003). All of these innovations bode well for individuals and groups

[41] For example, *An Taisce/WWF v. Commission* (ECJ 1994f); *Greenpeace v. Commission* (ECJ 1995c); and *Greenpeace v. Commission* (ECJ 1998c). This final decision was a test case brought by Greenpeace in an attempt to open up the rights provided to individuals and groups to bring environmental claims directly before the ECJ. It was unsuccessful.

[42] See nature protection cases mentioned above. Alongside these preliminary rulings, the Court had two particularly noteworthy infringement rulings regarding this issue. In *Commission v. Germany* (Case 361/88 1991 ECR 2567), the Court did attempt to improve the issue of individual rights, by arguing that EU environmental laws that also aimed at protecting human health must be interpreted in a way that enables individuals to make claims before national courts. Scholars highlight the potential this ruling offers for legal action on behalf of a "right to a clean environment" (Krämer 2000: 37). Unfortunately, little action has ensued. Further, although the Greenpeace decision mentioned above (ECJ 1998c)) has received considerable criticism in terms of allowable action by environmental NGOs under Article 230(4), the Court did explicitly suggest how these rights claims could successfully be made via another litigation strategy (e.g. Article 234):

"Although the subject-matter of those proceedings and of the action brought before the Court of First Instance is different, both actions are based on the same rights afforded to individuals by Council Directive 85/337/EEC, so that in the circumstances of the present case those rights are fully protected by the national courts which may, if need be, refer a question to this Court for a preliminary ruling under Article 177 [now Article 234] of the Treaty (paragraph 33)" [parenthetic comments added].

[43] The Commission issued a communication regarding the implementation of EU environmental law that addressed access to justice at the national level (rather than EU level) and the general need for further consultation and cooperation between EU organizations and the public to ensure the implementation and enforcement of EU law (CEC 1996c). A subsequent Council resolution would reiterate this (CEC 1997d).

[44] European Parliament and Council Directive 2003/4/EC *on public access to environmental information* and European Parliament and Council Directive 2003/35/EC *on public participation in environmental decision-making*.

to have enhanced rights to challenge before a court decisions made by both their national governments and EU organizations on environmental issues.

Political opportunities also came from the dramatic increase in legislative action: the average annual number of legislative acts increased from 14.4 in the 1980s to 37.5 per year in the 1990s. In large part, this was due to both the institutional changes that progressively widened and strengthened EU competence over environmental protection and the increasingly active transnational environmental lobby. The Treaty on European Union (TEU) in 1992 extended the formal basis for environmental protection. Such changes included Title 1, Article B which introduces the objective "to promote economic and social progress which is balanced and sustainable;" further, Article 2 now refers to integration as "a harmonious and balanced development of economic activities, sustainable and non-inflationary growth respecting the environment;" specifically, Articles 174–176 (ex 130r–130t) provide the environment with full status as an EU policy and finally the extension of qualified majority voting for most environmental matters. The TEU also gave increased powers to the EP by introducing the 'co-decision procedure', which entails a Conciliation Committee that can be convened at two different stages, and also the possibility of three different readings by the Parliament. As I will discuss below, this expanding competence was both cause and effect of the mutually empowering relationship that had begun to develop between EU organizations and NGOs.

While the EP gained new powers, DG Environment began seeing its autonomy shrink, even as its size grew. As environmental protection was mainstreamed into other policy areas, there were an increasing number of other DGs with a hand in environmental protection. For example, since 1993 each DG is required to submit an annual report on environmental performance and an Environmental Integration Correspondent housed in each DG oversees this process. While this presented environmental groups with a challenge by increasing the number of doors to knock on, this general increase in access points provided these groups with a greater chance to impact policy development.

Further, in 1993, the adoption of the *Fifth Environmental Action Programme* introduced for the first time that EU action could be taken on behalf of the "European Environment," a new construct that must be addressed in relation to processes of integration involving economic and social activity (CEC 1993d). This required significant broadening of the instruments available for EU environmental policy and also mainstreaming environmental policy into other EU policy areas. The program also explicitly reached out to the public sphere, calling for increased involvement of environmental NGOs, the development of green citizenship through education programs and the granting of individual rights, such as a right to access to environmental information and participation and eco-consumer rights (CEC 1993d: point 3.3 and 7.4). For example, the Commission extended formal policy access to environmental NGOs through the Consultative Forum on the Environment and Sustainable Development[45] and also began to develop a general plan to extend this type of public interest inclusion.[46]

Legislative action that followed from the program included the establishment of the European Environmental Agency,[47] a supranational organization bringing together scientists and environmentalists throughout the EU, and the Access to Environmental Information Directive,[48] which created a right to environmental information, giving ordinary citizens an opportunity for direct access to EU environmental politics. Together, these advancements illustrate how the Commission began to create both the formal policy access points and a new European social space to attain higher levels of public inclusion. The political opportunities were important not only for environmental mobilization, but also the larger European public.

The Treaty of Amsterdam, adopted in 1997, did not radically change the environmental basis in the Treaty, but did strengthen it. In particular, it extended the areas to which the co-decision procedure applied and the procedure was simplified (Article 175). Further, "sustainable development" was added as a formal objective of the Treaty (Article 2). And finally, a new article was added that explicitly calls for the integration of environmental protection and sustainable development into other EU policy areas: "Environmental protection requirements must be integrated into the definition and implementation of the EU policies and activities referred to in Article 3, in particular with a view to promoting sustainable development" (Article 6). Environmental activists were integral to these changes. Again, environmental groups seized the opportunities created earlier in the decade, and did so with the effect of gaining access to shape subsequent policy developments that would expand the opportunities available in the future.

The early 2000s also presented a series of innovations that would prove important for political opportunities. The *Sixth Environmental Action*

---

[45] Council Decision 93/701/EC, and later amended by Council Decision 97/150/EC. This guarantees 4–7 seats in the Forum to NGOs.

[46] [1997] O.J. C104/11.

[47] Council Regulation 1210/90/EEC. Rather than acting as an inspectorate or enforcement agency, after much debate this organization was to serve only as a "handmaiden" to policy makers by collecting and analyzing environmental data for EU policy development.

[48] Council Directive 90/313/EEC.

Programme (2002) was more ambitious than previous ones, laying out a ten-year plan that adopts a wide-ranging approach to environmental protection. Explicit in the program's mandate to improve the environment is the need to stimulate "participation and action of all actors from business to citizens, NGOs and social partners through better and more accessible information on the environment and joint work on solutions" (CEC 2002b: 1). As mentioned in Chapter 2, a series of directives regarding public access to information and access to decision-making and also a proposal for a new directive on access to justice resulted, all of which expanded the space for civil society to participate in the adoption and enforcement of EU environmental law.[49] Further, the European Parliament and Council continued to support an expansion in NGO involvement in developing and implementing EU environmental policy through the establishment and then renewal of the *Action Programme Promoting NGOs active in the Field of Environmental Protection*, which began in 1997 and was renewed in 2001.[50] Together, these opportunities would expand the space for civil society in the development, implementation and enforcement of EU environmental law.

Mobilization, institutionalization and political opportunities for public inclusion

By the 1990s, the Brussels environmental complex had institutionalized. EU environmental legislation focused on protection of a "European Environment" rather than individual national ecosystems. Similarly, the ECJ was increasingly asked to bring greater clarity and precision to this growing number of EU environmental rules. The growing density and formalization of a European environmental lobby during this time would be an integral component of this Brussels complex. As illustrated in Table 6.5, 35 transnational organizations involved in EU environmental issues were founded between 1990 and 2003. Following the trend from the last decade, these new organizations were most likely to be environmental associations (18 groups) or in the waste management/recycling sector (8 groups), reflecting (and at times shaping) the overall direction of EU environmental priorities.

[49] Directive 2003/4/EC on public access to environmental information, Directive 2003/35/EC on public access to decision-making on environmental matters and the Commission proposal for an access to justice in environmental matters directive (CEC 2003).
[50] Council Decision 466/2002/EC of the European Parliament and of the Council laying down a *Community Action Programme Promoting Non-Governmental Organizations Primarily Active in the Field of Environmental Protection*.

Table 6.5 *Transnational organizations involved in the area of environmental protection by organizational type and founding date, 1990–2003*

Organization	Founding date
Environmental/Natural resources/Sustainable development	
ELNI, ECEAE	1990
EN/IBI, IFAW, SPAN, ECE	1991
ENERO	1992
EarthAction Network	1992
Birdlife International	1993
EPE, EFNCP, CEEWEB, EAA	1994
IFN	1995
GAP	1997
OIKOS International	1998
EUCETSA	1999
AICA	2003
Waste management/Recycling/Energy	
ACE	1990
FEDARENE	1990
EuroACE, CEPI	1992
EUROPEN	1993
EEWC	1993
ACRR	1994
EUBIA	1996
ASSURRE	2000
Consumer rights	
ECAS	1990
Regional/Local authorities	
IULA-CEMR	1990
EUROCITIES	1993
Health	
EPHA	1993
EFH	1995
EEN	2003
Scientific research	
CEPS	1993
Other voluntary orgs.	
CENPO	1994

Source: Data compiled by author from *Directory of Pressure Groups in the EU*, Philip and Gray (1996), *Directory of Interest Groups* (Luxembourg: Office for Official Publications of the European Communities, 1996) and the database for *Consultation, the European Commission and Civil Society (CONECCS)* (European Commission, online database http://europa.eu.int/comm/civil_society/coneccs/.

Many of these new European groups originated from well-established international organizations and took on a new lobbying style. For example, Birdlife International (BI) established an office in Brussels in 1993, but its predecessor organization, International Council for Bird Preservation (ICBP) was started in the 1950s. However, both the structure and activities of BI have changed somewhat from the previous organization. Instead of serving solely as a depository for scientific and technical expertise on bird conservation, its Brussels office has become directly involved with policy development and advocacy.[51] Further, International Friends of Nature (IFN) was established in Austria in 1895 to help promote social tourism by "getting people to beautiful natural settings, awakening their love of nature and at imparting to them a knowledge about nature and culture" (IFN 1997a: 1). However, the growing changes in Europe in the early 1990s, both with the fall of the Berlin wall, the completion of the internal market, and an expansion in EU environmental competence prompted the group to refocus its campaigns and lobbying to the European level.[52] In 1995, the group would begin actively lobbying EU organizations and coordinating with other European level environmental organizations. Such activities included submitting policy proposals for the Intergovernmental Conference in 1996, that included the "Manifesto for a New Europe" (1993) and the "Manifesto for a Social, Ecological and Peaceful Future (1996)" and the "Green Paper – the Alps" (IFN 1997b: 2).

Coordinated efforts between environmental NGOs would reach new levels of formality between 1990 and 2003. Building on the initial links developed in the late 1980s through the Green 4 (G4), this collective action would increase in magnitude and formality by the end of the 1990s. In particular, mobilization involved regular meetings and joint lobbying campaigns, such as the "Greening the Treaty" campaigns, in which the NGOs lobbied for treaty revisions. (Stetter 2001). The G4 as a group led the first of these campaigns in 1990. The G4 came together and produced a document demanding various changes that would strengthen treaty provisions on the environment in the next round of amendments that led to the Maastricht Treaty in 1992 (WWF, EEB, FOEE 1990). The document was far-reaching and although many of the specific policy demands were not included in the Treaty on European Union, the NGOs agree that their campaign was successful at changing policy frames. The mobilization influenced the overall vision of the EU as reflected by the

---

[51] Interview with representative from BirdLife International, Brussels, March 2000.
[52] Following an IFN Congress in 1990, the group laid out this plan in the *Manifesto for a New, Ecological, Open and Social Europe* (IFN 1990).

inclusion of statements regarding sustainability and environmental protection in the opening articles of the Treaty.[53] Other specific successes included expanded use of qualified majority voting and an increased role in policy making for the European Parliament.[54]

The G4 expanded to the G7 in 1995, adding the environmental associations T&E, Climate Network Europe and Birdlife International to their ranks. Soon thereafter they embarked on the second campaign, *Greening the Treaty II*, in preparation for the Amsterdam Intergovernmental Conference in March 1996 (Stichting Natuur en Milieu 1995). This second campaign built on unfinished business from the TEU negotiations. These included the objective to attain the highest level of protection, inclusion of a right to the environment and extension of qualified majority voting. This campaign also introduced new proposals such as the inclusion of "sustainable development" in the treaty and its extension to other EU policy areas, as well as a more "effective form of right of initiative for the Parliament"(Stichting Natuur en Milieu 1995: 5). Observers agree that this second campaign, due to the larger number of NGOs, effective collective organization and the strategic use of EU opportunities promoting civil society, was able to successfully achieve some of their demands (Stetter 2001). In particular, inclusion of sustainable development and the integration principle were two of their biggest achievements. By 1999, the group would grow again, to the G8, including Friends of Nature International in their collaborative activities. Consistently these groups, both individually and as a whole, would take advantage of the political opportunities afforded them through formal consultations provided by the Commission and the Parliament, and would then push for greater inclusion.

Activists working through the European environmental law community were also influential during this time period. The increasing body of ECJ environmental case law and the conflicts that they highlighted became the basis of this mobilization. NGOs became increasingly active both in the dissemination of information regarding environmental rights and also in the implementation and enforcement of EU law. One example is the Environmental Law Network International (ELNI), which was set up in 1990 and has over 350 members including legal practitioners and academic lawyers worldwide. The group facilitates the discussion and transnational exchange of information on issues such as access to justice

---

[53] Interview with representative from WWF, Brussels, March 2000. See also Stetter (2001).

[54] Although the campaign had argued for qualified majority voting for all environmental issues, the end result of issues such as fiscal matters and town and country planning remaining subject to unanimity voting, makes this a compromised success.

and the effective use of the environmental impact assessment. The group often utilizes international conferences to achieve these ends and ECJ decisions often serve as talking points and subsequent policy recommendations.[55] This mobilization serves to change and maintain policy frames by keeping these issues alive and on the agenda of EU policymakers. Further, these discussions are an integral part of the social space that had begun to characterize a European environmental public sphere.

For example, in 1991, the ELNI held a conference entitled "Participation rights of environmental associations and their possibilities of taking legal action in European perspective." The proceedings were published in a volume that would be the first in a series of books covering similar topics, from environmental impact assessment procedures in Europe to citizen rights in European environmental law. While the conferences and publications provide detailed comparative data on current legal situations in the member states, they also made policy recommendations, such as on the right to bring actions before the ECJ (Führ and Roller 1991: viii). Similar to its support for other NGO activity, DG Environment co-sponsored three of these ELNI conferences (ELNI 2000: 1).

Similarly, NGOs, such as the earlier discussed Institute for European Environmental Policy (established 1976), were also actively shaping the EU environmental space by publishing reports that continued to raise concerns over pervasive non-compliance with EU environmental law.[56] These reports helped mobilize other environmental NGOs to utilize the Commission's complaint procedure to report member state implementation errors. Over time this mobilization and vigilance on behalf of environmental groups forced member state compliance through Article 226 legal proceedings and in effect reinforced EU competence over national environmental regulations.[57] This interaction between NGOs and EU

---

[55] ECJ rulings such as the *Kraaijeveld* decision and the failed *Greenpeace* cases would be included in the concerns raised at conferences. See conference proceedings as published in the volume edited by Führ and Roller (1991).

[56] For example, N. Haigh and F. Irwin (eds.) *Integrated Pollution Control in Europe and North America* (WWF/IEEP, 1990); D. Baldock and G. Bennett, *Agriculture and the Polluter Pays Principle* (Institute for European Enviromental Policy, 1991); *Liability for Contaminated Land in Germany, France, Netherlands and Denmark* (Institute for European Enviromental Policy, 1994).

[57] As discussed earlier, by the late 1980s the Commission began encouraging the use of the complaint procedure by citizens and NGOs as a way to help monitor compliance with EU environmental law. These groups would heed the call. Environmental complaints increased from 10 in 1982 to 315 in 1997. Following the Commission's communication encouraging the use of the procedure in 1987, there was a particularly high number, with an annual average of 522 between 1989–1992. Further, EU legislation such as the EIA Directive (Council Directive 85/313/EEC) had also created a complementary opportunity, as in 1996 the Commission stated that actions stemming from implementation

organizations illustrates how policy power was shifted away from member state governments.

Further, the G8 began to take a more active role in demanding greater legal rights when the opportunity arose. The ECJ's Greenpeace decision provided a new space to mobilize around an issue that had long been of concern to these environmental NGOs (as early as the first *Greening the Treaty* campaign) but had received minimal reception by EU decision-makers. In December 1999, the groups presented a joint letter to the European governments, Parliament and Commission demanding a Treaty amendment that would "provide individuals and public interest associations the possibility to defend environmental and other shared EU interests before the European Court of Justice."[58] They cited the *Greenpeace* cases as an example of why the current legal situation was unsatisfactory for Communty citizens.

By 2003, a dynamic relationship had evolved between transnational environmental NGOs and EU organizations. The Commission provided EU level access points both through its significant funding for NGOs and also by including them in expert groups and consultative forums (CEC 2000b: 3). Likewise, as we saw in the *Greening the Treaty* campaigns, these groups subsequently pushed for increased policy power for EU organizations; the Parliament in particular, which had been most sympathetic to their policy demands. While lobbying and framing proved to be the most successful tactics utilized by these groups, litigation became an increasingly successful tactic by the end of the 1990s and into the 2000s. Unlike the social provisions domain, the environmental NGOs only gained minimal success with individual legal claims, but instead were most successful by instigating legal proceedings via the complaint procedure, as well as utilizing unsuccessful litigation attempts (e.g. the *Greenpeace* decision) as policy talking points. Further, both the Commission and environmental NGOs would increasingly converge over the issue of greater public inclusion, if not for similar reasons, with a similar outcome. The institutionalization of EU environmental policy was acutely linked to the participation of citizens throughout the EU.

Conclusions

Much like the area of social provisions, as the EU began developing legislation and binding rules in the environment, transnational

---

problems with this Directive were the source of most of the complaints, petitions and infringement procedures in 1995 (CEC 1996d). Data compiled from *Annual Report on Monitoring the Application of Community Law*, various years, CEC.

[58] European Environmental Bureau, Press Release, 2 Dec 1999, Brussels.

environmental activists began shifting their lobbying activities to include the EU level. As these political opportunities afforded greater formal access and created new social spaces in EU politics, there were an increasing number of groups. Similarly, the findings in this chapter also illustrate that this mobilization became increasingly collective and collaborative as the EU expanded its competence over environmental protection. However, there is considerable variation in the general patterns of this mobilization. During the 1970s and 1980s, litigation had little interaction with environmental mobilization, despite the mobilizing potential embodied in these expansive rulings. This stands in stark contrast to the social provisions domain, as the litigation was both cause and effect of women's transnational activism both in Brussels and through national courts. Further, where environmentalists had formed a single European level lobbying organization by the mid 1970s, women's groups spent almost two decades attempting to form a similar organization, and were only successful by the 1990s. The findings suggest that even with similar opportunities, mobilization patterns were shaped by characteristics specific to the movement.

Further, in both domains, we saw how this mobilization changed the balance of power between ordinary citizens, EU organizations and national governments. As these groups became increasingly formalized and permanent actors in EU policy process, their mobilization impacted not only policy developments but also general public inclusion. These demands were often fostered and supported by EU organizations, such as the Commission and Parliament. Over time this interaction shifted the power away from member state governments as the policy trajectory was directly influenced by and remained accountable to this new European public sphere.

7 Conclusion: litigation, mobilization and governance

The European Court of Justice (ECJ) today is one of the main motors of governance in Europe. It has turned a relatively young body of law into a dynamic and coherent legal system governing and protecting public interests and civil society. This reality was exemplified by a vision put forth by Advocate General Trabucchi thirty years ago and reaffirmed by Advocate General Tesauro in the Court's courageous *P. v S.* decision (ECJ 1996d: paragraph 24):

> If we want Community law to be more than a mere mechanical system of economics and to constitute instead a system commensurate with the society which it has to govern, if we wish it to be a legal system corresponding to the concept of social justice and European integration not only of the economy but of the people, we cannot disappoint the [national] court's expectations, which are more than those of legal form. (ECJ 1975: 697)

All have not welcomed this evolution from the legal to the political, from economic to social justice; some critics have suggested that the Court suffers from "morbid megalomania" or a tendency of "running wild" or engaging in "revolting judicial behavior."[1] More accurately, one might describe the ECJ as dutiful worker, carrying out the ever challenging and increasingly complex job to which it was mandated almost fifty years ago: "The Court of Justice shall ensure that in the interpretation and application of the Treaty the law is observed" (Article 164 Treaty of Rome). The Court has taken this duty to uphold the rule of law very seriously, not hesitating to update the Treaty of Rome itself, secondary legislation and in effect national legislation and constitutions,[2] to ensure that the fundamental rights of European citizens are protected – even when they collide

---

[1] Criticisms of the Court mentioned in a lecture given by former ECJ Judge G. Federico Mancini (Mancini 1997).

[2] It is undisputable that ECJ judgments through the interpretation of the treaties and secondary legislation have led to significant changes in national law: from organization of national militaries in Austria, Germany and Greece (ECJ 1999a; ECJ 2000a) to national social security schemes in Portugal and Finland (ECJ 1990a); and access to employment opportunities in Germany (ECJ 1989b), to only name a few.

with the Community's sacred fundamental freedoms.[3] Despite the current on-hold status of the Constitutional Treaty[4] – these realities, and the analyses included in this book, illustrate that constitutionalism is alive and well in the European Union (EU). Indisputably, EU constitutionalism will be enhanced with a judicially enforceable constitution in the future, but for well over 40 years the ECJ has continued to construct and develop an unprecedented form of supranational constitutionalism dedicated to the protection of individual rights.

Civil society and transnational activists have also incrementally not only become a strong presence in Brussels, but a voice and hand in the process of European policymaking. In 1998, Padraig Flynn, Commissioner for Employment and Social Affairs, emphasized the importance of civil society and NGOs for integration:

We are here at this Forum because the European Union is committed to enriching the process of engagement. We are here today because the Union is committed to supporting the capacity of NGOs to be a prime interlocutor with the systems and structures which deliver our ability to enhance the basic rights of the citizens of Europe. (Flynn quoted in CEC 1999e: 12)

Similarly, a few years later in 2000, Margot Wallström, Commissioner for the Environment, spoke about DG Environment's latest action program that set aside €10.6 million to help finance environmental NGOs and aimed to further promote a European "civil society." She emphasized the need to facilitate a real dialogue with the public and DG Environment's commitment to this goal of public inclusion: "We are already doing this through a vision of sustainable development and sustainable society. And with this comes a democratic development – there is no greater task than to strengthen democracy" (Wallström quoted in CEC 2000b: 3). Further, this general trend in public inclusion is exemplified in the recent publication of the Commission's White Paper on European Governance

---

[3] In the *Schmidberger v. Austria* decision (ECJ 2003d) the ECJ did not hesitate to uphold human rights (freedom of assembly and association) over a Community fundamental freedom (free movement of goods), a case in which the ECJ created an equal constitutional ranking between the two principles. A protesting group of environmentalists were the recipients of this protection, despite the fact that their protest demonstration blocked a main cross-border roadway, prohibiting the free movement of goods by the international transport company who brought the claim. See Tridimas (2004) for a thorough discussion of this case.

[4] The Constitution for Europe (or Constitutional Treaty) was ratified by 14 member states in 2005: Austria, Belgium, Cyprus, Germany, Greece, Hungary, Italy, Latvia, Lithuania, Luxembourg, Malta, Slovakia, Slovenia and Spain. Following the rejection of the Treaty in public referenda in France (29 May 2005) and the Netherlands (1 June 2005), member states have decided to enter a "period of reflection, discussion and explanation" with the hopes of successful ratification in the future (European Council, 16–17 June 2005).

(CEC 2001), which calls for renewed commitment to fostering and developing a stronger civil society in EU politics (CEC 2001, 2000c).[5] The unprecedented formal inclusion of NGOs in the Convention on the Future of Europe (2002–2003) stands as another example – directly engaging civil society in the building of the Constitutional Treaty. Yet, much like the analyses illustrated, today this comes in the form of highly institutionalized mobilization, exemplified by the EU Civil Society Contact Group and their Act4Europe campaign, a European level organization comprised of umbrella organizations from the environmental, social, development, women, culture, human rights and public health sectors.[6]

The degree of power exerted by both the Court and civil society in expanding the scope and meaning of EU policy, today, is remarkable from the perspective of the original treaty makers in the late 1950s. Governance in the EU today is as binding over national equality laws and environmental regulations as it is over trade policies, and direct public participation in EU politics is becoming increasingly common alongside intergovernmental negotiations. The findings in this book suggest how the processes of litigation and mobilization influenced this development of supranational governance. In this chapter, I discuss the main theoretical and empirical findings of this study by focusing first on the individual processes of litigation and mobilization and then by evaluating these processes in terms of the extent of institutionalization and the implications for democracy in the EU. I end the chapter by discussing a set of lessons beyond the European experience.

Theoretical and empirical findings

This book elaborates a theory for understanding the interactions between individual activists, law and courts and the impact of this dynamic on governance. In particular, the research focuses on the emergence and evolution of supranational governance in Europe. I critically examine and suggest an answer to the question of how supranational governance emerges and institutionalizes. The approach brings into question dominant theories that argue integration is a function of the relative bargaining power of member state governments. Further, while the study builds on

---

[5] The Commission suggests the importance of greater public inclusion for participatory democracy in the EU as it provides "a chance to get citizens involved in achieving the Union's objectives and to offer them a structured channel for feedback, criticism and protest" (CEC 2001: 14). The White Paper states "it [participation] is about more effective policy shaping based on early consultation and past experience" (CEC 2001: 14).

[6] EU Civil Society Contact Group webpage: http://www.act4europe.org/code/en/hp.asp.

neo-functional theory by emphasizing the importance of EU organizations and transnational society in integration, it overcomes some of the inherent limitations to this approach. Neo-functionalism helped us understand why there was a functional demand for supranational governance, yet it tells us little about variation in this development. Instead, I argue that processes of institutionalization may vary across policy domains and procedures. This study elaborated an approach that conceptualizes integration as a result of the growing intensity of three factors: EU institutions (rules and procedures), EU organizations and transnational actors. Thus, we are able to evaluate any particular policy domain to determine if, how and why integration has evolved.

Further, I argued that institutionalization could take place through various processes. Moving beyond the existing integration literature that focuses on rule change through treaty negotiations and legislative processes, this book develops a generalizable framework for examining how governance is institutionalized through the mutually constituting processes of litigation and mobilization. The study focused on litigation pursuant to Article 234 and transnational mobilization. To test this approach, the study involved a cross-sector analysis between two EU policy areas, social provisions and environmental protection, and evaluated the extent to which institutionalization has occurred. Have national governments retained control over policy evolution or are EU policy spaces filled with EU organizations and transnational actors who increasingly possess their own impact on policy evolution? In the following sections, I elaborate these findings.

Litigation

Litigation begins with a legal claim. The findings in Chapters 3 and 4 suggest a set of general patterns that are occurring in legal claims arising through the Article 234 preliminary ruling procedure. First, concerning cross-national variation, the book revealed two main points. Cross-national variation is policy specific. Mobilized interests and legal resources, in the form of government agency legal support, were the two strongest variables in explaining why certain legal systems were the subject of social provisions preliminary references. Environmental reference rate was clearly more affected by the implementation problems occurring from a disparity between EU and national policy, as well as legal resources, but in the form of legal expertise and national standing rules, rather than government agency support.

Second, in terms of cross-sector variation between social provisions and environmental references, the findings confirmed the importance of

EU rules. In particular, the difficulty in bringing rights claims before national courts under EU environmental law, and the comparative ease permitted by equality rights embodied in EU social provisions, help explain the over two times the number of references in this later legal domain (148 environmental versus 307 in the social provisions sector between 1970 and 2003). Article 141 provided directly applicable rights that can be invoked and must be protected, whereas the direct effect of environmental directives was more difficult to claim, not least because there is no horizontal directive effect for directives, yet there is for treaty provisions. Finally, the analysis illustrated that ECJ precedent was a significant factor, in both legal domains, that may help us explain variation in litigation patterns over time. ECJ decisions, and the subsequent litigation and legislative acts they influenced, were integral in solving some of the policy tensions and vague measures that characterize both legal domains. Together, these findings suggest that the litigation dynamic begins with at least some EU rule, a necessary but not sufficient condition. Legal resources and the presence of mobilized interests help us to understand why, given this necessary rule, there is still considerable variation in national reference rates.

Given there is a legal claim that reaches the ECJ, I examined the Court's subsequent decision-making and suggest how this impacted governance and subsequent action. The research in Chapters 3 and 4 suggests that the ECJ functions to provide greater clarity to EU law and in doing so often expands EU competence while diminishing member state control over EU policy outcomes. Despite the belief of certain scholars, the policy positions of member state governments do not systematically shape ECJ decision-making. Time and time again, the ECJ is clearly informed of the preferences of powerful member state governments, and the ECJ does not hesitate to act in opposition to these interests. Instead, the data suggest that vague EU laws have given the ECJ the opportunity to make expansive rulings (rather than constrained it), regardless of member state opposition or national laws that currently govern these practices. The analysis also illustrates that the potential magnitude of the financial impact of an adverse ruling did not in any systematic way prevent the ECJ from making such a ruling.

Instead, preliminary rulings disproportionately involve vague EU laws and the ECJ operates to uphold EU interests and bring clarity by relying on EU law (be it its own case law or the legal argumentation embodied in the Commission's observations) rather than systematically preserving the national practices that are in question. It is through this dynamic that the Court is able to expand EU competence while maintaining its legitimacy. However, the book also illustrates that the legal basis of an adverse ruling can be critical to the relative power of member state governments to retaliate against these rulings. In particular, rulings involving secondary legislation (especially, those governed by qualified majority voting) rather than treaty based rights, presented national governments with a lesser degree of difficulty in reversing the decision. Amending such legislation poses a less difficult task than revising the treaty. While these retaliatory actions may have slowed the pace of institutionalization, generally the data illustrate how even this subsequent member state action fails to solve the problems and tensions that lead to future opportunities for action. The ECJ is once again activated.

A policy level discussion helps elaborate these conclusions. Institutional evolution in the sub-field of gender equality began with a legal claim traceable to the action of a Belgian stewardess and her lawyer who utilized Article 141 to invoke a right to equal protection. This led to the European Court of Justice transforming Article 141, a treaty provision governing equal pay and fair competition, into a positive right enforceable in national courts. The effects of this judicial rulemaking are legendary. Transformation into a positive right conferred on individuals the opportunity to bring claims before national courts, and the provision no longer simply placed duties on member state governments. Ordinary citizens were empowered in their own legal systems. Further, the ECJ rulings strengthened EU legislative action by providing a clear argument for why this treaty provision needed further elaboration. This gave activists operating in Brussels the social space to demand further rights. The consequences have required national governments to construct or change national policies to protect these rights. Positive integration has ensued. As the ECJ preliminary rulings expanded the rules and procedures (governance), this litigation affected the opportunities for action, both through the creation of new rights and subsequent legislative action.

Specifically, the case law analysis of pregnancy and maternity rights illustrates that through its preliminary rulings, the ECJ has in effect expanded the precision, scope and enforceability of EU institutions. More importantly, the constitutional basis (Treaty derived right to equal treatment) of these rulings has diminished the ability of member state governments to subsequently amend and change the policy effect of these rulings. The rulings impacted the construction of EU legislation, the Pregnancy Directive, but also a series of new claims brought before national courts. In light of this evolving dynamic among actors, organizations and institutions, it is not surprising that today the EU regulates national pregnancy and maternity policies despite a continual national government opposition to this expansion.

The environmental protection domain offers a variation of this pattern. Institutional evolution in the sub-field of nature protection began with the activism of national and transnational environmental groups demanding European-wide solutions to deteriorating national wildlife and habitats. Responding to this political pressure, member state governments began to develop at least some European-wide protective measures to address these concerns (the Wild Birds Directive). Despite this attempt at EU regulation, the pervasive non-compliance that ensued reflected the true intention of national authorities to maintain control over this sensitive and sometimes costly national issue. The judicial rulemaking of the ECJ would begin to change this.

Activated by environmental groups utilizing both the Commission's complaint procedure and legal action in national courts, the ECJ over time has come to expand the precision, scope and enforceability of EU nature conservation law. These ruling have been met with national government opposition and retaliation. Due to the fact that these rulings involved secondary legislation, member state governments did reverse a costly decision by adopting subsequent secondary legislation, the Habitats Directive. The immediate national consequence has been to weaken EU control over national conservation decisions. However, similar to the Pregnancy Directive, after the transposition period we do find legal claims invoking the Habitats Directive and demanding clarification, especially of the derogations in protection allowed by the law.

Comparing the two policy domains, the findings suggest a generalizable pattern to the litigation. First, ECJ rulings can provide litigants with new opportunities before national courts to pressure for and achieve national policy change to secure compliance with EU laws. For example, in the area of social provisions, pregnant workers in Spain were able to use national courts to secure protection that was not currently provided in Spanish legislation (a minimalist transposition of the Pregnancy Directive). Similarly, national environmental organizations in Italy utilized national courts to bring legal action against local authorities with the consequence of dismantling national hunting practices that were not in conformity with the Wild Birds Directive. Second, the extent to which these disputes involve vague aspects of EU law in which the Court subsequently provides clarity, these rulings can expand the precision, scope and enforceability of EU law. The ECJ's case law in the area of both pregnancy rights and nature conservation had this effect.

Third, the subsequent supranational and national policy impact of these decisions is acutely linked to the legal basis of the ruling. While both legal domains illustrate how expansive ECJ rulings can develop in tandem with subsequent legislation action, the legal domains varied in the relative power of member state governments *vis-à-vis* EU organizations that are activated by individuals, to control the trajectory of these policy developments. Rulings invoking treaty based principles and areas governed by unanimity voting present a greater challenge to EU policy makers interested in reversing adverse decisions through corrective legislation or treaty amendments. Despite the costly impact of numerous rulings in the gender equality domain, there was a higher degree of difficulty associated with reversing such a decision for this reason. On the other hand, in the area of nature conservation where rulings involved the interpretation of secondary legislation, member state governments were quick to retaliate against a particularly expansive ECJ ruling by amending a legislative proposal to reverse the decision.

Finally, the enforcement and utilization of ECJ rulings by national courts and a willingness of national courts to engage the EU legal system highlights how this policy trajectory can change despite member state opposition. As evidenced in both policy domains, ECJ rulings can enhance the power of national courts in their own legal system *vis-à-vis* the executive and legislative branches by providing the opportunity for review of national legislation. It is this action that ultimately can change the direction of both national and EU policy, despite the original intentions of national governments. Together, it is through this process of litigation that policy decisions have shifted away from member state governments.

Mobilization

The processes of litigation and mobilization are interconnected. The mechanisms involved in institutionalization through litigation hinged on strategic action by mobilized interests. Further, the research illustrates how ECJ precedent and subsequent legislative action can expand the opportunities for future action. However, I argue that this mobilization process is also analytically distinct. In the second half of this book, I focused on the process of institutionalization through mobilization in our two policy domains. How did EU political opportunities shape transnational mobilization? How did transnational activists change EU institutions? Did they alter the balance of power between EU organizations and member state governments? And finally, how did this process of mobilization impact the growing presence and permanence of public interests in EU politics?

The data reveal a general pattern in public interest mobilization in the EU. First, there was a general positive correlation between the numbers of EU political opportunities and level of transnational mobilization. In particular, as the EU policy process afforded public interest groups a greater number of formal access points and new social spaces to voice issues of concern, an increasing number of groups began engaging in full-time EU-level activities, whether opening offices in Brussels or regularly participating in transnational networks. Second, the study also illustrated how these political opportunities influenced the patterns of mobilization. In the early periods of EU development, public interest mobilization could be characterized as being less collective, as activists were often operating either individually, through informal networks or within a single group as these policy domains were evolving. By the end of the 1990s, as public interests were increasingly provided a permanent role in EU policy processes, activists optimized these opportunities by acting through highly organized campaigns and organizations.

Third, once mobilized, these group have systematically impacted EU governance, to the extent that their action alters the rules and procedures that serve as subsequent opportunities for action. In particular, mobilization was more effective at actually penetrating EU organizations and influencing policy developments when activists utilized tactics, such as lobbying, changing policy frames and litigation strategies that were compatible with the movement. These tactics posed relative challenges to a particular public interest group depending on pre-existing movement strategies. Generally, labor organizations had more difficulty surmounting national concerns to organize in a pan-European organization, whereas the environmental movement was able to build on similar international campaigns to organize at the EU level. The extent to which these groups influence EU rule change through lobbying campaigns, by altering policy frames to include public issues at the EU level, and utilizing EU law in litigation, the study illustrates that institutionalization can take place. Over time, this mobilization can lead to the construction of new rules and procedures, and thus can alter the institutional framework that governs individual and group action in the future.

Finally, the book reveals that this public interest mobilization and subsequent institutional change also had a more long-term impact on general public inclusion in the EU. Transnational activists were pressuring for specific policy goals and objectives, but their actions over time altered the policy space in a way that promoted greater public access. The litigation and legislative action that resulted from this action often expanded EU competence over a particular public policy and in doing so this facilitated greater civil society mobilization and discussion in EU politics. Further, greater public inclusion also paralleled a growth in the need for expert knowledge of and civil society support for complex public issues.

I now turn to specific findings from the two policy domains to elaborate these general conclusions. Litigation and legislative action were critical to the development of transnational mobilization in the area of social provisions. In the 1970s, the EU began forming the initial rights and opportunities that were necessary to provide a foundation for women's issues at the EU level. The ECJ's *Defrenne* decisions (ECJ 1971, 1976a, 1978) were instrumental to these opportunities, as were the individual women activists who began creating and utilizing opportunities within EU organizations, such as the Equality Unit in DG Employment and Social Affairs and the Women's Information Service in DG Information and Culture. By the 1980s, this activism would take the form of autonomous women's organizations whose creation was both cause and effect of the political opportunities created by the Commission and Parliament during this time. Further, transnational networks of legal activists would prove essential to ECJ litigation that eventually expanded the scope of allowable discrimination claims, thus enlarging the space for women's issues in EU politics.

Finally, in the 1990s, women's interests became an institutionalized sphere of EU politics. Transnational mobilization during this time period was characterized by formal lobbying organizations that were either solely or partially dedicated to women's issues. EU organizations continued to rely on the knowledge and expertise of individual activists similar to earlier time periods, but EU organizations also developed formal policy consultation procedures with these autonomous organizations. In the mid 1990s, the ECJ rulings would also begin to have a larger mobilizing effect amongst these transnational groups, as a result of rulings that presented a potential negative impact on the advancement of EU equality policy (e.g. the *Kalanke* decision, ECJ 1995a; the *Grant* decision, ECJ 1998g).

Generally, in the area of social provisions, the ECJ decisions have been integral to the development of transnational mobilization by creating new rights and changing the scope of EU equality law. The receptivity of women activists to these new opportunity structures may suggest the compatibility between these opportunities and the litigation strategies that are commonly utilized by the women's movement. Further, the absence of a formal European women's lobby until the 1990s, and instead the proliferation of informal organizing through networks and individual activism, is also consistent with characteristics of women's organizing more generally. Finally, the analyses also reveal that the opportunity structures provided by both the Commission and the Parliament were also both cause and effect of this activism. These EU organizations often created the funding and outreach that provided the initial space for women's organizing, but subsequently these activists were equally successful at expanding the space and opportunity for further inclusion in the future. Over time, women's transnational mobilizing has shifted from discrete individual action, as exemplified by the legal tactics of Elaine Vogel-Polsky, to more collective and permanent action, as illustrated by the some 4000 groups that coordinate their activities through the European Women's lobby, an organization that is granted considerable access to EU organizations.

Similar to the social provisions domain, environmental activists began shifting their lobbying activities to include the EU level as the Union began developing legislation and binding rules. However, these initial EU-level political opportunities would vary and so too would this mobilization. During the 1970s and 1980s, litigation would have a smaller impact on these mobilization patterns. While ECJ rulings began to resonate with environmental legal practitioners and academic lawyers during this time period, little environmental activism stemmed from these preliminary rulings. This stands in contrast to the social provisions domain. As the findings illustrate, this variation between policy domains is generally related to the difficulties experienced by activists making environmental rights claims despite the Court's expansive rulings. This general legal hurdle may be one explanation why environmental activists have generally had less success and thus less use of litigation tactics than women activists, leading to fewer overall numbers of environmental cases. Interestingly though, as we saw in Chapter 6, environmental nongovernmental organizations were consistently directly involved in a higher percentage of the preliminary rulings than women's groups. Instead, during this time period, transnational environmental activists were offered and took advantage of more advantageous and compatible EU political opportunity structures, such as Commission funding to support the development of Brussels based offices and participation with the Parliament's Environmental Committee.

On its face, transnational activism in both the environmental and social provisions sectors looked very different at this point. While grassroots activists operating in both EU policy areas had taken up permanent residence in Brussels and were active in EU policy development and implementation, the environmental movement already possessed a highly organized lobbying federation, whereas women activists were mobilizing through informal networks and acting individually within and through EU organizations. Women's groups were actively utilizing litigation and some lobbying to change policy frames, whereas environmental groups were engaging in highly organized lobbying campaigns and only secondary involvement in litigation (reporting member state noncompliance to the Commission for infringement proceedings) to change policy frames.

By the 1990s and early 2000s, these patterns would begin to converge. EU organizations were increasingly reaching out for greater civil society inclusion, even when member states sometimes hesitated to expand EU competence over public policies. The findings in this book illustrate that although these political opportunities often shaped the movements' actions, at the same time once the openings were created environmental activists and women's activists were a crucial component of creating opportunities and rights for greater public inclusion in the future. Over time, in both policy domains, this mobilization has become increasingly collective. The book illustrates that even the environmental movement, which began with comparatively greater collective mobilizing, as exemplified by the founding of the European Environmental Bureau in 1974, developed highly coordinated campaigns, as illustrated by the development of the G8 meetings and actions between transnational environmental groups. And again, the EU's Civil Society Contact Group is a perfect example of how highly institutionalized and collective civil society mobilization became by the mid 2000s. Brought together to participate in the Constitutional Treaty process of 2002–2003, this cross-sectoral group brought together the top umbrella organizations from the seven main rights- and value-based NGOs, including both women's groups and the environmental NGOs, to act in concert.[7]

Further, while women activists were on a whole more likely to utilize litigation, activists in both movements were increasingly mobilized in reaction to this litigation (in particular, the "negative" rulings in the *Kalanke* decision, ECJ 1995a and *Greenpeace* decisions, ECJ 1995c, 1998c). This mobilization in turn pressured for greater inclusion. Group action ended in a recommendation by the Commission clarifying the *Kalanke* decision and elaborating EU rules on women's inclusion through positive action programs or quotas. The ECJ would subsequently adopt this new position in the *Marschall* decision (ECJ 1997c). Similarly, the *Greenpeace* ruling, which denied an environmental group standing before the ECJ, led to a campaign led by the G8 environmental organizations that lobbied for new EU rules on access to justice. The result has been Community action with a series of new Directives[8] liberalizing access in environmental matters. Similarly, Community courts (the Court of First Instance in particular) continue to grapple

---

[7] EU Civil Society Contact Group webpage: http://www.act4europe.org/code/en/hp.asp.
[8] See discussion in Chapters 2 and 6. In particular, Directive 2003/4/EC on public access to environmental information, Directive 2003/35/EC on public access to decision-making on environmental matters and the Commission proposal for an access to justice in environmental matters directive (CEC 2003).

with this important issue of public access to justice (CFI 2002; ECJ 2002). National governments, industry and the agriculture lobby undeniably remain powerful actors in EU policy agenda setting, but by the early 2000s, civil society, as represented through both the environmental and women's movements, were equally permanent and at times very influential in the development and enforcement of EU law.

Institutional stability and democratic governance in the EU

The EU today governs what historically are protected national policy domains: social provisions and environmental protection. The study demonstrates that the creators of the treaty may not have foreseen this process of institutional innovation and the policy implications have not all been welcomed by member state governments. In contrast to intergovernmental arguments, the findings show that the relative power of national governments cannot explain the expansive logic that characterizes this policy evolution (for example, Garrett 1995; Garrett, Kelemen, and Schulz 1998; Garrett and Weingast 1993; Moravcsik 1998). This book has focused on the mechanisms of institutionalization. The evolution of governance resulted from a dynamic interaction between actors, organizations and institutions through the processes of litigation and mobilization. The above discussion highlighted the substantive policy outcomes of these processes. In this section, I would like to turn to a set of broader lessons regarding the stability of these processes of institutionalization and implications for democracy in the European Union.

Stability of institutionalization

To what extent are these processes likely to be rolled back? The answer is crucial for understanding the general trajectory of institutional change. Further, related to this, is the relative stability of these processes of institutionalization. What is the likelihood these processes will reproduce themselves? At first glance, when one looks at the processes of litigation and mobilization in the EU, there seems to be a host of mechanisms that could reverse or at least destabilize these processes. As illustrated in this book, member state governments are able to reverse the impact of adverse ECJ rulings, through the adoption of subsequent legislation or even through treaty amendments. Further, it is possible that member state governments could reduce the power of the ECJ by amending its jurisdiction. Similarly, limiting Community funding and formal EU access points available to civil society could discourage transnational mobilization. We might see these blockages at single points in time. Yet over time, the argument for roll-back and instability becomes increasingly difficult to sustain.

The findings illustrate that time and time again, regardless of member state action, ECJ precedent provided the opportunities for subsequent action. A crucial element of this dynamic is again the fact that the judicial rulings can be specific and retrospective, as well as general and prospective. Thus, when ECJ rulings are overturned by legislative action, this action may correct a specific rule that applied to a given dispute that took place in the past. Yet the general and prospective nature of court rulings enabled subsequent claims and litigation, despite member state action to correct the specific issue at stake in the ruling. The process is reproduced as the litigation created both the rights and the social space that fueled subsequent legal claims. The case law analysis of both pregnancy rights and nature protection illustrate this dynamic.

Short of abolishing the Court, member states can do little to stop this process of institutionalization. Rather, it can be slowed. Again, the Court was created to ensure that EU law is uniformly interpreted and effectively applied. Rather than a decreasing need for this interpreter of EU law, member states, EU organizations and individuals and groups are increasingly in need of this organization as EU rules expand. This study illustrates that as EU competence expands, these new rules can disadvantage individuals and businesses in one member state relative to others and legal claims arise. Further, EU legislative outcomes often result in lowest common denominator positions that possess vague policy prescriptions and there is a subsequent demand for clarification by those who are advantaged or disadvantaged by these provisions. In general, when one looks over time, despite considerable criticism of ECJ activism, member state governments have increased the Court's power.[9] I would expect this to continue.

---

[9] Although member state governments have voiced concern over unwieldy ECJ activism, these governments continue to strengthen the Court's capacity to fulfill these roles. In 1986, the Treaty of Rome was amended to include a Court of First Instance to allow greater examination of Commission activities in the area of competition policy. The Treaty on European Union further enhanced the ECJ's power in two ways. First, its capacity to check EU organizational power was extended by providing the European Parliament with the legal opportunity to challenge Council and Commission activities. Second, ECJ judicial decisions were given greater force by enabling the Commission to assess monetary penalties to member states that failed to implement ECJ decisions. A recent ruling by the Court against Greece for a significant monetary penalty illustrates the Court will not hesitate to assert these new powers (ECJ 2000b). Finally, the Treaty of Nice (2000) also strengthened the Community judicial system by upgrading the Court of First Instance (CFI) to a fully independent court and had its jurisdiction extended (OJ[2001] C 80, 1, new Article 220 EC). And this younger colleague of the ECJ has not hesitated to exert its new powers. In the *Jégo-Quéré* decision (CFI 2002), the CFI proposed a more liberal construction of the Community's standing requirements ("individual concern"), in effect widening judicial access for individuals and groups. The CFI referred to access to justice provisions in both the newly adopted (but judicially unenforceable) EU Charter of

The Constitutional Treaty, even in its current state – adopted but not ratified by all member states – can give us some idea of the institutional changes that may occur in the future, influencing the Court's power and maintaining the stability of institutionalization processes. Article I-28 (Title IV, Chapter I, Constitutional Treaty) provides a mandate to member states to "provide remedies sufficient to ensure effective legal protection in the fields covered by EU law", foreshadowing a continued use of the preferred mechanism for individual EU rights claims – via national courts through the Article 234 preliminary ruling procedure.[10] The article itself was also streamlined, defining clearly the Court's jurisdiction and with an added provision reflecting the Court's increased jurisdiction over criminal matters (Article III-369).[11] Importantly, the Court's authority is also unified and strengthened with the proposed abolishment of the three-pillar structure, which currently limits the ECJ's power over matters covered by the Treaty on European Union. Finally, the Constitutional Treaty made the EU Charter of Fundamental Rights[12] judicially enforceable, giving the ECJ formal jurisdiction over a body of constitutional rights and enhancing the privileged status that both the ECJ and Court of First Instance already, at times, place on fundamental rights.[13] It remains a question what institutional features will ultimately be included in a final document and when it will be ratified. Yet radical

---

Fundamental Rights and the European Convention on Human Rights – upholding the generally privileged status of these constitutional norms in domestic legal systems – despite their official lack of judicial enforceability by the EU courts.

[10] The ECJ's *UPA* decision (ECJ 2002; para. 40–41) upheld the Court's past case law taking a strict interpretation of *locus standi* under Article 230 (enabling direct actions by individuals before the Court) and mandated that member states instead must provide effective judicial protection and thus individuals seeking review of Community acts should utilize the preliminary ruling procedure.

[11] Article III-369 now states the Court's jurisdiction in giving a preliminary ruling as: "a) the interpretation of the Constitution; b) the validity and interpretation of acts of the institutions, bodies, offices and agencies of the Union." Further, it contains a new provision explicitly stating how the Court should respond, "if such a question is raised in a case pending before a court or tribunal of a Member State with regard to a person in custody, the Court shall act with the minimum of delay."

[12] The EU Charter of Fundamental Rights was adopted in December 2000 but was not formally incorporated into the Treaty so it technically remains judicially unenforceable by Community courts (OJ [2000] C 361, 1). Further, the limitations placed on the Charter in the Constitutional Treaty, that no individual could claim rights from the Charter that were not already present in their national legal system, may also limit the scope of power the ECJ has in interpreting and applying this document. That said, the case law analyses included in this book illustrate that clearly the ECJ has in the past expanded its own jurisdiction when it comes to the protection of fundamental rights.

[13] Again, both the *Jégo-Quéré* decision (CFI 2002) and the *Schmidberger v. Austria* decision (ECJ 2003d) are clear examples of both the Court of First Instance and the European Court of Justice invoking the EU Charter of Fundamental Rights to uphold individual rights, even when this requires limiting Community fundamental freedoms.

modifications to these proposed changes to ECJ power are not foreseeable, given that public outcry to the Constitutional Treaty did not target provisions for a more powerful Court. Instead, these institutional changes are in fact the recipe for greater EU democracy, legitimacy and accountability in the future – a move welcomed by European civil society.

Public interest mobilization presents a similar logic. Although minimizing EU policy developments and limiting the funding available to groups in Brussels could affect their operations, this action would not necessarily cause the mobilization dynamic to turn back and destabilize. As the study illustrates, even in a time when there was minimal expansion in Community legislative advancements in social provisions, women activists were increasingly organizing in Brussels. Further, when EU funding for transnational expert networks on equality issues was limited in the 1990s, these activists continued to collaborate over issues of shared concern. Once the space is created and the links are formed, these individuals and groups increasingly become a permanent part of the European landscape. In both policy domains, the findings reveal that over time the EU expanded its competence over these areas of public policy. This expansion led to a functional demand for public support. The Commission relies on these groups and individuals for their expert knowledge on complex public issues. Once these groups gain access, it becomes increasingly difficult for member state governments to take action that would limit public inclusion. Denying access could damage civil society support, and the success of controversial issues such as the common currency, enlargement and importantly, the ratification of a Constitutional Treaty, are intimately linked to this support.

A second issue regarding the stability of institutionalization further explores this question of path dependence. In particular, how much of the present and future is determined by what happens in the past (e.g. Thelen 2004; Pierson 2000)? The litigation dynamic illustrates a distinct pattern. The ECJ often justified its rulings in light of its past case law, a pattern observed readily in the American experience, but one that is generally new but very much on the rise even in civil law systems (Stone Sweet 2002). In particular, the case law analysis of pregnancy rights and nature protection illustrated how the Court expanded EU competence over these policy domains, but did so incrementally by slowly building on previous case law to justify rulings. These decisions then served to shape judicial outcomes in the future. Further, as the body of case law in a particular policy domain increased in density, so did the density of future decisions. ECJ rulings pursuant to Article 234 in the area of nature protection, continually cited previous case law resulting from infringement proceedings, and these rulings in turn were cited in later preliminary rulings. The pregnancy rights case law illustrates how ECJ precedent proved to be a more powerful tool for litigants even after the Pregnancy Directive was adopted into national law. Member state governments decided to limit the scope and protection provided under the directive due to a lack of consensus on sensitive issues such as night work by women. Yet failure to resolve these issues legislatively only provided claimants and the ECJ the opportunity to expand this protection in the future. The Court continued to rely on its past case law to justify this expansion.

The mobilization dynamic introduces a similar albeit less powerful relationship. The data from both the social provisions and environmental protection domains reveal a pattern that suggests the power of past action to generate future mobilization. In the early years of the EU, there were few public interest groups operating in Brussels, with less than twenty groups in both domains combined. By 2003, the policy domains were characterized by a flourishing network of groups with 134 organizations across the two domains. This growth was cumulative. Women organizing through grassroots organizations and informal networks such as CREW, WEAG and ENOW in the 1970s and 1980s provided the connections and collaboration that were necessary for the development of a formal women's lobby in the 1990s, EWL. Similarly, environmental organizations such as WWF and Friends of the Earth initially participated in EU politics through its membership in the umbrella organization, the European Environmental Bureau. By the early 2000s, these groups had developed their own independent European offices, an action that was made possible by this early mobilizing. In both policy domains, as EU competence expanded, groups could not afford to be left out as other organizations mobilized to exploit these new opportunity structures. Thus, the decision to organize was often motivated by the pre-existing levels of mobilization in a given policy domain. Further, as the findings illustrated, once the Community made the decision to provide at least some support for these groups, the connections were formed and sustained, regardless of changes in funding in the future. The path was paved, the doors were opened and a public sphere had begun to develop.

Litigation, mobilization and democratic governance

The expansive nature of these processes of institutionalization of supranational governance may tell us something about democracy in the European Union. In particular, the findings enlighten various concerns raised in a continuing debate over the Union's democratic deficit.[14] First, the "distance

---

[14] There is a rich body of scholarship devoted to this topic. See for example, Weiler et al. (1995); Weiler (1999); Craig (2001); Curtin (1997) and Andersen and Eliassen, eds. (1996), Scharpf (1999).

issue" has long troubled both scholars and practitioners, fearing that the EU is inherently undemocratic as policy decisions are being decided at a greater distance from the scrutiny and direct participation of civil society. Yet both the litigation and mobilization processes illustrate how citizens are increasingly directly engaged with the EU legal system and policy process, with the effect of narrowing the distance that might otherwise exist between national and EU politics. The Court's supremacy and direct effect doctrines provided a new opportunity for ordinary citizens to invoke EU law before their own national courts. Further, the transnational networks associated with both of these processes, be it activists working through Legal Experts Network or conservationists in Birdlife International, reached out to citizens at the national level informing them of their rights and opportunities under EU law. While the vast majority of EU citizens are not directly involved, but instead rely on the work of these transnational activists, this mobilization over time can begin to make EU politics more reachable to the ordinary citizen.

Second, and somewhat related to the first, the EU policy process has been criticized for being unintelligible to ordinary citizens due to its complexity and lack of transparency. As the distance shrinks, so too does this concern. Activists working through CREW and even from within the Commission's Women's Information Service, were providing detailed, readable and accessible information for women throughout the EU in an attempt to educate them about how their lives were affected by EU policies, and how they could go about utilizing EU resources and procedures to protect these rights. Further, the exchange of information between environmental groups in Spain and the Netherlands regarding how to bring claims before the ECJ illustrates how activists shared their expertise in order to diminish the complexities associated with lodging a complaint for the first time. While a large number of EU citizens may still remain uninformed and confused by EU politics, this book illustrates how transnational public interest groups have made considerable strides towards making the EU a more transparent and less complex place for the ordinary citizen.

Third, others criticize the EU for possessing a "substantive imbalance" in policy priorities for disproportionately favoring capital over labor. Thus the argument goes that even as the European Parliament is strengthened to be more representative of the interests of European citizens, this imbalance persists due to the overwhelming dominance of policies related to economic integration. Again, the findings in this book illustrate that despite the intentions of member state governments, EU policies often had significant unintended consequences. Fair competition policies can have consequences that do not always favor capital. The transformation of

Article 141, the Equal Pay Principle, is a case in point. This treaty provision placed duties on member state governments and was intended to protect businesses from unfair competition that could result from lower paid female labor. Instead, an activist labor lawyer utilized this general provision to expand women's rights and provided the ECJ with concrete situations to apply this abstract EU rule. The outcome was legendary. The Court transformed this treaty provision into an enforceable right, granting women throughout the EU a new legal basis to seek protection from discriminatory practices. This provision was not designed to protect women, but instead benefit business. Litigants activated the ECJ's judicial rulemaking capacity and over time these decisions altered the balance of power and empowered ordinary citizens.

Together, this study illustrates the importance of moving the debate about democracy and the EU, and even more generally in global governance,[15] away from a discussion that is solely focused on electoral and executive deficiencies to one including the interaction between courts and society. There is clearly opposition to such an assertion. The *judicialization* of policy-making (Shapiro and Stone Sweet 2002), as exemplified by this study, has not surprisingly deepened long-standing debates over the tenuous relationship between courts (as counter-majoritarian organizations) and representative democracy (e.g. Bickel 1962; Black 1960; Bobbit 1982). These concerns are equally salient in the international context as scholars raise the question whether courts and constitutionalism at the international level may in reality promote or undermine democracy at home and internationally (Rubenfeld 2004). While these are important theoretical and empirical questions we should continue to explore, this book suggests the positive effects of such judicial empowerment.

By examining the interaction between the European Court of Justice, civil society and governance, this study highlights how courts can provide important democratic participatory opportunities for citizen and groups by engaging them in the development, monitoring and enforcement of law. Again, these processes of litigation and mobilization do not replace the importance of representative institutions, but instead complement the work of executives and the legislature. The study adopts a key principle that the enhancement of democratic governance is defined as greater accountability, transparency and individual participation in political processes. There are multiple approaches to accountability (Keohane and Grant, 2005), and this book illustrates how supranational legal mechanisms can contribute to accountability, through enforcing the

---

[15] See special issue of Government and Opposition dedicated to the topic (Held and Koening-Archibugi 2004).

law, rights claiming and greater legal protection for individuals. This dynamic is not unique to the European Union but instead is a pattern of democratic participation that we see taking place around the globe (see Cichowski 2006a, 2006b; Cichowski and Stone Sweet 2003; Alter 2006; Börzel 2006; Conant 2006; Kelemen 2006; Scheppele 2003).

Beyond the European experience

I would like to conclude by suggesting a set of broader lessons for scholars concerned with processes of institutional change and evolving political spaces. In particular, I argue that courts and social movements are increasingly shaping the direction of domestic and international political processes – a reality that challenges our current theoretical understandings of comparative and international politics.

First, beyond substantive policy creation, courts can exert significant consequences on social power relations. Throughout the world, courts and processes of legalization are incrementally transforming international and domestic politics – from human rights to the adjudication of trade disputes (Alter 2001; Kelemen 2001; Keohane et al. 2000; Tallberg 2002). Our scholarship illustrates how judicial organizations both empower and constrain nation-states – the dominant actors in global governance. Courts can also exert potentially powerful effects on political reform and individual empowerment in countries around the world (Cichowski and Stone Sweet 2003; McCann 1994; Shapiro 1981; Stone Sweet 2000; Scheppele 2003, 2004). This book illustrates how a supranational court is able to empower disadvantaged individuals *vis-à-vis* powerful interests. This legal action relies on a necessary rule, be it legislation or a treaty (constitutional) provision and the ability of a given interest to mobilize and utilize this opportunity. Given an independent judiciary with judicial review powers, a court's resolution of this legal claim may lead to the expansion of governance. Through judicial rule-making, the rules and procedures can become more binding and precise, altering the opportunity structures for future claims. Put simply, altering the institutions in a given policy arena can change who has access to that policy space. The extent to which courts continue to achieve greater autonomy, as reflected in the global trend to create and empower constitutional courts (Tate and Vallinder 1995; Kenney et al. 1999; Ginsburg 2003), and the greater equality achieved in access to justice, the greater likelihood this pattern of mobilization will continue.

Second, these court rulings do not just float in space. Instead, they impact the emergence of new social spaces. Beyond serving as the basis for new legal claims, judicial decisions can bring attention to important policy issues, creating the space for new discussions. Individuals reorient their activities as a result of this new opportunity and over time the space is, so to speak, filled in. From an international perspective, we see this happening over issues such as the tensions arising between global free-trade norms and environmental protection. At both the national and international level, judges have been asked to adjudicate between these seemingly disparate interests, as businesses demand protection for their enterprises, which are increasingly constrained by varying domestic environmental regulations. Disputes over issues as diverse as US tuna conservation policies to EU labeling requirements of genetically modified foods have resonated loudly with environmental activists (Kelemen 2001). As the opportunity is created for a global discussion of free trade and environmental protection, environmentalists have mobilized quickly for fear of being left out of these increasingly important policy decisions. Today, the environmental movement is increasingly active across and above nations, from the protest activities of Greenpeace and its flagship the Rainbow Warrior, to the environmentalists whose international lobbying led to the adoption of the Bio-Safety Protocol, an international treaty with an unprecedented level of environmental protection. Once the space was created, the actors continued to exploit these opportunities.

Third, a key lesson of this study was the reciprocal effect of this mobilization. That is, once actors were mobilized by new political opportunities, their action could over time alter the institutions and the boundaries of politics. This trend is not unique. Instead, social movements have historically served to widen domestic political spaces to include previously disadvantaged or excluded public interests.[16] Given this reality it remains surprising that only a handful of studies examine the impact of social movement activism on political structures (Giugni, McAdam and Tilly 1997; Gamson and Meyer 1996). This study contributes to understanding how movement action can change governance. The implications for public inclusion and democratic politics make this an increasingly important research agenda.

This book also highlights the importance of studying the effect of mobilization not only on governance structures in domestic politics but at the supranational and international level. Increasingly, international organizations provide the formal access and space for the input of non-governmental organizations and transnational activism is on the rise (Keck and Sikkink 1998; Tarrow 2005). Utilizing these spaces, individuals and groups have subsequently pressured for greater public inclusion

---

[16] The American civil rights movement is a clear example of this dynamic (e.g. Morris 1984).

and attention to public concerns in a policy arena, which is traditionally dominated by nation-states. Rights to a hearing, transparency and civil society participation are increasingly an integral part of global governance institutions (Bignami 2005). Today, levels of public activism akin to domestic politics increasingly characterize international politics. The public mobilization surrounding the World Trade Organization's (WTO) general meetings serves as a case in point. Further, national executives have begun to respond to civil society demands by integrating public issues, as exemplified by the success of women activists to achieve gender-mainstreaming policies in three powerful international organizations, the World Bank, the United Nations and the European Union.[17] Yet even beyond these policy changes, as this study illustrates, international governance can be altered, the extent to which these groups become more collective and formal, and more permanent in transnational and international spaces.

It is through these evolving dynamics of litigation and mobilization that institutionalization of governance can occur. Certain rules are created and through the actions of individuals and organizations these rules can be expanded in a direction that leads those governed by these rules down a path that becomes increasingly hard to change (Pierson 2000; North 1990). Powerful actors produce rules and organizations that embody their interests, yet these opportunities can be used in unintended ways. These consequences are not all welcomed by national executives. In domestic politics, it can enable disadvantaged individuals to change state sanctioned inequalities through the (alleged) non-political interpretations of the judicial branch. From the international perspective, these outcomes can change who controls the trajectory of global politics. Over time, the legitimacy of international organizations may rely more on the support of ordinary citizens throughout the world, rather than the national executives that (allegedly) control these organizations (Cichowski 2006b). Governance does not only hinge on a series of executive and legislative choices, but has evolved as the accumulation of strategic activism by courts and social activists, operating above and below the nation-state.

---

[17] See World Bank (1997) and UNDP (1997).

References

Court of Justice of the European Communities Decisions cited in the text

Social provisions

ECJ 1970. Internationale Handesgesellschaft, Case 11/70, European Court Reports (ECR) 1970: 1125.
ECJ 1971. Defrenne I, Case 80/70, ECR 1971: 445.
ECJ 1976a. Defrenne II, Case 43/75, ECR 1976: 455.
ECJ 1978. Defrenne III, Case 149/77, ECR 1978: 1365.
ECJ 1980. Macarthy, Case 12/79, ECR 1980: 1275.
ECJ 1981a. Jenkins, Case 96/80, ECR 1981: 911.
ECJ 1981c. Worringham, Case 69/80, ECR 1981: 767.
ECJ 1982b. Garland, Case 12/81, ECR 1982: 359.
ECJ 1984b. Hoffman, Case 184/83, ECR 1984: 645.
ECJ 1985b. Case 19/83, ECR 1985: 457.
ECJ 1986a. Bilka, Case 170/84, ECR 1986: 1607.
ECJ 1986b. Von Colson, Case 14/83, ECR 1986: 1891.
ECJ 1986c. Johnston, Case 222/84, ECR 1986: 1651.
ECJ 1989b. Rinner-Kühn, Case 171/88, ECR 1989: 2743.
ECJ 1989d. Danfoss, Case 12/54, ECR 1989: 345.
ECJ 1990a. Barber, Case 262/88, ECR 1990: 1889.
ECJ 1990c. Dekker, Case C-177/88, ECR 1990: 3941.
ECJ 1990d. Hertz, Case C-179/88, ECR 1990: 3979.
ECJ 1991b. Stoekel, Case C-345/89, ECR 1991: 4047
ECJ 1993a. Marshall II, Case C-271/91, ECR 1993: 4367.
ECJ 1993b. Moroni, Case C-110/91, ECR 1993: 6591.
ECJ 1993c. Ten Oever, Case C-109/91, ECR 1993: 4879.
ECJ 1993d. Neath, Case C-152/91, ECR 1993: 6935.
ECJ 1994c. Haberman-Beltermann v. Arbeiterwohlfahrt, Case C-421/92, ECR 1994: 1657.
ECJ 1994d. Webb, Case C-32/93, ECR 1994: 3567.
ECJ 1995a. Kalanke, Case C-450/93, ECR 1995: 3051.
ECJ 1996a. Gillespie, Case C-342/93, ECR 1996: 475.

ECJ 1996d. P v. S and Cornwall County Council, Case C-13/94, ECR 1996: 2143.

ECJ 1997a. Draehmpaehl, Case C-180/95, ECR 1997: 2195.

ECJ 1997b. Larsson, Case C-400/95, ECR 1997: 4135.

ECJ 1997c. Marschall, Case C-409/95, ECR 1997: 865.

ECJ 1997d. Commission v. French Republic, Case C-197/96, ECR 1997: 1489.

ECJ 1997e. Commission v. Italy, Case C-207/96, ECR 1997: 6869.

ECJ 1998a. Boyle, Case C- 411/96, ECR 1998: 6401.

ECJ 1998b. Pedersen, Case C-66/96, ECR 1998: 7327.

ECJ 1998d. Brown v. Rentokil Ltd., Case C-394/96, ECR 1998: 4185.

ECJ 1998e. Thibault, Case C-136/95, ECR 1998: 2011.

ECJ 1998g. Grant, Case C-249/96, ECR 1998: 346.

ECJ 1998h. Commission v United Kingdom, Case C-106/96, ECR 1998: 2729.

ECJ 1999a. Sirdar, Case C-273/97, ECR 1999: 7403.

ECJ 1999b. Lewen, Case C-333/97, ECR 1999: 7243.

ECJ 1999c. Abdoulaye, Case C-218/98, ECR 1999: 5723.

ECJ 2000a. Kreil, Case C-285/98, ECR 2000: 69.

ECJ 2000d. Mahlburg, Case C-207/98, ECR 2000: 549.

ECJ 2001a. Melgar, Case C-438/99, ECR 2001: 6915.

ECJ 2001b. Tele Danmark, Case C-109/00, ECR 2001: 6993.

ECJ 2003a. Busch, Case C-320/01, ECR 2003: 2041.

ECJ 2004a. Gómez, Case C-342/01, ECR 2004: 2605.

ECJ 2004b. Alabaster, Case C-147/02, ECR 2004: 3101.

ECJ 2004c. Sass, Case C-284/02, ECR 2004: 11143.

ECJ 2005. Mayer, Case C-356/03, ECR 2005: 295.

Environmental protection

ECJ 1976b. Handelskwekerij GJ Bier, Case 21/76, ECR 1976: 1735

ECJ 1981b. Van Dam & Zonen, Case 124/80, ECR 1981: 1447.

ECJ 1983. Inter-Huiles, Case 172/82, ECR 1983: 555.

ECJ 1984a. Rhône-Alpes Huiles, Case 295/82, ECR 1984: 575.

ECJ 1985a. ADBHU, Case C-240/83, ECR 1985: 531.

ECJ 1987a. Pretore di Salo (Anglers' Assoc.), Case 14/86, ECR 1987: 2545

ECJ 1987b. Commission v. Belgium, Case 247/85, ECR 1987: 3029.

ECJ 1987c. Commission v. France, Case 262/85, ECR 1987: 3073.

ECJ 1987d. Commission v. Germany, Case 412/85, ECR 1987: 3503.

ECJ 1987e. Commission v. Netherlands, Case 236/85, ECR 1987: 3989.

ECJ 1987f. Angler's Association, Case 14/86, ECR 1987: 2545.

ECJ 1988a. Commission v. Denmark (Danish Bottles), Case 302/86, ECR 1988: 4621.

ECJ 1988b. Commission v. France, Case 252/85, ECR 1988: 2243.

ECJ 1989c. Nijman, Case 125/88, ECR 1989: 3533.

ECJ 1990b. Gourmetterie Van den Burg, Case 169/89, ECR 1990: 2143.

ECJ 1990e. Vessosso and Zanetti, Cases 206 & 207/88, ECR 1990: 1461.

ECJ 1990f. Zanetti and others, Case 359/88 ECR 1990: 1509.

ECJ 1990g. Commission v Netherlands, Case 339/87, ECR 1990: 851.

ECJ 1991e. Commission v. Germany (Leybucht Dykes), Case 57/89 ECR 1991: 903.

ECJ 1991f. Commission v. Italy, Case 157/89, ECR 1991: 57.

ECJ 1991g. Commission v. Italy, Case 334/89, ECR 1991: 93.

ECJ 1991h. Commission v. Italy, Case 361/88, ECR 1991: 2567.

ECJ 1991i. Commission v. Council (Titanium Dioxide), Case 200/89, ECR 1991: 2867.

ECJ 1993e. Vanacker, Case C-37/92 ECR 1993: 4947.

ECJ 1993f. Commission v. Spain (Santoña Marshes), Case 355/90 ECR 1993: 4221.

ECJ 1994a. Association de Animaux, Case C-435/92, ECR 1994: 67.

ECJ 1994e. Difesa della Cava, Case C-236/92, ECR 1994: 483.

ECJ 1994f. An Taisce/WWF v. Commission, Case 585/93, ECR 1994: 733.

ECJ 1995b. Commission v. Germany, C-422/92 ECR 1995: 1097.

ECJ 1995c. Greenpeace v. Commission, C-461/93 ECR 1995: 2205.

ECJ 1996b. Ligue belge des oiseaux, Case C-10/96, ECR 1996: 6775.

ECJ 1996e. WWF Italia and others, Case C-118/94 ECR 1996: 1223.

ECJ 1996f. Lappel Banks, Case C-44/95 ECR 1996: 3805.

ECJ 1996g. Vergy, Case C-149/94 ECR 1996: 299.

ECJ 1996h. Van der Feesten, Case C-202/94, ECR 1996: 355.

ECJ 1996i. Kraaijeveld, Case C-72/95, ECR 1996: 5403.

ECJ 1997f. Tombesi, joined Cases C-304/94, C-330/94, C-342/94 and C-224/95 ECR 1997: 3561.

ECJ 1997g. Commission v. Greece, Case C-329/96, ECR 1997: 3749.

ECJ 1997h. Commission v. Germany, Case C-83/97, ECR 1997: 7191.

ECJ 1998c. Greenpeace v. Commission, Case C-321/95, ECR 1998: 1651.

ECJ 1998f. Dusseldorp BV, C-Case 203/96 ECR 1998: 4075.

ECJ 1999d. Commission v. France, Case C-166/97, ECR 1999: 1719.

ECJ 1999e. Commission v. France, Case C-96/98, ECR 1999: 8531.

ECJ 2000b. Commission v. Greece, Case C-387/97, ECR 2000: 3214.

ECJ 2000c. First Corporate Shipping Ld. (FCS), Case C-371/98, ECR 2000: 9235.

ECJ 2000e. Commission v. France, Case C-374/98, ECR 2000: 10799.

ECJ 2001c. Tridon, Case C-510/99, ECR 2001: 7777.

ECJ 2003b. Nilsson, Case C-154/02, ECR 2003: 12733.

ECJ 2003c. League for the Protection of Birds & others, Case C-182/02, ECR 2003: 12105.

Other Decisions

ECJ 1963. Van Gend en Loos, Case 26/62, ECR 1963: 1.

ECJ 1964. Costa, Case 6/64, ECR 1964: 585.

ECJ 1974. Van Duyn, Case 41/74, ECR 1974: 1337.

ECJ 1975. Mr. and Mrs. F v. Belgium, Case 7/75, ECR 1975: 679.

ECJ 1979. Ratti, Case 148/78, ECR 1979: 1629.

ECJ 1982a. Becker, Case 8/81, ECR 1982: 53.

ECJ 1989a. Wachauf, Case 5/88, ECR 1989: 2609.

ECJ 1991a. Ellinkiki, Case C-260/89, ECR 1991: 2925.
ECJ 1991c. Commission v. Germany, Case C-131/88, ECR 1991: 825.
ECJ 1991d. Commission v. Germany, Case C-361/988, ECR 1991: 2567.
ECJ 1994b. Graff, Case C-351/92, ECR 1994: 3361.
ECJ 1996c. Bosphorus, Case C-84/95, ECR 1996: 3953.
ECJ 2002. Union de Pequeños Agricultores (UPA), Case C-50/00, ECR 2002: 6677.
ECJ 2003d. Schmidberger v Austria, Case C-112/00, ECR 2003: 5659.

Court of First Instance of the European Communities Decisions cited in the text

CFI 2002. Jégo-Quéré, Case T-177/01, ECR 2002: 2365.

Official European Union Documents cited in text

Commission of the European Communities (CEC) 1960. *Bulletin of the European Communities*, No. 6/7. Luxembourg: Office of the Official Publications of the European Communities.

CEC 1962. *Bulletin of the European Communities*, No. 1. Luxembourg: Office of the Official Publications of the European Communities.

CEC 1963. *Bulletin of the European Communities*, No. 2. Luxembourg: Office of the Official Publications of the European Communities.

CEC 1972. *Bulletin of the European Communities*, No. 10. Luxembourg: Office of the Official Publications of the European Communities.

CEC 1973a. *First Community Action Programme on the Environment.* OJ No. C 112, 20/12/73. Luxembourg: Office of the Official Publications of the European Communities.

CEC 1973b. *Report of the Commission to the Council on the Application of the Principle of Equal Pay for Men and Women, situation on the 31 December 1972.* SEC (73) 3000. Luxembourg: Office of the Official Publications of the European Communities.

CEC 1977. *Second Community Action Programme on the Environment.* OJ No. C 139, 13/6/77. Luxembourg: Office of the Official Publications of the European Communities.

CEC 1978. *Women of Europe* (1992), No. 6/78. Brussels: Women's Information Service, Directorate-General Audiovisual, Information, Communication, Culture.

CEC 1979. *Official Journal of the European Communities* (annual index edition, 1979). Luxembourg: Office of the Official Publications of the European Communities.

CEC 1981. *A New Community Action Programme on the Promotion of Equal Opportunities for Women* (1982–1985), COM(81) 758. Luxembourg: Office of the Official Publications of the European Communities.

CEC 1982. *Council Resolution on the promotion of equal opportunities for women.* Official Journal C 186, 21.7.82, p. 3. Luxembourg: Office of the Official Publications of the European Communities.

CEC 1983. *Community Law and Women, Women of Europe*, Supplement No. 12. Brussels: Women's Information Service, Directorate-General Audiovisual, Information, Communication, Culture.

CEC 1984. *Report of a Comparative Analysis of the Provision for Legal Redress in member states of the European Community in Respect of Article 119 of the Treaty of Rome and the Equal Pay, Equal Treatment and Social Securities Directive.* Brussels: European Commission, Directorate General V Employment, Industrial Relations and Social Affairs.

CEC 1985. *Community Law and Women, Women of Europe*, Supplement No. 19. Brussels: Women's Information Service, Directorate-General Audiovisual, Information, Communication, Culture.

CEC 1987a. *Community Law and Women, Women of Europe*, Supplement No. 12. Brussels: Women's Information Service, Directorate-General Audiovisual, Information, Communication, Culture.

CEC 1987b. *Fourth Environmental Action Programme.* O.J. C328/1. Luxembourg: Office of the Official Publications of the European Communities.

CEC 1988. *Proposal for the Habitats Directive*, COM (88) 381. Luxembourg: Office of the Official Publications of the European Communities.

CEC 1989. *A Community strategy for waste management.* SEC (89) 934. Luxembourg: Office of the Official Publications of the European Communities.

CEC 1990a. *Proposal for a council directive concerning the protection at work of pregnant women or women who have recently given birth.* COM (1990) 406. Luxembourg: Office of the Official Publications of the European Communities.

CEC 1990b. *First Commission Report on the Implementation by Member States of EEC Environmental Law.* Commission Document P-5. Luxembourg: Office of the Official Publications of the European Communities.

CEC 1990c. *Equal Opportunities for women and men: The Third Medium Term Community Action Programme 1991–1995.* COM (90) 449. Luxembourg: Office of the Official Publications of the European Communities.

CEC 1991. *Eighth Annual Report on the Monitoring of the Application of Community Law* (1990), COM (91) 338. Luxembourg: Office of the Official Publications of the European Communities.

CEC 1992. *Women of Europe* (1992), No. 70. Brussels: Women's Information Service, Directorate-General Audiovisual, Information, Communication, Culture.

CEC 1993a. *Sex Equality Litigation in the Member States of the European Community: A Comparative Study.* Brussels: European Commission, Directorate General V Employment, Industrial Relations and Social Affairs.

CEC 1993c. *Second Report on the Application of Directive No. 79/409/EEC on the Conservation of Wild Birds.* COM (93) 572 final.

CEC 1993d. *Fifth Environmental Action Programme.* O.J. C138/1. Luxembourg: Office of the Official Publications of the European Communities.

CEC 1995a. *Utilization of Sex Equality Litigation Procedures in the Member States of the European Community: A Comparative Study.* Brussels: European Commission, Directorate General V Employment, Industrial Relations and Social Affairs.

CEC 1995b. *Opinion on the planned A20 motorway in Germany which will intersect the Trebel and Recknitz Valley.* OJ EC 1995: C 178/3. Luxembourg: Office of the Official Publications of the European Communities.

CEC 1995c. *European Social Policy: Options for the Union.* Luxembourg: Office of the Official Publications of the European Communities.

CEC 1996. *Directory of Interest Groups.* Luxembourg: Office of the Official Publications of the European Communities.

CEC 1996a. *Commission communication to the European Parliament and the Council on the interpretation of the judgment of the Court of Justice on 17 October 1995 in Case C-450/93, Kalanke v. Freie Hansestadt Bremen.* COM (96) 88. Luxembourg: Office of the Official Publications of the European Communities.

CEC 1996b. *Commission Opinion on the intersection of the Peene Valley by the planned A20 motorway pursuant to 6(4) of Directive 92/43/EEC.* OJ EC 1996 L 6/14. Luxembourg: Office of the Official Publications of the European Communities.

CEC 1996c. *Commission Communication on Implementation of EU Law.* COM (96) 500. Luxembourg: Office of the Official Publications of the European Communities.

CEC 1996d. *Thirteenth Annual Report on Monitoring the Application of Community Law, (1995).* O.J. C303/1. Luxembourg: Office of the Official Publications of the European Communities.

CEC 1996e. *Incorporating Equal Opportunities for Women and Men into all Community Policies and Activities.* COM (96) 67 final. Luxembourg: Office of the Official Publications of the European Communities.

CEC 1997a. *General Report 1996 of the Legal Experts Group on Equal Treatment of Men and Women. Monitoring Implementation and Application of Community Equality Law 1996.* Brussels: European Commission, Directorate General V Employment and Social Affairs.

CEC 1997b. *First Annual Survey on the Implementation and Enforcement of Community Environmental Law.* Working Document of the Commission Services. Brussels. European Commission, Directorate General XI Environment.

CEC 1997c. *Commission Communication On the Promoting the Role of Voluntary Organizations.* COM (97) 23. Luxembourg: Office of the Official Publications of the European Communities.

CEC 1997d. *Council Resolution on Access to Justice in the Implementation of EU law.* O.J. C321/1. Luxembourg: Office of the Official Publications of the European Communities.

CEC 1998a. *Directory of the Projects 1998. Medium-term Community Action Programme on Equal Opportunities for Women and Men.* Luxembourg: Office of the Official Publications of the European Communities.

CEC 1998b. *Equality Quarterly News. Newsletter of the Expert Legal Group on the Application of European Law on Equal Treatment between Women and Men,* Spring 1998, No. 2. Brussels: European Commission, Directorate General Employment, Industrial Relations and Social Affairs.

CEC 1998c. *Equality is the Future.* Congress Summary 21–22 September 1998. Brussels: European Commission, Directorate General Employment, Industrial Relations and Social Affairs.

CEC 1998d. *Fifteenth Annual Report on Monitoring the Application of Community Law (1997)* COM (98) 317. Luxembourg: Office of the Official Publications of the European Communities.

CEC 1999b. *Monitoring, implementation and application of Community Equality Law. General Report 1997 & 1998 of the Legal Experts' Group on Equal Treatment of Men and Women.* Brussels: European Commission, Directorate General Employment and Social Affairs.

CEC 1999c. *On the Implementation of Council Directive 92/85/EEC of 19 October 1992.* COM (1999) 100. Luxembourg: Office of the Official Publications of the European Communities.

CEC 1999d. *Sixteenth Annual Report on the Monitoring of the Application of Community Law (1998),* COM (1999) 301 final. Luxembourg: Office of the Official Publications of the European Communities.

CEC 1999e. *European Social Policy Forum 1998 – Summary Report.* Luxembourg: Office of the Official Publications of the European Communities.

CEC 2000a. *Bulletin – Legal Issues in Equality,* 1/2000. Directorate General for Employment and Social Affairs. Luxembourg: Office of the Official Publications of the European Communities.

CEC 2000b. *Environment For Europeans.* No. 3, July 2000. Luxembourg: Office of the Official Publications of the European Communities.

CEC 2000c. *White Paper on European Governance: Enhancing Democracy in the European Union Work Programme.* SEC (2000) 1547/7. Luxembourg: Office of the Official Publications of the European Communities.

CEC 2000d. *Community Framework Strategy on Gender Equality.* COM (2000) 335 final. Luxembourg: Office of the Official Publications of the European Communities.

CEC 2001. *European Governance: A White Paper.* COM (2001) 428. Luxembourg: Office of the Official Publications of the European Communities.

CEC 2002a. *Access to Justice in Environmental Matters.* Final Report prepared by Nicolas De Sadeleer, Gerhard Roller and Miriam Doss. ENV.A.3/ETU/2002/0030.

CEC 2002b. *Summary. The Sixth Environmental Action Programme of the European Community 2002–2012.* Luxembourg: Office of the Official Publications of the European Communities.

CEC 2003. *Commission Proposal for a Directive on Access to Justice.* COM (2003) 624. Luxembourg: Office of the Official Publications of the European Communities.

CEC 2004. *Proposal for a Directive of the European Parliament and of the Council on the Implentation of the Principle of Equal Opportunities and Equal Treatment of Men and Women in Matters of Employment and Occupation. Extended Impact Assessment. Commission Staff Working Paper.* SEC (2004) 482. Luxembourg: Office of the Official Publications of the European Communities. http://www.europa.eu.int/comm/employment_social/gender_equality/legislation/legalacts_en.html.

CEC 2005a. *Directory of Community Legislation in Force and other acts of the Community Institutions.* Luxembourg: Office of the Official Publications of the European Communities. http://www.europa.eu.int/eur-lex/lex/en/repert/index.htm

CEC 2005b. *Bulletin – Legal Issues in Equality*, 2/2005. Directorate General for Employment and Social Affairs. Luxembourg: Office of the Official Publications of the European Communities.

European Parliament (EP). 1961. Rapport interimaire su l'egalisation des salaries masculins et feminins, Document 68, (October 1961). Luxembourg: Office of the Official Publications of the European Communities.

EP 1981. *The Report of the Ad Hoc Committee on Women's Rights* (Maij-Weggen Report), Document 1–829/80–11. Luxembourg: Office of the Official Publications of the European Communities.

EP 1984. *Reports of Enquiry, European Parliament Working Documents*, 1–1229/83/C (Jaunary 1984). Luxembourg: Office of the Official Publications of the European Communities.

Other Government Documents cited in the text

British Equal Opportunities Commission (EOC). 1980. *Equality for Women, Assessment – Problems – Perspectives, a European project.* Manchester: Equal Opportunities Commission.

United Nations Development Program (UNDP). 1997. *Global Umbrella Programme for Gender Equality and the Advancement of Women: Gender Mainstreaming and the Advancement of Women.* New York: United Nations Office for Project Services.

United Nations Economic Commission for Europe (UNECE). 1998. *Convention on Access to Information, Public Participation in Decision-Making and Access to Justice in Environmental Matter.* Århus, Denmark, 25 June 1998. http://www.unece.org/env/pp/documents/cep43e.pdf

World Bank. 1997. *Mainstreaming Gender in World Bank Lending: An Update.* Washington D.C.: World Bank Operations Survey.

Non-Governmental Organization Publications/ Information cited in the text

(Interviews with Non-Governmental Organizations are documented in the text.)

Bureau of International Recycling (BIR). 1996. BIR. In A. B. Philip and O. Gray (eds.), *Directory of Pressure Groups in the EU.* 2nd Edition. London, UK: Cartermill International Ltd.

Centre for Research on European Women (CREW). 1983. *CREW Reports*, Vol. 3, No. 1. Brussels: CREW Publications.

1985. *CREW Reports*, Vol. 5, No. 2. Brussels: CREW Publications.

1989. *CREW Reports*, Vol. 9, No. 11/12. Brussels: CREW Publications.

1991. *CREW Reports*, Vol. 11, No. 5. Brussels: CREW Publications.

1993. *CREW Reports*, Vol. 3, No. 8/9. Brussels: CREW Publications

1994. *CREW Reports*, Vol. 14, No. 8/9. Brussels: CREW Publications.

1996. Centre for Research on European Women. In A. B. Philip and O. Gray (eds.), *Directory of Pressure Groups in the EU*. 2nd Edition. London, UK: Cartermill International Ltd.

Council of European Municipalities and Region (CEMR). 1996. CEMR. In A. B. Philip and O. Gray (eds.), *Directory of Pressure Groups in the EU*. 2nd Edition. London, UK: Cartermill International Ltd.

European Anti-Poverty Network (EAPN). 1996. EAPN. In A. B. Philip and O. Gray (eds.), *Directory of Pressure Groups in the EU*. 2nd Edition. London, UK: Cartermill International Ltd.

European Bureau of Consumer Unions. 1996. BEUC. In Alan Butt Philip and Oliver Gray, *Directory of Pressure Groups in the EU*. 2nd Edition. London, UK: Cartermill International Ltd.

European Community of Consumer Cooperatives (EURO COOP). 1996. EURO COOP. In A. B. Philip and O. Gray (eds.), *Directory of Pressure Groups in the EU*. 2nd Edition. London, UK: Cartermill International Ltd.

European Environmental Bureau (EEB). 1998. *Global Assessment of the Fifth Action Programme on Sustainable Development*. Brussels: EEB.

1999. *Annual Summary of Activities*. Brussels: EEB.

2004. The EU's New Constitution: Assessing the Environmental Perspective. Brussels: EEB. http://www.eeb.org/activities/european_constitution/EU-new-Constitution-Assessment-081104.pdf.

European Federation of Waste Management (FEAD). 1996. FEAD. In A. B. Philip and O. Gray (eds.), *Directory of Pressure Groups in the EU*. 2nd Edition. London, UK: Cartermill International Ltd.

European Ferrous Recovery and Recycling Federation (EFR). 1996. EFR. In A. B. Philip and O. Gray (eds.), *Directory of Pressure Groups in the EU*. 2nd Edition. London, UK: Cartermill International Ltd.

European Metal Trade and Recycling Federation (EUROMETREC). 1996. EUROMETREC. In A. B. Philip and O. Gray (eds.), *Directory of Pressure Groups in the EU*. 2nd Edition. London, UK: Cartermill International Ltd.

European Network of Women (ENOW). 1985. *Assessment of the Community Action Programme on the Promotion of Equal Opportunities for Women*. Brussels: ENOW.

1996. ENOW. In A. B. Philip and O. Gray (eds.), *Directory of Pressure Groups in the EU*. 2nd Edition. London, UK: Cartermill International Ltd.

European Recovery and Recycling Association (ERRA). 1996. ERRA. In A. B. Philip and O. Gray (eds.), *Directory of Pressure Groups in the EU*. 2nd Edition. London, UK: Cartermill International Ltd.

European Solidarity Towards Equal Participation of People (EUROSTEP). 1996. EUROSTEP. In A. B. Philip and O. Gray (eds.), *Directory of Pressure Groups in the EU*. 2nd Edition. London, UK: Cartermill International Ltd.

European Union Migrant Forum. 1996. The Forum. In A. B. Philip and O. Gray (eds.), *Directory of Pressure Groups in the EU*. 2nd Edition. London, UK: Cartermill International Ltd.

European Union of Women (EUW). 1996. EUW. In A. B. Philip and O. Gray (eds.), *Directory of Pressure Groups in the EU*. 2nd Edition. London, UK: Cartermill International Ltd.

European Water Pollution Control Association (EWPCA). 1996. EWPCA. In A. B. Philip and O. Gray (eds.), *Directory of Pressure Groups in the EU.* 2nd Edition. London, UK: Cartermill International Ltd.

European Women's Lobby. 1996. *EWL Newsletter*, Vol. 10. Brussels: EWL.

　2005. *EWL Communication Strategy for the European Convention.* Brussels: EWL.

Friends of the Earth Europe (FOEE). 1996. FOEE. In A. B. Philip and O. Gray (eds.), *Directory of Pressure Groups in the EU.* 2nd Edition. London, UK: Cartermill International Ltd.

　1999. FOEE Brochure. Brussels: Friends of the Earth Europe.

Greenpeace. 1998. *International Annual Report, 1998.* Brussels: Greenpeace International, European Unit.

　2000. *Greenpeace International's European Work.* Brussels: Greenpeace International, European Unit.

Institute for European Environmental Policy (IEEP). 1996. IEEP. In A. B. Philip and O. Gray (eds.), *Directory of Pressure Groups in the EU.* 2nd Edition. London, UK: Cartermill International Ltd.

International Friends of Nature (IFN). 1990. *Manifesto for a New, Ecological, Open and Social Europe.* Austira: International Friends of Nature.

　1997a. *Friends of Nature: Tradition.* Austria: International Friends of Nature.

　1997b. *Friends of Nature: Commitment to Sustainable Development.* Austria: International Friends of Nature.

International Union of Local Authorities (IULA). 1996. IULA. In A. B. Philip and O. Gray (eds.), *Directory of Pressure Groups in the EU.* 2nd Edition. London, UK: Cartermill International Ltd.

Oil Companies European Organization for the Environment, Health and Safety (CONCAWE). 1996. CONCAWE. In A. B. Philip and O. Gray (eds.), *Directory of Pressure Groups in the EU.* 2nd Edition. London, UK: Cartermill International Ltd.

Platform of European Social NGOs. 1998. *Summary Newsletter.* Brussels: Platform.

　2003. *Social Platform Response to the Part III. The Policies and Functioning of the Union of the Draft Constitution.* Brussels: Platform. http://www.socialplatform. org/module/filelib/responsetothepartiii19june2003.doc

Public Services International (PSI). 1996. PSI. In A. B. Philip and O. Gray (eds.), *Directory of Pressure Groups in the EU.* 2nd Edition. London, UK: Cartermill International Ltd.

Stichting Natuur en Milieu (1995). *Greening the Treaty II: Sustainable Development in a Democratic Union, Proposals for the 1996 Intergovernmental Conference.* Document prepared by Ralph Hallo for Climate Network Europe, European Environmental Bureau, Transport & Environment, Friends of Earth Europe, Greenpeace, World Wildlife Fund, Birdlife International.

Transport & Environment. 1998. *T&E and European Transport: The importance of a voice for the environmental and future generations.* Brussels: T&E.

World Wide Fund for Nature (WWF). 1997. *At Cross Purposes: How EU Policy Conflicts Undermine the Environment.* Surrey: WWF United Kingdom.

2000. *WWF's European Policy Programme*. Switzerland: WWF International.
World Wide Fund for Nature (WWF), European Environmental Bureau (EEB), and Friends of the Earth Europe (FOEE). 1990. *Greening the Treaty*. Brussels: WWF European Policy Office.

General references

Alter, Karen. 1996. The European Court's Political Power: The Emergence of an Authoritative International Court in the European Union. *West European Politics*, 19: 458–487.

1998. Who are the "Masters of the Treaty"?: European Governments and the European Court of Justice. *International Organization*, 52: 121–47.

2001. *Establishing the Supremacy of European Law: The Making of an International Rule of Law in Europe*. Oxford, UK: Oxford University Press.

2006. Private Litigants and the New International Courts. *Comparative Political Studies*, 39: 22–49.

Alter, Karen and Jeannette Vargas. 2000. Explaining Variation in the Use of European Litigation Strategies: European Community Law and British Gender Equality Policy. *Comparative Political Studies*, 33: 452–482.

Andersen, S. and K. Eliassen (eds.). 1996. *The European Union: How Democratic is It?* London: Sage.

Arnull, A. 1995. Private Applicants and the Action for Annulment under Article 173 of the EC Treaty. *Common Market Law Review*, 32: 7–49.

Arranz, Fátima, Beatriz Quintanilla, and Christina Velasquez. 1999. *Predicting the Impact of Policy: Country Report, Spain*. Liverpool, UK: Feminist Legal Research Unit, University of Liverpool.

Aspinwall, Mark and Justin Greenwood. 1998. Conceptualizing Collective Action in the European Union: An Introduction. In J. Greenwood and M. Aspinwall (eds.), *Collective Action in the European Union: Interests and the new Politics of Associability*. London, UK: Routledge.

Baldock, David. 1992. The Status of Special Protection Areas for the Protection of Wild Birds. *Journal of Environmental Law*, 4: 139–144.

Bamforth, N. 1993. The Changing Concept of Sex Discrimination. *Modern Law Review*, 56: 872–880.

Barnard, Catherine. 1999. EC 'Social' Policy. In P. Craig and G. de Búrca (ed.), *The Evolution of EU Law*. Oxford, UK: Oxford University Press: 479–516.

Barnes, Pamela M., and Ian G. Barnes. 1999. *Environmental Policy in the European Union*. Cheltenham, UK: Edward Elgar Publishing Limited.

Baumgartner, Frank. and Bryan Jones. 1991. Agenda Dynamics and Policy Subsystems. *Journal of Politics* 53, 1044–1074.

1995. *Agendas and Instability in American Politics*. Chicago: University of Chicago Press.

Bickel, Alexander. 1962. *The Least Dangerous Branch*. New York, NY: Bobbs and Merrill.

Bignami, Francesca. 2005. Creating European Rights: National Values and Supranational Interests. *Columbia Journal of European Law*, 11, 242–353.

Black, Charles. 1960. *The People and the Court*. Englewood Cliffs, CA: Prentice Hall.

Bobbitt, Philip. 1982. *Constitutional Fate*. New York, NY: Oxford University Press.

Boch, Christine. 1996. Case Law: Court of Justice. *Common Market Law Review*, 33: 547–67.

Börzel, Tanja. 1998. The Greening of a Polity? The Europeanisation of Environmental Policy-Making in Spain. *South European Society and Politics*, 2(1): 65–92.

1999. Why There is No Southern Problem: On Environmental Leaders and Laggards in the European Union. RSC Working Paper No. 99/16. Florence: European University Institute.

2001. *States and Regions in the European Union: Institutional Adaptation in Germany and Spain*. Cambridge: Cambridge University Press.

2006. Participation Through Law Enforcement: The Case of the European Union. *Comparative Political Studies*, 39: 128–152.

Börzel, Tanja and Rachel Cichowski, eds. 2003. *State of the European Union: Law, Politics and Society*. Oxford: Oxford University Press.

Bowman, M. J. 1999. International Treaties and the Global Protection of Birds 87–119: Part I. *Journal of Environmental Law*, 11: 87–119.

Braithwaite, Mary and Catherine Byrne. 1995. *Women in Decision-making in Trade Unions*. Brussels: European Trade Union Confederation.

Bretherton, Charlotte and Liz Sperling. 1996. Women's Networks and the European Union: Towards an Inclusive Approach? *Journal of Common Market Studies*, 34: 487–508.

Brockett, Charles D. 1991. The Structure of Political Opportunities and Peasant Mobilization in Central America. *Comparative Politics*, 2: 253–274.

Burley, Anne-Marie and Walter Mattli. 1993. Europe Before the Court: A Political Theory of Legal Integration. *International Organization*, 47: 41–76.

Burstein, Paul. 1991. Legal Mobilization as a Social Movement Tactic: The Struggle for Equal Employment Opportunity. *American Journal of Sociology*, 5: 1201–1225.

Button, James. 1989. The Outcomes of Contemporary Black Protest and Violence. In T. Gurr (ed.), *Violence in America*. Newbury Park, CA: Sage.

Byrne, Paul and Joni Lovenduski. 1978. The Equal Opportunities Commission. *Women's Studies International*, 1: 131–147.

Caporaso, James. 1998. Regional Integration Theory: Understanding Our Past and Anticipating Our Future. In W. Sandholtz and A. Stone Sweet (eds.), *European Integration and Supranational Governance*, Oxford: Oxford University Press: 334–351.

Caracciolo di Torella, Eugenia. 1999. Recent Developments in Pregnancy and Maternity Rights. *Industrial Law Journal*, 28: 276–82.

Caracciolo di Torella, Eugenia and Annick Masselot. 2001. Pregnancy, Maternity and the Organisation of Family Life: An Attempt to Classify the Case Law of the Court of Justice. *European Law Review*, 26: 239–260.

Casqueira Cardoso, João. 1999. *Predicting the Impact of Policy: Country Report, Portugal*. Liverpool, UK: Feminist Legal Research Unit, University of Liverpool.

Chalmers, Damian. 1999. Inhabitants in the Field of EC Environmental Law. In P. Craig and G. de Búrca (ed.), *The Evolution of EU Law*. Oxford, UK: Oxford University Press.

2000. 'The Much Ado about Judicial Politics in the United Kingdom: A Statistical Analysis of Reported Decisions of United Kingdom Courts invoking EU Law 1973–1998.' *Jean Monnet Paper 2000/1* Harvard University Press.

Cheyne, Ilona and Michael Purdue. 1998. Fitting the Definition to Purpose: The Search for a Satisfactory Definition of Waste. *Journal of Environmental Law*, 7: 149–168.

Cichowski, Rachel A. 1998. Integrating the Environment: The European Court and the Construction of Supranational Policy. *Journal of European Public Policy*, 5(3): 387–405.

2001. Judicial Rulemaking and the Institutionalization of EU Sex Equality Policy. In A. Stone Sweet, W. Sandholtz and N. Fligstein (eds.), *The Institutionalization of Europe*. Oxford, UK: Oxford University Press.

2002. 'No Discrimination Whatsoever:' Women's Transnational Activism and the Evolution of European Sex Equality Policy. In N. Naples and A. Desai (eds.), *Women's Community Activism and Globalization*. New York: Routledge.

2003. Law, Politics and Society in Europe. In T. Börzel and R. Cichowski (eds.), *State of the European Union: Law, Politics and Society*. Oxford: Oxford University Press.

2004. Women's Rights, the European Court and Supranational Constitutionalism. *Law and Society Review*, 38: 489–512.

2006a. Introduction: Courts, Democracy and Governance (Special Issue Introduction). *Comparative Political Studies*, 39: 3–21.

2006b. Courts, Rights and Democratic Participation. *Comparative Political Studies*, 39: 50–75.

Cichowski & Stone Sweet. 2003. Participation, Representative Democracy and the Courts. In R. Dalton, B. Cain and S. Scarrow, (eds.) *New Forms of Democracy? Reform and Transformation of Democratic Institutions*. Oxford: Oxford University Press, pp. 192–220.

Cockburn, Cynthia. 1996. Strengthening the Representation of Trade Union Women in the European Social Dialogue. *The European Journal of Women's Studies*, (3): 7–26.

1997. Gender in an International Space: Trade Union Women as European Social Actor. *Women's Studies International Forum*, 20: 459–470.

Cohen, Sue. 1998. Body, Space and Presence: Women's Social Exclusion in the Politics of the European Union. *The European Journal of Women's Studies*, 5: 367–380.

Collins, Ken and David Earnshaw. 1992. The Implementation and Enforcement of European Community Legislation. *Environmental Politics*, 1(4): 213–249.

Conant, Lisa. 2002. *Justice Contained: Law and Politics in the European Union.* Ithaca: Cornell University Press.

2006. Individuals, Courts, and the Development of European Social Rights. *Comparative Political Studies*, 39: 76–100.

Costain, Anne N. 1992. *Inviting Women's Rebellion: A Political Process Interpretation of the Women's Movement.* Baltimore, MD: Johns Hopkins University Press.

Craig, Paul. 2001. The Nature of the Community: Integration Theory and Democratic Theory, Two Discourses Passing in the Night. In P. Craig and G. de Burca (eds.), *EU Law: An Evolutionary Perspective.* Oxford: Oxford University Press.

Craig, Paul and Gráinne de Búrca. 1998. *EU Law: Text, Cases and Materials, 2nd Edition.* Oxford, UK: Oxford University Press.

Curtin, D. 1997. *Postnational Democracy, The European Union in Search of a Political Philosophy.* London: Kluwer.

Dalton, Russell. 1994. *The Green Rainbow.* New Haven: Yale University Press.

Dalton, Russell, Manfred Kuechler and Wilhelm Burkin. 1990. The Challenge of New Movements. In R. Dalton and M. Kuechler (eds.), *Challenging the Political Order: New Social and Political Movements in Western Democracies.* Oxford, UK: Polity Press.

Dalton, Russell and Robert Rohrschneider 1999. Transnational Environmentalism: Do Environmental Groups Cooperate Globally? CSD Working Paper 32/99. Irvine: University of California, Irvine.

de Certeau, Michel. 1984. *The Practice of Everyday Life.* Berkeley, CA: University of California Press.

de Groote, Jacqueline. 1992. European Women's Lobby. *Women's Studies International Forum*, 15: 49–50.

de la Mare, Thomas. 1999. Article 177 in Social and Political Context. In P. Craig and G. de Búrca (ed.), *The Evolution of EU Law.* Oxford, UK: Oxford University Press.

della Porta, Donna. 1995. *Social Movements, Political Violence and the State: A Comparative Analysis of Italy and Germany.* New York, NY. Cambridge University Press.

Demiray, D. A. 1994. The Movement of Goods in a Green Market. *Legal Issues of European Integration*, 1: 73–110.

Deshormes, Fausta. 1992. Women Of Europe. *Women's Studies International Forum*, 15(1): 51–52.

Donnelly, Mary, Siobhán Mullally, and Olivia Smith. 1999. *Predicting the Impact of Policy: Country Report, Ireland.* Liverpool, UK: Feminist Legal Research Unit, University of Liverpool.

Downs, Anthony. 1967. *Inside Bureaucracy.* Boston: Little Brown and Co.

Doyle, Alan and Tom Carney. 1999. Precaution and Prevention: Giving Effect to Article 130r Without Direct Effect. *European Environmental Law Review*, 8: 44–47.

Ellis, Evelyn. 1993. Protection of Pregnancy and Maternity. *Industrial Law Journal*, 22: 63–67.

1998. *European Community Sex Equality Law.* 2nd Edition. Oxford, UK: Oxford University Press.

1999. Court of Justice. *Common Market Law Review,* 36: 625–633.

Epp, Charles. 1990. Connecting Litigation Levels and Legal Mobilization: Explaining Interstate Variation in Employment Civil Rights Litigation. *Law and Society Review,* 24: 145–163.

1998. *The Rights Revolution: Lawyers, Activists, and Supreme Courts in Comparative Perspective.* Chicago: The University of Chicago Press.

Fligstein, Neil. 1997. Social Skill and Institutional Theory. *American Behavioral Scientist,* 40: 397–405.

Forbath, William E. 1991. *Law and the Shaping of the American Labor Movement.* Cambridge, MA: Harvard University Press.

Francioni, Francesco and Massimilliano Montini. 1996. Public Environmental Law in Italy. In R. Seerden and M. Heldeweg (eds.), *Comparative Environmental Law in Europe.* Maklu: Metro.

Freeman, Jo. 1973. The Origins of the Women's Liberation Movement. *American Journal of Sociology,* 78: 792–811.

Fuente Vázquez, Dolores de la. 2000. Spain. In Commission of the European Communities (CEC), *Bulletin – Legal Issues in Equality,* 1/2000. Directorate General for Employment and Social Affairs. Luxembourg: Office of the Official Publications of the European Communities.

Führ, Martin and Gerhard Roller, eds. 1991. *Participation and Litigation Rights of Environmental Associations in Europe: Current Legal Situation and Practical Experience.* New York: Peter Lang.

Galanter, Marc. 1974. Why the "Haves" Come Out Ahead: Speculations on the Limits of Legal Change. *Law and Society,* 9: 95–160.

1983. The Radiating Effects of Courts. In K. D. Boyum and L. Mather (eds.), *Empirical Theories of Courts.* New York, NY: Longman: 117–142.

Gamson, William and David Meyer. 1996. Framing Political Opportunity. In D. McAdam, J. D. McCarthy and M. Zald (eds.), *Comparative Perspectives on Social Movements.* Cambridge, UK: Cambridge University Press: 275–290.

Garrett, Geoffrey. 1992. International Cooperation and Institutional Choice: the European Community's Internal Market, *International Organization,* 46: 533–560.

1995. The Politics of Legal Integration in the European Union. *International Organization,* 49: 171–181.

Garrett, Geoffrey, R. Daniel Kelemen and Heiner Schultz. 1998. The European Court of Justice, National Governments and Legal Integration in the European Union. *International Organization,* 52: 149–176.

Garrett, Geoffrey and Barry R. Weingast. 1993. Ideas, Interests, and Institutions: Constructing the EC's Internal Market. In Judith Goldstein and Robert Keohane, (eds.) *Ideas and Foreign Policy.* Ithaca: Cornell University Press, pp. 173–206.

Geddes, Andrew. 1992. Locus Standi and EEC Environmental Measures. *Jounal of Environmental Law,* 4: 31–39.

Ginsburg, Tom. 2003. *Judicial Review in New Democracies: Constitutional Courts in Asian Cases.* New York: Cambridge University Press.

Giugni, Marco, Doug McAdam and Charles Tilly (eds.). 1997. *How Movements Matter*. Minneapolis, MN: University of Minnesota Press.

Goldfield, Michael. 1989. Worker Insurgency, Radical Organization, and New Deal Labor Legislation. *American Political Science Review*, 83: 1257–1282.

Golub, Jonathan. 1996. The Politics of Judicial Discretion: Rethinking the Interaction between National Courts and the European Court of Justice. *West European Politics*, 19: 360–385.

Graber, Mark A. 1993. The Non-majority Difficulty: Legislative Deference to the Judiciary. *Studies in American Political Development*, 7, 35–72.

Granger, Marie Pierre. 2003. Towards a Liberalisation of Standing Conditions for Individuals Seeking Judicial Review of Community Acts: *Jégo-Quéré et Cie SA* v *Commission* and *Union de Pequeños Agricultores* v *Council*. *Modern Law Review*, 66: 124–138.

2004. When Governments go to Luxembourg: The influence of the governments on the European Court of Justice. *European Law Review*, 29: 1–31.

Guttieres, Mario and Guy R. Bayley. 1994. Country Report: Italy. *European Environmental Law Review*, 3: 8–10.

Haas, Ernst. 1958. *The Uniting of Europe: Political, Social and Economic Forces, 1950–1957*. Stanford, CA: Stanford University Press.

1964. Technology, Pluralism and the New Europe. In S. Graubard (ed.), *A New Europe?* Boston, MA: Houghton Mifflin Co.

Haas, Peter. 1990. *Saving the Mediterranean*. New York, NY: Columbia University Press.

1993. Protecting the Baltic and North Seas. In Peter Haas, Robert Keohane & Marc Levy (eds.), *Institutions for the Earth: Sources of Effective International Environmental Protection*. Cambridge, MA: MIT Press.

Haigh, Nigel and David Baldock. 1989. *Environmental Policy and 1992*. London: Institute for European Environmental Policy.

Hall, Peter A. and Rosemary C. R. Taylor. 1996. Political Science and the Three New Institutionalisms. *Political Studies*, 44: 936–957.

Handler, Joel. 1978. *Social Movements and the Legal System: A Theory of Law Reform and Social Change*. New York, NY: Academic Press.

Harding, Christopher. 1980. The Private Interest In Challenging Community Action. *European Law Review*, 5: 354–361.

Harlow, Carol. 1992a. Towards a Theory of Access for the European Court of Justice. *Yearbook of European Law*, 54: 32–45.

1992b. A Community of Interests? Making the Most of European Law. *Modern Law Review*, 55: 331–351.

Harlow, Carol and Richard Rawlings. 1992. *Pressure Through Law*. London, UK: Routledge.

Harte, J. D. C. 1997. Nature Conservation: The Rule of Law in European Community Environmental Protection, Analysis. *Journal of Environmental Law*, 9: 139–180.

Hartley, T. 1988. *The Foundations of European Community Law*. 3rd Edition. Oxford, UK: Claredon.

Hattam, Victoria C. 1992. Institutions and Political Change: Working-class Formation in England and the United States, 1820–1896. In S. Steinmo,

K. Thelen and F. Longstreth (eds.), *Structuring Politics: Historical Institutionalism in Comparative Analysis*. Cambridge, UK: Cambridge University Press: 155–187.

Held, David and Mathias Koening-Archibugi (eds.) 2004. Introduction to Special Issue. *Government and Opposition*, 39(2): 125–131.

Héritier, Adrienne. 1999. *Policy-making and diversity in Europe: escaping deadlock.* Cambridge, UK: Cambridge University Press.

Hildebrand, Philipp M. 1992. The European Community's Environmental Policy, 1957 to '1992': From Incidental Measures to an International Regime? *Environmental Politics*, 3: 14–44.

Holder, Jane. 1997. Case Law: Case C-44/95. *Common Market Law Review*, 34: 1469–1480.

Hoskyns, Catherine. 1992. The European Community's Policy on Women in the Context of 1992. *Women's Studies International Forum*, 15: 21–28.

　1996. *Integrating Gender: Women, Law and Politics in the European Union.* London: Verso.

Imig, Doug and Sidney Tarrow (eds.). 2001. Studying Contention in an Emerging Polity. In D. Imig and S. Tarrow, eds. *Contentious Europeans: Protest and Politics in an Emerging Polity.* New York: Rowman and Littlefield.

Jackson, Donald W. and C. Neal Tate (eds.). 1992. *Comparative Judicial Review and Public Policy.* Westport, CT: Greenwood Press.

Jenkins, J. Craig. 1983. Resource Mobilization Theory and the Study of Social Movements. *Annual Review of Sociology*, 9: 527–550.

Judge, David. 1992. 'Predestined to Save the Earth': The Environment Committee of the European Parliament. *Environmental Politics*, 1(4): 186–212.

Katzenstein, Mary. 1998a. *Faithful and Fearless: Moving Feminist Protest inside the Church and Military.* Princeton: Princeton University Press.

　1998b. Stepsisters: Feminist Movement Activism in Different Institutional Spaces. In D. S. Meyer and S. Tarrow (eds.), *The Social Movement Society: Contentious Politics in a New Century.* Lanham, MD: Rowman & Littlefield Publishers, Inc.: 195–216.

Katzenstein, Mary and Carol McClurg Mueller (eds). 1987. *The Women's Movements of the United States and Western Europe.* Philadelphia: Temple University Press.

Keck, Margaret and Kathryn Sikkink. 1998. *Activists Beyond Borders: Advocacy Networks in International Politics.* Ithaca, NY: Cornell University Press.

Kelemen, R. Daniel. 2001. The Limits of Judicial Power: Trade-Environment Disputes in the GATT/WTO and the EU. *Comparative Political Studies*, 34 (6), 622–650.

　2006. Suing for Europe: Adversarial Legalism and European Governance. *Comparative Political Studies*, 39: 101–127.

Kenney, Sally. 1992. *For Whose Protection?: Reproductive Hazards and Exclusionary Policies in the United States and Britain.* Ann Arbor: University of Michigan Press.

Kenney, Sally, William Reisinger and John C. Reitz (eds.). 1999. *Constitutional Dialogues in Comparative Perspective.* New York: St. Martins Press Inc.

Keohane, Robert. 1984. *After Hegemony*. Princeton, NJ: Princeton University Press.

Keohane, Robert, & Ruth W. Grant. 2005. Accountability and Abuses of Power in World Politics. *American Political Science Review*, 99 (1): 29–43.

Keohane, Robert, Andrew Moravcsik, & Anne-Marie Slaughter. 2000. Legalized Dispute Resolution: Interstate and Transnational. *International Organization*, 54 (3): 457–88.

Kirchner, E. 1977. *Trade Unions as Pressure Groups in the European Community*. Farnborough, UK: Saxon House.

Kluger, Richard. 1975. *Simple Justice: The History of Brown v. Board of Education and the Black America's Struggle for Equality*. New York, NY: Vintage.

Knill, Christoph and Lenschow, Andrea. 1998. Coping with Europe: the Impact of British and German Administrations on the Implementation of EU Environmental Policy. *Journal of European Public Policy*, 5(4): 595–614.

Krämer, Ludwig. 1991a. The Implementation of Community Environmental Directives within Member States: Some Implications of the Direct Effect Doctrine. *Journal of Environmental Law*, 3: 39–56.

1991b. The Implementation of Environmental Law by the European Economic Communities. *German Yearbook of International Law*, 34: 13–53.

1996. Public Interest Litigation in Environmental Matters Before European Courts. *Journal of Environmental Law*, 8: 1–18.

2000. *E.C. Environmental Law*, 4ᵗʰ Edition. London: Sweet and Maxwell.

Kriesi, Hanspeter, Ruud Koopmans, Jan Willem Duyvendak, and Marco G. Giugini (eds). 1995. *New Social Movements in Western Europe: A Comparative Analysis*. Minneapolis: University of Minnesota Press.

Lenaerts, K. 1990. Constitutionalism and the Many Faces of Federalism. *American Journal of Comparative Law*, 38: 205–64.

Liefferink, Duncan and Mikael Skou Andersen. 1998. Greening the EU: National Positions in the Run-up to the Amsterdam Treaty. *Environmental Politics*, 7: 66–93.

Lodge, J. 1989. The European Parliament. In J. Lodge (ed.), *The European Community and the Challenge of the Future*. London: Pinter.

Lovell, George. 2003. *Legislative Deferrals: Statutory Ambiguity, Judicial Power, and American Democracy*. New York, NY: Cambridge University Press.

Lowe, Philip and Jane Goyder. 1983. *Environmental Groups in Politics*. London: Allen & Unwin.

Macroy, Richard. 1992. The Enforcement of Community Environmental Laws: Some Critical Issues. *Common Market Law Review*, 29: 347–369.

Mancini, Federico G. 1989. The Making of a Constitution for Europe. *Common Market Law Review*, 24: 595–614.

1997. An Analysis of the Public and Private Purposes of the Court of Justice of the European Communities. Paper given to the University of New South Wales, Australia, 27 October 1997. http://www.lawfoundation.net.au/resources/mancini/analysis.html.

Mancini, G. F. and S. O'Leary. 1999. The New Frontiers of Sex Equality Law in the European Union. *European Law Review*, 24: 331–53.

March, James G. and Johan P. Olsen. 1989. *Rediscovering Institutions: The Organizational Basis of Politics*. Boulder, CO: Lynne Reiner.

Marks, Gary and Doug McAdam. 1996. Social Movements and the Changing Structure of Political Opportunity in the European Union. In G. Marks, F. Scharpf, P. Schmitter, and W. Streek (eds.), *Governance in the European Union*. London, UK: Sage Publications: 95–120.

Mattli, Walter and Anne-Marie Slaughter. 1995. Law and Politics in the European Union: A Reply to Garret. *International Organization*, 49: 183–190.

1998. Revisiting the European Court of Justice. *International Organization*, 52: 177–209.

Mazey, Sonia. 1998. The European Union and Women's Rights: From the Europeanization of National Agendas to the Nationalization of a European Agenda? *Journal of European Public Policy*, 5(1): 131–52.

Mazey, Sonia and Jeremy Richardson. 1992. Environmental Groups and the EC: Challenges and Opportunities. *Environmental Politics*, 1(4): 109–128.

1999. Introduction: Transference of Powers, Decision Rules, and Rules of the Game. In Sonia Mazey and Jeremy Richardson (Eds.), *Lobbying in the European Community*, 2nd edition. Oxford: Oxford University Press.

2001. Institutionalizing Promiscuity: Commission-Interest Group Relations in the EU. In A. Stone Sweet, W. Sandholtz and N. Fligstein (eds.), *The Institutionalization of Europe*. Oxford, UK: Oxford University Press.

McAdam, Doug. 1982. *Political Process and the Development of Black Insurgency, 1930–1970*. Chicago, IL: University of Chicago Press.

1996. Political Opportunities: Conceptual Origins, Current Problems, Future Directions. In D. McAdam, J. D. McCarthy and M. N. Zald (eds.), *Comparative Perspectives on Social Movements*. Cambridge, UK: Cambridge University Press: 23–40.

McAdam, Doug, John D. McCarthy and Mayer N. Zald. 1996. Introduction: Opportunities, Mobilizing Structures, and Framing Processes – Toward a Synthetic, Comparative Perspective on Social Movements. In D. McAdam, J. D. McCarthy and M. N. Zald (eds.), *Comparative Perspectives on Social Movements*. Cambridge, UK: Cambridge University Press: 1–20.

McCann, Michael W. 1994. *Rights at Work: Pay Equity Reform and the Politics of Legal Mobilization*. Chicago: University of Chicago Press.

1998. How Does Law Matter for Social Movements. In B. Garth and A. Sarat (eds.). *How Does Law Matter*. Evanston: Northwestern University Press.

McGlynn, Clare. 1996. Pregnancy Dismissals and the Webb Litigation. *Feminist Legal Studies*, IV: 229–42.

2000. Pregnancy, Parenthood and the Court of Justice in Abdoulaye. *European Law Review*, 25: 654–662.

Micklitz, H. W. and N. Reich, eds. 1996. *Public Interest Litigation before the European Courts*. Baden-Baden, Germany: Nomos Verlagsgessellschaft.

Miller, Christopher. 1998. *Environmental Rights: Critical Perspectives*. London, UK: Routledge.

Moravcsik, Andrew. 1991. Negotiating the Single European Act: National Interests and Conventional Statecraft in the European Community. *International Organization*, 45: 19–56.

1995. Liberal Intergovernmentalism and Integration: A Rejoinder. *Journal of Common Market Studies*, 33: 611–628.

1998. *The Choice for Europe: Social Purpose and State Power from Messina to Maastricht*. Ithaca, NY: Cornell University Press.

More, Gillian. 1999. The Principle of Equal Treatment: From Market Unifier to Fundamental Right? In P. Craig and G. de Búrca (eds.), *The Evolution of EU Law*. Oxford, UK. Oxford University Press.

Morris, Aldon. 1984. *The Origins of the Civil Rights Movement*. New York, NY: The Free Press.

Mossuz-Lavau, Janine. 1988. Women of Europe: Mirroring the Course of Women's Rights in Europe, 1977–1987. *Women of Europe: 10 Years)*. Brussels: Women's Information Service, Directorate-General Audiovisual, Information, Communication, Culture, 27: 3–59.

Nettesheim, M. 1996. Article 173 of the EC Treaty and Regulations: Towards the Development of Uniform Standing Requirements. In H. W. Micklitz and N. Reich (eds.), *Public Interest Litigation before the European Courts*. Baden-Baden, Germany: Nomos Verlagsgesellschaft.

Neuwahl, N. 1996. Article 173 paragraph 4 EC: Past, Present and Possible Future. *European Law Review*, 21.

Nollkaemper, André. 1997. Habitat Protection in European Community Law: Evolving Conceptions of a Balance of Interests. *Journal of Environmental Law*, 9: 271–286.

North, Douglass C. 1990. *Institutions, Institutional Change and Economic Performance*. New York, NY: Cambridge University Press.

O'Connor, Karen. 1980. *Women's Organizations' Use of the Courts*. Lexington, MA: Lexington Books.

Olson, Mancur. 1965. *The Logic of Collective Action*. Cambridge, MA: Harvard University Press.

Olson, Susan M. 1984. *Clients and Lawyers: Securing Rights of Disabled Persons*. Westport, CT: Greenwood.

Pagh, Peter 1999. Denmark's Compliance with Europe Community Environmental Law. *Journal of Environmental Law*, 11: 301–319.

Pescatore, Pierre. 1974. *The Law of Integration*. Leyden: Sijthoss.

Philip, Alan Butt and Oliver Gray. 1996. *Directory of Pressure Groups in the EU*. 2nd Edition. London, UK: Cartermill International Ltd.

Pierson, Paul. 1996. The Path to European Integration: A Historical Institutionalist Approach. *Comparative Political Studies*, 29: 123–63.

2000. Increasing Returns, Path Dependence, and the Study of Politics. *American Political Science Review*, 94: 251–267.

Pierson, Paul and S. Liebfried. 1992. Multi-tiered Institutions and the Making of Social Policy. In S. Liebfried and P. Pierson (eds.), *European Social Policy: Between Fragmentation and Integration*. Washington, D. C.: Brookings Institute.

Piven, Frances F. and Richard A. Cloward. 1977. *Poor People's Movements: Why They Succeed, How They Fail*. New York: Vintage.

Pollack, Mark A. 1997. Delegation, Agency and Agenda Setting in the European Community. *International Organization*, 51: 99–134.

1998. The Engines of Integration? Supranational Autonomy and Influence in the European Union. In W. Sandholtz and A. Stone Sweet (eds.), *European*

Integration and Supranational Governance, Oxford: Oxford University Press: 217–249.

2003. *The Engines of European Integration: Delegation, Agency and Agenda Setting in the EU*. Oxford: Oxford University Press.

Prechal, Sacha. Kalanke Ruling. 1996. *Common Market Law Review*, 33: 45–52.

Rasmussen, H. 1980. Why is Article 173 Interpreted Against Private Plaintiffs? *European Law Review*, 5: 112.

1986. *On Law and Policy in the European Court of Justice*. Dordrecht: Martinus Nijhoff.

Rehbinder, Eckard and Richard Stewart. 1985. Legal Integration in Federal Systems: European Community Environmental Law. *The American Journal of Comparative Law*, 33: 371–446.

Richardson, Jeremy. 1998. *The EU as an Alternative Venue for Interest Groups*. Paper presented to the American Political Science Association, Annual Meeting, Boston, 3–6 September 1998.

Rosenberg, Gerald. 1991. *The Hollow Hope: Can Courts Bring about Social Change?* Chicago, IL: University of Chicago Press.

Ross, G. 1995. *Jacques Delores and European Integration*. London: Polity.

Rubenfeld, Jed. 2004. Unilateralism and Constitutionalism. *New York University Law Review*, 79, 1971–2028.

Rucht, Dieter. 1996. The Impact of National Contexts on Social Movement Structures: A Cross-Movement and Cross-National Comparison. In D. McAdam, J. D. McCarthy and M. N. Zald (eds.), *Comparative Perspectives on Social Movements*. Cambridge, UK: Cambridge University Press: 185–204.

2001. Lobbying or Protest? Strategies to Influence EU Environmental Policies. In D. Imig and S. Tarrow (eds.), *Contentious Europeans: Protest and Politics in an Emerging Polity*. Lanham, MD: Rowman & Littlefied Publishers Inc.

Russell, Peter H. and David O'Brien (eds.) 2001. *Judicial Independence in the Age of Democracy: Critical Perspectives from around the World*. Charlottesville: The University Press of Virginia.

Ruzza, Carlo. 1996. Inter-Organizational Negotiation in Political Decision-making: EC Bureaucrats and the Environment. In C. Samson and N. South (eds.), *The Social Construction of Social Policy*. London: Macmillan.

Sacks, Vera. 1987. The Equal Opportunities Commission – Ten Years On. *Modern Law Review*, 49: 560–592.

Sanchis Moreno, Fe. 1996. Spain. In R. E. Hallo (ed.), *Access to Environmental Information in Europe. The Implementation and Implications of Directive 90/313/EEC*. London: Kluwer Law: 225–248.

Sandholtz, Wayne. 1998. The Emergence of a Supranational Telecommunications Regime. In W. Sandholtz and A. Stone Sweet (eds.), *European Integration and Supranational Governance*, Oxford: Oxford University Press: 134–163.

Sandholtz, Wayne and Alec Stone Sweet (eds.). 1998. *European Integration and Supranational Governance*. Oxford, UK: Oxford University Press.

Sands, Peter. 1990. European Community Environmental Law: Legislation, the European Court of Justice and Common-Interest Groups. *Modern Law Review*, 53: 685–698.

Sbragia, Alberta. 1996. Environmental Policy: The "Push-Pull" of Policy-Making. In H. Wallace and W. Wallace (eds.), *Policy-Making in the European Union*. Oxford: Oxford University Press: 235–255.

Scharpf, Fritz. 1996. Negative and Positive Integration in the Political Economy of European Welfare States. In G. Marks, F. Scharpf, P. Schmitter, and W. Streek (eds.), *Governance in the European Union*. London, UK: Sage Publications: 15–39.

  1999. *Governing in Europe: Effective and Democratic?* Oxford, UK: Oxford University Press.

Scheingold, Stuart. 1974. *The Politics of Rights: Lawyers, Public Policy and Political Change*. New Haven, CT: Yale University Press.

Scheppele, Kim Lane. 2003. Constitutional Negotiations: Political Contexts of Judicial Activism in Post-Soviet Europe. *International Sociology*, 18(1): 219–238.

  2004. A Realpolitik Defense of Social Rights. *Texas Law Review*, 82(7): 1921–1961.

Schermers, H. G. and C. W. A. Timmermans (eds.). 1987. *Article 177 EEC: Experiences and Problems*. North-Holland.

Schneider, Ann. L. and Helen Ingram. 1997. *Policy Design for Democracy*. Lawrence: University Press of Kansas.

Schubert, G. 1965. *The Judicial Mind*. Evanston, IL: Northwestern University.

Seerden, René and Michiel Heldeweg. 1996. Comparative Remarks. In R. Seerden and M. Heldeweg (eds.), *Comparative Environmental Law in Europe*. Maklu: Metro.

Sewell, William. 1990. Collective Violence and Collective Loyalties in France: Why the French Revolution Made a Difference. *Politics and Society* 18: 527–552.

Shapiro, Martin. 1981. *Courts: A Comparative and Political Analysis*. Chicago, IL: University of Chicago Press.

  1988. *Who Guards the Guardians: Judicial Control of Administration*. Athens, GA: University of Georgia Press.

Sidjanski, D. 1970. Pressure Groups in the EC. In C. Cosgrove and K. Twitchett (eds.), *The New International Actors: The United Nations and the EC*. London, UK: Macmillan.

Silverstein, Helen. 1996. *Unleashing Rights: Law, Meaning, and the Animal Rights Movement*. Ann Arbor, MI: University of Michigan Press.

Slaughter, Anne-Marie. 2003. A Global Community of Courts. *Harvard International Law Journal*, 44, 191–219.

  2004. *A New World Order*. Princeton, NJ: Princeton University Press.

Slaughter, Anne-Marie, Alec Stone Sweet and Joseph H. H. Weiler (eds.) 1998. *The European Court and the National Courts – Doctrine and Jurisprudence: Legal Change in its Social Context*. Oxford, UK: Hart Press.

Slot, Pierre Jan. 2003. Case C-510/99. Procureur de la République v. Xavier Tridon. *Common Market Law Review*, 40: 169–178.

Snow, David A. and Robert D. Benford. 1988. Ideology, Frame Resonance, and Participant Mobilization. In B. Klandermans, H. Kriesi and S. Tarrow (eds.), *From Structure to Action: Social Movement Participation Across Cultures.* Greenwich: JAI Press.

Sorauf, Frank J. 1976. *The Wall of Separation: The Constitutional Politics of Church and State.* Princeton, NJ: Princeton University Press.

Stein, Eric. 1981. Lawyers, Judges, and the Making of a Transnational Constitution. *American Journal of International Law*, 75: 1–27.

Stetter, Sebastian. 2001. Maastricht, Amsterdam and Nice: The Environmental Lobby and Greening the Treaties. *European Environmental Law Review*, 2: 150–159.

Stone Sweet, Alec. 1998. Constitutional Dialogues in the European Community. In A. M. Slaughter, A. Stone Sweet and J. H. H. Weiler (eds.), *The European Court and the National Courts – Doctrine and Jurisprudence: Legal Change in its Social Context.* Oxford, UK: Hart Press.

1999. Judicialization and the Construction of Governance. *Comparative Political Studies*, 31: 147–84.

2000. *Governing with Judges.* Oxford, UK: Oxford University Press.

2002. Path Dependence, Precedent and Judicial Power. In M. Shapiro and Alec Stone Sweet, *On Law, Politics and Judicialization.* Oxford, UK: Oxford University Press.

2004. *The Judicial Construction of Europe.* Oxford, UK: Oxford University Press.

Stone Sweet, Alec and Tom Brunell. 1998a. Constructing a Supranational Constitution: Dispute Resolution and Governance in the European Community. *American Political Science Review*, 92: 63–81.

1998b. The European Courts and the National Courts: A Statistical Analysis of Preliminary References, 1961–95. *Journal of European Public Policy*, 5: 66–97.

1999. *The Alec Stone Sweet and Thomas L. Brunell Data Set on Preliminary References in EC Law, 1958–98.* Florence, Italy: Robert Schuman Centre for Advanced Studies, European University Institute.

2000. The European Court, National Judges and Legal Integration: A Researcher's Guide to the Data Base on Preliminary References in European Law, 1958–98. *Särtryck ur EuroparättsligTidskrift* (Swedish Journal of European Law) 3: 179–92.

Stone Sweet, Alec and James Caporaso. 1998. From Free Trade to Supranational Polity: The European Court and Integration. In W. Sandholtz and A. Stone Sweet (eds.), *European Integration and Supranational Governance.* Oxford: Oxford University Press: 92–133.

Stone Sweet, Alec and Wayne Sandholtz. 1998. Integration, Supranational Governance, and the Institutionalization of the European Polity. In W. Sandholtz and A. Stone Sweet (eds.), *European Integration and Supranational Governance.* Oxford: Oxford University Press: 1–26.

Stone Sweet, Alec, Wayne Sandholtz and Neil Fligstein (eds.). 2001. *The Institutionalization of Europe.* Oxford, UK: Oxford University Press.

Tallberg, Jonas. 2002. Paths to Compliance: Enforcement, Management, and the European Union. *International Organization*, 56 (3): 609–943.

Tarrow, Sidney. 1998. *Power in Movement: Social Movements and Contentious Politics*. Cambridge, UK: Cambridge University Press.

2005. *The New Transnational Activism*. New York: Cambridge University Press.

Tate, C. Neal and Torbjorn Vallinder. 1995. The Global Expansion of Judicial Power: The Judicialization of Politics. In C. N. Tate and T. Vallinder (eds.), *The Global Expansion of Judicial Power*. New York: New York University Press.

Thelen, Kathleen. 2004. *How Institutions Evolve: The Political Economy of Skills in Germany, Britain, the United States and Japan*. New York: Cambridge University Press.

Tilly, Charles. 1975. Reflections on the History of European State-making. In C. Tilly (ed.), *The Formation of National States in Western Europe*. Princeton, NJ: Princeton University Press.

1978. *From Mobilization to Revolution*. New York, NY: McGraw-Hill.

1982. Britain Creates the Social Movement. In J. Cronin and J. Schneer (eds.) *Social Conflict and the Political Order in Britain*. New Brunswick, NJ: Rutgers University Press.

Tomlins, Christopher L. 1985. *The State and the Unions: Labor Relations, Law, and the Organized Labor Movement in American, 1880–1960*. New York, NY: Cambridge University Press.

Tridimas, Takis. 2004. The ECJ and the Draft Constitution: A Supreme Court for the Union? T. Tridimas and P. Nebbia, (eds), *EU Law for the 21st Century: Rethinking the New Legal Order*. Oxford: Hart Publishing.

Tsebelis, George. 1994. The Power of the European Parliament as a Conditional Agenda Setter. *American Political Science Review*, 88: 128–142.

Tsebelis, George and Geoffrey Garrett. 2001. The Institutional Foundations of Intergovernmentalism and Supranationalism in the European Union. *International Organization*, 55: 357–390.

Tsebelis, George and Amie Kreppel. 1998. The History of Conditional Agenda Setting in European Institutions. *European Journal of Political Research*, 33: 41–71.

Tyrrell, Alan and Zahd Yaqub (eds.). 1993. *The Legal Professions in the New Europe*. Oxford, UK: Blackwell Publishers.

Vallance, Elizabeth and Elizabeth Davies 1986. *Women of Europe: Women MEPs and Equality Policy*. Cambridge, UK: Cambridge University Press.

Vogel, David. 1993. Environmental Policy in the European Community. In S. Kamienecki (ed.), *Environmental Politics in the International Arena*, Albany, NY: SUNY Press.

Vose, Clement E. 1959. *Caucasians Only: The Supreme Court, the NAACP, and the Restrictive Covenant Cases*. Berkeley, CA: University of California Press.

Walker, Jack L. Jr. 1991. *Mobilizing Interest Groups in America: Patrons, Professions and Social Movements*. Ann Arbor, MI: University of Michigan Press.

Walker, Samuel. 1990. *In Defense of American Liberties: A History of the ACLU*. New York, NY: Oxford University Press.

Weiler, Joseph H. H. 1981. The Community System: The Dual Character of Supranationalism, *Yearbook of European Law*, 1: 268–306.

1991. The Transformation of Europe, *Yale Law Journal*, 100: 2403–2483.

1994. A Quiet Revolution: The European Court and Its Interlocutors. *Comparative Political Studies*, 26: 510–34.

1998. European Models: Polity, People and System. In P. Craig and C. Harlow (eds.), *Lawmaking in the European Union*. London: Kluwer.

1999. *The Constitution of Europe*. Cambridge, UK: Cambridge University Press.

Weiler, Joseph H. H., U. Haltern and F. Mayer. 1995. European Democracy and its Critique. In J. Hayward (ed.), *The Crisis of Representation in Europe*. London: Frank Cass.

Westlake, M. 1994. *A Modern Guide to the European Parliament*. London, UK: Pinter.

Wils, Wouter P. J. 1994. The Birds Directive 15 Years Later: A Survey of the Case Law and a Comparison with the Habitats Directive. *Journal of Environmental Law*, 6: 219–242.

Winter, Gerd. 1997. Nature Conservation: The Rule of Law in European Community Environmental Protection, Footnote. *Journal of Environmental Law*, 9: 139–180.

World Jurist Association. 2002. *Law and Judicial Systems of Nations*, 4th edition. Washington D.C.: World Jurist Association.

Wyatt, Derek. 1998. Litigating Community Environmental Law – Thoughts on the Doctrine of Direct Effect. *Journal of Environmental Law*, 10(1): 9–19.

Zemans, Frances Kahn. 1983. Legal Mobilization: The Neglected Role of the Law in the Political System. *American Political Science Review*, 77: 690–703.

Index